GOD
ON TRIAL

A Brief History of Atheism

by Georg Siegmund

TRANSLATED BY ELINOR CASTENDYK BRIEFS

DESCLEE COMPANY
New York - Tournai
Rome - Paris

Originally published in German under the title *Der Kampf um Gott.*

(© 1957 Morus-Verlag Gmbh, Berlin).

The present English translation is an adaptation of the third German edition.

Imprimatur
Tornaci, die 25 mars 1967
J. THOMAS, vic. gen.

Library of Congress Catalog Card Number : 68-26913.

Printed in Belgium by Desclée & Cie, Éditeurs, Tournai.

TABLE OF CONTENTS

TRANSLATOR'S NOTES

One of the classic difficulties in translating from the German is that of selecting the right English word for *Geist* or its adjective *geistig* from among a score of possibilities. Constantly confronted as one is in a book of this kind by a single German word for spirit, Holy Spirit, mind, intellect, intelligence, wit, imagination, genius, soul, morale, essence, ghost, specter, and even "body of alcoholic beverages," the English translator begins to envy his German counterpart happily privileged to translate so many terms with the one accommodating word *Geist*. *In this book,* wherever the choice clearly narrowed to "intellectual" or "spiritual" in its current religious or moral sense, the problem solved itself, but in a few cases neither word alone sufficed. In these, where *geistig* seemed to imply both the "spiritual" of current usage and spiritual in the intellectual, 18th- century sense of *un homme spirituel,* I have used both words, spiritual and intellectual.

The Siegmund text of the chapters on Nietzsche seemed to demand the use of the familiar English word, superman, for *Uebermensch,* despite Walter Kaufmann's use of "overman" in his brilliant translation of *Zarathustra,* which I have quoted. Mr. Kaufmann's reason for the change is valid for his purpose, a clear fresh translation, but in the context of *God on Trial* I believe that the reader's familiarity with the words superman and superhumanity is important enough to warrant their use outside the quotations even at the cost of sacrificing the consistency that would require "overman" throughout.

Wherever feasible, I have quoted from English translations of the writings under discussion; where existent, from authorized translations, for instance of Marx and Lenin. Obviously it is not always possible to find a single, isolated sentence in collected works, which are frequently arranged differently in the English version, or among random "selections from" the book quoted in German. Such passages, as wel as those from books translated but out of print, I have translated myself as literally as possible. Very brief or fragmentary sentences in quotation, above all those from German works that do not exist in English, I have not included in the reference notes, although Professor Siegmund has been scrupulously correct about acknowledging every one; in most instances I have integrated the name of the author into the text instead. I have also added a supplementary English booklist to this second edition, which the author has enlarged for English readers.

I should like to express my gratitude to all those whose patience and cooperation have made this translation possible, above all to Goetz and Regina Briefs; also to Christa von Bomhard for months of painstaking quotation-tracking at Georgetown University Library and the Library of Congress, Elizabeth Kirtland for her generous editorial assistance, and to Elizabeth Beverly for typing her way undaunted through all the complications of enlargement, revision, and a labyrinth of English and German references.

E. C. B.

PREFACE

> The real, the deepest, the sole theme of the
> world and of history, to which all other themes
> are subordinate, remains the conflict of belief
> and unbelief. *
>
> —Goethe

In recent years this quotation from Goethe has often been cited to indicate the temper of the times. To date, however, the details of the struggle between belief and unbelief, history's real, deepest, and sole theme, have not been fully delineated. Therefore we cannot arrive at a basic understanding of the ideological contentions of our time or an understanding of the positions of both fronts and their tactics. In this struggle, the inwardly divided and contending powers of the human spirit, itself unchanging regardless of changing times, are deployed on a grand scale. Hence our study must of necessity become first of all an analysis of the motivating psychic forces that doggedly assault the bastions of belief.

To be convincing, this study had to allow witnesses of each age to testify at length, since in ideological argument the rationalistic preconception that only rational elements are involved still largely prevails. The result is that the emotional forces are purposely ignored. According to this view, shared with F. Th. Vischer, the moral element is always to be taken for granted. In reality, however, we cannot take it for granted. On the contrary, right here lie the forces that drive the mind to make common cause with the one side or with the other. In this sense, what is really involved is a psychoanalysis of belief and unbelief.

The author has revised and enlarged the text of the second German printing for this English-language edition.

Georg Siegmund

* Gœthe, Der West-œstliche Divan, d. Gesamtausgabe 5 (1961), p. 200.

I. *The present situation in the battle for belief*

INTRODUCTION

On a scale hitherto unknown in human history, " unbelief " has launched into battle against " belief. " When we speak of " unbelief, " we are using a negative characterization that can be easily mistaken for an evaluation that is negative from the start. Actually, in itself, this " unbelief " is usually true belief. The conviction that the old faith is vanishing forever gives modern man's new belief in himself its driving power. Today almost as many people stand in the ranks of anti-faith as in the ranks of Christianity. To a superficial observer, the fronts of the great political power-blocks presently aligned against each other seem to coincide with their ideological fronts; but the more closely we examine this opinion the more questionable it proves to be.

The contemporary world view of many Westerners schooled in the natural sciences is also a kind of atheism. For men like Julian Huxley, Director General of UNESCO from 1946-48, God has become an unnecessary hypothesis whose term of heuristic authority has expired; no longer scientifically tenable, God has become an obstacle to thought. In the wake of a callous secularization, an ever spreading loss of faith has rendered industrial society godless in the sense of God dethroned and forgotten.

Atheism as the event of the age is given by some of its representatives a certain time-construction patterned on progress, whether in the sense of a prolonged biological evolution (Huxley), or that of a super-individual destiny (Heidegger). According to this theory, the time has come for the last god, the god of the Christians, to abdicate.

Though tidings of the death of God have been trumpeted across the world not only by Nietzsche, but also by others before and after him, many people refuse to listen, says Huxley. This is because "religious beliefs and practices have a very strong time-lag."[1] Ernst Juenger and others corroborate Nietzsche's message that "God is dead." According to Juenger, this is both the basic fact in the present world-catastrophe and the premise for the monstruous unfolding of man's power now in progress. Heidegger interprets the nihilism of Nietzsche's message as the "fate" of man today, a fate which it is his to shoulder resolutely. If atheism is "an event of high order, similar to breaking out of a magnetic field," as Juenger says, there can be "no virtue in belief, or sin in unbelief."

Diametrically opposed to this opinion is that which holds belief and unbelief to be neither a matter of fate nor the doom of a particular age, but a responsible act rooted deep in man's personal existence. This is how Goethe meant his famous: "The real, the deepest, the sole them of the world and of history, that to which all others are subordinated, remains the conflict between belief and unbelief."[2]

In the West, 19th century philosophers felt more and more the need to proclaim the "death of God," with the result that many cultivated circles have long been permeated by the sometimes vague, sometimes perfectly clear feeling that the drama of the West's struggle for emancipation from God is now at an end; that therefore the time has come to write the history of the dying god "while there are still witnesses to his vital reign."[3]

To be sure, typical Western atheism is quite different from that of the East. If the latter is primarily an act of aggression against

[1] J, Huxley, *Man in the Modern World* (Chatto & Windus: London, 1947), p. 132.
[2] J. W. Gœthe, *Der West-œstliche Divan, Gesamtausgabe* 5 (1961), p. 200.
[3] F. Mauthner, *Der Atheismus und seine Geschichte im Abendland* (I. Band, 1963), p. 3.

God and belief in God, the chief characteristic of the Western brand is a skepticism that keeps man firmly tethered within the confines of this world. Hence to a large extent faith in God is lost or dead, and the void that results terrifies. Meanwhile there is no dearth of angry young men organizing to help the new, outspoken unbelief to victory.

If also the leaders of current existentialism are godless, their godlessness is often a painful void which they hope to fill with a fresh discovery of God.

For all their significant differences, the bonds between Eastern and Western atheism are much closer than we care to admit. Anyone who digs into the literary sources of dialectical materialism will find the famous German philosophers of the past century constantly cited as its crown witnesses. As early as 1882 Friedrich Engels declared: " We German socialists are proud of our descent, not only from St. Simon, Fourier, and Owen but also from Kant, Fichte, and Hegel. " [4] A few years later he wrote: " The German working class is the inheritor of German classical philosophy. " [5] Lenin sees in dialectical materialism " the legitimate and necessary product of the whole recent development of philosophy and the social sciences. "

One should not overlook the fact that the man who " alone and unaided succeeded in combining the idea of proletarian Messianism with that of a Russian Messianism, and so transformed vague Russian longings into an explosive power capable of blasting to fragments centuries-old bastions " [6] considered himself first and foremost a philosopher, and constantly returned to the philosophical sources of Marxism. For Lenin had studied his Hegel with what was for him unusual thoroughness. He accused the German Social Democrats of having out of opportunism left the path which leads from the great German philosophy of the 19th century straight to Marx and Engels. This, he continues, is evident chiefly in their

---

[4] F. Engels, Die Entwicklung des Sozialismus von der Utopie zur Wissenschaft (1882).

[5] F. Engels, *Ludwig Feuerbach and the Outcome of Classical German Philosophy* (London: Martin Lawrence, 1934), IV, p. 70.

[6] E. von Kologriwof, *Die Metaphysik des Bolschevismus* (1934), p. 56.

relaxation of the critical struggle against religion. In a pamphlet published in 1917, *State and Revolution,* he writes:

> "It is well known that German Social Democracy, in proportion as it began to decay and become more and more opportunist, slipped more and more frequently into the philistine misinterpretation of the celebrated formula: 'Religion is a ... private matter.' That is, this formula was twisted to mean that the question of religion was a private matter *even for the party of the revolutionary proletariat!* It was against this utter betrayal of the revolutionary programme of the proletariat that Engels protested. In 1891 he saw only the *very feeble* beginnings of opportunism in his party, and, therefore, he expressed himself on the subject very cautiously: ... 'for the free activity of the working class — such as the realization of the principle that *in relation to the state,* religion is a purely private matter....' Engels deliberately emphasized the words 'in relation to the State,' as a blow straight at the heart of German opportunism, which had declared religion to be a private matter *in relation to the Party,* thus degrading the party of the revolutionary proletariat to the level of the most vulgar 'free-thinking' philistinism, which is prepared to allow a non-denominational status, but which renounces the *Party* struggle against the religious opium which stupefies the people. "

Note the lordly consciousness of mission, the ringing pride in possessing and propagating " pure " doctrine! This attitude of superiority spread from Lenin to all champions of dialectical materialism. From the outset they declined to examine seriously the standpoint of their opponents. Apparently they already sensed the danger of its mollifying their own revolutionary position.

THE WESTERN ROOTS OF BOLSHEVISM

We must not shrink from the discovery that Bolshevism demasks not so much the face of Russia as our own Western past. The roots of Bolshevist philosophy are to be sought among us. "It is characteristic of the superficial way in which the whole 'white' worlds thinks, " Oswald Spengler said decades ago, "that this Bolshevism is regarded as a Russian creation, threatening to conquer

Europe. Actually, it was born in Western Europe as the last triumph of the presumptuous intention to control living history by thumb rule systems and ideals. " [7]

We must not forget that " Communism came to Russia as a legitimate offspring of Western intellectual and social history, that Lenin dreamed of making Berlin, not Moscow, the capital of the world revolution. " [8]

Contrasted with Communism's authoritatively determined *Weltanschauung* based strictly on clear uniform suppositions, the philosophical thought of the West is a hodgepodge of conflicting doctrines. Frequently operative here is a skepticism which no longer recognizes the solid, objective norms that are the backbone of all religions but considers all norms historically and psychologically qualified. The fact is that in the Western world the same basic philosophical positions prevail as in the Eastern world. To be sure, the West lacks the courage to draw the revolutionary consequences that the East has drawn and continues to draw. Moreover, as warning voices keep reminding us, in the West a practical materialism runs rampant. Usually dismissed as politically innocuous, it nonetheless represents a fateful sign of spiritual disintegration. Certainly among the masses, it produces a shortsighted delusion which conceals the range and gravity of the philosophical conflict now raging.

The apparent relaxation of the fist with which the East has hitherto pommelled world revolution and belligerent atheism along their way further screens the real issue in this battle for belief. What has really taken place is a significant change in tactics. Brute force is being replaced by more refined and flexible methods. Many have tried to interpret these methods as evidence of a new spirit of appeasement and amelioration. Again and again there have been discussions as to whether the legitimate plea for social reshuffling and development could not be stripped of its obviously unessential mantle of religious persecution. Indeed, even churchmen have gone so far as to brand the view that Communist rule places the church under a death sentence as " infamous heresy "

---

[7] O. Spengler, *The Hour of Decision*, " Germany and World-Historical Evolution, " p. 115.

[8] K. Mehnert, *Peking and Moscow*. Translated from the German by Leila Vennevitz (G. P. Putnam and Sons: New York, 1936), p. 6.

(Martin Niemoller). Against all this stands the cold fact that in
Bolshevist-ruled countries the screws of the ideological struggle are
being systematically turned tighter and tighter — obviously to
implement universal atheism. Noteworthy too is Henri Chambre's
comprehensive and often penetrating study [9] of Russian documents
which enabled him to substantiate his theory that although since
the 1917 Revolution Soviet ideology has undergone many radical
changes of method, in the area of religion not one of these expedient
shifts has altered Communism's theoretical-ideological stand. Today
as yesterday, Leninist Marxism wages the same aggressive war
against God and all that reminds men of God. However, even if
there were to be some unpredictable change of Bolshevist leaders,
the new would still be mere exponents of a total, self-implementing
system which has been thought through to the end and which
cannot relinquish its fundamental position without contradicting
itself.

How little we can speak of a change in the established goal is
clear from Khrushchev's programmatic speech to the 22nd Congress
of the Communist Party in 1961. He declared:

> " Communist education presupposes the emancipation of the con-
> sciousness from religious prejudices and superstitions which will still
> prevent some Soviet people from manifesting their creative forces to
> the full. We need a well-considered and orderly system of scientific-
> atheist education that will embrace all strata and groups of the popula-
> tion and will prevent the dissemination of religious concepts, especially
> among children and adolescents. "

In the new program of the Communist Party of 1961 the struggle
against superstitions and religious prejudice has clearly been made
a major issue and the special concern of Bolshevist education: " The
Party regards the combatting of manifestations of bourgeois ideology
and morality and the remnants of private-property psychology,
superstitions, and prejudices, to be an integral part of the work of
Communist upbringing. "

> ... " The Party employs means of ideological influence to rear
> people in the spirit of the scientific-materialistic world view, to over-
> come religious prejudices without permitting the sentiments of be-

---

[9] H. Chambre, *Le Marxisme en Union Soviétique* (Paris, 1955), p. 354.

lievers to be insulted. It is necessary to systematically conduct broad
scientific-atheist propaganda. "

The State spares no effort to attain its confirmed goal: eradication
of the last trace of religion by 1980.

Until now, analysis of dialectical materialism on the intellectual
level has been crippled by typical prejudice. Strangely enough,
those in responsible circles continue to react to the dangers of
materialism with strangely ostrichlike tactics. A whole battery of
questions arising from the materialistic view of man and the world
is simply dismissed by the high priests of scientific philosophy as
irrelevant. "Materialism—a fossil of science," writes Barbara
Morgan. All too easily, downgrading of this kind seems to excuse
people from taking the Eastern world-view seriously. Besides, we
are told, materialism as a scientific explanation of the world has
long been outstripped; it is merely a calcified "by-product of
science" possible only in a period without a great philosophy, as
was the second half of the preceding century. Furthermore, materialism never was a genuine world view, but only a surrogate for
one and bound to collapse the moment a steadily advancing knowledge of nature once again concentrated more on the essence of
nature itself. Admittedly, the argument continues, materialism continues to exercise remarkable power over the masses, but this is to
be accounted for by the law of historical aftereffects, according to
which a played-out intellectual system becomes fully effective among
the masses only a generation or two later. "To call a philosophy
a fossil does not, unfortunately, mean that it is dead. The philosophy
of materialism was never more alive than it is today. It has filtered
down from the intelligentsia to the power seekers and from them
to the victims, " [10] writes Barbara Morgan, adding that one can
admit materialism's far-reaching effects without feeling any obligation to tackle the problem seriously and objectively.

One is particularly loath to grant dialectical materialism in the
official party form that is valid in the East the rank of any of the
Western philosophies. Western intellectuals have often simply
refused to bother their heads about it.

[10] B. Morgan, *A Skeptic's Search for God* (New York: Harper & Brothers,
1947), p. 14.

Objective thinkers refuse to take such pretensions seriously because they are revolted by the arrogance of Bolshevist "philosophers" who insist that they possess the sole scientific philosophy—all others being based on a mere pseudo-science manufactured "upon orders from American imperialists and the Vatican to deceive the proletariat, the better to exploit them," as I. M. Bochenski writes in his book on Soviet Russia's dialectical materialism.

Three decades ago, in a paper entitled "The Collapse of Materialism," the famous biologist and philosopher, Hans Driesch, seemed to have had the final word on the subject of the materialism then current. Since then, it has become a platitude to say that materialism's pseudo-scientific explanation of the world has totally broken down.

In the course of our reflections it will become evident that there is much more behind present-day materialism than the word first suggests. This is reason enough to dig deeper, to expose the uncritically chosen underpinnings on which the whole system stands and to test their strength. It is also worth noting that during the course of man's history, materialistic world views have frequently followed in the wake of moribund idealistic systems; further, that today, dialectical materialism is amazingly well received in Western intellectual circles. The philosophy of Communism exercises such fascination, and not only over the proletariat, which it continues to celebrate as the pillar of the future, but also over intellectuals. Western atom-physicists have been known to risk their lives to place secret information at the disposal of Eastern Communists. Nor can one say that these men simply succumbed to promises of material compensation. Even Lenin jeered at the professors and "revisionists" who "with indulgent smiles murmured...that materialism had long since been 'refuted'." [11]

[11] W. I. Lenin, *Collected Works* (New York: International Publishers, 1963).

THE INADEQUACY OF DEFENSE ALONE

There certainly does exist, and not only among the masses but also among the educated as well, a myopic infatuation with the pressing concerns of daily living. Coupled with little awareness of responsibility for important decisions, this shortsightedness becomes downright blindness oblivious to danger. In Nietzsche's metaphor, we stroll heedlessly over frozen waters, unconcerned that a thaw-wind has been blowing for days, and that the ice is already thin. The heedlessness of the crowd forces the intellectual watchmen at the outposts of the age to assume the responsibilities of the thoughtless.

In the intellectual confrontation which the present situation demands, it is not enough merely to intercept and parry blows. Nor is it permissible to stoop to the level of dialectical materialists and employ their tactics. Emotional outbursts of fanatical aggressiveness must not be allowed to infect objective thought. Dispassionately, we must take the trouble to distinguish clearly between the substance of the argument and its emotional by-products, to examine it quietly without prejudice while tracing the psychic causes behind the fanaticism.

Without condescension, without underestimating the strength of the adversary, unimpressed by the argument that dialectical materialism today is only an insignificant variant of a long-refuted materialism which flourished in the late 19th century, we must first catch up with our antagonist and analyze him more deeply than he does himself. For in the onslaught from forces confident of victory, those under fire must never allow themselves to be pushed into a defensive position, or to limit their action to repairing the breaches in their own bastions. Rather they must roll back the aggressor's entire front in order to attack on his own territory. This classic rule is particularly valid in the present intellectual conflict. When Karl Marx declares that thorough Germany cannot revolt without revolting thoroughly, from the ground up; that emancipation of the German is emancipation of the whole mankind; and that the spearhead is philosophy, [12] we had better prick up ours ears and take Communism's philosophical draught seriously. As for the radicalness of our antagonist, we should go deeper and get down to the roots, " radices, " from which the whole tree springs.

Too often we try to attack Marxism on its forefront, misreading it as merely social-economic doctrine, although Marxism itself claims unequivocally to be more. Today even economic theoreticians perceive the depths of the problem and try to understand Marxism as a counterreligion. Thus Eduard Heimann observes: " Atheism is integral to all Marxist thought and is, in a way, its climax and the test of its perfection. " [13]

For Marx, atheism is anything but a mere superstructure or façade that can be removed from his intellectual system without essentially changing it. We have his own statement that, for him, atheism is more fundamental than Communism; that it is indeed " an absolutely essential ingredient of Marxism. "

True, the " new faith " indignantly rejects all attempts to label it religion or even counterreligion. It considers itself a philosophy, proclaiming to be the most progressive philosophy of the day. Had some bourgeois contemporary of Marx questioned him on his intellectual origins, Marx would certainly have described himself as a student of Hegel, whose dialectical methods he had revived and applied to economic phenomena, thereby creating the ideological means for a " thorough " revolution. Similarly Lenin, the Russian disciple of German Marx, and Stalin, Lenin's Caucasian disciple, would have called themselves above all philosophers and engineers of humanity.

THE IMPACT OF MARXISM

Nonetheless, any evaluation of Marxism solely as a philosophy is totally inadequate. The extraordinary drive which ended in the

[12] K. Marx-F. Engels, Hist. Krit. Gesamtausgabe im Auftr. des Marx-Engels-Instituts Moskau. Erste Abt .Bd, (I. I. Halbband, 1927), p. 621.

[13] E. Heimann, Reason and Faith in Modern Society (Middletown, Connecticut, 1961).

victory of Bolshevism came from the powerful Messianic faith which pounded through its veins, a faith confident of attaining the secular fulfillment of its longings through Marxism. For decades, especially in Russia, a footloose, confused, yet arden Messianism had sought a way out, not only from material distress, but also out from under general subjugation by an exodus into some promised land. Everywhere great masses of men and women whose spirit had not yet been completely broken feverishly awaited the establishment of a "kingdom of God," about which the most incredible rumors were spread and credited. An oppressed people, convinced that it has been chosen, sincerely hoped in the wake of the most radical of revolutions and the dictatorship of the "proletariat" to establish the Messianic Kingdom. Once Karl Marx's ideology, already borne on the high winds of genuine belief in the saving power of revolution, merged with the ardent Messianic longing of the Russian people, it swelled to a hurricane that could stop at nothing short of the triumph of world revolution.

In the West, after centuries of falling away from Christianity (a movement identifiable with Machiavelli, Hobbes, Voltaire, Napoleon, Nietzsche, Hitler, and Mussolini), Marxism succeeded in attracting the unemployed spiritual forces of the day. For the animating spirit of this counterfaith proclaims: We are the power of the future! With us marches progress, irresistible as a law of nature!

Basic to this pseudo-religion is its sacrosanct faith in an historical progress supposedly allied with dialectical materialism. Meanwhile, the wheel of history has turned things upside down too often to justify any such primitive faith in one-directional progress. Since this faith does not rest on arguments—indeed categorically rejects them—the only thing that could expose it as delusion would be an actual historical development that runs counter to Marxist expectations. Already there have been disappointments that can no longer be concealed. Moscow has repeatedly convened congresses of experts on atheistic propaganda, who have been forced to admit that "obsolete superstition" is still a vital force which dominates large sections of the population, and which, in spite of all the pressures against it, continues to make fresh converts. At any rate, faith in the catchword, "superannuated religion," (which,

once outside aid is withheld, dies a natural death) has been badly
shaken. It is senseless to argue about which side possesses the
stronger, potentially more creative forces or to attempt a prognosis.
Ultimately decisive will be not the vital power to enlist but the
spiritual power of the truth to which that faith is bound.

Too easily discussions of timely problems degenerate into heated
controversies whose timeliness passes very quickly. Later examination of the same issues, once settlement has taken the emotional
wind from their sails, usually reveals that the positions of simple
pro and *con* were too short-range. For this reason, our considerations of the religious conflict today must reach beyond the isolated
context of the present. We must view the momentary fronts as but
one act of the ideological epic struggle which runs through all
human and world history. By thus broadening the basis of our
question, we can steer clear of the sandbars and shallows on which
most contemporary debate on this subject becomes grounded. Thus
our turning to Goethe for guidelines. Now we must examine the
history of Western thought to see whether the conflict between
belief and unbelief really is " the true, the deepest. . .the only
theme. . .of human history. "

2.   *The struggle between belief and unbelief*

THE REVOLT OF THE TITANS

For us of an enlightened age Etna's volcano is like a vision of primordial grandeur. From Sicily's eastern coast the mountain lifts its snowy head ten thousand feet above the sea. As we watch the smoke clouds curl from the main crater ringed by two hundred lesser ones, we shudderingly recall that since antiquity, this volcano has vomited fire and stone eighty times. For the great Greek tragedian Aeschylus who had seen Etna's massif for himself, while on a voyage to Western Greece, the mountain was mystically alive. Men believed that the Titan Typhon of the hundred hands, brother of the rebel Prometheus, lay imprisoned under Etna, and from time to time gave vent to his helpless rage. From Aeschylus' *Prometheus Bound* we learn that Typhon too had rebelled against the gods:

> " Pity too filled my heart when once I saw
> swift Typhon overpowered,
> Child of the Earth was he, who lived
> in caves in the Cilician land,
> a flaming monster with a hundred hands,
> who rose up against all the gods.
> Death whistled from his fearful jaws.
> His eyes flashed glaring fire.
> I thought he would have wrecked God's sovereignty. " [1]

[1] E. Hamilton, *Three Greek Plays* (W. W. Norton and Co., Inc., 1937), p. 111.

But the supreme God's lightning bolt had struck him down and his mammoth frame pinned fast by the mountain's bulk still sprawls near the coast there where the sea narrows to the Straits of Messina. Even in the bolt-scorched Titan, hatred of Zeus continues to simmer, occasionally showing licks of flame. One day it will boil over, utterly destroying the fertile slopes of the entire island.

All myths with their epic breadth and colorful details will be misunderstood as long as we see in them nothing more than the play of uninhibited, creative imagination rather than the poetic expression of man's age-old awareness of himself and his place in the world. Only when we search deep within ourselves for our own answers to similar experiences will we be able to grasp the myths. Only one who himself has known the torture of inner tensions stretched beyond human endurance, and their explosion in a burst of wild rebellion sweeping everything from its path with elemental disregard, knows how naturally such experiences come to be imagined on a gigantic supernatural scale. Such projections of man's spirit into nature are convincing only when the ancient poet himself has experienced the elemental, explosive power of wild rebellion. An occasional, fleeting vexation is not enough; Titanic rebellion springs from an inmost wound, from the throbbing indignation of the creature writhing helplessly in his creaturely chains, yelling curses against the gods. Only thus, as a symbol torn from man's deepest experience, is the natural phenomenon " volcano " comprehensible in human terms. How lacerating for the man of antiquity the over-powering tensions he suffered must have been, making him turn at last against the highest god and, in an outburst of rage, accuse him of injustices of such enormity that only the mythical image of an Etna-bound Titan could convey his despair.

The figure of Prometheus is part of the mainstream of Greek mythology. The myth that envelops his name was there from the beginning, not woven later. Originally the Greeks had considered him a god, though never one of the Olympian pantheon who enjoyed an effortless, paradisiacal world. Prometheus' deeds, like those of the other Titans, are accomplished by a supreme effort of the will. They are born of heavy labor quite unknown for instance to Zeus, " For Thee doth all this universe that circles round the earth obey, moving whithersoever Thou leadest, and is gladly swayed by Thee. " [2]

In spite of their descent from Gaia, the Earthmother and her firstborn son, Uranus—at least according to the theogany of Hesiod—the Titans' sympathies were with man; indeed, they constitute paradigmatically man's way of existence. Prometheus is credited with two primordial deeds with which he confronts the gods: the establishment of the sacrificial meal, and the theft of fire. With these he took man's yoke upon himself representing " the wretched ones " before the carefree gods. Again typically human, Prometheus is convinced that he can attain his goal only by devious means. Through slyness and trickery he tries to balance the scales tipped against man. To assert himself as a man he thinks he must act unjustly, even though the resulting punishment is terrible. This is the tragedy of human existence.

Because the Titans are able to accomplish their deeds only through unspeakable effort, they are touchy about resistance, inclined to bitterly misinterpret difficulties as personal wrongs, until their thwarted energy finally explodes into active revolt. Hence all Titans are disposed to criminal excesses. They are what today would be called supermen, the apotheoses of man contemplating himself, oversized and idealized.

How profoundly neo-humanism misunderstood the essence of the Greek, into whom Winckelmann projected his own dreams of perfect harmony [3]—the peace of quiet greatness and noble simplicity, of blithe beauty and sensual pleasure! Even a thinker usually as unimpressionable as Hegel succumbed to the dream-image of his day and took his turn at hymning the Attic essence. He held that the spirit of Greece, the " image of a people's genius, fortune's and freedom's child nurtured by the beautiful imagination " [4] was beamed into the soul receptive to human beauty and greatness. No! Greek reality was quite different. Greeks sighed no less than we under

---

[2] Hymn of Cleanthes, Professor Mahaffy, *Greek Life and Thought*, English Translation by E. H. Blakeny in " Texts for Students, " Vol. XXVI (London, 1921). T. W. Rolleston, *The Teaching of Epictetus* (George Rowtledge and Sons, Limited, 1891).

[3] C. Kerenyi, *Prometheus, Archetypal Image of Human Existence*. Translated from the German by Ralph Mannheim. Bollingen Series LXVI (Pantheon Books, 1963).

[4] W. Dilthey, *Die Jugendgeschichte Hegels* (1905), p. 71.

the burden of uncertainty, discord, disappointment, and bitterness.
It was to exhort them never to let wanton frivolity make them forget
the underlying tragicalness of life that the tragedies were enacted
every year with cultic solemnity.

TWO BASIC FORMS
OF THE CULTURAL "SOUL"

False as it is to consider ethnologically ancient peoples "savage,"
it is equally one-sided to think of the primitive cultures as realizations of unperturbed harmony: man at peace with himself and the
world. Still, we can make some rough comparisons. The culturally
primitive Congo pygmies, for instance, live in a state of relative,
childlike contentment with themselves and their surroundings. Even
when pressure from stronger tribes has led to a certain cultural
impoverishment, it is far from the truth to call them degenerate.
An expert writes of them: "Never do they allow a feeling of
helplessness towards the raging elements to prevail; they know
neither dread nor fear of nature's manifestations. Harsh, joyless,
drab, and monotonous as their existence may seem to us, they
themselves feel no sense of privation; on the contrary, they consider
themselves, so to speak, undefeated victors in the struggle for
existence. Hence the cheerful pluck and stubborn tenacity with
which they set about their daylong tasks; hence their unflagging
resilience in the daily hunt, although they come home with empty
bags almost as often as with heavy; hence their unbroken spirit
even when they are profoundly shaken by illness or death. Fear or
worry about the future are unknown, and their young people are
strangers to the dark intellectual torments of youth elsewhere. This
indomitable courage towards life wings their feet far into old age." [5]
Some pygmy tribes live in a kind of childhood still outside the
threshold of genuine culture—if by culture we mean the achieve-

[5] M. Gusinde, *Die kongo-Pygmaeen in Geschichte und Gegenwart* (1924),
p. 232.

ments of civilization. Many have not yet reached the real stone age, since they do not systematically make stone tools, but are satisfied with wooden ones. Even when they adopt tools from neighboring peoples, they still lack the incentive necessary for rapid cultural development; instead they have preserved a childlike contentment. Naturally this is not true of all pygmies—even here we find the converse attitude so much more common in other races.

This converse attitude is most pronounced where an intense will strives titanically to bring the earth to heel and to exploit the forces of nature by means of clever inventions. If ethnologists still distinguish primitive peoples from civilized, the difference referred to does not lie in any intellectual capacity nor in the notion that the primitive race lacks certain talents which the civilized possesses. Basically, all races have the same intellectual capacity. What of course characterizes primitive peoples is their use of extremely simple resources in their pursuit of a livelihood and their limited understanding of natural phenomena, whereas typical of the civilized races is a strong leaning to technical mastery and the exploitation of natural resources. But if the intellectual capacity of both is the same, the question arises: why does a people content itself with simple means of livelihood; why does it not develop its own technology; why this hesitant, often downright negative attitude towards the ready technological means developed by neighboring peoples and within easy reach? Right here we have the two diametrically opposed basic attitudes which spiritually stamp whole tribes, whole races. These attitudes appear as different formative powers. One might call them cultural entelechies, or with Frobenius, cultural "*Paideuma.*" According to him, "cultural souls" achieve a certain independence from the individual members of the community. "As an independent being the *Paideuma* has a life of its own."[6] Impersonal spirit, it governs a whole community, reacting formatively upon each member.

If we take the contradiction between the two basic attitudes described as a kind of crimson string and follow it through the maze of the world's religious phenomena, we distinguish a cor-

[6] L. Frobenius, *Paideuma. Umrisse einer Kultur- und Seelenlehre* (1953), p. 56,

responding pair of opposite attitudes that point to a remarkable discovery. The ethnologist Richard Mohr calls attention to the curious fact that we find, " particularly among peoples with few technological interests a highly developed religion, ritual, and art, " which leads us to suspect that " these people display little interest in the development of technical accomplishments because their psychic attention is absorbed by other things. " [7]

RELIGION:
MORE THAN A PRODUCT OF EVOLUTION

For decades religious research has made intensive efforts to fit the confusing multiplicity of myths, beliefs, and religions into some sort of comprehensive whole by means of a schema that would make it easier to see them as a unit and to understand their relationship. One such schema was the biological world view so widespread in the heyday of Darwinian thought; a schema, so it seemed, that could be stretched to apply universally. Unquestionably, in the field of living organism (animalcubes, for instance) the evolutionary theory is of primary importance; one must marvel at the number of different forms which the metamorphosis of a single organism —for all the limitation of genus—is able to develop. Must not therefore (through ever higher development of the animalcules) even the most diverse forms of plant and animal life have come into being, each stemming from the one before it? Impressive arguments for the development of animate being in this manner, at least within certain form boundaries, can be cited.

Nonetheless, we must not fail to recognize that what is meant by evolution is above all a category of vitality, and the living actualization of originally imperceptible potentialities. Such evolutionary development is a natural process; it represents a prehuman event, yet one that we too still experience because we are also organic

[7] R. Mohr, *Die Christliche Ethik im Lichte der Ethnologie* (1954), p. 3.

beings. Because of the link between our essential and physiological levels, our spiritual life also participates in the evolutionary process through growth and maturation, although here, as compared with mere physiological development, qualitatively new factors play a role. At any rate, the truly personal life is not exhausted by the evolutionary process but finds fulfillment in acts of personal recognition, affirmation, and choice. Thus the dimension of natural processes (characterized by fixed lines of development in nature) is left behind, and a new dimension entered in which present conditions cannot be used to predict future states. For it is in selective acts that " pure rationality " can never quite explain that the courses of development to be followed are set.

In man, because of his intellectual self-possession, there exists a multidimensional range of possibilities within which he is free to choose for himself. Wherever we meet man, in history or in prehistory, it is always as one who has long since ceased to be a mere product of the purely natural and unilinear processes of evolution. Always he is true man, awakened to self and capable of forming his own attitude toward that self, toward the world, and the ground of the universe. Closer examination reveals that from the start a mysterious inner dissension is at work in man, which splits his " evolution " into different directions. Hence purely physical laws and theories — the moment they presume to account for the whole man, his specifically human and historical world included — become questionable, misleading, and clearly pseudo-scientific. Above all, attempts to illuminate the inmost province of human life (i.e. religion in all its uniqueness) completely miscarry when approached from purely biological categories. To say that religion evolves is to imply that it results from given potentialities like those that unfold in physiological processes, whereby environmental influences are capable of causing variable departures in form. But even variations of environment are provided for in the play of such potentialities, which are the results, more or less automatic, of inheritance plus environment without intervention from higher authority. When Hegel has his absolute spirit evolve, for all his dialectical shuttling, he is utilizing what is really a pre-intellectual and subpersonal category that has no connection with spirit in the full independence and initiative of the word. " Evolution " is only the " coming to " (closely connected with organic development) of a yet latent, not yet actual mind or spirit *(Geist)*. Spirit in the full sense, however, is not a coming to, but an arrival at self. Freed from natural necessity, man's spirit can so line up and survey its life's possible directions, as to enable it to choose objectively from among them. Though total intellectual freedom is never a goal fully obtained by a culture, it always exists (at least incipiently) wherever genuinely human beings work out for themselves in custom, ethics, art, and religion the supreme forms of human existence.

MAN'S DIVIDEDNESS

If man today is conscious of being a creature of inner tensions whose natural impulses tug him in opposing directions, he has learned from just such painful ambivalence that two souls live within his breast. Very likely this characteristic schizoidism was always in man, at least potentially, and hence from the start his life was more than a mere natural process, was always genuine history in which his own decisions played at least a part. Always it is conscious man, or man on the way to consciousness of self, who attempts to explain his place in the world through myth and religion, and thereby fits himself one way or another into the world order, even though he by no means grasps the magnitude of his conclusions or suspects their consequences.

The primary characteristic of conscious man is the complexity of his life; he is forced by his own nature to assume an attitude towards himself, even if initially and for a long time that attitude is embedded in the collectivity of the tribe. To his own wonder man discovers himself on earth. Deep within him is the voice of a mysterious joint-knowledge (conscientia) of a world order in which he is to take his place. He is free to follow the promptings of his conscience, and he is also free to succumb to the promptings of a selfish rejection of the world and his place in it. Only men, not animals, can commit suicide. If man obeys the impulse to reject existence as it is, to reorganize it according to his will and for his purposes, he will be tempted to find some nefarious means of getting to the heart of the world's secret and of discovering the hidden fulcrum from which it is supposed to be possible to lever history according to his desires. It is from such attempts that magic is born.

RELIGION AND MAGIC AS OPPOSITES

A comparative study of cultures is bound to reveal that psychic tendencies differ not only from individual to individual but from race to race. Inner perceptiveness varies with different peoples. " Psychic needs and intellectual interests determine what a particular people will respond to, and their attitude towards reality determines a culture's ' face ', " says ethnologist Richard Mohr. Thus Leo Frobenius, tracing the psychic roots of cultures, found everywhere two converse attitudes, the mystic and the magic, a division we find also in *The Golden Bough* [8] by the famous ethnologist Frazer. " Since the beginning, " writes Evelyn Underhill, " the spiritual history of man reveals two distinct fundamental attitudes towards the unseen; and two methods whereby he has sought to get in touch with it. " [9]

Apparently the conflicting directions which the cultures of different peoples take result in a deep cleavage which can draw them in at least two directions in a schizoidism that offers an inborn freedom of choice so that man is never forced by nature into any one direction. Not that the choice is always clear and simple. More often, indeed typically for that enigmatic being, man, we find the strangest compromises, overlappings, criss-crossings of the lines of the often more colorful than comprehensible cultural patterns. None-

---

[8] Sir J. G. Frazer, *The Golden Bough; A Study in Magic and Religion* (1890).

[9] E. Underhill, *Mysticism. A study in the nature and development of man's spiritual consciousness* (New York, 1955).

theless, the two general directions are unmistakable. Richard
Mohr confirms that the whole of cultural history moves along one or
the other " track " indicated by Frobenius, the word for him imply-
ing an " abstraction, " for although theoretically the two *Paideumen*
are distinct, in colorful reality they often blend and mix, piling
one upon the other, touching and influencing each other mutually.

The point of departure is the same for both directions: experience
of the frailty of man's own existence; amazement that existence is a
matter merely of fact rather than necessity; existential fear in the
face of threats on all sides; powerlessness to direct his life alone;
man's unavoidable dependence on the rest of the world; awareness
of the inevitability of death; the duty (imposed by conscience as well
as by the law of blood) to subordinate the self to the many-structured
order of kinship; finally, the conflict between should and would—
all these experiences force man to confront the invisible.

The true religious attitude consists in personally affirming one's
own limitations, in lifting one's eyes (trust) to the surmised
Limiter, in recognizing a Supreme One " above, " in accepting the
duties to which man knows himself bound. Because the religious
man's relation to the Supreme One is marked by a certain diffidence,
he does not wish his devotions to be unprepared or extemporaneous.
He employs formal rites, and prefers to pray carefully formulated
prayers. He addresses his Lord with short, spontaneous words that
spring from his private momentary mood. Fear of failing to appear
before his God in the proper manner inclines him to lay down hard
and fast rules of religious deportment and to select suitable medi-
ators. In religious cults, the prayer mediator is the priest, who is
essentially different from the magician.

There are many reasons for man's failure to rise to the fully
human, personal religious attitude expected of him and his letting
himself slip or be pressured into the opposite position. First of
these is the inertia and sloth of the human spirit resulting from its
union with sensible nature. It costs man an effort to attain to a
fully human religious attitude; many never arrive at it. Instead
of pushing his way through intellectually to the powerful One behind
all nature, the unspiritual man remains so impressed by the natural
forces at work in his immediate world, that he takes them for
anonymous ghostly powers, or even animal spirits which he reveres.

Also primitive man knows himself divinely challenged by the blows of fate which befall him. Somehow he must assimilate the blow. First he cries out in pain to Him from whom he believes the blow has come. If he feels himself deserted by the supreme heavenly Being he has venerated with childlike trust all his life, his relation to Him may cool. If similar experiences are repeated time and again, his original warm and lively trust in a Heavenly Father may recede into the background. The image pales. Instead, the individual feels himself delivered over to the impersonal, unfeeling forces of fate. The primitive man can consent to revolt, bitterness, even malediction. Although in the remote beginning of man's history a warm, childlike relation to a Heavenly Father prevailed, apparently in the course of the centuries frequently there came a cooling of the once warm relations to the divine. This must have been true also of the Germanic tribes, who at the time of their entry into world history universally believed in fate, even though their ancient Aryan heritage had been faith in Dyaus-Pitar, the radiant Father in Heaven.

Frazer distinguishes clearly between magic and religion as two fundamentally different attitudes. Despite their essential difference, he allowed them to evolve in two directions. In this he was unable to transcend the evolutionary standpoint of his day. Frazer speaks of the deep-rooted battle of principles between magic and religion, which explains the merciless enmity with which so often in history priest persecuted magician. The magician's haughty self-complacency, his presumptuous behavior towards the higher powers, and his unabashed claim to equality with them are bound to revolt the priest, whose reverence for divine majesty and deep humility towards it, must consider such claims and behavior godless, and a blasphemous attempt to usurp rights that belong to God alone.

From all this there appear among primitive peoples two opposing forms of belief; in the one, belief in a " religious god-man "; in the other, belief in a " magical god-man. " More correctly, one could say, on the one hand, belief in a god-man, on the other, in a man-god. Whereas the first belief is in the embodiment of a divine being in human form, the magical man-god, thanks to a secret sympathy with nature, considers himself a being who exercises extraordinary powers.

VARIOUS DISPOSITIONS

Only from the viewpoint of their fundamental difference in attitude is a clean line between religion and magic discernible, since their outer forms are often so closely interwoven as to appear identical. For it does happen that forms of expression that were originally religious degenerate into traditional rites performed with magical rather than religious intent. In religion, the reverent and conscientious attitudes dominate; the religious man seeks to establish conscious contact with the divine world-mover, to fit into the unique sacred order of things. The religious attitude thus cements the community on which it has a strong moral impact.

With magic it is quite different. Here there is no personal reaching up to the divine. All the magician aspires to is autonomous power over the forces of earth. Departure from the sacred order unleashes dark passions. It is for private, selfish reasons that the sorcerer is consulted. The activity of the priest lies on a higher plane. Sorcery turns round such things as rain-making, healing, money-making, power, and child-bearing. But whether the aim is the conjuring of a spirit, the overcoming of a danger or the curing of a disease, magic's ultimate aim is always an intensification of the powers of the will beyond the limits of the natural in order to obtain some particular favor for oneself or one's group. Self-interest is always paramount.

To be sure, the religious attitude is not free from self-interest; also the religious man seeks his own happiness but that happiness is a part of and subordinate to the general, greater good. It is accompanied by a spirit of devotion and selflessness.

Where the differences between religion and magic are clear-cut, the result is uncompromising enmity between priest and sorcerer. Their implacability springs from their essentially contrary attitudes. True, in daily life with its many compromises the borderlines frequently overlap. Where both employ the same language, customs, and accoutrements, an anthropologist can easily become confused and report mysticism where magic pervades. Notwithstanding, religion and magic are opposite poles of one and the same world.

Between these poles lie various gradations of religions, cults, and magical practices which the history of religion has so far tried in vain to classify rectilinearly.

Love of God is prevalent in the religious attitude even when that love is still searching for God, is yet unconscious or unable to explain itself. Its exact opposite is self-love, magic's ultimate aim. Where religion builds community, magic shatters it.

Magic's cardinal tenets may be summed up as follows:

1. There exists " a supersensible and real ' cosmic medium ' which interpenetrates, influences, and supports the tangible and apparent world. "

2. There is " an established analogy and equilibrium between the real (Plato's unseen) world and the illusory manifestation which we call the world of sense. "

3. " This analogy may be discerned, and this equilibrium controlled by the disciplined will of man which thus becomes master of itself and of fate. "

" Magical operations, " says Eliphas Levi, a modern magician, " are the exercise of a power which is natural, but superior to the ordinary powers of nature. " The same magician admits that the main weakness of the magical attitude is " the cold intellectual arrogance, the intensely individual point of view which occult studies seem to induce by their conscious quest for exclusive power and knowledge, their implicit neglect of love. " [10]

The magician's greed for power through knowledge poisons and destroys his relations to God.

EVOLUTION, NO BRIDGE

Richard Mohr is right to reject as impossible any " evolution from religion to magic or vice versa. The intrinsic difference between the two attitudes is too great and too diverse. It does happen that religion may degenerate into magic, understandable enough in view

[10] *Ibid.*, pp. 160-62.

of the cleavage in man himself which keeps his magical and religious attitudes perpetually at war. Admittedly no mere collection of facts suffices to get to the root of the contradiction; this can be done only by illuminating the *Paideuma* or guiding soul that lies there. The religious attitude always relates itself somehow to personally apprehended powers outside or above the world, which it approaches with reverent awe, trust, and love. The magical attitude is entirely different. It is really concerned not with metaphysical but with physical, earthly forces which the practitioners of magic attempt to control. Their whole effort is aimed at acquiring as many of these powers as possible and utilizing them for their own purposes."

Where the religious attitude considers God the real center of the world, magic places man there, either individual man or mankind. Where the religious man accepts the family as the natural and proper unit of a social order into which it is the task of the individual to integrate himself, the man of magical tendencies creates for himself an artificial social order, a totemistic clan-organization for example, or some arrangement which splits the tribe according to sex, into two groups which in daily life are kept unnaturally isolated. Above all, the values of the two positions are placed entirely differently. In the one, appreciation of transcendent values has a positive, appeasing effect on people; whereas exclusive interest in earthly values tends to swell desires far beyond the limits of the individual need. Desire then degenerates into greed and callousness.

We can still observe this among the pygmies, especially when two tribes with completely different attitudes live next door to each other. The difference between them is traceable even to the smallest details of daily life. Mohr describes some that typify the difference in attitude. When a severe thunderstorm rages over all their heads, the members of one pygmy tribe will try to disperse it by magic, like the blowing of a horn, and vociferously deny any guilt for which the storm might be a punishment. During the same storm, members of a neighboring tribe will mutually confess their guilt and perform propitiatory rites. Where a distinctly religious cult governs the life of a tribe, there is no magic at all. Magic runs rampant in other pygmy races which show little interest in religious ideas and no need for God in their daily lives. Egotism is a flagrant characteristic of such tribes.

SIGNIFICANCE OF THE OPPOSITION

Typical of the religious research of the last decade was its concern with the spiritual content of religions and myths. Comparing them, it often allowed itself to be misled by certain outward resemblances into assuming intrinsic similarities. Above all, it tried to bring order into the motley spectacle of existence by arranging it along the lines of evolutionary thought. The predominant idea behind research of this kind is a rationalistic basic attitude, which in the sense of Vischer's " the moral life is always self-understood, " considers it unseemly to examine the affective roots and the substance of morality. Yet genetic studies of great world views reveal that these often grow out of emotional predispositions, and that what is true of the *Weltanschauungen* of the great philosophers is valid also for the world views *(Weltanschauungen)* of peoples. Here again religious research is easily distracted from its original purpose by the pressing task of amassing material. The herbalist's enthusiasm often exhausts itself in the task of collecting, and he forgets to reflect on the archetypal, which Goethe made the chief objective in his memorable search for the prototype of all plant life.

He who wishes to get to the psychic roots of religious and philosophical phenomena cannot simply line them all up as equals when he remembers that man's eternally unchanging essence conceals a deep split that runs all the way through him, and that cannot fail to affect above all else his profoundest thinking and believing. The classification of races according to their basic world views *(Weltanschauungen)* provided a simple, natural system " so permanent, that even in the face of changes in the remaining culture, its validity remains, as Tessmann proved in the specific case of the Tschama. . . . For all his cultural changes man remains essentially the same " (Mohr, p. 20).

It is understandable that the fundamental religious attitude is by nature conservative; it inclines man towards contentment, thus fostering fewer impulses to further cultural progress. By contrast, the magical attitude is man-centered; indeed, in the last analysis, not only anthropocentric but egocentric. Thus the absolute, the "one and only" is sought not outside or beyond the world but in the world. Precisely this positing of the things of the world as absolutes must suffer from the very real limitations of all human endeavors. Its reaction to disappointment is an inordinate impulse to reform life autonomously.

Not improperly, magic has been called the first stammerings of natural science. Magic can shift easily, even naturally into technical inventiveness to which mankind owes its elementary and basic inventions. In sum, to the magically inclined, inventors are heroes, whereas to the religious conservative, they are apt to seem blasphemers. It was the impious, Titans, supermen, who dared to break out of the old accepted pattern and to take existence into their own hands.

TECHNOLOGY AND RELIGION

It is necessary to say a word here about technology's attitude toward religion because there has been a great deal of argument lately over its relative drawbacks and blessings. In this debate the full significance of technology is seldom appreciated. Technology's purpose, it is said, is to facilitate life. Theoretically it aims at relieving man of arduous and unpleasant chores. In reality, technological science is far more; it belongs essentially to man's nature.

Deeply impressive and full of profound significance is the account in Genesis of man's integration into the "*Hexaemeron*" or six days of labor. Here God is described as the Originator of the work-pattern with its rhythm of labor and rest intended for men. By observing this first law, man acquiesces to the same divine will and word by which, in the beginning, heaven and earth obediently

came into existence. This law is valid only for man, (not for plants
and animals) because, thanks to his God-given reason, man resembles God himself. He cannot live uncomplicatedly like the animals.
He is obliged by necessity and duty to create through his own
intelligent efforts the basis for his own way of life. Thus from
the beginning, man as a cultural being is set apart from the rest
of creation, a fact which the Bible reports with the simple and
evocative words " The Lord took the man and placed him in the
Garden of Eden to till it and to keep it " (Gn 2,15). Even before
the Fall this law was valid for man. After it, to be sure, the command
to work becomes harsh necessity. " In the sweat of your brow you
shall eat bread, till you return to the ground, since out of it you
were taken " (Gn 3,19).

Even in this first generation the road forks in two completely
different directions designated by the names Cain and Abel. This
separation is not a biological one but is the result of intellectual
choice. Cain's wildness lives on in his descendants, who like him
constantly overstep the bounds set by God. Lamech is but one
expression of their defiance, Lamech who was the first to take two
wives, thus arbitrarily introducing a new custom directly at odds
with the marriage pattern established in Eden. With menacing
bravado he sings his proclamation of immoderate, self-glorifying
revenge. Cain's violent, degenerate line is contrasted with that of
Seth, founder of another, a more pious tribe which began " to call
upon the name of the Lord " (Gn 4,26).

The Bible differentiates between nations on which God's blessing
rests, and those which lie under his curse. But here again there
can be no question of an unmerited fate, rather it is the consequences
of their own choice. On the basis of this choice, curse can be
turned into blessing, and blessing into curse. Although Seth's
descendants had found favorable conditions in the fruitful plains
of Sinar, with their increase a daring spirit of enterprise made itself
felt which soon degenerated into an inordinate desire for autonomy.

The attempt to build a tower reaching into the heavens was not
in itself punishable. What was punishable was the avowed intention
behind it: " let us make a name for ourselves lest we be scattered
all over the earth " (Gn 11,4). " What they wanted was fame, a
ringing name for having established a great center of political,

cultural, and economic power with an enormous temple for idols
in its midst. In other words, they wanted to become a world power
that worshipped idols and was alien, indeed hostile, to the one true
God. At the heart of that great power was to be the enormous
temple of idolatry. This is the concrete meaning of their being of
one tongue, their wishing to remain so, and their beginning to build
the tower. " [11]

Biblical accounts of God's direct intervention in the undertakings
of presumptuous men may sound naively anthropomorphic, yet in
them we already have the workings of the inner law: the quantitative
propagation of human plans, when it becomes excessive, renders
them uncontrollable and hence unrealizable. Wherever God intervenes in the Bible, it is with the explicit purpose of destroying some
concentration of God-inimical power on earth potentially capable
of producing ever more monstruous works. This time it was the
technology of city construction which had so inflamed man's pride
that he attempted to make himself the sovereign center of the world.
God, whom nothing can resist, shatters the inventions of ambitious
man.

Man's desire to perpetuate his name is not in itself sinful; it
becomes so only when it deteriorates into an autocratic greed for
power. There is a striving that is permissible and good. Endeavors
of this kind the Lord God himself furthers, as when he said to
Abraham, " I will show you; I will make a great nation of you "
(Gn 12,2). " In the kingdom of God, a great name is a gift of the
Lord, not a result of personal accomplishment. It is ' grace,' not
' works ' " (Closen, p. 34). Likewise man's attempts to break
through the barriers of his finite world are not in themselves evil.
To be sure, heaven can never be stormed by any wilful construction
of soaring towers, but only by seizing the " Jacob's ladder " which
heaven itself lets down in our hours of grace. After this vision of
the ladder, the Patriarch Jacob was overwhelmed by a genuinely
religious experience of God's nearness. " How awesome is this
place! This is none other than the house of God; this is the gate of
heaven " (Gn 28,17).

It is understandable that man's new self-confidence, born as it is

---

[11] G. Closen, *Wege in die Heilige Schrift*, Vol. 2, p. 33.

of his taste of technical mastery of life, easily becomes a craving for power which seizes technology to achieve its ends. Herein lies the demonic aspect of a technology that leads man away from God's will to do his own.

On the other hand, it is also understandable that religious people fearing technological excess are inclined to underestimate God's command to cultivate the earth, i.e. their cultural mission, and frequently neglect it. The religious attitude leans to preservation, conservation, with its negative counterpart: paralysis. In judging the history of mankind's religious decisions, this dialectical seesaw must be carefully considered if we are not to succumb to a sweeping condemnation of technology.

ANIMOSITY TOWARD GOD

Because the magic self-contained attitude aims at elevating man, because his happiness is its chief concern, a slight sensitivity and irritability are natural to it, which in turn gives rise to a typical phenomenon which Tessmann calls " animosity toward God. " [12]

Among very primitive peoples we notice that outbursts of rage against the godhead are no rarity. Sometimes we find a bitterness against God so widespread that people avoid speaking his name, that they, so to speak, cancel him out. Thus it was possible for so pure, clear, and morally superior a religion as the monotheism of the Indians of Tierra del Fuego (Yamana) to remain totally indiscernible to the outside world. Not only for Darwin did these Patagonians seem to be a typically religionless people, but even for a missionary who lived among them for decades. Not until a certain explorer gained so much of their confidence that he was allowed to undergo the youth-ritual by which he was made a member of the tribe and lived as one of them did he, after many years, discover their carefully guarded secret of faith in Wataninewa. Patagonian Indians are inclined to blame this heavenly God for

[12] G. Tessmann, *Die Bubi auf Fernando* (1923), p. 227.

sudden death. Above all, women who have lost little children consider themselves to be unjustly punished and refuse to speak his name. Everyone complains to him, reproaches him, quarrels with him, scolds him, and demands a settling of accounts. Of course, they also make their peace again. One cannot be angry with God forever; one also repents of violence, of the anger that carried him away.

Such irritation with God tends to weaken faith in God, indeed to cancel him out of the picture. It is important to discern this. One example: " It happens with the Bhils that someone who is quite overcome by sorrow turns against Bhagwan, expressing his revolt by curses and maledictions. Those women especially who have lost their husbands early can, on occasion, completely forget themselves and burst into blasphemy. But when they are called to account, they generally try to pretend that they have said nothing of the kind. ' Did you hear me say it? ' they will ask angrily or ' When and where am I supposed to have said that? ' They are afraid to ' risk their heads ' as the Bhil says. Here is a more or less free translation of such a blasphemy: ' God, may thy trace disappear because thou hast taken aim at my house. The harm of my house thou wouldst have set about, and Thou hast taken my husband's life '. " [13]

In the joy of everywhere finding traces of a primordial mono-theism, one was inclined to stress the brighter aspects and to ignore the dark ones. Rarely do we find descriptions of negative aspects included. [14] We certainly give far too little consideration to the extent to which such blasphemies might be the turning-point in an originally warm and vital trust in God, the beginning of the decline and death of faith. The wording of the malediction quoted above should make us prick up our ears. " God, may thy trace disappear. " Once it has been pronounced, the possibility must be reckoned with that a permanent bitterness takes over, which poisons the relationship to God. Then natural " growing cold "; indeed, desire to " cancel God " becomes reality. Like mildew, this resentment settles upon

[13] W. Koppers, *Primitive Man and his World Picture*. Translated by Edith Raybould (London and New York), pp. 79-80.
[14] W, Schmidt, *The Origin and Growth of Religion. Facts and Theories* (London, 1931), XII, p. 179.

man's faith, and the wider, deeper, more generally it spreads, the more faith in the one transcendent God languishes. This condition also explains how it can become difficult to discern the remains of an original monotheism which lingers on under such a blanket of disease. That a permanent attitude of bitterness against God can become an occasion for black magic is not only plausible, but has been explicitly reported, by Tessmann for one, in his book on the "Bubi." [15] To this Mohr comments: "here the origin of magic rites is an immoral, presumptuous revolt against God. Very likely the psychological foundation of all magic may be sought here" (Mohr, p. 25).

From the preceding, it is understandable that in the consciousness of mankind, reaching as far back as memory itself, the origin of the crafts everywhere seems somehow linked with blasphemy. It is the Titans who by their own efforts advance human destiny. They consume themselves in the violence of their effort to achieve, whereas Zeus reigns in sublime repose from which his every act unfolds. He whose attention is directed at achievement alone at the expense of being is prone to sudden outbursts, to blasphemous excesses, to acts of violence.... Face to face with Aetna one understands that the Titanic essence is the unpredictable violence of the volcano, not the river's steady flow. Technology's mythical origin is to be found among the Titans. The essence of technology, superman with his catastrophic outbursts, his frenetic achievements and hectic restlessness come straight from the Titanic world. That is why it was the Titan Prometheus who with his theft of fire made technical development possible. " [16]

MAN'S REMONSTRANCES WITH GOD
IN EARLY EGYPTIAN RELIGION

Along with the unmistakable reverence which shines through early man's fundamental attitude toward the godhead, we find also

[15] G. Tessmann, *Die Bubi auf Fernando Po* (1923), p. 227.
[16] G. Nebel, *Weltangst und Goetterzorn* (1951), p. 53.

evidence of the temptation in times of trial to reprove God. Above all, people who have grown self-confident through the development of their own creative powers are susceptible to this temptation and in danger of rejecting God completely and turning away from him. Evidence of this temptation is to be found also in the religion of ancient Egypt.

Through the jumble of Egyptian deities (mostly local gods) an inclination to monotheism is clearly discernible. Egypt's oldest religious treasure is Amon, a god of heaven whose symbol is the sun. H. Junker is convinced that Ur, whose name means "the great," is recognizably a very ancient heavenly *Allgott*. Apparently, his loss of supremacy was due to the inclusion of more and more local gods in the celestial ranks. [17]

In the 22nd century B.C. when the Old Kingdom (the first comprehensive, unified state on Egyptian territory) collapsed, more than a form of government collapsed with it. The entire pyramid of society with its firm belief in the continuity of the state in a timely beyond, and its faith in the immortalization of earthly life in achievement and monument all underwent a crisis which threatened the very existence of Egypt as an historical entity. Understandably, in this period a profound skepticism developed toward the whole question of immortality. The convulsions of a hitherto unshakable confidence in life are reflected in lamentations over the shattered order of existence and lead to impassioned debate on the fate of the country and on the personal fate of the questioner. Who is really, ultimately responsible for the general breakdown is the question of questions. "It is only natural that this controversy is essentially religious," says the Egyptologist Eberhard Otto, "for it is while it is being fought, and on Egyptian soil, that man takes the initial step out of the magical-natural coherence in which he found himself into the awareness of his unique existence as man." The profound question as to the why of pain and disorder must be addressed to someone. The deeper it gnaws, the more completely it works its way through things transient until at last it stands face to face with Heaven's Highest. Thus controversy becomes dialogue. Man complains, reasons, doubts, and accuses; and the power which

[17] M. Eliade, *The Sacred and the Profane. The Nature of Religion.* Translated from the French by Willard Trask (New York, 1959).

he believes determines his life replies. As in the Book of Job, arguments for and against are not presented as intellectual abtrac- tions, but in lively metaphor. Granted, today such plasticity of speech hinders more than it helps true understanding. This is one reason why the aid of an expert is essential. Eberhard Otto's work [18] expressly treats of God reproached, a common theme in early Egyptian literature.

Impotent in a creation that is out of joint, man is inclined to hold the Creator responsible for an original flaw in creation, thereby putting the blame also for his own personal misery on God and his accomplices, the lesser gods who in obedience to his command sustain creation. What the believer really expects of God, Otto points out, quoting from ancient Egyptian texts, is that he be " a shepherd for each one, a stranger to evil. Though his flock be small, yet he spends the day leading it to pasture. " But man is disappointed in his hope. God should never have allowed such a corrupt generation as the present one to flourish. He should have prevented the gods from preserving their seed. " Oh, if only in the first generation he had seen them for what they were! He would have hurled curses at them, would have lifted his mighty arm against them! Their seed, their heirs he would have destroyed. Instead, he desired that they be continually born. Thus every- where heartlessness and oppression arose. That is the trouble! There could be no end to it as long as these gods had a hand in things. It is they who allow the corrupt seed to continue to pour out of Egyptian women; after all, they hardly find it lying in the street! Violence and oppression—that is what the gods have created. There was no pilot in that day. Where is he today—asleep perhaps? Look about—there's not a sign of his power! "

God created man inadequate and now He has even lost control over him; this is the sum of the Egyptians' complaint. The reverent man is overpowered by the violent. Inordinate and perverse, that is the man God made!

In melancholy resignation to the vanity and hopelessness of life one weary sojourner finally suggests that men should simply enjoy life in order to forget its sorrows.

[18] E. Otto, *Der Vorwurf an Gott* (1951), p. 4.

Despite all this, in Egyptian intellectual and spiritual circles doubt and dissatisfaction with God have apparently not yet led to the rejection of God. Fragmentary warning words, ascribed to the " all-Lord " or " one-God, " have been preserved and are evidence of Egyptian belief in a single, absolute Lord. He was the One, even before creation with its duality: before heaven-earth, man-woman, farm-desert. Before all such " double things " existed, there was the One. (Similarly Plato speaks of God as the ONE.) In a small Egyptian fragment from an admonition attributed to God we find: " I have put glory in place of sensuality, generosity in place of greed, the heart's peace in place of bread-eating. " In a " heavenly discourse " between Atum and Osiris, man's complaints and reservations are put in the mouth of Osiris, who, though a god, is the mythical representative of man, whose complaints he lays before the Sun God, Amon. Here again God's answer is that earthly lust is to be supplanted by heavenly glory.

In another reply, the Supreme One reminds man of all the good that he has given him. Explicitly he points out that evil goes back not to the will of God but to the willfulness of men. Evil springs from the human heart; it has no place in the plan of creation. Finally, he calls attention to the secret which God reserves for himself. Man does not know the beyond and is not meant to know it. Through suggestive images God stressed his inscrutability. In his even stronger reply to Job's complaints, God deliberately takes Job to task: as creature, man in his ignorance should not presume to remonstrate with his Creator.

After a period of skepticism, when trust in the God-given order of things had reestablished itself in the Egyptian world, the point is emphasized that God's efficacy embraces all creatures, even those animals outlawed by cult. Yes, the great One-Lord surrounds his countless creatures with his all-embracing life-giving love—symbolized by two widespread arms.

We have a papyrus from the last century of the third millenium B. C. which seems to indicate that at this time trust in divine providence has been restored. A complete, self-contained hierarchy supports all living things, from Creator to the least creature. It appoints to each, man and animal, his definite place, and bestows upon monarchy, as a divine institution, meaning and justification.

Even magic has its place. " Well ordered are the lives of men,
God's cattle. For their sake he created heaven and earth. For
them he put an end to darkest chaos. He created the air that their
noses might breathe. Men are God's images, issue of his body.
Atum rises in the heavens for their sake. He made plants for
them, and animals, bird and fish to nourish them. God slew his
enemies and destroyed even his children when they attempted to
rebel. He also set himself up among men in images for their
protection. He chose their rulers for them, predestined them from
the egg, that they might strengthen the backs of the weak. He gave
them magic as a weapon against the strong arm of events, and
dreams to warn them by day and by night. The blasphemers
among them he slew as a man strikes down his son for his brother's
sake. God knows every name " (Otto).

In the Egyptian world view, God is an attentive shepherd from
whose care nothing is excluded. Faith in God's indulgent providence
transcends the doubts of the disappointed and embittered heart.

The Old Testament presents an incomparably livelier and more
dramatic account in the Book of Job of this temptation to rail
against God. Job's triumph over the temptation is also more
impressive. Nevertheless, basically it is the same temptation that
confronts man, now here, now there. When man succumbs, he
rebels against God, in turn renouncing him.

HOMERIC POLYTHEISM

Only against the background of Homeric man's faith in the gods
does the real meaning of the Titans and their supposed labors
become clear. Homer's gods and goddesses are so completely
integrated into man's world that they bear human traits. The
gods of antiquity have frequently been a cause of scandal, and
Homer, describing them, is often accused of being in reality
irreligious. It is true that Homer's gods live in discord, and in the
grip of sensual passions, that they slyly, constantly try to hoodwink

one another. To judge by their immoral behavior, they seem
determined to sink even lower than man. Whereas the chief
attribute of the God of the Old Testament is holiness, in Homer,
man's moral greatness far surpasses that of the gods.

Among Homer's mortals we find radiant examples of marital
faithfulness, as in Penelope; Andromache's fervent love of husband;
the bridal modesty of Nausicaa. Homer proclaims, not as a heavenly
but as an earthly ideal, nothing is better or more desirable on earth
than man and wife united in heartfelt love, quietly managing their
household to the envy of their enemies, and the joy of their friends.
Though even Zeus and Hera, like other Olympians, are constantly
making heaven resound with their quarreling, on Homer's earth
we find close, knit fathers and sons, like Odysseus and Telemachus.
Family and friendship are ennobled by ethical bonds. In this
respect, human life seems to be superior to Olympian. The theory
that the Homeric gods are nothing but magnified projections of the
world of men is understandable enough. However, we must not
forget that essentially, the tragic world of mortals is clearly distinct
from that of the carefree and blissful gods. Even when in myth
men are begotten by gods, the borderline between god and man
cannot be more sharply drawn than it is by the classic poets. In
fact their main purpose seems to be to draw that line as uncompromisingly as possible (Schrade). [19]

Perhaps Homeric man does not as yet dare to consider himself
the author of his own decisions. When he considers a situation
and makes a decision, he is convinced that the gods have prompted
him. Whenever a man says or does something out of the ordinary,
Homer explains this by the intervention of a god. Bruno Snell [20]
exaggerates when he claims that Homeric man lacks self-confidence
in the sense that he does not regard himself the author of his own
thoughts and actions. Self-confidence is certainly there, but in the
Greek epic, events do seem to be prompted by the gods. Even
human emotion, thought, and will appear to be of divine origin.
It is a mistake, however, to conclude that Homer's gods are no more
than a projection of the best in man who, not daring to claim

[19] H. Schrade, *Goetter und Menschen Homers* (1952), p. 179.
[20] B. Snell, *The Discovery of the Mind. The Greek Origins of European
Thought.* Translated by T. G. Rosemeyer (Oxford: Basil Blackwell, 1953).

heroic virtue as his own, ascribes it to imaginary beings. In spite of their often all too human traits, essentially at least, the complete "otherness" of the godhead is apparent. Homer's gods are in essence different from men. True, man's fate is largely determined by the gods. In Homer there are only the beginnings of the soul's dialogue with itself. Stepping up behind him, Pallas Athena grabs Achilles by the hair; the hero whirls round. Amazed, he recognizes "his good spirit."

Once man gained a livelier self-awareness, the Homeric view of the gods had to change—and change it did in proportion to the growth of that awareness. Thus a religious crisis was inevitable. Whereas Achilles still interprets his decision as a divine intervention, the Greek of the 5th century B. C. knows himself to be the father of his own acts; accordingly, he holds himself responsible for the choices he makes.

THE CRISIS IN POLYTHEISM

With man's growing knowledge of himself comes a refinement of his sense of justice toward the godhead. Whereas the simple man unquestioningly submissive to his gods accepts everything from them without reflection, the man of increased self-awareness expects certain things from his gods. Disappointed, he grows more and more easily offended by them. For although he is freed from the old belief that everything he did was determined by the gods, he is not yet free enough to stop holding them responsible for the evils that befall him. With his growing sense of justice, man's estrangement from the gods also grows. He begins to reflect on their too human shortcomings as described in the ancient tales of gods and heroes. Feelings refined enough to appreciate the noble and the sacred begin to find fault with the undignified and anthropomorphic traits of the deities. Thus a critical attitude toward the real essence of divinity gains momentum.

Even the earliest thinkers on record attempted to spiritualize the concept of God. Though modern interpretations of pre-Socratic thought persist in neglecting its theological implications, so widely recognized a scholar as Werner Jaeger has made the theology of the early Greek philosophers his special field, selecting Heraclitus' " Enter in; here too are gods " [21] as the leitmotif of his analysis.

The crisis in the old belief had two results. On the one hand, it led to an attempt to recapture the divine by personal and intellectual effort; on the other, to a vain, frivolous withdrawal from belief in general, a complacent disavowal of the gods and arrogant insistence on individual reason. For the first time in history, man is loudly proclaimed to be " the measure of all things ": of existing things, because they exist; of non-existing things because they do not exist (Sophists). Shocked by the implicit threat to the spiritual foundations on which the State stood, the guardians of the old order attempted to summon the deserters to trial on charges of godlessness *(asebeia)*. How to counter *asebeia* and to crush the Sophists' attempt to establish the absolutism of the human mind—this was essentially what Plato came to consider his appointed task.

THE PROMETHEAN MYTH

In the Greeks' process of achieving intellectual independence the Titans typify the trail blazers. If before them men were " dreamers and dull-witted, " the Titans' deeds stirred them to self-confidence and a sense of power. [22]

Even in chains Prometheus boasts of his accomplishments:

> " Enough of that. I speak to you who know.
> Hear rather all that mortals suffered.
> Once they were fools, I gave them power to think.
> Through me they won their minds.
> I have no blame for them. All I would tell you
> is my good will and my good gifts to them.

[21] W. Jaeger, *The Theology of the Early Greek Philosophers* (Oxford, 1947).
[22] Aeschylus, *Prometheus Bound.*

Seeing they did not see, nor hearing hear.
Like dreams they led a random life. " [23]

Prometheus awakened man's mind; now at last he could grasp reality, his own as well as the reality of the world about him. Without understanding, man is a vacillating dream-figure. Without intellect he has no world. Only when he no longer loses himself in every sense-impression, no longer pursues every inclination, does he acquire a self that commands the passing moment; only then does he really see—not only with his senses, but with his mind as well.

What the Titans brought mankind was not merely technology as a means to better living, but above all, through and with technology, an intellectual awakening or coming to. Until then man had dreamed away his existence undisturbed. Only through this awakening, which goes hand in hand with the invention and use of technical aids, above all that of fire, does man's life become a self-directed *vita humana*. This advance was possible only through unspeakable effort, through ceaseless labor. That is why Typhon and his brood are referred to as the " hundred handed. " The Titans are capable of working quietly and inconspicuously, but there is in them an uncontrollable passion for progress which, when it encounters resistance, easily flares up into frenzy. For the elements do resist; they fight stubbornly and long before they surrender to man. He must force them with tremendous effort.

The first to break out of the unity of existence—often even out of the clan in order to be completely independent—are the smiths. " The smith is the cunning outwitter. Promethean intelligence is forge-understanding divinely exalted. Prometheus is the driving and corruptive mythical power behind the Western development of recent centuries. When we contemplate Atlas, whose bulging muscles uphold the pillars of heaven, we begin to understand that strain is an essential Titanic characteristic. In all its forms the Titanic is heavily burdened and can assert itself only by pushing with all its force against the load. Titanic exertion is always pain; that is why industrial man is simultaneously pain-bearer and giant

---

[23] E. Hamilton, " Prometheus Bound, " *Three Greek Plays* (New York: W. W. Norton and Co., Inc., 1937), p. 115.

of the will.   The misery which accompanies industrial development is another intrinsic part of Titanism, as is voluntarism, the passion to compel the vanished presence of the divine by force, to establish Paradise by means of struggle and organization " (Nebel, p. 67).

Never content, the Titans work unremittingly to attain what the blissful gods above eternally enjoy to the full without effort.   What the Titans do achieve never brings them the peace of the Olympians. On the contrary, achievement seems to acquire an existence of its own that compels further effort, on and on to the never-ending labors of Sisyphus.   Under the circumstances it is quite understandable that the sorely tried Titan is inclined to view unexpected resistance—the lightning's all-destroying bolt, flood, or other unleashed elements that demolish his appointed work—with profound distrust.   Surely one had only the jealousy of the gods to thank. They pounce enviously on the works of men in order to destroy them!   At such interference the flame of revolt flares high in those who feel themselves cheated out of the reward of their sweat and toil.   It was psychological situations of this kind that engendered the myth of Prometheus.

In the theogony of Hesiod, who lived about a century after Homer, we have the first coherent account of the Promethean myth. In it we find the beginning of a reaction totally absent in the world of Homer's gods: contradiction and revolt.   Prometheus has brought fire from Olympus not only to help men physically, but also intellectually to lift themselves by their own endeavors.   In the Aeschylus myth, Prometheus is the symbol of the provident man. Even his name signifies one who looks ahead.   This myth of man as his own helper rocks the old belief in gods.   Self-help, self-redemption liberates man from his fear of the gods.   Thus the Roman poet Lucretius calls the philosopher Epicurus the new Prometheus who frees man from the shackles of the old fear of the gods.   Even in Aeschylus, there is a hint of what has become much clearer in our own day: technology as the secularized doctrine of redemption, an outright ersatz for religion.   As Wilamonitz-Moelendorf points out, it was in Aeschylus' Promethean trilogy (of which only Part II, *Prometheus Bound*, has survived) that Prometheus first appeared as the powerful contestor of the omnipotence of Zeus familiar to us through world literature.   With Prometheus, so-called civilization began. Before he taught mortals to build houses, they had lived like ants in holes in the ground. For men Prometheus invented writing and numbers; he taught them to compute the seasons, to work metals, the art of healing. He brought them the Muses to inspire them. According to Aeschylus he was the first to bend the necks of wild animals to the yoke, that these might relieve men of their heaviest toil; he harnessed the horse to the wagon, set sails to the mariner's craft to catch the wind. Again and again these deeds are lauded as tremendous.

The gift of prophesy is particularly stressed as one of Prometheus' gifts to mankind. He taught the art of divining the favor or disfavor of the gods and of foretelling the future by interpretation of dream, bird-flight, entrails and sacrificial flame. Here a light is thrown on magic that clearly reveals its non-religious origin, thus confirming our foregoing interpretation. Augury is considered " not a religious event, but a technical ability, " says Nebel (p. 79).

Proud though enchained, Prometheus sums up his own defense in one sentence: " All human skill and science was Prometheus' gift " (Aeschylus, *Prometheus Bound*, p 35).

He openly confesses his theft of fire for man's good. Picking a quarrel with Hermes (who has been sent him by Zeus), he finally shouts in fury: " In one word, I detest all gods who could repay my benefits with such outrageous infamy " (Aeschylus, *Prometheus Bound*, p. 49). But Prometheus' pride does not yet exalt itself to the point of absolute arrogance. Though he tends to exaggerate, what he is insisting on to Zeus is his right. Even he (a paltry figure who hardly embodies the principle of justice) can proudly remain obdurate in the name of justice, because Zeus is in the wrong. That in the no longer extant Part III of the Aeschylus trilogy it can come to mutual compromise and reconciliation is evidence that in the Zeus of poetry, absolute, transcendental holiness has not yet been conceived, and Promethean revolt has not yet hardened into absolute, metaphysical arrogance. To be sure, in the Olympian Zeus, the poet was attempting to portray absolute deity far removed from any taint of earthliness. But Nebel is right to call it " an abortive attempt at a transcendent God " (p. 66).

Instead of becoming adamant in their pride, both sides make concessions and reach an agreement. In the poet's own opinion, the ultimate and profound purpose of tragedy is to warn against *hybris* or sinful pride. Prometheus then is not yet a figure of absolute rebellion; however, he does indicate the road along which the Promethean revolt of the West will one day march toward full-fledged metaphysical revolution.

SOCRATES AND PLATO

Compared with the Promethean tragedy of Aeschylus, the myth of Epimetheus and Prometheus which Plato has the Sophist Protagoras recount barely touches on what in the Aeschylus myth is the main theme: revolt. Here Prometheus is the great benefactor of man who in sorry contrast with the animals has been imperfectly endowed by nature. Only with the artificial aids of civilization, as supplied by Prometheus, does man become fit for existence. Only incidentally are we told that Prometheus was later punished for the theft he committed for his brothers. The Protagoras account stresses another point: civilization had not yet made men truly prosper. For this they had first to gather together in groups for mutual protection from wild beasts, groups that were inwardly united by the individual's Zeus-given sense of right and justice.

In the course of Greek intellectual self-discovery the issue of man's deep sense of righteousness, his conscience, was bound to divide thinkers into two camps. In the one, a refined conception of right and wrong became the impulse to purify and spiritualize the concept of God, as we have it in Socrates' *Daimonion,* with which a new relation to the godhead came into being. In spite of man's growing awareness of his transitoriness, age-old customs of veneration continued to bind him to his ancient gods. Philosophical reflection was needed to make a truly spiritual God-concept possible, the goal round which all of Plato's intellectual efforts ultimately revolved.

On the other hand, progressive intellectual independence caused a large number of the enlightened to cast off old ties completely and to display all those unpleasant aspects of godlessness that so disturbed Plato. The State was quite justified in attempting to prevent such libertinism. The State's inability to distinguish between the libertinism of godless agnostics and the maturation of a Socratic faith in God based on awareness of the ethical (Socrates knew himself bound in conscience to God) was what opened the eyes of a shocked Plato to the depravity of his day and made him ponder ways and means to check the impending catastrophe. Plato realized that what was needed first of all was an extremely sober examination of reality. Only then could one begin to tackle the problems involved. The fact that the existence of such a situation could be interpreted as a divine mandate (and that as a result of that mandate a definite, albeit not yet thorough knowledge of the absolute could emerge) threw human limitations into sharp contrast with the omnipotent otherness of the godhead, permitting the humbly reverent a glimpse of a divine existence totally different from man's own. Plato's intellectual efforts were rewarded with a clarification of the concept of God that comes close to the Christian. His philosophy leads to the " ONE " who as the Absolute, the Unconditional, utterly transcends the world. God is " the other, " totally unlike anything on earth. [24] Indeed, if in spite of man's efforts, events continue to move toward catastrophe and the ultimate " plunge into the abyss, " one must implore God to intervene, to take the reins again and pull a stumbling world back to its feet. [25]

In his last work, *The Laws,* a Plato purged and clarified by age demands that philosophy (which in *The State* he had still described as the redeemer from the ungodly life) be replaced by " *religio.* " The climax of *The Laws* comes in Volume X with its defense of religion against the irreligion of the Sophists, the enlightened expounders of natural philosophy, and against the half-educated, who eagerly absorb any atheistic notions they are exposed to. In his debate with these unbelievers, Plato works himself into a state which, as he himself admits, makes his speech more passionate than it was meant to be. On the other hand, he adds, strong language

[24] K. Schilling, *Plato, Eine Einfuehrung in seine Philosophie* (1948), pp. 85, 271.
[25] *Ibid.*

is necessary; otherwise the godless might needlessly conclude that the better arguments were on their side! For Plato unbelief is much more than an erroneous opinion on the existence of the godhead, a mistake that dialectical arguments can correct. No! Atheism is a moral attitude based on affective grounds, an attitude that can be interpreted rationally not only from a particular point of view but generally. Since belief in God is the foundation of incorruptible law, belief and unbelief are not merely private matters. Hence the question of religion cannot be left to the whim of the individual. This would only cause people to underestimate its importance. What is at stake is the very foundation of communal existence: law and order.

Basic to communal existence is respect for authority. Plato points out that in the city of Athens the question of authority has long since taken a fateful turn. Whereas in Persia freedom has been destroyed by the stranglehold of despotism, in Athens the bounds established by authority are being overthrown by unrestrained freedom. The theater, once an important school of culture, where the people reverently listened to their spiritual leaders and accepted their instruction, has now become an arena for insolent passions. This was the first field that the aristocracy had been forced to surrender to the mob. Today the masses deem themselves competent to evaluate the beautiful and the unbeautiful, feel called upon to pass judgment on matters of art, indeed, on all matters. Once unleashed, they soon lose all reverence and fall into that nasty bumptiousness which disdainfully dismisses the judgment of the wise. No wonder that evil, once introduced, continues to spread! First to go was obedience to the authorities, then respect for parents, for the aged, and for the law. Men lost their natural sense of right and wrong, which forbids perjury and perfidy. They acquiesced in what can only be called Titanic defiance, and like the Titans plunged themselves into hopeless misery.

The State must be strengthened by a stable system of law. This is Plato's aim throughout *The Laws*. It must provide a plumb-line to straighten from within men's leaning toward degeneracy and destruction. The first word in the book is *GOD*, written large. For as the old maxim says, God is the beginning, middle, and end of all being. Irresistible, unswerving, he proceeds upon his way led by punitive justice, which exacts penance from those who disobey his law. The results of the Sophists' liberalism should open the eyes of all reasonable men, for indissolubly bound to unbelief is unbridled sensuality, which consents to every kind of enticement and debauchery. Most dangerous of all is the self-glorification of the unbeliever. He brags of his wealth, of his bodily strength and fitness; he lives under the illusion that he has been called not to serve but to rule; his head is stuffed full of foolish presumptions; he is lost, and his companions in godless arrogance perish with him. Though he may for a while happily delude himself into believing his pose of superman, in the end punitive justice will overtake him and hurl him and his cohorts to destruction.

Through all of Plato's arguments on irreligion runs the bright thread of his basic thought: good and evil are everlastingly at war, a war that is simultaneously the struggle between belief and unbelief. Caught between the battle-lines, the average man must be ripped out of his sluggish indifference by those who are morally mature. Otherwise his indolence will allow him to be crushed by the weight of avid passions, and he will simply succumb to evil. Uncompromisingly Plato opposes the least denial of the absolute antagonism between good and evil. He suffers no dialectical conciliation of the two standpoints, no metamorphosis of the ethically negative into the ethically positive. In Plato's world, divine providence does permit evil to contribute to the plan of the world as a means to the fulfillment of the whole. But for the individual who must choose between belief and unbelief it is a question of the well-being of his immortal soul. Thus for Plato, belief in the soul's immortality is part and parcel of faith in God. All his dialectical energies are directed toward furnishing proofs of that immortality. He does not hesitate to remind men of the absolute, eternal consequences of their decisions. The lot of the soul after death is determined by its own decisions and efforts during life. God, Lord of the cosmos, knows the works of each soul, the good and the evil. He has placed every human being in the world precisely where he can contribute most to the victory of good and the defeat of evil; the soul does not select its own domain. In its place each soul either strives upward toward the light or sinks down into darkness. When the soul nears its highest degree of purity after the death of the body, it receives a blissful everlasting abode. In the opposite case, it finds itself face to face with the terrors of the underworld.

Plato addresses himself directly to tempted youth not yet aware of the full consequences of decision: " O youth or young man, who fancy that you are neglected by the Gods, know that if you become worse you shall go to the worse souls, or if better to the better, and in every succession of life and death you will do and suffer what like may fitly suffer at the hands of like. This is the justice of heaven, which neither you nor any other unfortunate will ever glory in escaping, and which the ordaining powers have specially ordained; take good heed thereof, for it will be sure to take heed of you. If you say, ' I am small and will creep into the depths of the earth, or I am high and will fly up to heaven, ' you are not so small or so high but that you shall pay the fitting penalty, either here or in the world below or in some still more savage place whither you shall be conveyed. This is also the explanation of the fate of those whom you saw, who had done unholy and evil deeds, and from small beginnings had grown great; and you fancied that from being miserable they had become happy; and in their actions, as in a mirror, you seemed to see the universal neglect of the Gods, not knowing how they make all things work together and contribute to the great whole. And thinkest thou, bold man, that thou needest not to know this? He who knows it not can never form any true idea of the happiness or unhappiness of life or hold any rational discourse respecting either. " [26] If you try, he adds encouragingly, the godhead itself will come to your aid.

Thus Plato unequivocally supports the basic teaching of revealed religion both of the Old and New Testaments: faith is what decides a man's ultimate good fortune or disaster. Springing from a fundamentally ethical attitude, faith expresses itself in moral striving. In Plato we find the same basic aim present in the Christian proclamation: the well-being of the soul

Plato's unbelievers include not only those who deny the existence of gods but also those who claim that the gods pay no attention to the affairs of men, indeed, even those who imagine that the gods

[26] *Plato Selections*, edited by R. Demos (New York: Charles Scribner's Sons, 1955), p. 445.

are easily appeased by prayers and offerings. Because unbelief is more than an intellectual error or misconception of the existence and the essence of the godhead but is rooted deep in individual affective choice, it is, Plato admits, difficult to combat. Nevertheless, he considers demonstrations of the proofs of the gods' existence based on the intelligent order of the world as well as proofs of the immortality of the soul important and necessary. For this reason he himself takes great pains to provide such proofs. With them he opposes the claim of the natural philosophers that everything has come into existence by chance, a claim that today's natural philosophers attempt to uphold in the name of Darwin.

Above all, Plato attacks the hypothesis revived in modern times by the Neo-Hegelians: God did not create the world, rather, man created gods. For this hypothesis destroys the foundations of justice. If the gods are mere figments of man's imagination, unbelievers must promptly conclude: then law cannot be founded on the gods. Therefore instead of gods, nonbelievers advocate a legal positivism. At their own discretion, lawgivers should appoint for different times and places different gods as the supposed pillars of their own man-made laws. In reality, justice does not rest on any god-given natural law; rather it grows either out of the conflicts of men or out of compromise or force. For this reason justice is subject to constant change; whatever law has succeeded in enforcing itself is considered just until it has been overthrown by a new law. Unfortunately, Plato's own sorry experience with precisely this doctrine, that might makes right, proved that it all too deeply impresses the young, seducing them to acts of godlessness and revolt. Supposedly their only desire is for a " natural " life. But this is only a threadbare excuse and mask for their real objective—to subjugate others rather than place themselves voluntarily with those others at the service of the law.

It is the stern duty of the lawgiver to combat unbelief, for unbelief is the source of all lawlessness. The justice of God is at stake. How then is the lawgiver to combat the evil of unbelief, which threatens man and the State? Should he limit himself to laws and threats of punishment, or should he not first make an attempt in all kindness to teach men something better? Everything possible must be done to convince men of the existence of God.

Plato bases one proof of that existence on the primacy of the soul. Even though Plato's individual proofs as he presented them largely fail to convince today, his basic thought is still valid. In any case, Plato is absolutely convinced that denial of God is closely related to denial of the human soul, in other words, denial of the non-material, the spiritual, and the immortal in man. It is only with the denial of the soul that unbelief acquires its acutely immoral aspects, which are based on disrespect for God and on arrogance.

The theogonies of certain writers, Plato continues, have discredited the whole idea of God; their frivolous fables about the gods have done faith in the godhead more harm than good. Deep in the human heart lies a sense of the divine that forbids ascribing human weaknesses to gods. The gods cannot be carefree, lighthearted debauchees. If even for human leaders, doctors, ships' captains, generals, statesmen, and *patres familiae,* unconditional loyalty in small things is the prerequisite of success, how much more is seriousness in great issues to be expected of the immortals?

To an ethically effective faith in God belongs also faith in his providence which watches over the preservation and fulfillment of the whole and fits the seemingly least important detail into the universal plan. Plato knows that the so-called theodicy-problem (How can the fact of evil in the world be reconciled with the existence of a good God?) is the most frequent stumbling block to belief, and that bitterness over some supposed divine injustice leads soonest to unbelief. According to Plato, one should address such a doubter more or less as follows:

My dear young man, very possibly it was your profound sense of the divine that led you down the path of doubt. You allowed yourself to be impressed by the gods' supposed injustice in the world. Many blasphemers live in seeming good fortune; many evil-doers reach a ripe old age unpunished; miserable creatures succeed in scaling the pinnacles of tyrannic power. All this affronts your sense of nobility. Because you cannot hold the godhead responsible for such things, you prefer to believe that the gods live far removed, in blissful ignorance of the ways of men. [27]

Plato then replies to this doubt with the heart's testimony to the

[27] *Ibid.,* pp. 437-38.

unconditional goodness and loving care of the godhead. Gods cannot be like men, who allow themselves to be duped by flattery. The gods are the incorruptible guardians of justice. To impute injustice to them is the most dangerous form of godlessness. Plato is well aware of the fundamental temptation that all men must face, the temptation of Job born of disgust with the world's injustice, the temptation to question the most divine attribute of the godhead. Like Job, all men are tempted to wrangle with God on the principle of absolute justice in order to convict Him of injustice, which is the same as denying Him.

Out of his deep concern for the common good, Plato pleads for strict laws that would severely punish attempts to degrade wholesome fear of the gods. Doubters still open to reason should of course be reasoned with and their concept of God corrected. But once unbelief is coupled with the wickedness and malice of a corrupted heart, as with the Sophists, tyrants, and deceiving magicians, punishment should not be spared. An incurable blasphemer should even be punished by death.

At the end, Plato once again insists on the importance of "unshakable fear of the gods" based on the twin truths of belief: in the uniqueness of the soul as compared with the body and with matter in general, and in a God-permeated order within the cosmos as the basis of the simultaneously visible and moral order of the cosmos as a whole.

"Above all," Plato explains, "God should be to us the measure of all things, far more so than any kind of man, as we are taught at present. For whosoever tries to be pleasing in the sight of the Supreme Being must of necessity become like him. For this reason, it is the considerate man who pleases God because he is like God; the inconsiderate man is unlike God; he clashes with God and so falls into injustice; so it is in all things" (Schilling).

This is the aged Plato's reply to the Sophists' dictum that man is the measure of all things; it is the ripe fruit of a long philosopher's life, a philosopher, moreover, who ranks as one of mankind's greatest, the one to whom men always return in times of intellectual and spiritual crisis.

It was probably while under the impact that Socrates' death had made on his enemies, accusers, and judges, as well as on his own disciples that Plato drew his portrait of the just man who has proved himself not only in right-willing and right-doing but who also has the courage to endure unshaken, even to the death, the gloating of his scoffers.   For though the sufferer of injustice be bound, scourged, blinded, and ultimately crucified, moral victory is always on his side, not on the side of those who commit the injustice.   With this insight, Platonic thought comes closer to the Christian concept of expiatory suffering than does any other pre-Christian thought with the exception of a few books of the Old Testament.   On this high plain not even the fact of his own unjust sufferings can shake Plato's conviction that God and absolute justice are one and the same; quite the contrary.   According to this concept, it is precisely the distinction of such suffering that makes a return to the just order of things possible.   With this the last trace of revolt is eradicated, clearing the way for absolute obedience to the godhead.

EPICURUS - FATHER OF WESTERN ATHEISM?

Neither the wholesome " fear of the gods " that the great tragedians taught, nor the intellectually mature God-fearing piety that Plato proclaimed as the beginning of true human wisdom was to be the power that shaped the spirit of the Hellenic age and maintained its order.   Instead, an " enlightenment " which aimed at dissipating the sinister clouds of fear by the bright light of human reason carried the day.   This enlightenment is closely linked with the name of Epicurus.

Epicurus is considered the father of Western atheism.   His own disciples exalted the Master to a hero, to man's liberator from the burdensome yoke of fear of the gods.   With extravagant enthusiasm the Roman Epicurean, Titus Lucretius Carus, celebrates Epicurus in his didactic poem *De Rerum Natura* as the first Greek who dared to relieve man of religion's oppressive load.   He lauds Epicurus as the first mortal courageous enough to look the freakish gods in the eye and challenge them. He was not one, says Lucretius, to be intimidated by heaven's lightning bolts. These only spurred his brave heart to unlock nature's secrets with the key of Democritus' philosophy of nature and its processes. For Lucretius, Epicurus is the hero with heel dug deep in the neck of the monster, Fear-of-the-gods, which he has overcome. " His victory, " boasts Lucretius, " has raised us to the heavens. " This evaluation of Epicurus has survived. Like Lucretius, Karl Marx celebrates Epicurus as the first Greek enlightener, as the one who supplanted the old idols by the new divinity, human self-consciousness. [28] For Marx and Engels Epicurus was the really radical enlightener of antiquity, who publicly attacked the old religion; it was from Epicurus that atheism sprang. Insofar as atheism existed among the Romans, it drew from the same source. This view is reflected throughout the article on atheism in the *Great Soviet Encyclopedia*. [29]

Was Epicurus really the defiant hero of a public atheism for which he has been celebrated from antiquity to the present day? If the historical Epicurus was such a hero, how did he ever escape the wrath of his contemporaries? Why was he not accused of " *asebeia*, " when even Socrates (who according to Xenophon's *Memorabilia*, tried to stir up in young people faith in and fear of the gods) did not escape charges of trying to seduce youth by the introduction of new gods? Not only godlessness but even the introduction of new gods was considered sufficient grounds for the death penalty. Agnostic remarks were enough to cause the Athenians to ban Protagoras from city and country. According to Cicero, this had made many people cautious about expressing atheistic views openly since even doubt was punishable. Cicero seems to include the Epicureans among his " many. " [30]

A single chance selection from Epicurus might lead us to suspect that his so-called atheism is in fact only a misunderstood attempt to supplant the naive popular conception of the gods by a more spiritual one, a goal that the great thinkers had been working

[28] K. Marx and F. Engels, *Complete Works*, I, 1, 1 (1927), *Dissertation*, pp. 1-144.

[29] Oleschtschuk, *Atheismus. Grosse Soviet-Enzyklopaedie*. Reihe Geschichte und Philosophie 49 (1956), p. 5.

[30] Cicero, *On the Nature of Gods*. Translated by Hubert M. Poteat (Chicago, 1950), I, 23, 201.

toward from Thales to Aristotle. Werner Jaeger [31] calls those who
attempted to spiritualize the concept of God, and who consequently
were suspected of "*asebeia,*" the first creators of a philosophical
theology (Jaeger, p. 17). In a letter to Menoeceus after his explicit
assurance that gods do exist, Epicurus continues: "The irreligious
man is not the person who destroys the gods of the masses but the
person who imposes the ideas of the masses on the gods." [32]

Was Epicurus perhaps, like Xenophanes, really what Jaeger calls
"a spiritual revolutionary" who accepted as a moral duty the
pressing need for a philosophical clarification and deepening of
naive popular conceptions and who loudly proclaimed the views of
his day incompatible with an intellectually and morally purged world
view? For an answer we must examine the whole process of
philosophical spiritualization closely. Today we know better than
we did half a century ago that the reflection of the early Greek
thinkers circled round the problem of God. For Xenophanes God
was the very heart of the discussion. Xenophanes declared war on
the gods of popular belief with the grandiose words: "*One* God
is the greatest among gods and men: neither in form nor in spirit
does he resemble mortals" (Jaeger, p. 55). By establishing this
negation from the start, Xenophanes stimulates and clarifies further
search for an understanding of God. God is completely different
from all earthly creatures. With this the colorful world of
Homer's and Hesiod's anthropomorphic gods collapses. As the
ground of being *(Weltgrund)* God must be far removed from such
vain imaginings. Though no full-fledged monotheism is reached,
what emerges is a philosophical realization of the fundamental
oneness of the *Weltgrund*. For Xenophanes it is indisputable that
the human spirit will never be capable of comprehending the infinite
all-directing One recognized by philosophers as the principle of all
being, that here man's powers of conception simply fail him. All
human attributes of God are to be denied; then there will be room
for more exalted concepts. In any case, the one, all-embracing God
who is the Word-principle is exalted far above all partly divine

[31] W. Jaeger, *The Theology of the Early Greek Philosophers* (Oxford and
Clarendon Press, 1947).

[32] Lucretius, *The Philosophy of Epicurus.* Translated by George K. Stro-
dach (Northwestern University Press, 1963), p. 179.

powers in the world. Granted, one attribute of the Supreme God is conscious spiritual self-possession; nevertheless it is important to clear our understanding of the divine of all anthropomorphic slag. God sees, thinks, and hears omnisciently. His awareness is not dependent on the sense-organs or a nervous system. With absolute conviction Xenophanes speaks of the one God who is more than all others, different from all Titans, for whom indescribable toil is a prerequisite of achievement, whereas absolute repose and tranquillity characterizes the Highest. " Merely with the power of the spirit, effortlessly, he effects all things " (Jaeger).

Precisely this divine combination of repose and power strongly influenced the period after Xenophanes. Aeschylus was obviously influenced by him. In the supplicants' magnificent prayer for protection, Zeus is the all-holy God beyond man's comprehension.

> " May God good issue give!
> And yet the will of Zeus is hard to scan:
> Through all it brightly gleams,
> E'en though in darkness and the gloom of chance
> For us poor mortals wrapt.
>
> Safe, by no fall tripped up,
> The full-wrought deed decreed by brow of Zeus;
> For dark with shadows stretch
> The pathways of the counsels of his heart,
> And difficult to see.
> It has been truly said
> ' The strong desire of Zeus is hard to hunt '.
> For him all things shine clear,
> Though he hide them in black darkness
> From the eyes of men that perish.
>
> When by the nod of Zeus
> It is decreed that a thing be accomplished,
> The event falls firm on its feet.
> For the paths of his purposing heart
> Stretch dark and tangled, baffling sight and thought.
> " From their high-towering hopes
> He hurls mortals to their destruction;

And there is no immortal
Who unsheathes against him the effortless power of godhead,
But Zeus in a moment punishes his pride,
Though throned in the worship of men. " [33]

Even Pindar, though not yet free from polytheism, called Zeus
lord of all, rescuer, ruler, judge and holy one. No human act
escapes his divine attention. In the metaphysical reflections that
followed, efforts toward a more ethical conception of God become
increasingly apparent. Xenophanes criticizes Homer and Hesiod
for heaping disgraceful human acts—stealing, lying, adultery—upon
the gods. As the deity must be above every mortal frailty, so must
its universal power surmount national borders. Not only penetrating
thought that attempts to bore its way through to the ultimate ground
of being, but also reverence before the exaltedness of the divine
is a rich source of the spiritualizing process of the God-concept.
In Plato and Aristotle the trend toward spiritualization of the deity
reaches its climax and a certain conclusion.

Is Epicurus, then, with his criticism of the godhead and his so-
called atheism part of this same process of spiritualization of the
God-concept? The answer must be No. In the first place, his
philosophy is something quite different from that of the early
thinkers including Plato and Aristotle. What determined and
directed their thought was the will to clear a passageway to being
and truth by means of philosophical cognition. Because of the
will's insistence on unqualified objectivity, the place their philosophy
occupies in world philosophy is unique. For beginning with the
Sophists, men's disposition to philosophy had changed essentially.
A weary agnosticism had caused a slackened interest in truth *per se*,
focusing attention more on the pragmatic uses to which philosophical
teachings could be put.

Epicurus swings the rudder in the opposite direction. Here is
no passionately objective search for truth. No refined, consciously
ethical intelligence inquires how God should be conceived. In
Epicurean philosophy the secret of the universe has become a

---

[33] Aeschylus, *Prometheus Bound, The Supplicants, Seven Against Thebes,
The Persians.* Translated with an Introduction by P. Vellacott (Penguin
Books, 1961), p. 57.

secondary matter. With Epicurus comes the shift from the essential to the personal, from the objective to the subjective. For him philosophy is a kind of hygiene of the soul, an art in which the suffering of the soul is explained as the result of fear—of men's fear of Fate, fear of the gods, fear of death. The lack of objectivity in Epicurus' teaching is clearly evident in his non-objective treatment of his opponents. For Epicureans, the views of the opposition are " not the mature convictions of philosophers, but, rather the disordered dreams of maniacs. "[34] They dismiss Stoic teachings, for instance, as the gossip " of ignorant old crones "[35] and accuse men held in the utmost esteem of being imbeciles, fools, and lunatics. Even in Epicurus' own day, the lack of depth and objectivity in Epicurean thought was deplored. " The violence of Epicurus' philosophical polemics, " says Olof Gigon, " stands in striking contrast to an otherwise warm philanthropy. We have inherited whole lists of Epicurus' malicious nicknames for other philosophers. In the existent texts there is hardly a page free from polemics. "[36]

If for Epicurus philosophy is no more than concern for the health of one's own soul (a kind of search for mental health) there is no question of fortifying the soul with a manly vigor unafraid to shoulder the burdens of one's calling and of earthly limitations in general. What the Master teaches is a sophisticated, ostrichlike technique of dissuading men from their fears of life and of " death, this the most horrifying of evils, " which hangs over every man's head like the boulder over Tantalus. Epicurus rejects the yoke of an eternal master who must be feared. There is not a trace of *religio* is his thought, of secret awe before the mystery of the *Weltgrund*, the inscrutable ground of being that sustains the world. He seems to feel no need to know ever more clearly, purely, spiritually a God he has surmised, and to purge him of the unworthy features of popular fancy.

In spite of all his admirers' attempts to make Epicurus a great hero with the courage to defy the gods, to mock their punitive lightning bolts, and to liberate men from their deep fears, the historical Epicurus was not a man to run risks for his convictions.

---

[34] Cicero, V. d. Wesen d. Goetten, I, 16, p. 79.
[35] *Ibid.*, I, 20, p. 87.
[36] O. Gigon, Einleitung zu: Epikur. Von der Ueberwindung der Furcht XV.

Instead of intrepidly defending his atheistic tenets, Epicurus cleverly adapted his view to popular belief, as is evident from an enlightening fragment of a letter to Thyrson. Stobaeus writes: " There are times when one should cultivate reflection on the gods. Epicurus not only thought this but also practiced it in his own life by participating in all the traditional feasts and sacrifices. Thus during the archontate of Aristonymous he writes to Thyrson through a fellow citizen, Theodotus, that together they have celebrated all the celebrations...including the feast of Choen, the Athenian mysteries, and all the rest of them. . . . " (Gigon, *Fragmente*). Even Epicureans were of the opinion that " in order not to offend Athenian sensibilities. . . Epicurus theoretically allotted to the gods a place in his system " though in reality he denied them. Indicating the Epicureans, Cicero adds that at the mere appearance of cant, genuine religion is completely cancelled. The ambiguity of Epicurus' doctrine on the gods is mentioned again and again. By slight shifts of emphasis one can claim either that Epicurus accepted the existence of the gods, or that he in reality disavowed them. Thus Posidonius in his work on the essence of the gods can say " that Epicurus was in fact an atheist, and that his statements about immortal gods were designed only to avert from himself the hatred of the people. " [37]

In documents as old as those of the Philodem Collection we find the pointed remark that in Epicurus' equivocal position fear of man has replaced fear of the gods, whereby the man-fearing really have less to hope than the God-fearing.

" 'One must pretend,' says Epicurus, '. . .in order not to spoil the peoples' pleasure and be hated for disapproving acts that they enjoy.' The Epicureans also believe that the pious bring offerings and hold initiations not joyfully, but in fear, whereas in their own case it is no different, for they certainly act out of fear without sharing in the comforting hopes of the others. Indeed they act only out of fear and the worry that their confusing and deceiving game with the masses might be discovered. For these, they have also written books about the gods and piety—twisted, unclear,

[37] Cicero, *On the Nature of Gods.* Translated by Hubert M. Poteat (Chicago, 1950), I, 33, p. 225.

completely distorted books to protect themselves, because they are afraid to reveal their real opinion. " [38]

With these twisted speeches belong also the occasional statements that Epicurus had taught " knowledge of the gods, " that he alone had acknowledged that gods exist. In so doing he had resorted to an argument much in use at the time, namely, the " *consensus gentium* ": " The greater part of mankind are united in acknowledging that which is most probable, and which we are by nature led to suppose, namely, that there are gods. " [39] Proofs of the gods' existence are based on a primitive sensuality, largely on " dream visions. " Epicurus believes that men's notions of god spring from dreams. " For, " says he, " when great images of human shape impressed them during sleep, they supposed that some such god of human shape really existed. " [40] Epicurus draws his naive, heavy realism from Democritus, who held that dreams were actual material images that had freed themselves from the original objects, which they represented. The gods were portrayed entirely anthropomorphically. They were even supposed to speak Greek. Although the gods were assigned to *Intermundia* (supposedly completely isolated from Earth) Epicurus, untroubled by the obvious contradiction, claims that gods, exiled there, prowl about the earth at night confounding men with nightmares. If gods exist, they can only be sensual, material forms, for according to Epicurus' philosophy of nature, there is no reality but sensual, material reality. The only divine attribute of the many all too human gods is their carefree and effortless way of life. Divine freedom would be impossible were the gods to take upon themselves the burdens and worries of ruling the world. Burdened gods would be like men. In other words, divine world government is incompatible with divine bliss (Gigon, *Fragmente*, p. 26).

Epicurus agitated specifically against teleology as a basis for recognition of a divine universal planner and ruler. Apparently he was familiar with Socrates' detailed arguments in the *Memorabilia*,

---

[38] O. Gigon, *Fragmente*, p. 65,
[39] Bohn's Classical Library. Treatises of M. T. Cicero. Lit. translated by C. D. Yonge (London 1878), I, p. 1.
[40] The Loeb Classical Library. Sextus Empiricus. With an English translation by R. G. Bury. Against the Physicists. Against the Ethicists. I, 25, p. 13.

in which the ingenious formation of the organs of the human body
are taken as a point of departure. To this Epicurus expressly
objects: " The system of providence, " he says, " contrived nothing
in the production of animals. For neither were the eyes made for
seeing, nor the ears for hearing, nor the tongue for speaking, nor
the feet for walking; inasmuch as these were produced before it
was possible to speak, to hear, to see, to walk. Therefore these
were not produced for use; but use was produced from them "
(Gigon, *Fragmente*, p. 79).

Any predominance of the conscience in man's relation to the gods
is completely absent from Epicurus' thought. Vigorously he denies
that gods are watchmen over the deeds of men. Hence qualms of
conscience and terror of punitive gods are superfluous. With this
also the myth of the Titans, who were severely punished for defying
the gods, loses its substance. Epicurus' words of wisdom are
supposed to bring comfort, to break the bondage of superstition
by rejecting popular notions.

> " And so conclude that it is just that those,
> (After the manner of the Gigants), should all
> pay the huge penalties for monstruous crime,
> Who by their reasonings do overshake
> The ramparts of the universe and wish
> There to put out the splendid sun of heaven,
> Branding with mortal talk immortal things. " [41]

No serious assessment of Epicurus leaves any doubt that his
ambiguity (on the one hand stripping the gods of power, on the
other, pretending to recognize their existence) really destroys genuine
religion, which in justice renders the Deity its due.

The fact of evil in the world (a fact supposedly incompatible with
an all-governing Deity) is the foundation of Epicurean atheism,
that is, Epicurean rejection of the gods' providence in the world.
The " famous argument of Epicurus, " as it was called in the
Fragments, which has been adapted by the *Great Soviet Encyclopedia*
for its article on atheism runs: " God, " he says, " either wishes
to take away evils, and is unable to; or he is able and is unwilling;

[41] T. L. Carus *De Rerum Natura*. Of the Nature of Things (Los Angeles,
1957), V, p. 202.

or he is neither willing nor able, or he is both willing and able. If he is willing and unable, he is feeble, which is not in accordance with the character of God; if he is able and unwilling, he is envious, which is equally at variance with God; if he is neither willing nor able, he is both envious and feeble, and therefore not God; if he is both willing and able, which alone is suitable to God, from what source then are evils, or why does he not remove them? " [42]

It is weary, resigned protest, not daring heroic revolt, which leads to Epicurus' rejection of Providence. In the *Fragments* we read: "Epicurus saw that the good are always subject to adversities, poverty, labors, exile, loss of dear friends. On the contrary, he saw that the wicked were happy.... But what especially moved him was the fact that religious men were especially visited with weightier evils, whereas he saw that lesser evils or none at all fell upon those who altogether neglected the gods, or worshipped them in an impious manner; and that even the very temples themselves were often set on fire by lightning.... Therefore, when Epicurus reflected on these things, induced as it were by the injustice of these matters (for thus it appeared to him in his ignorance of the cause and subjects), he thought that there was no providence. " [43]

Yet as we have seen, Epicurus' rejection of divine providence does not go as far as atheism with its express denial of the godhead. In the *Fragments*, we find hints that Epicurus would have been more consistent had he denied the gods completely. "The disputation of Epicurus extends thus far: he was silent as to the other things which follow; namely, that because there is in him neither care nor providence, therefore there is no reflection nor any perception in him by which it is effected that he has no existence at all. Thus, when he gradually descended, he remained on the last step, because he now saw the precipice. But what does it avail to have remained silent and concealed the danger? Necessity compelled him even against his will to fall. " [44]

Similarly in another passage: "When Epicurus describes the goal of his teachings on the gods as fearlessness, lack of worry

[42] Ante-Nicene Christian Library. The Works of Lactantius. Translated by William Fletcher (Edinburgh, 1871), 13, p. 28.

[43] *Ibid.*, I, 17, p. 8.

[44] *Ibid.*, II, p. 6.

concerning them, it seems as if that goal would be more surely attained by assuming no goal at all than by learning to accept a god who desired neither to help nor to harm. " [45]

It is then his own disciples who propose the more consistent conclusion. Epicurus diplomatically avoids this conclusion in order to play safe.

What significance does Epicurus' attempt to dispel fear of the gods have for natural science, the great instrument of enlightenment? Much as in the French Revolution, enlightenment is praised as the great, enthusiastically welcomed light with which Epicurus, torchbearer and rescuer of mankind—albeit not the first—banned the specter of man's fear of the gods. In the process of disposing of the gods, Epicurus cares little whether his natural explanations of nature's various phenomena are individually correct or incorrect. On the contrary, he insists that often several explanations are possible. All that matters is that some completely natural explanation can be given, so that it is not necessary to transcend the limits of earth. Again and again Lucretius celebrates the Master as the torchbearer of enlightenment. "This darkling terror in the mind must then be routed not by the sun's rays, not by the bright shafts of day but by the observation and rational inspection of nature. Nothing is created out of nothing and nothing passes into nothing. " [46]

In order to clarify his leaning to atheism, Karl Marx chose as the theme for his doctor's dissertation *The Difference Between the Nature Philosophy of Democritus and that of Epicurus*. Here he characterizes admirably Epicurus' interest in the scientific explanation of nature. Marx says: "Epicurus proceeds with a boundless nonchalance. Clearly he is not interested in examining the real causes of things. At the end, Epicurus admits that his explanation aims only at *ataraxia* (quietude of mind), not at a knowledge of nature for its own sake. In Epicurus, therefore, materialism with all its contradictions as the science of self-knowledge, is carried to its ultimate consequence and perfection.... " [47]

[45] O. Gigon, *Attikos*, p. 81.

[46] The Philosophy of Epicurus. Letters to Herodotus. Parallel Passages from Lucretius, p. 156.

[47] K. Marx and F. Engels, *Hist. krit. Gesamtausgabe*, I, pp. 23, 52.

The goal that Epicurus is trying to reach via liberation from fear of the gods and of death is pleasure. However, he does not seek pleasure, as do Plato and Aristotle, in the joys of speculation *(bios theoreticos)* but rather in the unbroken enjoyment of bodily pleasures. Since ethical restraint is disavowed, pleasure is sought purely for its own sake, including the pleasures of " the belly. "

Yet Epicurus is no apostle of a sensual, uncurbed hedonism. He knows and demands limits, but only those of a utilitarian nature. For in the long run licentious enjoyment punishes itself, causing more pain than pleasure. Epicurus' goal is uninterrupted self-indulgence, in other words, self-indulgence that is restricted when this is necessary for continued pleasure. Thus he can say, " On bread and water, man's bliss can compete with that of Zeus. " [48] Always the ultimate goal of pleasure is " to live like a god among men. " In the foreword to Karl Marx's *Dissertation,* we have an echo of this challenge to men to make knowledge of self their supreme, indeed their only god.

The peculiar effect of Epicurus' life is important to any assessment of his essential contribution. Not his so-called truths, but rather Epicurus the man with his attitude of protest against the gods is what intrigued and continues to intrigue the imagination. In the history of Epicureanism, the Master has been idealized, hero-worshipped, and deified. Lucretius Carus writes, " . . .then a god was he—hear me, illustrious Memmius—a god. " [49] And from one of his pupils we have, " Compared with other men's lives, that of Epicurus with its mildness and self-content, is mythical. " The motto of the Epicureans is in much the same vein: " Do everything as if Epicurus were watching you. " [50]

In his didactic poem, *De Rerum Natura,* Lucretius revives the flagging protest against the gods with unparalleled harshness. The work closes with a long-drawn-out description of a world bedecked with the corpses of cholera victims. Protest flares up against the gods, who have brought murder into the world. Before Lucretius

[48] O. Gigon, *Fragmente,* p. 112.
[49] T. L. Carus, *De Rerum Natura.* Of the Nature of Things. Translated by William Leonard (Los Angeles, 1957), V, p. 417.
[50] The Loeb Classical Library. Seneca. *Ad Lucilium Epistulae Morales.* Translated by Richard Cummere (London, New York, 1917). Epistle XXV 5, p. 185.

expunges the existence of the gods utterly, he breaks off in disgust, the poem unfinished. The mentally deranged poet took his own life. What a light this tragic end throws on the alleged blissfulness of victory over fear of the gods proclaimed with so much pathos! Blissful man exalted to the heavens—is this not empty pathos vainly trying to stifle a profound inner conflict? It was Cicero who first published the unfinished work, still without a conclusion.

Though the Epicureans lacked the courage to draw conclusions consistent with their own doctrine, there did exist among the ancients men who openly confessed to a real atheism. According to Cicero, Diagoras of Melos, "surnamed the Atheist," and the Cyrenaican, Theodorus, unequivocally denied the gods. The originally pious poet Diagoras, master of the dithyramb, was so shaken by the gods' failure to punish a perjurer that he became a fanatical atheist.

A later, much used argument against belief in divine providence goes back to him. Once when a friend called his attention to the many votive-images donated by grateful survivers of shipwreck, he retorted cynically, "Quite so, but where are the tablets of those who suffered shipwreck and perished in the deep?" [51] Even on shipboard during violent winds and in the face of threats and accusations, Diagoras courageously clung to his atheism.

From all this we begin to see the real origin of Western atheism. In addition to its affective or emotional grounds, there is the theodicy-problem of God's justice, which confuses man with his will to absolute justice, and often leads him to deny divine providence altogether. Atheism is not founded on empirical considerations of the world and of human life. It does not possess conclusive arguments that the world exists in itself, that its reality needs no origin in God.

The fact that Karl Marx's radical criticism of the existing order is traceable not to mere political or social desire for change, but rather to his own declared "Promethean" revolt against the divine order, best reveals the historical range of the Epicurean revolution. In the preface to his dissertation on the difference between the

[51] M. T. Cicero, *Complete Works*, III, 37, p. 330.

nature philosophy of Democritus as opposed to that of Epicurus, it is above all Prometheus, hater of all gods, whom Marx acknowledges. Embryonically all the basic themes of his philosophy are in the *Dissertation*: It is the task of the expressly godless believer in the self alone to re-create the world!

Like Lucretius, Marx celebrates Epicurus as the greatest enlightener of the Greeks, the first mortal who dared to defy the gods of heaven. Basic to Marxian philosophy is man's knowledge of self as the supreme godhead. Hence for Marx the prerequisite to a new world in which man is lord is the destruction of the old Christian world.

THE LOGOS OF THE STOA

By different roads the Stoics and Epicurus aspired to the same goal: to make man and human behavior absolute norms. The Stoic seeker of wisdom has discovered his *logos*, which is only part of the cosmic *logos* and essentially no different from it. This *logos* is one's own nature as the law of reason, obedience to which implies an autonomy shadowed by autocracy. The law requires of man nothing but that which is suitable to his nature and what his own *logos* demands of him. In Chrysippus' strictly monistic psychology the pure *logos* is the inmost voice of the soul; no accompanying autonomous, a-logical impulse is valid. Emotions are simply weaknesses of a not yet fully conscious *logos*. They are objectionable *per se* because they are the folly of a man who has not yet perceived true good and evil. Fools are like men drowning in the tides of mere opinion; the wise man has found refuge in the pure air of fullness-of-life bright with the knowledge of truth. The Stoics never tire of stressing the point that the difference between the fool and the wise man is not merely one of degree; it is qualitative. The wise man has entered into the *polis* of reasonable beings to which also the gods belong. Like earthly city-states, this one too is united and protected by the law of reason, equally binding for all.

As Max Pohlenz points out in his book on the Stoa, " This great
polis does not offer the Stoic a mere superficial substitute for the
concrete political state. The *polis* is a religious experience without
which a man cannot become fully aware of his godlike sovereignty
and of his responsibility. "

In his absolute knowledge of good and evil, which is identical
with virtue, the wise man enjoys the priceless possession of inner
peace and harmony, a possession that renders him sufficient unto
himself. The wise man has already made the right attitude completely his own; hence he is also free. No longer can any stroke
of fate rob him of his peace. In his knowledge and virtue he
possesses the one true good with which reasonable beings can be
endowed, " And this possession puts him on a level with the
godhead. . .he is himself divine. " For this reason the *logos* of a
man who has become fully autonomous has the right, if need be,
to decide on his own future existence; hence, should his life no
longer seem worth living, he is perfectly free to end it. Truly the
sage has become the *logos* incarnate; he is the ideal man, the
absolute model beyond the reach of all human frailties. Imper-
turbably the Stoa stood by this myth of the sage, thus establishing
for man a similarity to the gods that elicited their opponents'
ridicule: Oh these wondrous ones, whose likeness to Zeus can be
shattered by a cold in the head! Nowhere in Zenon and Chrysippus,
says Pohlenz, is there an inkling that Zeus is more than a name to
them. Here man himself has become God. Seneca's *Homo homini
res sacra* anticipates Feuerbach's theme of man become his own
god. By an intellectual grasp of himself, man can save himself.
His salvation and happiness lie in his own reason. " To creatures
endowed with a rational nature what better guide can be offered
than reason? " asks Seneca. Although certain Stoic phrases including some of Seneca can be interpreted as faith in the gods,
the wise man who has become godlike has cast out fear of the
gods. Thus absolute humanism, from its Stoic breakthrough on, is
as Heinrich Weinstock calls it in his book, *Die Tragoedie des
Humanismus*, " a humanitarian religion, and whatever forms it
takes will remain so though it will not always admit it even to itself.
The believers in pure humanity with the courage to be absolutely
honest with themselves will take pride in their doctrine of absolute

humanism as the noblest of all the revolts that have appeared in an unbroken chain throughout the history of Western thought since the Serpent's first whispered temptations. "

The high intellectual and moral level of Stoic self-liberation has bound even earnest and pious souls in its spell. " With the loftiness of Stoic claims, one proud spirit infected another, as with a burning fever capable of mounting to a delirium of self-destruction. For Western *homo sapiens,* the chief lure of the Serpent's song has always been its promise of godlikeness through knowledge of good and evil. As early as 250 B. C. Chrysippus, who revived the first Stoic School, staked out the wise man's claim to absolute power by virtue of his ' possession of knowledge of good and evil. ' He can attain such knowledge because men are rational beings, and as such, equal to the gods. Man's only obstacle to godlikeness is always the subhuman in him, his animal-like sensuality. If he can overcome this by the power of his reason, which is his true humanity, Chrysippus insists, he becomes absolute and " no longer need fear any god " (Weinstock).

With this we have touched upon the essential forms of unbelief that were to attach themselves to the belief of the Christian era like so many shadows. After the self-revelation of the Christian God in his unfathomable personal love, the antagonist too steps forward, ever more crassly consummating himself in revolt and unfathomable hate.

THE HOLY GOD OF THE OLD TESTAMENT

Amazing presentiments of and parallels to the teachings of revealed religion may be found in Plato. Even the early Christians noted the correspondences and described Greek philosophy as a phenomenon analogous to Mosaic Law. As the Law had been a " tutor unto Christ " for the Jews (Gal 3,24), now philosophy is to fulfill a like mission among the heathen. Clement of Alexandria even went so far as to explain the similarities between the two by Greek philosophy's dependence on the Old Testament. Above all in Platonic doctrine, he saw the intellectual link between the world of Greek thought and Christian faith. For Clement, Plato was a disciple of Moses. Yet in spite of their unquestionable relationship, a large gulf exists between the Hebrew world and the Greek. Slowly, gropingly, an intellectual consciousness of self began to stir in Greek philosophy a new confidence which critically refined popular mythological notions of God and succeeded in defining a nobler, more spiritual concept of the Deity. In its mature form this effort pushed its way through to a concept which the revealed religion of the Old Testament simply took for granted.

Inherent in every such process of spiritualization is a danger that should not be overlooked: the more highly abstract the concept of God becomes and the more rigorously all anthropomorphisms are banned, the greater the danger of that religion's becoming abstract and unreal. For the sake of God's living nearness to man, for the vitality of man's existential encounter with God, anthropomorphisms cannot be avoided entirely. As long as man recognizes them as mere figures of speech, presentations of this kind do not damage genuine faith. This danger does exist when, crassly humanized, they are taken literally by the naive. On the other hand, increasing abstractness weakens the vital concept of God, and the warm conviction of his absolute reality fades. Here the danger is that God is reduced to a shadowy concept that is bandied about dialectically. Men grow less and less convinced of his reality. The Greeks too were aware of this danger. [52]

In sharp contrast to the great explorers of the Greek intellectual world, the leaders of the Israelites were not the least concerned with philosophical clarifications of popular conceptions of God, nor did they attempt to arouse sleeping consciences with dialectical discussions of basic ethical concepts. They appear rather as envoys of the one holy God of the universe who through them addresses his Chosen People. The faithful of the Old Covenant never doubted the existence of this God; hence their prophets never felt the need to argue his case or supply proofs of his existence. For the Prophets, God was no vague, remote abstraction. Their task was

[52] Martin Buber, Eclipse of God, Studies in the Relation between Religions (New York: Harper & Brothers, 1952), pp. 39-46.

rather to pound into the people of the Covenant, who under the influence of their pagan surroundings tended to slip off into idolatry, that there is but *one* God, and that the idols of the heathen are vanities. Furthermore, that the one God is at the same time the unconditionally Holy One who demands that man, as his creature, become holy.

In the world of the Old Testament there was never a real denial of God. When the Psalms repeatedly upbraid the fools who claim that there is no God (Ps 10,4; 14,1; 53,2), they mean people who live as though God did not exist or as though he paid no attention to them—did not punish their sins. It was not until the last century B. C., when the Israelites in Egypt came into contact with people influenced by Hellenism who denied the very existence of God and the continuity of the soul after death (Democritus, for instance, defines spiritual activity as a purely material process) that a change of approach became necessary. The closing book of the Old Testament, the Book of Wisdom, met that need. Taking the greatness and beauty of creatures as the starting point of a logical sequence of thought, Wisdom demonstrates the necessity of a divine Creator (Wis 13,5).

Although the Judaic concept of God has little to do with speculative abstractions, nonetheless, in its original form, the name used for God in the Old Testament is superbly suggestive of his essential being, indeed, an unexcelled expression of the unique nature of divine existence. When the Lord God appeared to Moses to delegate to him the task of leading his people out of Egyptian slavery, Moses dared to ask God his name. The Israelites, he explained, would doubt that he, Moses, really had a mandate from the God of their fathers and would insist on knowing in whose name he was sent. According to Exodus, God replies to Moses' request:

" I am who am. Thus shall you say to the Israelites I AM sent me to you...this is my name forever; this is my title for all generations. " With this self-definition of God we have in the most concise form once and for all time Divinity's own self-identification, the perfect expression of that absolute self-possession which so radically differentiates divine being from creaturely existence. Human existence is only a brief span beginning and ending within the endless stream of time. In the Second Book of the prophet

Isaiah the name *Yahweh* is used to testify to the everlastingness of God. *Yahweh* is an eternal God (40,28). He is the First and also the Last (44,6; 48,12).

Through all the books of the Old Testament runs the command to recognize *Yahweh* alone as God and to desist from worshipping other gods. Here is the fundamental difference between the religion of the Old Testament and the religious concepts of Israel's neighbors. Although in other races isolated religious thinkers were able to transcend popular concepts and to make a breakthrough to the personal acceptance of a single divine world-governor, their views never succeeded in penetrating and permeating the thought of whole cultures. In Egypt, for instance, Pharaoh Amenophis IV (c. 1375-1358 B. C.) attempted to establish a cult of the one god with the sun as his symbol (Aten). Amenophis changed his own name to Akhenaton ("He pleases Aten") and tried to found a new center for the God Aten in Tell el-Armana. But the masses rejected the king's concept of the divine. Soon after his death, Akhenaton's religious accomplishment was undone. His grave was desecrated, the temples to Aten in Tell el-Armana were razed, and Akhenaton's memory was pursued with implacable hatred. [53]

The Israelites too were not immune from gravitating toward easier, polytheistic cults. That they nonetheless managed to preserve through centuries their faith in the one God with its high moral demands was due largely to the efforts of God-sent leaders, who threw their whole moral weight against backsliding and led the people, grown unfaithful over and over again, back to the God of their fathers.

The first and fundamental duty of the people of the Covenant as a whole as well as of the individual believer was to recognize and venerate the *one* God. To render divine worship to any other being was considered a crime worthy of death.

In the religion of the Old Testament we find astonishing unions of opposites which anywhere else would have blasted unity to bits. For one thing, the cult of *Yahweh* was imageless. Not only was the making and worshipping of heathen idols forbidden by law, but also forbidden was any kind of representation of the Divine. This

[53] H. Schaefer, *Amarna in Religion und Kunst* (1931).

prohibition stressed the absolute sublimity of God: nothing in all the visible world exists that could be appropriately used as a symbol for God. And actually, archeological diggings in Palestine have not uncovered a single image of *Yahweh*. Yet the lack of images never led to an abstractionism that reduced the reality of God to a concept. On the contrary, the God of the Old Testament is a uniquely real, vital personality who maintains specific contacts with men. In order to keep God a living personality, anthropomorphic language seems to be necessary. In this, the writings of the Old Testament reach the limits of the possible. Even the Prophets, who possessed a purified conception of God, made use of metaphor in their exhortations to the people. Apparently there was no need to fear they would be misunderstood. Martin Rehm points out that it is in Isaiah II, the high point of Old Testament theology, that the humanizing of God goes farthest. Isaiah has God say (literally), " I will cry out, moaning and panting like a woman in labor " (Is 42,14). The prophet's aim was the genuinely religious desire to sharpen the contrast between God and man, and to do this it was important to present God as a living personality. God is no impersonal foundation of the universe oblivious of and utterly disinterested in the world. With a strong hand he intervenes in world history; nothing on earth escapes his eye and ear. His wrath makes earth tremble. Yet never does God in his anger become exorbitant, senseless, or arbitrary as man does. Always the norm of divine wrath is absolute justice. It is precisely this identification of justice with holiness, God's most central and divine attributes, which is stressed.

Over and above the holiness of Levite, cult, and priest stands an ethical holiness which (expressly referring to the holiness of the God of the Covenant) demands holiness of the people of that Covenant. The towering greatness of the Old Testament's conception of God is revealed in its high moral standards. It is no neutral moral code, but the Person *Yahweh* who demands obedience to his laws. That is why the prophets usually begin with the words, " Thus speaks Yahweh! " The most basic requirements of society, respect for the life and property of others, honesty, and uprightness in all dealings are commanded by God himself. He who breaks the law commits a sacrilege against God's explicit will. Thus ethics become God's personal concern; He commands obedience to the ethical code expressed in the laws and punishes those who neglect them.

Since the people are *Yahweh's* possession, it behooves them to behave in a manner befitting God's own, as he has commanded. Sanctified above all by their election as the people of the Covenant, it follows that this people must become holy, even as God Himself is holy. Thus in the Book of Leviticus we find a whole list of commands, each beginning: "Be holy, for I, the Lord, your God, am holy" (Lv 19,2). Through this interlocking of the ethically good with the qualities of holiness, the moral order of the Old Testament reached a high point unmatched by any other religion of the ancient world.

Al worldly holiness is but derivative, consequent holiness; real holiness, in its original and fullest sense, belongs to God alone. In the great vision which inaugurated his vocation, the prophet Isaiah beheld the thrice Holy One. Thronged before the lofty throne of God, the Seraphim prostrate themselves crying: "Holy, holy, holy is the Lord God of hosts...all the earth is filled with his glory" (Is 6,3). What divine holiness means is that God is supremely himself, unaffected by the narrowness and pettiness of the world. Exalted above all things, he cannot be used by anyone for non-divine ends. God remains free from all ties and considerations; he is Lord of his own will; he commands his wrath and his love. He is himself supreme Right and Justice and not answerable to any principle of absolute justice contrived outside himself. No earthly created being can litigate against him. It is God's exalted holiness that renders him unapproachable and beyond the reach of earthly beings. Yet here again, it does not follow that God remains aloof from his world. Utterly different from anything earthly, he can be simultaneously remote and intimate. There is no people—joyfully boast the prophets of the Old Covenant—whose God is as near to his people as *Yahweh!*

The holiness of God, rooted in his greatness and sublimity, is not one divine attribute among others; it is his essential attribute, that which renders God godly. Thus in the Old Testament it was possible for "the Holy" to become his name, full substitute for the expression "God." Isaiah, the Prophet of divine holiness par excellence, uses the appellations " God of Israel " and " The Holy One of Israel " interchangeably.

When one compares the other religions of the ancient world with that of the Old Testament from the viewpoint of the holiness of its God, the deep gulf between the Biblical and pagan conceptions of God is clearly revealed. The ethical purity and greatness of the Divine as it shines forth from the pages of the Bible simply does not exist among the pagans. In the Old Testament it is in the Godhead itself that holiness has simultaneously its most exalted model and its ultimate foundation. Holiness permeates and dominates the whole field of religion. For this reason the religion of the Old Testament has been designated the religion of holiness.

Much as the Judaic religion stresses man's absolute subordination to his Creator, it is anything but a religion of man's subjugation, as Hegel accuses it of being. On the contrary, it is precisely the absolute sovereign dominion of God over His people which guarantees their human dignity and freedom. For in God's kingdom, the dignity of the individual is preserved by absolute justice, which no despot may warp. Furthermore, all social, all civic life bear the stamp of that divine sovereignty. The people belong to God with whom all power lies. Hence the demands and laws of Judaic justice are presented as divine ordinances, which as a rule begin with the words: " Thus speaks *Yahweh.* " In the early period, God's sovereignty was given tangible expression by the fact that no earthly kingdom existed beside it. There were only judges to execute God's precepts. Gideon rejected the crown that was offered him with the stern admonition: " I will not rule over you, nor shall my son rule over you. The Lord must rule over you " (Jgs 8,23). When the people insisted on a strong hand and clamored for a king like their neighbors, Samuel was angered because he recognized in their desire for a king disregard for God's kingship (3 Kgs 7,1; 1 Sam 8,7).

Occasionally of course, selfish human commands could be given in the name of a falsely claimed, divine authority. Some such abuses unquestionably occurred. But in principle, the individual lived under the aegis of divine justice. The Judaic world's exemplary social legislation testifies to his. At a time when unrestrained paternal authority ruled among the Greeks, and the setting out of newborn babies to die of exposure was common, not a single case—not even that of a female infant—is recorded in the Old Testament. The love of children was so great that barrenness was considered a divine punishment, and laws against abortion were superfluous. To prevent exploitation of the poor by those grown rich, a law was passed which required the return of purchased land to its original owner after 50 years (Lv 25,8-16). Thus an attempt was made to preserve the original and equal distribution of land among the individual families. At harvest-time the poor enjoyed gleaning rights. To take interest on loans was illegal, whereas in other oriental cultures inordinate usury, sometimes demanding interest as high as 50 per cent, was common. Even the lot of slaves was alleviated by the law. A slave was never considered a mere chattel, but always as a person made in the image of God.

Most important of all, the Sabbath was a major social measure; it provided even the poorest with a regularly recurring day of rest and prevented selfish exploitation of his labors with damage to his health. At the same time, it was a day which man was urged to use for contemplation of his non-earthly calling. Benefits of this kind, which fell to all, freeman and slave alike, were unknown in any other religion of the day.

Although the books of the Old Testament reveal a unique faith in God that on the one hand demands absolute obedience from man, that on the other promises man, as the image of God, the absolute protection of his law, all too frequently the actual lives of men were far from that lofty ideal. But even man's culpable falling away from God is integrated into the Biblical world view. The people of the Covenant have chosen their own fate; it is their unfaithfulness that led to their rejection by God.

JOB: THE TEMPTATION TO REVOLT

In the world of the Old Testament, the battle between belief and unbelief assumed a special form befitting that world's unique concept of God. It is described for us in the Book of Job, that document

of human greatness which can well challenge Aeschylus' *Prometheus
Bound*, and which like it remains one of the pinnacles of world
literature.   With breath-taking boldness Job tackles the ultimate
questions with which stricken man passionately wrestles.   As Paul
Claudel says, "...of all the books of the Old Testament it is the
most sublime, the most poignant, the most daring, and at the same
time the most enigmatic and disappointing—I would almost say,
the most repugnant.   The language is so powerful that like a
lightning bolt it touches off a deflagration of light, images, sense,
and sound, leaving the reader simultaneously confounded and
gripped to his very entrails when the man from the land of Ur raises
his voice.   And what a voice!   Who has ever pleaded man's cause
with such intrepitude, such energy?   Who has ever found at the
depths of his faith cause for such a cry, such vociferous protest,
such blasphemy? ... " [54]

Though in Prometheus there is only indignant rebellion, the
outcry of revolt; though he will admit no more than a comparison
between himself and Zeus, never unconditional subordination to the
god (to whom he does not concede absolute justice), his is the
same rebellion that stirs in Job.   But in Job rebellion is curbed
by faith's unshakable conviction: God is the absolutely holy,
absolutely just One.   Thus ultimately, Job's rebellion is molded
into a hard-wrought yet clearly triumphant faith in the rescuing
God.   Job may hurl accusations against God, "But here is no
philosopher or lawyer cleverly arranging his arguments in tight,
mutually protective cohorts.   Here it is a question not only of a
man stricken in heart and in his flesh, but of a just man perturbed
and scandalized to the depths of his faith, who in a convulsion of
his whole being, vomits his entrails.   In the respites torn from Job's
terrible sobs, all is disorder, contradiction.   He despairs and he
hopes, hopes with mad hope; he blasphemes and adores; he is
sinner and innocent; he appeals to God against God; to the known
against the unknown; to justice against the Law; to the conscience
against imputation; and confronting the Holy of Holies with the
holiness of his own existence, he quotes him and he impugns him.
What hurls itself upon Job twisting and ravaging him is the spirit

---

[54] Paul Claudel, *Le Livre de Job*, Paris: Plon, 1947, p. 1.

of prophecy. "Should he slay me, he cries, I will hope in him. I know that my Vindicator lives, and that on the last day I shall rise and see him with my own eyes, I and no other. For the works of his hands he is there, with his strong right arm! This hope is rooted in my bones " [55]

This is the greatness of Job, that even when rocked by the fearful blasphemy which he must spew out if it is not to poison his soul, in the end he is caught up again into his absolute faith in the infinitely alive, infinitely Holy One, who metes out justice whether man understands it or not, who redeems life even if only in a distant future. Thus in the last analysis, life in this world is not split into two inimical parts; it is not an existential paradox. It is only that man's thinking, reflecting emotions are so shaken by the contradictions within himself that he tries to shift the dichotomy to the ground of existence, and in so doing he succumbs to a world view whose tragedy is absolute. Job resists the quicksands of such existential pessimism and real (the only real) nihilism. He heroically confronts them with his unbroken faith in a personal God behind the enigmas of this world. Like a sun blotted out by the dark clouds of earthly existence, God nonetheless is and remains absolute Light.

In Job knowledge of his own creatureliness, which dares not remonstrate with God the omnipotent, omniscient One, clashes with the bitter rebelliousness of a heart that must remonstrate: " For he is not a man like myself that I should answer him, that we should come together in judgment..." (9,32). "To the Almighty I say: all I want is that I be permitted to discuss this with him. Oh you gathered round me, be still a little that I may sort out my thoughts! Why do I gnaw my flesh and clutch my soul in my fists? Though he should slay me, I will hope in him—but I insist on telling him to his face what I have to tell him—and he will be my Vindicator. Let him judge me! I am innocent! I demand a judge! It is this holding my tongue that is killing me! Do not intimidate me! Show yourself uncovered that we may discuss this together. Why do you hide yourself? Who makes you believe I am your enemy? " [56]

[55] *Ibid.*, p. 6.
[56] *Ibid.*, p. 4.

Beyond a doubt, here is one who must blaspheme, yes, who must wildly proclaim his rebellion but who cannot refrain from worshipping, from proclaiming also his devoted trust. This is what eases the mortal tension within him, and deflects the temptation to lacerate himself and thereby harden his heart.

Against the background of Job's temptation, which is fundamentally the temptation of every believer, one begins to understand why the authors of the Old Testament, especially the Psalmists, insist again and again on man's trusting God as the just Judge even when he reels aghast at God's inscrutable ways. Were such a thing as a lawsuit against the Lord possible, God would be acquitted (Ps 50,6). For the believers of the Old Covenant, true faith consists in recognizing divine justice. "Thou art just, Oh Lord, and all your judgments are just..." (Tb 3,2). "A just judge is God" (Ps 7,12). "Of justice your right hand is full" (Ps 48,11). Innumerable passages assert and reassert God is absolutely just even when men cannot understand. When the Old Testament believer repeatedly asserts his belief in God the just judge, he speaks from personal experience of the great temptation that leads away from God to unbelief: to that questioning of Divine justice, that bitterness which no longer can or will trust, and therefore hardens into such animosity against God that it ultimately attempts to eradicate him.

3.

The God
of revelation

PAUL IN ATHENS

Two worlds met in a decisive encounter when the apostle Paul, challenged by Stoic and Epicurean philosophers, proclaimed his message of the God of Revelation. The main ideas that he developed in his speech before the Areopagus have been preserved for us in the Acts of the Apostles (17,22-51). Paul: "Men of Athens, I see that in every respect you are extremely religious. For as I was going about and observing objects of your worship, I found also an altar with this inscription: 'To the Unknown God.' What therefore you worship in ignorance, that I proclaim to you. God, who made the world and all that is in it, since he is Lord of heaven and earth, does not dwell in temples built by hands; neither is he served by human hands as though he were in need of anything, since it is he who gives to all men life and breath and all things. And from one man he has created the whole human race and made them live all over the face of the earth, determining their appointed times and the boundaries of their lands; that they should seek God, and perhaps grope after him and find him, though he is not far from any one of us. For in him we live and move and have our being, as indeed some of your own poets have said, 'For we are also his offspring.' If therefore we are the offspring of God, we ought not to imagine that the Divinity is like to gold or silver or stone, to an image graven by human art and thought. The times of this ignorance, God has, it is true, overlooked, but now he calls upon all men everywhere to repent; inasmuch as he has fixed a day on which he will judge the world with justice by a Man whom he has appointed, and whom he has guaranteed to all by raising him from the dead. " This proclamation of the God of Revelation, masterfully woven into the spiritual heritage of the auditors, led to a preliminary crisis, to a sorting of souls. For when Paul began to speak of the resurrection of the dead, he was interrupted. Some mocked him, others suggested, " We would hear this, but another time. " The *epigoni* of Epicurus had learned their master's teaching well and having rejected fear of the gods once and for all, they refused to let themselves be disturbed by religion again. But some of the hearers of these first Christian tidings in Athens joined Paul and believed... " among them Dionysius of Areopagus, and his wife Damaris, and others. "

As Paul walked through the streets of Athens for the first time he was deeply moved—the Acts stress this point—by the statues of the gods he saw everywhere. This evidence of the religious aspect of the Greek spirit (a spirit obviously familiar to him through Greek literature) gave him the opening he needed for his speech before the Areopagus. Among the Greek poets and thinkers Paul refers to were probably the Stoic philosopher Cleanthes, from whom we have the magnificent *Hymn to Zeus*, and the poet Aratus of Sicily.

PRECHRISTIAN AWARENESS OF GOD

It was in Cleanthes' *Hymn to Zeus* that Stoic fervor found its warmest and most characteristic expression. Although composed for group recitation during religious celebrations in schools, both the form and content of the hymn betray the completely personal creed of a believer for whom, as he himself says, prose can only inadequately express his feelings for the sublime God. Hearing the opening lines of praise to Zeus-of-the-many names, the congregation senses the appellations Zeus, Logos, Thysis, Pronoia, and Heimarmene to be but different names for the one all-god. Zeus is praised not only as lord of nature and wellspring of all being, but also as upholder of the law, as a king obeyed not as despots are obeyed, but as one before whom the cosmos freely bows. Confronted by divine majesty, man's proud awareness of his own strength vanishes, and the crushing weight of his spiritual and moral plight unburdens itself in heartfelt prayer to Zeus, giver of all good and " benevolent father "—though Xenophon and Chrysippus would hardly have named Zeus so! The hymn opens with the words:

" Most glorious of Immortals, many named, Almighty forever.
Zeus, ruler of Nature, that governest all things by law,
Hail, for lawful is it that all mortals should address Thee.
For we are Thy offspring, taking the image of Thy voice, as many
    things that live and move upon the earth.
Therefore I will hymn Thee, and sing Thy might forever. "

It concludes:

" But Thou, O Zeus, the All-giver, dweller in darkness of cloud,
Lord of thunder, save Thou men from their unhappy folly,
Which do Thou, O Father, scatter from their souls:
and give them to discover wisdom, in whose assurance
Thou governest all things with justice:
So that being honored, they may pay Thee honor,
Hymning Thy words continually, as it becomes a mortal man. "

" Father "—thus, from the heights of his piety, the reverent Greek addresses the unknown God. And basically he is unknown, a nameless power, this Zeus of many names; he is no self-revealed, absolutely personal, divine thou, who from a totally different world addresses man and demands a reply. Cleanthes' Zeus is a power; true, a power poetically personified; but it is still unclear to what extent a really personal being is meant. Basically, this Zeus exists on the same level as man, as the hymn specifies in closing: on the level of " the law " that mutually binds God and man. Such a Zeus is not the God of Job, not the absolutely Holy One with whom no creature dare contend.

Nonetheless, Cleanthes is one of the few Greeks who, pushing his way through the crowd of functional gods and local *Numina,* succeeds in lifting his eyes to the light, recognizable to the mind alone, in which God dwells. As a result his heart overflows in prayer. Of course, we have no certainty that more is meant here than a poetic fiction. Among the Stoics early presentiments of a supreme, personal God were ultimately destroyed by their pantheistic solution to the question of God's relationship to the world. Stoic providence is only a poetic transcription of *Heimarmene,* Fate, which no one could take seriously or personally enough to address in prayer, whereas even the philosophical schools with a purified notion of God continued to make constant concessions to a polytheism which the educated were supposed to have outgrown. This eternal compromising by enlightened philosophers with religious views and forms of a bygone day, which only increased as paganism declined, proves that man's deepest yearning cannot be satisfied by what Prueman calls pantheism's hazy notions of some cosmic *Allgott.* Because the search was on for a living God in a concrete religion, the return to crude popular conceptions was countenanced and intellectualized with religious-philosophical underpinnings.

This quest for God, unquestionably real in much of Greek thought, was the classical world's " foreschooling " or " *Propaideutia* " (Clement of Alexandria) which prepares the soul to receive the word of God eager to reveal itself. Even if the altar inscriptions " to an unknown God " did originally mean one of the many gods to be feared and appeased, Paul gave it the new dimension of the unknown God long sought by the human spirit. Yet the Pauline proclamation was never meant to be a mere continuation and further intellectual clarification of the hazy concept of God already familiar to Greek thought. Paul's message belongs to another realm entirely; it comes from above. For it is precisely in the name of this unknown God that Paul speaks of that God who lowers the barriers between himself and man and addresses him. " Him who you do not know and yet honor, him I proclaim to you! " Overlooking centuries of man's shrouded un-knowing, God lets it be proclaimed that all men, everywhere, should now turn to him. For now the day of Judgment has been set, which one universally confirmed by his resurrection from the dead will consummate.

Although the new tidings find a suitable prerequisite to their understanding in the half-knowledge of God already existent in Greek
thought, these tidings do not address themselves to the mind in
order to clarify and spiritualize its notion of divinity. Rather
they appeal to the whole man, challenging him to take his stand
with the self-revealing God.

Paul himself had been called from the Jewish faith to the new
tidings. He had once been a Scribe of the Torah and was well
acquainted with the *Book of Wisdom's* evaluation of those tragic
souls who, though capable of perceiving the master hand of the
Creator in creation, leave the clearly indicated path to him, preferring to lose themselves in the drifting fogs of passion and
insincerity.

THE BOOK OF WISDOM
AND KNOWLEDGE OF GOD

In the 13th chapter of the Book of Wisdom, a so-called deutero-
canonical document written shortly before the beginning of the
Christian era, we have a presentation of man's tragic predicament
halfway between darkness and light. The author was obviously
familiar with Greek philosophy, and Wisdom tellingly describes
man's alternatives: the joyful achievement of his true goal, or his
turning away from it. Man is misled by the seductiveness of things
intended only as guideposts, but which so beguile the wayfarer
with their beauty that he forgets that they are only markers and
loves them for their own sake. The result is a profound schizophrenia: simultaneously man desires and does not desire his goal.
Things in their beauty are reflected bits of infinite beauty and
must remain so, or they fail in their appointed task which is to
lure men's hearts to Him. All too easily, the reflection becomes
temptation. Eye and heart are captivated by the outward form
of the object and ignore its essence. Man is satisfied with the
messenger and misses the message: the Creator's first and fundamental self-revelation is his creation. In his lust for things, man

rips them out of context and hugs them to him, thus violating their true purpose and significance.

In the general confusion, one fact stands firm: the human spirit's original orientation remains constant. Despite man's ever deeper entanglement with error and his infatuation with creatures, his elemental desire remains strong. Man needs only to disentangle himself from overhasty commitments and set out on his way again to the proper goal. Thus the 13th chapter of the Book of Wisdom offers a first psychoanalysis of the interlacing of belief and unbelief. In its mellow wisdom it does not reject erring man or completely condemn him. The whole tenor is one of indulgent mildness. Apparently the author was well acquainted with the colorless pantheism and tired agnosticism in which the philosophical attempts to overcome popular polytheism had stranded. Unquestionably, his own choice is belief in the personal God.

" For all men were by nature foolish who were in ignorance of God, and who from the good things seen did not succeed in knowing Him who is, and from studying the works did not discern the artisan; but either fire, or wind, or the swift air, or the circuit of the stars, or the mighty water, or the luminaries of heaven, the governors of the world, they considered gods. Now if out of joy in their beauty they thought them gods, let them know how far more excellent is the Lord than these; for the original source of beauty fashioned them. Or if they were struck by their might and energy, let them from these things realize how much more powerful is he who made them. For from the greatness and the beauty of created things their original author by analogy is seen.

" But yet, for these the blame is less; for they indeed have gone astray perhaps, though they seek God and wish to find him. For they search busily among his works but are distracted by what they see, because the things seen are fair. But again, not even these are pardonable. For if they so far succeeded in knowledge that they could speculate about the world, how did they not more quickly find its Lord?

" But doomed are they, and in dead things are their hopes, who termed gods the works of human hands: gold and silver, the product of art, and likeness of beasts, or useless stone, the work of an ancient hand " (Wis 13, 1-10).

Here is no violent outburst of that holy wrath so familiar to us in the Prophets, but a tired melancholy paired with sympathy which in its balanced sense of justice seeks to excuse wherever possible. In view of earth's magnificent beauty, the error most easily condoned is that of nature worship, which by contrast with the hideous fetishes of idolatry, has preserved a bright and conciliatory note. But even nature worship, though indulgently reckoned as little more than a shortcoming, is not blameless. This early analysis of unbelief reveals that the root of unbelief is to be found not in some misjudgment but rather in the lack of inclination and will to break through the surface of existence in order to reach its divine ground, in a blindness of heart which, though understandable, is not without blame in the real sense. Not evil intent but heedlessness, childish impatience, and shortsightedness are what mislead men to nature worship.

Young Christianity's message to the pagans took the insights of the Old Testament's "*Sapientia*" and developed them in the light of Revelation. Careful reading makes it abundantly clear that the Book of Wisdom addresses itself to half somnambulant man dazed by earth's narcotic fragrance and reeling from wanton lusts. It pleads with those who have lost their moral freedom and become slaves to their own perverse desires. Wisdom is one long clarion call to awaken from the torpor of lasciviousness and from the dark thralldom of things to a manly, sober grasp of the light of truth, which continues to shine through man's delirium.

When the soul, long deceived by false teachings, sickened by unrestrained appetites and lusts, and enslaved by false gods is suddenly jolted awake by joy or by dread, and coming to—as out of drunkenness or coma—returns to health, it joyfully proclaims its half-buried yet living knowledge of God, naming him "with this name alone because, properly speaking, he alone is true."

This challenge to a consciously ethical self-possession recalls another quite different philosophy of self-confidence: that proclaimed by Prometheus, prehistory's boundless dreamer; by Lucretius, disciple of Epicurus, who teaches the god-fearful to shake off their fears and find themselves in order to forge their own lives in courageous self-glorification; it is traceable today in much that modern preachers of autonomy suggest to the "intellectually mature. " Though all these philosophies, like that of Tertullian, are intended to rouse sleepers to conscious self-possession, the kind of self-possession suggested by them is completely different from his. All three doctrines of autonomy attempt to rouse men to a consciousness of their absolute, personal freedom, which as we shall see, invariably pushes them in the opposite direction towards absolute bondage to Fate. Christian apostles to the pagans, on the other hand, are convinced that never and nowhere does God allow his tracks to disappear completely; that seeds of the divine Logos can always be found; that God's will to direct souls to him guides them even along the most tangled paths and leads them all at last to a common center. They insist that there is in all the world no spot of life so Godforsaken that it does not reflect some ray of divine light. Basically, God's truth is independent of people and tribe, of temple and holy place, of birth and social position; it is a common good meant to be the possession of all. To be sure, here is a God who requires the hearty will to seek and find. Since men have drunk of the intoxicant of sin, the Lord God lets them stagger their own way that they may experience how " it is an evil and bitter thing for thee to have left the Lord thy God " (Jer 2,19). Yet God never ceases to summon. Even the lacerating suffering that comes from sin is a call to grace and to return to his deserted order.

ST. PAUL ON THE LOSS OF GOD

Very probably St. Paul had an intimate acquaintance with the views of the Book of Wisdom and purposely utilized them; very probably his thought reaches back to the same sources from which Wisdom had drunk. Be this as it may, the tenor of the judgment he passes on pagan godlessness is totally new. For him it by no means suffices sadly and wearily to excuse what cannot be changed. Paul stresses God's pressing will to be known. God does not merely permit men to find him. He commands them to seek him. Paul speaks not only of men's ability to recognize God and of the possibilities of doing so; he goes much further. By the mere fact of their human nature and reason, the pagan already possesses true knowledge of God. "What is invisible in him," in other words, the divine not visible to the eye of flesh, becomes visible to the understanding mind. With his intellect man is able to pierce the many-colored façade of the purely sensual. He can transcend the sensually visible and penetrate to the invisible, in which the world around him has its origin and duration. Mortal himself, and despite whatever partial and transient powers man may manage to obtain, he remains helpless against the world, which, although transitory, he knows must be rooted in a completely different realm of existence, in the everlasting power of God, who as God, is totally different from anything worldly. When despite this knowledge, which cries out for acceptance all around them, men persist in godlessness, the real reason lies not in any lack of knowledge, but in a perversion of heart. To escape the vital consequences of the truth about God, the godless suppress and violate the truth. Hence they are not blameless. To know God is not only an intellectual matter; it includes the whole person's acknowledgment of God as him to whom man owes praise and thanksgiving.

With the godless, then, it is not primarily the mind that errs but the heart that strays. "Heart" here means the individual's inmost realm, the core of his personality, which selects something, becomes attached to it, and ultimately exalts it to his highest value. This explains the consequences of godlessness: the heart that has rejected God is unable to find a substitute among creatures, who disappoint him. Refusal to acknowledge God in daily life leads to a darkening of the heart, to a first and real nihilism. The godless "lose themselves in vanities." As early as Jeremiah we read that those who turned away from Jehovah "pursued nothingness," and so themselves fell victim to nothingness (Jer 2,5). Paul points out that just as Israel's turning from Jehovah was a turning to gods who were nonentities, the voluntary turning away from the God who makes himself unmistakably recognizable damages men's powers of perception and fixes their attention upon empty things. Those who rebelled "lost themselves in vain thoughts." Darkness enters the heart that foolishly denies itself the knowledge it has experienced.

Thus came an appalling substitution of folly for wisdom. Paul's accounts are written under the impact of the Roman Empire's frightening depravity, which had taught him the close connection between knowing and living and made him realize the awful responsibility that weights every spark of recognized truth. Mercilessly he pillories the consequences of man's perversion. Sin is inseparable from shame, as even the heathens, for all their error, know. Therein, visible to the eyes of all, lies the wrath of God upon the heathen.

Paul says: " For the wrath of God is revealed from heaven against all ungodliness and wickedness of those men who in wickedness hold back the truth of God, seeing that what may be known about God is manifest to them. For since the creation of the world his invisible attributes are clearly seen, his everlasting power and divinity being understood through the things that are made. And so they are without excuse, seeing that although they knew God, they did not glorify him as God or give thanks but became vain in their reasonings, and their senseless minds have been darkened. For while professing to be wise, they have become fools, and they have changed the glory of the incorruptible God for an image made like to corruptible man and to birds and four-footed beasts and creeping things. Therefore God has given them up in the lustful desires of their heart to uncleanness, so that they dishonor their own bodies among themselves—they who exchanged the truth of God for a lie and worshipped and served the creature rather than the Creator who is blessed forever, amen.

" For this cause God has given them up to shameful lusts; for their women have exchanged the natural use for that which is against nature, and in like manner the men also, having abandoned the natural use of the women, have burned in their lusts one towards another, men with men doing shameless things and receiving in themselves the fitting recompense of their perversity. And as they have resolved against possessing the knowledge of God, God has given them up to a reprobate sense, so that they do what is not fitting, being filled with all iniquity, malice, immorality, avarice, wickedness; being full of envy, murder, contention, deceit, malignity; being whisperers, detractors, hateful to God, irreverent, proud, haughty, plotters of evil; disobedient to parents, foolish, dissolute, without affection, without fidelity, without mercy. Although they have known the ordinance of God, they have not understood that those who practice such things are deserving of death. And not only do they do these things, but they applaud others doing them! " (Rom 1,18-32).

To judge from this, the history of pre-Christian religion is anything but the story of mankind's continuous spiritual ascent to maturity; rather it is the story of a decline of the first magnitude. The ways of God are obscured by the wrong tracks of man's guilt, so that from this standpoint, his end is really to be compared with night and the darkness of death. It is such perversion that provokes God's wrath, not the state of the world or its events as such, but the wantonness of men who, preferring wickedness, reject truth. Men have only themselves to blame for their lack of light because they love darkness more. Instead of surrendering themselves to truth, they attempt to obtain power over it through magic. All they are really doing is suppressing truth and banishing it from their lives.

Natural recognition of God, which should gradually ripen through a man's experience of himself and the world, granting him knowledge (even if this knowledge is still confused and uninterpreted) of the transcendancy and personalness of God is a prerequisite for man's receptiveness to revelation. Unlike all other creatures, man is the one being who can count on God's speech or silence, on his revealing or concealing himself. To allow him to choose personally light or darkness, man is placed halfway between the two: in the twilight of a dawning knowledge of God still far from the full light of noon. In the final analysis, sin consists in the refusal to let God be God; in embracing the world instead, tricking worldliness out in all the resplendence of the numinous. From this standpoint, all other than Christian religions, to the extent that they are marred by such sin, not only cannot be placed on a par with the Christian religion, but cannot even be positively evaluated. When polytheistic, they misinterpret God's infiniteness by translating it into an infinitude of earthly forces and powers; when pantheistic, they attempt to merge the world's endless variety of deified forces and powers into a metaphysical religious unit. In both cases the personalness and freedom of God, who through his Word revealed himself to the world in an historical act, is guiltily forgotten. The religious will to worship, which, owing to a natural predisposition in man, must worship something, ignores the one living God and in his stead places the things of the world upon its altars.

DIVINE SELF-REVELATION

It is from the higher standpoint of Christian faith that nonrevealed, nascent knowledge of the transcendent and personal God can best be confirmed and natural truth sifted from any blameworthy admixture of error. Christianity carefully preserves natural religion's preparation for supernatural history and sees in man's predisposition for divine knowledge, in his inborn and indestructible nobility, a godlikeness not shared by any lesser creature. Christian faith in God cannot fail to guard against every kind of polytheistic and pantheistic idolatry of the world, which stems from the blinding effects of the Fall, and which are just as effective in today's neo-pagan thought as they were in the old pagan world. Christianity proclaims that in his sovereign freedom and mercy to man, which is undeserved, the personal and transcendent God has revealed himself. These tidings force man into a unique position where he is confronted by an absolute choice. Once a man has heard God's summons in the voice of revelation, he can no longer ignore it; he must reply—with a yes, to his eternal well-being, or with a no, to his eternal harm.

By its very essence, revelation must become history. Natural reason may be able to anticipate the existence of a sovereignly free, utterly divine Person, but reason is incapable of advancing from a mere concept to a possible, still less to an actual revelation of a personal and divine Being. Natural reason is dependent on God's concrete revelation of himself in human history without which genuine religion, man's response in free obedience to the divine summons, has no foundation. A " natural religion " that in the name of an absolute, unchanging, metaphysical essence of God bars all historical factors on principle and attempts to explain man's relation to God from the earthly standpoint solely by means of

general metaphysical categories, can only be regarded as a surrogate
for genuine religion.

Since God is the absolute personality—or as the mystics call him,
Superpersonality—his revelations are acts of free self-disclosure.
History is founded on such acts which can never be predetermined
like a natural process with its functioning of given parts. In true
history there is always the unpredictable factor of the freedom of
two persons' dialogue of action, that of God with a man. God's
addressing himself to a person is never dictated by the elements of
that particular person's life and nature. Always revelation and
man's response to it remains an independent event.

THE ORIGINALITY OF THE
EVANGELISTS' PROCLAMATION

Comparison between the Evangelists' faith in God and the Greek
sages' reflections on the divine at once reveals their differences.
For the Evangelists of the New Testament, God's existence is self-
understood. They are never bothered by the question: does God
really exist? There is not the slightest trace of any need to assure
themselves first of the existence of the divine by laborious speculation; to analyze man's intrinsic need for and groping presentiment
of God, a process which He seems to shun, retiring again and again
from the inquisitive probing of men's minds. There is no fear that
fundamentally God might be an illusion, a projection into the
cosmic of man's own desires and needs. In the New Testament
there is not a trace of the anguished questions characteristic of the
modern conception of God. " God is in the first place simply there.
He is there in spite of all his incomprehensibility and sublimity,
all the fear and trembling and the overwhelming joy which this
divine Reality may have in store for men, there simply as the
most evident fact of all, the fact in no need of proof or explanation. He is really there. For the men of the New Testament the
question is not whether the reality of the world which they can see

and touch might perhaps point beyond itself to the infinite darkness
of a wholly Other; all they are concerned with is how this God,
who has always been given and self-evident, actually behaves, so
that man might for the first time learn how things really stand with
himself and the world. It is not the immediate reality of the world
and its visible magnitude which serve as a kind of permanent base
from which, subsequently as it were, God is going to come within
reach, but just the reverse: it is only under God that men find their
own reality, and the reality of the world becomes clear and comprehensible. This unquestioning assurance of God's existence does
not arise from any properly metaphysical considerations, nor is it
troubled or put off balance by the awareness that this kind of
genuine knowledge of God is absent in the rest of the New
Testament world. " [1]

It is important to appreciate the originality of this new perception of God which went hand in hand with extraordinarily high ethical
standards. It does not spring from metaphysical reflection, nor
does it claim to answer a particular religious need, although in the
thought of the Old Testament there is room for both. Still the
existential ground of the Evangelists' new knowledge of God is
neither completely human experience nor completely earthly insight.
They are conscious of being messengers, " apostles, " who have
been " sent. " They speak in the name of Another from whom their
own authority stems. They consider themselves delegated to convince all men who do not know God of the blameworthiness of their
omission, their " sin. " And although they demand a conversion
or reorientation of heart to the living God, they do not base that
demand on metaphysical considerations but on a mandate from
God, who revealed himself in Jesus Christ. The Evangelists are
not in the least daunted by the otherness of the world around them.
For them the pagan way of life is characterized essentially by
privation, and by the absence of all that should be and is not.
Hence they are not tempted to become part of it themselves.

Neutral, purely problematical theorizing about God is completely
unknown in the New Testament. To know God is always a matter

[1] Karl Rahner, S. J., " God, Christ, Mary, and Grace, " *Theological Investigations*, Vol, I. Translated with an Introduction by Cornelius Ernst, O. P.
(Baltimore: Helicon Press, 1961), p. 94.

of the whole man: not of his reason only, but equally a moral decision, a personal turning to or away from God. Hence it is more realistic to search the New Testament for a psychology, more precisely, for a psychoanalysis of belief or disbelief in God than for a theory of cognition of God. For it is impossible to explain logically the peculiar coexistence of what basically *is* knowledge of God with the determined will not to know God. This can be explained only psychologically by the tensions between conflicting levels deep within man from which opposing forces contend with one another. Already in the Bible we find the phenomenon of " repression, " of a dissembling self-deception. Delusion is the central problem of any psychoanalysis of the New Testament. Because the Evangelists saw through the dishonesty of delusion, their own knowledge of God could remain unchallenged by both the polytheism and the skepticism of the pagan world in which they lived and preached. They realized that their mission lay neither in doctrinal instruction, nor in the rational development of the incipient awareness of God which basically everyone possesses; that it was more important to tear away the veils of self-deceit, to extricate men's knowledge of God from the rubble of original and personal sins so that they could return to the living God. " The revealed Word presupposes men who really know something of God in spite of their lying and being lost through sinfully idolizing the world; and on the other hand this concealed knowledge of God only becomes really conscious of itself when it breaks through men's hardness of heart and is released by the Word of the God who reveals himself as utterly beyond the world. " [2]

The messengers of the New Testament are understandable only from the standpoint of their conviction that the personal living God had revealed himself to them, taking hold of their lives in order that through them he might participate in the history of all mankind. After having already revealed himself in various ways to his people of the Old Covenant, God had last spoken to them through his Son. In Jesus Christ God proclaims his redemptive grace to all men. Through Christ, the Apostles themselves had come to believe. They had personally witnessed his reality; they had seen him with their

[2] *Ibid.*, p. 98.

eyes and heard him with their ears; they had touched him with
their own hands. Above all, they were witnesses of Jesus' resurrection. In the risen Christ they had beheld the glory of God. For
them personal experience of the reality of Christ was inextricably
bound to their belief in the living God. Therein is true life: to
know God and him whom God has sent. Basically therefore, the
content of their preaching circles round the demand that men turn
away from their idols in order to turn to the service of the true God
and the expectation of his Son's return.

NEW UNDERSTANDING OF THE WORLD

Christian faith throws an illuminating light on the world. The
world is entirely creature. For all the New Testament's appreciation
of field lilies and weather signs in the heavens, nowhere do we find
a trace of that sentiment, that numinous *Weltgefuehl* which invests
the world and its beauty and splendor with the sheen of the divine.
The lily's loveliness puts Solomon's raiment to shame, but one is
also reminded that lilies quickly fade and are tossed into the fire
like so much straw. All creation is affected by man's sinfulness
which isolates him from God, and the whole of nature sighs
longingly for the revelation of his glory of which its own glory
is a part.

Godliness, an attribute which Homeric man and the men of
antiquity in general are prone to confer upon the things of the
world, belongs solely to the living God of Revelation. His godliness
is apparent above all in the part he plays in human history. God's
sacred participation in history is a new liberating kind of action
which neither evolves from nor is limited by earthly conditions,
though it takes place in a specific here and now. It is in such
historical acts that God's purposeful and personal sovereignty proclaims itself. Poignantly it pervades the whole man demanding his
yes or no. By a sovereign decision the Lord has set human history
a definite goal. Now at last Hellenic man is offered release from

the hopeless tedium of ever recurring historical cycles. No longer need the lead weight of *Heimarmene,* whom none can unriddle and none escape, crush men and gods; totally impersonal *Heimarmene,* the real godhead of pre-Christian man. The Christian has shed this weight. His life has acquired a splendid teleology; he has a goal, for he knows himself called in all the freedom of grace to enter into the glory of God and participate in the intimacy of his love. Even the least impressive, the least free life acquires unqualified value by direction to an absolute goal. To the extent that it contributes to the realizations of a man's eternal welfare or eternal disaster, every moment now possesses a hitherto undreamed-of significance. With this the Christian has become a new man, for whom the old life has lost its appeal.

Though man remains completely creature, clay in the hands of the Potter, and should not presume to argue with him, the true godliness of the Christian God consists precisely in his inviting this same clay to become person, to become one worthy of dialogue with his Creator and his God. Herein lies the Christian's new dignity which is stamped even upon his body, now become the temple of the Holy Spirit. The Christians of the first centuries are exhorted again and again to esteem that dignity, never to forfeit it by vulgar contamination with pagan life.

Karl Rahner rightly stresses this dual relationship of God and the spiritual creature as something uniquely Christian, a fact which pure metaphysics easily loses sight of. He says: "Further, this relationship between God and man, which is so obscure for metaphysics, is seen at its clearest precisely in the saving history of God's dealings with man. Man takes part in a real dialogue with God. He gives God's Word the answer which he, man, wants to give. And this may turn out contrary to God's will. Man can harden his heart, he can resist the Spirit of God, he can obey or not obey God's will, he can contradict God, he can set his will in opposition to God's plan of salvation. The existence of powers in the world which are hostile to God and which are yet creatures of the one God cannot be separated from this reality of a personal independence of the created spirit; the reality of sin, its inexcusability before God, God's wrath over sin, his summons to reconciliation, prayer, the existential genuineness of which depends on man's having a genuine initiative with regard to God—all these realities witnessed to in the New Testament presuppose the same bi-personal relationship between God and man. God's activity in the course of saving history is not a kind of monologue which God conducts by himself; it is a long, dramatic dialogue between God and his creature, in which God confers on man the power to make a genuine answer to his Word, and so make his further Word dependent upon the way in which man does in fact freely answer. God's free action never ceases to take new fire in the activity of man. History is not just a play in which God puts himself on the stage and creatures are merely what is performed; the creature is a real co-performer in this human-divine drama of history. And so history has a real and absolute seriousness, an absolute decision, which is not to be relativized as far as the creature is concerned with the remark—at once true and false—that everything rises from God's will and nothing can resist it. " [3]

In this bilateral relationship between God and men, prayer is the natural expression of the creature's turning to his Creator. Joyful acknowledgment of God is the highest form of prayer, not the invocation for help and strength. Praise gives God due honor and thanks him for his glory revealed to us in Jesus Christ. Prayer indicates quite naturally to what degree belief in God has become a truly vital, truly personal relationship with God. When in an intellectual age proofs of the existence of God are fashionable, but prayer is disdained as something childish, it is high time for a fundamental change in men's faith.

DIVINE LOVE—AGAPE

The love of God, his merciful and kindly grace which unexpectedly seeks out the wayward sinner and honors him with his companionship is *the* great experience of the early Christians; behind it, however,

[3] *Ibid.*, p. 110.

looms an equally great earnestness. God's love is the reverse of
his wrath and his absolute hatred of sin, particularly of the renewed
sin of the backsliding Christian. Once awareness of these two
aspects of God fades, and the tremendous deed of God's love is
sentimentalized, when the infinite, transcendent God becomes a
grandfatherly dear Lord, enlightened man, proud of his own reason,
must protest.

We see at once from the nomenclature that the love of the self-
revealing God is something completely new and different from love
as interpreted by ancient Greek wisdom. The Greek *Eros* is
inflamed by beauty, wills its own fulfillment, and strives towards
the primeval source of absolute beauty, "*das Urschoene.*" The
agape of the Christian God is a free world-transcending act which
takes effect in a manner that for human understanding is sovereignly
paradoxical. Whereas the human quest for God leads up steps of
spiritualization and sublimation, God's love is not shared primarily
with those who, metaphysically speaking, have climbed the closest
to him: not with the wise, the powerful, the successful, the self-
assured, the morally whole. God chooses precisely that which the
world calls folly. His love turns to the weak, the failures, the
inwardly broken, clearly reflecting the sovereign selectivity of his
grace. No mortal shall boast that God's grace was called down by
his personal righteousness! From the world's point of view there
is nothing which in itself can lay claim to the grace of God. The
highest is as far removed from it as the lowest. And precisely
because a man's over-confident sounding of his own trumpet makes
it difficult for him to hear God's voice, God selects the weak and
the foolish so that all "flesh" may fall silent before him. The
godliness of God's love is demonstrated above all by his outpouring
of Self in the form of a servant, in the lowness of poverty, in his
inexplicable death on the cross. When the Christian believer avows
that God is love, he does not mean some abstract concept of love,
nor is he calling attention to some ontological attribute of God.
His reverent knowledge stems from his own experience of the living
God's free infinite act of love by which, out of sheer grace, he
uplifts a man to Him. Thereby God invests man with a new
dignity.

God's love replaces the "*Heimarmene*" of antiquity. The love of God, not the inexorably wheeling stars, determines the fate of the world and of men.

By that love, countless gods and powers, genii and demons which had trapped and bound men in the nets of their tyrannical capriciousness and scattered terror wherever they went were tumbled to the ground. Man's holiness, once misled, has found its way back to the One Holy Lord, the Redeemer God. No longer may a few chosen ones hope to escape the endless treadmill of Fate by the door of some esoteric doctrine. God's love stands open to all mankind. Thus night brightens into day, and men awaken to a kingly awareness of their freedom.

CLEMENT OF ALEXANDRIA

Just as the thirsting Greek spirit, languishing in its chronic fever for truth, had clutched at each new cult from the East and syncretized it (without succeeding in quenching its thirst), it grasped also at the new Christianity, hopeful of assimilating it too. Gnosticism was the attempt to adapt Christianity to Greek needs by rationalizing and mythologizing it. Had gnosticism succeeded in its real intention, the spirit of antiquity would have stripped Christianity of the new, i.e. the God of Revelation, and would have totally absorbed it. But the early guardians of Christian truth recognized and withstood this temptation to pull their faith in God down from its heights. To be sure many Christians reacted with a certain uneasiness to this refusal to compromise with the spirit of the world and took cover in the merely defensive position of faith alone. It was Clement of Alexandria who steered the faithful through these dangerous straits. He knew the nuggets of gold scattered by the *Logos* over the pagan world, and he appreciated Greek philosophy as God's propaedeutic for Christianity, a preparation which would play as providential a role for the Greeks as the Old Testament had played for the Jews. In his " *Protrepticos* ", his " *Admonitium* " to the pagans, Clement contrasts the new faith with the old:

"See how mighty is the new song! It has made men out of
stones and men out of wild beasts. They who were otherwise dead,
who had no share in the real and true life, revived when they but
heard the song. " [4] In the face of God's revelation, all the old
myths, oracles, mysteries must fade away like *Fata Morgana*. "And
the Word himself now speaks to you plainly, putting to shame your
unbelief, yes, I say, the Word of God speaks, having become man,
in order that such as you may learn from man how it is even
possible for man to become a god. " [5]

Clement's description of the moral perversion of the ancient
Greeks is frightful. We see how lascivious passions, above all,
inordinate sexual desires, projected themselves unbridled into the
world of the gods—truly an analysis of the human libido equal to
Freud's analysis of the dream world of his neurotics. The perversion
grew, at length finding an outlet in the public cult of the genital
organs.

"These are the mysteries of the atheists. And I am right in
branding as atheists men who are ignorant of the true God, but
shamelessly worship a child being torn to pieces by Titans, a poor
grief-stricken woman, and parts of the body which, from a sense of
shame, are truly too sacred to speak of. It is a twofold atheism
in which they are entangled, first, the atheism of being ignorant
of God...and...of believing in the existence of beings that have
no existence, and calling by the name of gods those who are not
really gods,—nay more, who do not even exist, but have only got
the name. " [6] The two opposite summits of folly are denial of God
and superstition.

Men, says Clement, continued to invent new gods, gods spawned
to a large extent by unhealthy licentiousness, mere archetypes of
man's own lust.

The Christian knows that he has been rescued from the world of
such perversion. Clement continues: "We are they who, according
to John, are not 'from below,' but have learnt the whole truth from

[4] T. F. Clement (Alexandrinus), *Exhortation to the Greeks*. Translated by
G. W. Butterworth (New York: G. P. Putnam's Sons, 1919), p. 11.

[5] *Ibid.*, p. 23.

[6] *Ibid.*, p. 47.

him who came from above, who have apprehended the dispensation of God, who have studied ' to walk in the newness of life. ' " [7]

But Clement also knows how to assemble and validate the basically noble and profound glimpses of God which the philosophers in their wisdom had formulated again and again. Hellas testified eloquently to man's deeply buried, better self. True, Clement tends to see the philosophers' wisdom as originally inspired by the Old Testament. " It may be freely granted that the Greeks received some glimmerings of the divine word, and gave utterance to a few scraps of truth. Thus they bear witness to its power, which has not been hidden. " [8]

If towards the end Clement makes generous use of the Prophets, it is to shock the spiritually torpid back to awareness of the sober truth. He finds it necessary to echo the prophetic warnings constantly because the pagans really are like drug addicts. " But verily, you who do not understand are like men who have drunk of mandrake or some other drug. God grant that one day you may recover from this slumber and perceive God. " [9]

One result of their well-deserved blindness, Clement continues, is a curious loss of human feeling. In their insensitivity the godless resemble Lot's wife who was turned to a pillar of salt. The great danger then is lack of feeling, which renders man insensible to the word of God. Blindness and deafness are more dreadful than other evils, for the one robs men of the sight of heaven, the other of the possibility of hearing about God.

Here is indeed deeply concerned exhortation. In his powerful plea that men return to health, Clement begs them over and over again to vomit up the deadly poison and take " the medicine of immortality, " to find true life in the new knowledge of holy sobriety. Far from appealing only to the mind, Clement also proffers the ailing strong medicine, antitoxin to the serpent's poison on which sinful man has sickened. Only thus can the convalescent dispel the fever of their illusions and arrive at the full truth. " Away then, away with our forgetfulness of the truth! Let us remove the ignorance and darkness that spreads like a mist over our sight; and let us get a vision of the true God, first raising to

[7] *Ibid.*, p. 137.
[8] *Ibid.*, p. 167.
[9] *Ibid.*, p. 223.

him this voice of praise, 'Hail, O Light!' Upon us who lay buried in darkness and shut up in the shadow of death a light shone forth from heaven purer than the sun and sweeter than the life of earth. That light is life eternal, and whatsoever things partake of it, live. But night shrinks back from the light, and setting through fear, gives place to the day of the Lord. The universe has become sleepless light and the setting has turned into a rising. This is what was meant by, 'the new creation.' For he who rides over the universe, 'the sun of righteousness,' visits mankind impartially, imitating his Father, who 'causes his sun to rise upon all men,' and sprinkles them all with the dew of truth. " [10]

[10] *Ibid.*, p. 243.

4. *Faith of the middle ages*

FAITH AND KNOWLEDGE

If medieval man ordinarily possessed an unbroken faith in God, the characteristics of that faith are understandable only from a knowledge of the formative power of Christianity. True, the Germanic tribes were sometimes Christianized without coming to grips with religion and the spiritual reorientation considered necessary today. However, the faith of the governing class was founded on the paradogmatic experiences and insights of those men of the spirit revered as "Fathers": Justin, Tatian, Lactantius, to name but a few, and above all on Augustine, whose impact on medieval spirituality was enormous.

As the apostle Paul pointed out, there is a pronounced difference between Greek wisdom and Christian faith. For anyone who has received the light of Christian truth, Greek wisdom is pseudo-wisdom, if not folly; whereas for the self-confident Greek Christianity is folly. At first glance ancient Greek philosophy seems to have been completely cancelled by the new total otherness of the Christian attitude. However, we must guard against exaggeration; Paul's antitheticalness should not become an unbridgeable antithesis. For Paul subscribes fully to the light of natural reason by which a true knowledge of God can be attained. If before Christ men had no true faith in the living God, this was not because their minds were ill equipped to attain it, but because their hearts were corrupt. Their unbelief is blameworthy because their natural morality was sufficient to lead them to the true God had they really desired it.

That a bridge between Greek wisdom and Christian faith existed is to be seen in the simple fact that Greek philosophers did find the way to Christ. Justin, for instance, who died a witness to his faith in Christ in 165 A.D., had been instructed in Aristotle's Peripatetic, as well as in Stoic, Pythagorean and Platonic philosophy. After his conversion to Christianity, Justin, a wandering teacher, did not discard his Greek philosopher's mantle. Philosophers who like Justin saw in Christianity the only dependable and profitable philosophy were not concerned with knowledge for its own sake as are so many philosophers today. For them, as for Plato, philosophizing was merely a means to an end, a way out of the painfully experienced evils of their day. But if also certain ancient philosophers indicated belief in God, they were not in a position to lead the way to the attainment of its end: true happiness. The paths they followed were but timber tracks, which did not lead out of the woods. Although the old philosophies contained elements of truth, they did not possess truth itself, the *Logos*. The seeds they offered were insufficient for the sowing of a sustaining harvest. Justin's overwhelming experience was his discovery that Christianity garnered the scattered grains of truth into one magnificent store. Without the aid of divine revelation man fails in his attempt to attain salutary knowledge of redemption in its full sense. In his need, faith comes to him with its offer of truth; once he accepts it, he realizes that faith does not violate reason. Indeed, he revels in the blissful realization that philosophical truths flow to the believer through nonphilosophical channels, and that through faith what previously had suffered from disorder now falls into place. Purely philosophical knowledge is of necessity fragmentary and uncertain. Fundamentally, it is by " the word of God " that good is effected, whereas evil is effected by attacks against the word. Thus Justin can exclaim jubilantly, " the truths which men in all lands have rightly spoken belong to us Christians. " It is Christian faith resting on God's personal revelation which first lifts the fog that hangs over all merely philosophical knowledge of God. Only in faith was the clarity of an unquestionable monotheism possible, which was never achieved when men strove to reach God unaided. The lines of Greek thought at its best do point toward the concept of a single universal God but without ever quite attaining it.

Not until the coming of the Christian faith does the point of convergence move into such clarity that later it was argued again and again that Christian thinkers had actually got their monotheism from Greek philosophy. In reality, nowhere in antiquity was the insight ever attained that God (the only Being man has ever dared name absolute Being) is the principle of existence, who alone deserved the designation Being in the sense of He Who Is. All other being exists only in relation to the first principle of existence, which is God. Greek philosophy never reserved the name " God " for a single being, nor did it create a God concept in which an entire world view was anchored. Though its highest exponents may have been on the way to monotheism, monotheism never was the dominant principle of existence in Greek philosophy. In their struggle against anthropomorphism, Greek poets and thinkers built the foundations of a natural theology, but it was a theology that was unable to abrogate polytheism. If according to Xenophanes there existed a great and powerful god, he was only the highest among gods and men. And the other Greek thinkers got no further. Plato's doctrine of the good certainly led to important insights for Christian speculation; still, his concept of God is not that of the supreme and perfect origin of existence in whose godliness a certain class of beings participate—to some extent possibly all being. In *Timaeus* Plato makes a significant attempt to understand a divine father and cause of the world. But even this god, giant that he is, still has a rival aside and apart from him, the intelligible realm of ideas. Moreover, he reveals distinct similarities to other members of the Platonic family of gods. Plato's demiurge is not the Christian Creator of the world.

With Aristotle it is much the same. The fact that in his will he left offerings to Demeter, Zeus Soter, and Athena Soteira is unmistakable evidence that even Aristotle was not proof against polytheism. Hence the " prime unmoved mover " of Aristotelian speculation is by no means unique as the Christian God is unique, but according to Aristotle's cosmic world view, merely one of about fifty equals. From this it is clear how far removed the imposing intellectual monument of Aristotelian truth is from ultimate truth which the Old Testament puts into God's mouth. "Hear, O Israel! The Lord is our God, the Lord alone! " (Dt 6,4). And when Jesus was asked which of the commandments was the greatest, his reply was an acknowledgment of Biblical monotheism: "Hear, O Israel! The Lord our God is one God " (Mk 12,29). Gilson comments on this pertinently: " Now this *Credo in unum Deum* of the Christians, this first article of their faith, appeared at the same time as an irrefragable rational truth. That if there is a God, there is only one God is something which after the seventeenth century will be taken for granted as self-evident; nobody will any longer trouble himself to prove it. The Greeks did not realize it however. What the Fathers had never ceased to affirm as fundamental belief because God himself had said it, is also one of those rational truths, and most important of all, one which did not enter philosophy by way of reason. " [1]

In order to know who God might be, Moses asked God himself for his name, upon which he received the unequivocal answer, "I am who am " (Ex 3,13-15). It was not human reason that succeeded in laying the foundations from which Christian philosophy could soar. God himself laid them. Not until the coming of medieval Christian philosophy was the full scope of this new unmistakable principle, God is true being, seized upon and thought through to the end. From it follows that in God life and being, existence and essence must be identical, whereas all other existence exists only through its relation to and on the strength of the source of Absolute Being. In all nondivine existence, essence and existence are not really identical, though the medieval thinkers were unable to explain their precise relation to one another. From the supposition that God is the absolute principle of existence it follows that only one God can exist. This cornerstone of Christian philosophy was laid not by Plato nor by Aristotle but by Moses.

From the foregoing we begin to see the true relation between faith and knowledge. They are certainly no mutually exclusive either-or. Nor can the one be swallowed up by the other as in the case of rationalism and fideism. True, such one-sided notions have appeared again and again in the course of Christian religious history,

---

[1] E. Gilson, *The Spirit of Medieval Philosophy* (Gifford Lectures, 1931-32). Translated by A. H. C. Downes (London: Sheed & Ward, 1950), pp. 46- 47.

but each time dialectical discussion ended in a balanced doctrine which, without intermixing, preserved the full rights of both reason and revelation. Augustine's treatise, *On the Advantages of Belief (De utilitate credendi)* points out that among the advantages of faith is its ability to safeguard even the rationality of reason. Over and over again he quotes Isaiah: " If you do not believe, you will not understand, " a thought which corresponded perfectly to his own personal experience. Anselm of Canterbury received his most powerful stimulus from Augustine to whom he felt related. His principle " *credo ut intelligam* " has been consistently misunderstood, and for that reason calumniated. The faith that is meant here is far from being a " *sacrificium intellectus,* " a blindfolded faith that accepts from the start unexamined, paradoxical, even contradictory doctrines. The Scholastics were anything but what Nietzsche tried to label Pascal: " Christianity's most instructive victim, " and their faith was the opposite of anything that " so terrifyingly resembles a continuous suicide of reason. "

No helpless desperation lurks behind the Schoolmen's will to faith, urging it to plunge blindly into irrational belief. On the contrary, Scholasticism is based on stouthearted confidence in a human reason freed from certain limitations by revelation. St. Anselm, for instance, set for himself the task of demonstrating, as far as possible, the reasonableness of faith. Always his reflections are presented with an eye to unbelievers whom he hopes to persuade. In his attempt to rationalize faith he went too far, as his own master, Lanfrank, objected. Yet St. Anselm can be accused neither of rationalism nor of fideism. The Scholasticism that followed him restored balance to Anselm's method and justly regarded him as the father of their school. Behind his principles (taken from Augustine) stands his own blissful experience: where mere reason no longer suffices, revelation steps in. For the Scholastics, as for the early Fathers, it was a high point of their experience, when light, breaking in on their prayerful meditation on the faith, simultaneously blazed down upon their reason, wonderfully illuminating the enigmas of life and the world, whereas philosophy alone became hopelessly entangled in a net of unanswerable antinomies. The significance of a Thomas Aquinas lies in his clean separation of faith and knowledge with their objective differences; in his recognition of

the rights of natural reason to the discoveries of science, to which
he allots the rank of *praembula fidei,* in other words, gateways to
faith, that in no way compromise faith's essential otherness.

MEDIEVAL FAITH AS A PHILOSOPHY OF CONFIDENCE

Intellectually the Middle Ages and the modern age contrast sharply
with each other although their contrariety is not always immediately
clear. Not only Plato and Aristotle, but also Thomas Aquinas teaches
that philosophy begins with wonder. Wonder is the natural impulse
of a mind on which some fact has dawned; amazement that there is
anything at all, and that it is as it is. The fact that I (who observe
and am aware of observing) exist, like that other fact, that a world
I have not devised exists in itself around me, is likewise cause for
wonder. With wonder comes reverence for that which is and from
reverence stems the will to understand. That is why philosophy
born of wonder and reverence is a philosophy of being. To it
belongs confidence in one's reasoning powers, which are considered
capable of unravelling the enigmas of existence by concentrated
effort, of comprehending the ground of being.

Diametrically opposed to this attitude of confidence in human
reason, the typical modern philosophy starts off from doubt. It
naturally mistrusts given conditions, even as it mistrusts the range
of its own powers of perception, considering itself obliged first to
examine the instrument of perception. Thus it finds itself in the
awkward position of being obliged to use a questionable instrument
to examine that instrument. Critical philosophy's growing mistrust
of all alleged being ends in outright agnosticism, which declares the
ground of being, God, to be unknowable. As a result, the remaining
metaphysical positions are cancelled by a radical positivism.

In the process the bracing tension of polar opposites which hold
the world together is broken. Now, once self-understood opposites
become contradictions, which expunge one another in a dialectical

seesaw of play and counterplay. One striking example of such a dialectical switch may be found in the contrast between the high-spirited optimism and absolute affirmation of life and the world during the Renaissance with which the modern age began, and the gloomy pessimism of the late modern age, our own day. For soon, fired by the questionableness of personal existence, criticism of the moral behavior of human beings and of the world and world events sets in. Man mistrusts the government of the world and feels himself called to blacklist all the incongruences of history and present a catalogue of crimes committed in the name of religion. As a parting shot, he fires the ironic question: And such a world is supposed to be the creation of a good God? Out of protest against a botched world, man goes to the extreme of abrogating that world's Creator. Logically enough, this attitude must conclude by denying any possible significance of the world and of life. Ultimately, the unquestioned a priori on which all such philosophizing is based (see Albert Camus) is the absurdity of the world. As Nicholas Hartmann sees it, the world suffers from splitting contradictions, antinomies that cleave it to the core.

When a philosophy attempts to culminate in a radical contradiction, it only cancels itself. If it nonetheless continues to philosophize, it can do so only by not believing its own claims and unconsciously clinging to man's original confidence in existence.

One typical form of modern intellectual concern with the world no longer poses the ultimate questions at all, as a matter of principle. " Philosophy " has become a positivistic natural science, which—wherever possible by experiment and measurement—collects positive substances from the world and simply relates them, ignoring the problem of being *per se* and the ground of being. No path leads from the self-imposed limits of this purely natural science to any metaphysical concern with the characteristics or foundations of being. All such questions are dismissed as unscientific. Natural science holds that its task is to test the functional dependency of events and, if possible, to express the results in mathematical formula. In modern scientific circles the problem of being is ignored.

Yet for the medieval intellectual this was the question of questions. He posed it with all the strength and high courage of a sound and youthful mind undissipated by the toxins of doubt. In his considerations of the problem of being, he stressed first principles which are as much principles of being as they are of thought; indeed, which *can* be principles of thought only because, first, they are principles of being. He who dispassionately devotes himself to the problem of being in all its significance cannot fail to recognize the absolute perceptibility and unconditional validity of first principles according to which being really " is ": is what it is. From this it is evident that an absolute contradiction of being is not reconcilable with being. Contradiction may exist for a man incapable of embracing the fullness of being, for one prone to inflate part views to whole views with contradictory results; but in being itself, such contradiction is impossible.

Medieval philosophy, including its extension into theology, is a philosophy of being *(Seinsphilosophie)* in its fullest sense. On the basis of God's self-designation as being: " I am who am, " that philosophy perceived a depth and metaphysical dimension undreamed of by antiquity. Ever after, as von Fuerstenberg points out, medieval philosophy was aware that being " has the tendency to relapse into the absolute. " In other words, there are two kinds of being: relative, qualified, contingent being and absolute being, being *a se, ens ut ens,* the power that enables being to be. If anything exists at all—and that it exists, no one submitting a thesis can deny—there must also be such a thing as absolute being. And this Being is God. Hence for the philosopher confident of the reality of being, the existence of God as Being *a se* is an assumption so essential that to deny God would be a self-contradiction which is impossible when one grasps the full dimensions of the thesis. True, medieval thinkers were not proof against positing far-fetched notions about the essence of God: for one, the pantheistic assertion that he is the totality of existence. But such notions inevitably aroused healthy opposition and were the occasion of further clarification of the concept of divine *Ursein* or primal being so completely different from created, contingent being; for to divine Being nothing can conceivably be added, and from it nothing subtracted.

Much has been accomplished in the way of clearly formulating details and clarifying questions of reciprocal origins among first principles; yet the paradox remains the clearest and most important of all first principles. When we consider the difference between absolute and contingent being, contingent being—insofar as it exists—must have received its being from the absolute, or in a very general sense must have been caused by the absolute. Primal being must be the cause of all other being. The only being compatible to all contingent being, which does not contain its own sufficient ground of being, is being that is radically inconstant; that includes possibilities of change which may be realized in time. This inconstancy Aquinas calls potency and act. God alone is pure ACT, always constant and intrinsically necessary. In him there can be no mere possibility of further actualization; otherwise he would be on the same level with created things. The general principles which are concerned with contingent being are unconditionally valid, but because along with created things they are given, they are for Aquinas *veritates creatae.*

Among the essential differences between divine Being and created being belong the totally different way in which each is effective. All that God, the First Cause, creates is a reflection of his own essence and existence; second causes are not and never could be capable of such creativity. Second causes can only be contingent causes; dependent on already existent material, they are capable only of effecting changes in things that already exist. Although the differences between first and secondary causes are necessarily and generally valid, this by no means implies that from given, secondary causes specific results necessarily follow. Actual effects are themselves contingent, as are the particular processes by which they are effected, for instance in the laws of nature, the forms of which are not necessarily as they are but could be otherwise. In modern philosophy, inasmuch as it is concerned with the principle of causality, the radical difference between divine and creaturely operations is often misunderstood. Thus it was supposed that one could speak of a real cause only where it was question of a total cause. But total causes do not exist in the created world; however, secondary causes are real causes capable of operating autonomously. St. Thomas states clearly that with the conclusion: God is the Prime Mover of the world, the existence of a First (creative) Cause has been proved. Though he refers to Aristotle and even quotes him, Aquinas' "First Cause" is not the same. Aristotle does not distinguish his first cause unequivocally from the chain of secondary causes. He does not explore the radical origin of things in the totality of their being, as does classical medieval metaphysics and later the philosophy of Leibnitz. In Leibnitz, even as in Schopenhauer, looms the utterly un-Greek question: Why is there anything rather than nothing at all?

Gilson has demonstrated in detail that as a result of the famous medieval controversy over the nature of the proofs of the existence of God, Christian philosophers move on an entirely different level from Aristotle even when they are quoting him. For Averroës, who remains bound by Greek tradition, God and world are eternal opposites, as they are in the Platonic and Aristotelian view, in which God is merely the crownpiece of the cosmos and world-mover. God is the first link in the chain, but not in the sense that he radically transcends the rest of the chain. By comparison, for Avicenna, who comes from the Jewish tradition, God is strictly and absolutely first among all being. God is before and beyond all other being. Whereas Averroës never leaves the ground of the physical, Avicenna clearly represents the metaphysical view. To be sure, Aquinas still begins as a physicist, but he ends as a metaphysicist. It could be proved, says Gilson, " that even his general interpretation of Aristotle's metaphysics transcends authentic Aristotelianism, for in raising our thoughts to the consideration of Him Who Is, Christianity revealed to metaphysics the true nature of its proper object. " [2] If God is Being in the fullest and unique sense: Being *a se,* the question must immediately arise: How can there be any other being besides and outside him?

Other being can exist at all only because it is sufficiently grounded in the only true Being. Except for God, there can be no self-empowered being. At this point the medieval thinker does not capitulate to the seemingly insoluble antinomy of being; he knows that a real solution exists in being, even if human understanding is incapable of grasping it fully. For all that, he is familiar with the main lines of such a solution. If God is Being itself, in him existence and essence must coincide, must be identical. God cannot " become " because nothing from outside can be added to him; by necessity he contains everything within himself. Consequently, he

[2] *Ibid.,* p. 80.

is the absolute perfect Being, far above all changeableness. The radical variability of the things of earth is evidence that they do not exist in themselves, that with them existence and essence do not coincide. They can claim for themselves no autonomy of being.

From the essential difference between original divine Being and creaturely partaken being, it is clear that the nature of God's creating must be the bringing into existence of being. To create means: to cause being to be. A being is capable of creating only in proporton to his own being. The total cause of any being can only be God; only he is Creator. Greek philosophy never achieved this clear concept of God as Creator because the uniqueness of divine Being was never fully clarified. All contingent things are contingent because the origin of their being is not in themselves; they receive their being merely through participation in divine Being; hence they are incapable of imparting being. Thanks to the being they have received, they can only effect changes in things that already exist. Secondary beings can be but secondary causes. They can only change the conditions of things under their control, can only pass on certain qualities of being; never can they bring things into existence. *Homo faber* can never become *homo creator*. Man's so-called works consist only in re-working, rearranging, developing what already exists. " Works " in the full ontological sense are God's alone; man is incapable of usurping them.

If the world was created by God, if it received the totality of its being—existence and essence—from him, participation in God's perfection is an intrinsic necessity. It is a rationalistic exaggeration to assert that God *could* only create the best of all possible worlds. Such an assertion is an unseeming limitation of God's omnipotence. Since no one ever sat in God's council, no one can say what possibilities were open to God and which were rejected as unworthy of him. Nonetheless, every world that he creates must by virtue of its necessary and intrinsic relation to God as Creator be good. Humanly speaking, nothing but the goodness of God can be called the " motive " for the creation of the world. Only supreme goodness could have induced divine emanation.

For an understanding of modern atheism, it is of fundamental importance to underscore God's relation to the world as the Middle Ages understood it, for contemporary atheism by no means begins

by denying God and his existence. Rather its theoretical denial of
God comes only as the end of an intellectual movement which, from
its beginning, was something more properly called unbelief. It
begins by criticizing the world, by slandering God's creation. With
typically short-circuited reasoning, it relates the world so closely
to God's total causality as to render it the sole causality. Second
causes are for the time being denied, thus making God directly
responsible for all the shadows of existence, for all evil, ultimately
even for human wrongdoing. Shortsightedness of this kind, which
began before the Reformation, flatly contradicts the medieval conception of God.

In spite of all the misconceptions currently paraded as " Christianity, " true Christianity is basically optimistic: the world, a work
of God, is good and remains good, even when perverted by human
sin. The contempt of the world so often preached in the Middle
Ages springs not, as is claimed, from the senseless longing of whole
generations for the void, but from the will to purge a fallen world.
Even the purgative asceticism of the Middle Ages with its realistic
recognition of evil springs from belief in the fundamental goodness
of the world, whereas the modern affirmation of life which began
with the Renaissance and continued until Nietzsche accepts the
world unconditionally. Like any other idolatry, this must end in
disappointment and in the emotional repugnance we find in today's
atheistic existentialism with its disillusionment with the world and
the absurdity of world events. By its own logic, unrealistic and
exaggerated optimism degenerates into extreme pessimism. In spite
of all its variations of mood, Christianity's ever realistic conception
of the world remains untouched by such extremes. It roots deep
in the Scriptural assurance we are given in Genesis (1,31): "God
saw that all he had made was very good. "

Since early Christianity (Irenaeus) this passage from Scripture
has been the cornerstone of an optimistic Christian *Weltanschauung*.
With it, all Gnostic attempts at world calumniation were dismissed
as unchristian. (The Gnostics tried to make some *demiurge* the
creator of the world in order to relieve God of the responsibility
for having created an intrinsically evil world.) The world in itself
is not the result of a primal error, of ontological malice, of any
fall or worldwide faithlessness. Rather, it is the good God, who

made all things out of nothing, who, blameless, gave his creatures not only life but ordered existence. God alone bears the responsibility for the world he created. Christianity does not deny evil in the world, either physical or moral; it does not make a bagatelle of evil; nor does it consider evil some sort of ingredient necessary to keep the world going. However earnestly it condemns evil, Christianity considers it only accidental [dis-order], a fact which permits the hope that it will one day be overcome.

Antiquity lacked the initial categories necessary for complete understanding of moral evil in the world. In Aristotle and Plotinus it is ultimately matter which is to blame for the contingency and disorder of the world. For Christianity it is clear that the real evil does not come from matter but entered the world through the reprehensible act of a spiritual being. It was not the body that led the spirit into sin, but rather the spirit that brought death to the body.

As the noblest creature in the world, man is called to community with God, a summons that is addressed to the mind with its freedom of decision. This vocation places man high on the peak of creation, but simultaneously in danger of plunging—through his own fault—into the abyss. Only man possesses personal freedom and can therefore be addressed by God's personal love. Without an understanding will, there would be no possibility of community with God. In order to be eligible for the call to the bliss of divine love, man must have freedom of personal decision. This freedom is the supreme existential gift, which God alone can give. It is also a fearful gift, for whoever possesses it possesses the power to abuse it. Inconstant as every creature is (provided with a will to decide for or against God) man has fallen from the peak of existence into truly original or primal sin. This transgression did not consist in man's striving for something evil in itself; rather it was that he chose a lesser good where he had been called to choose a greater. Created for God, man preferred creatureliness to God. The result of this first false step was a breach in the original order of things through which the virus of disorder could easily continue its attack. Christianity was first to clarify to the root the concept of moral evil. This is not a matter of a failing of nature, of erroneous and defective happening, but ultimately of the personal revolt of a

creature created free *against his Creator*. That is why in the
Christian view moral evil has a special name: sin. Sin is man's
refusal to acknowledge his existential and moral dependence on
God. It is man's attempt to establish himself on his own, to glorify
himself, to break out of his role of *homo faber* in order to presume
to that other role of *homo creator*. Basically, every sin is a revolt
against God.

Deeply as the acids of sin have eaten into the world, according
to the great medieval thinkers, nature's core nonetheless remains
sound because nature remains God's creature, hence it cannot lose
its fundamental characteristic of essential goodness. Sin has by no
means destroyed all goodness, because it has not destroyed all
being. The whole concept of a nature essentially corrupted is self-
contradictory. It was under the influence of Luther, Calvin, and
Jansenius that the notion that the rot of sin had affected the world
radically came to be considered the true Christian interpretation.

It is only since the end of the Middle Ages that—for all its
polaric tension—the unified view of the world split into dialectical
antipodes: the one view, that of the Renaissance, with its worship
of nature as it is; the other, the view of the Reformers, which
preaches nature's rottenness to the core of her created being. The
true type of medieval believer was St. Francis of Assisi; for this
undistorted unfalsified Christian soul to love God and to love God's
world were one and the same thing.

When modern atheism denies the clear-cut faith in the one God
whom Christianity revealed, a revelation which medieval scholarship
developed, it is forced to set itself up against that faith as its
antithesis. Hence only as such an antithesis is modern atheism
understandable. Historically speaking its doctrine has been written
not on a blank, but on an already closely written page—to be sure,
one on which the attempt was made (as so often with rescripts)
to erase the original letters. As we have already pointed out, in
the near future this slowly developing antithetical doctrine is not
likely to turn against God directly. Its initial offensive is directed
against God's world: it refuses to accept the world as God's.
Indirectly it makes God responsible for the world's shortcomings
in order to conclude that such a world cannot be the creation of
a good God!

Not even the Middle Ages were free from currents of unbelief, but that unbelief did not stem from philosophy. Its foundations were laid on what Fritz Valjavec calls " completely different spiritual powers. " For a long time superstition and unbelief were close neighbors. It was particularly the de-classed, (people without tradition), men and women of so-called bad faith, the dishonorable, the knackers and hangmen, vagrant scholars, and mercenaries who were the purveyors of superstition and of a merciless and ugly criticism of the entire existing order. Only gradually did these " freethinkers " come to attach importance to a philosophical foundation for their attitude, thereby resurrecting many pagan influences.

As early as the late Middle Ages the broad stream of Christian faith was divided by conflicting currents. On one side the concept of divine majesty was exaggerated to a sole, arbitrary regimentation by an all-efficating God, a deviation which prepared the way for the Reformers' later deviation from the God concept. In extreme reaction to this, the Stoic will to absolute self-mastery and autocracy was revived by the Renaissance philosophers. For the medieval believer, God was Lord of life and death; life was not only a gift, but a task entrusted to him by God to whom he had to render an account. Hence in the Middle Ages, suicide was rare. In 1524 Pietro Pomponazzi, a famous Renaissance philosopher, died not as a Christian, but as a Stoic philosopher. He decided to die (instead of a thousand times) only once. Disdainful of death, he refused nourishment. He carried out his decision despite the forceful opposition of the faithful around him. A last attempt to make him change his mind met with an angry, " Let me alone, I *want* to die! "

For the true believer the will to absolute autocracy is the most dangerous of all the temptations that lie in wait for the creature. All presumed autocracy kicks against the creature's radical dependence on God in all that he is and does. Without the positive, creative will of the Creator the creature can neither exist nor act. When recognition of the contingency of his own existence is crowded out, man attempts to make himself lord of the earth by setting aside the order which his conscience knows to be as old as creation. Thus he commits afresh the original sin and opens yet another breach for the attack against the divine order. This is certainly the approach of modern atheism.

5. *The metaphysical revolt*

THE THEOCRATIC WORLD VIEW AND ITS DISINTEGRATION

The fundamental idea behind the medieval world view is that of a God-willed hierarchical order in which everything has its place or at least ought to have. As the Apostle Paul had said, all things are from God, through God, and directed to God. Christians are called to effect the kingdom of God; they are to establish spiritual unity; the great goal is one body, one soul, all united in the one Lord, one faith, one baptism, one God and Father (Eph 4,1-6). Because God has adopted them as his children, all men are members of one family whose historical existence on this earth, like themselves created by God, is to be perfected in God. Everything has a place where it can best serve that great goal. Hence the idea of a God-given *ordo* as the central concept of medieval thought. Antiquity's most valuable achievements (Greek philosophy and the Roman concept of the state) are taken out of isolation and woven into the great cosmic tapestry of that order. For the Middle Ages the world really was a cosmos, a well-ordered whole in which each part had validity and worth through its position in the eternal order to which it belonged. Thus man was offered the many-faceted satisfaction of his personal striving for harmonious form and effect—the whole man, including his intellect, emotions, and will. All revolve round one true Center. By contrast, the intellectual and spiritual life of the modern age, though it will long continue to feed on the heritage of the Middle Ages, is characterized ever more markedly by drastic dialectical reversals that harden into mutually excluding opposites. On the one hand, these produce dynamic unrest and tremendous achievements; on the other, such spiritual dismemberment that schizophrenia has become the hallmark of modern man.

The metaphysics of the hierarchy of being also shaped medieval ethics. The concept of the eternal harmony of the cosmos gave birth to the further concept of a world order and moral order that were closely interwoven. Nature's—above all human nature's—gravitation to the goal established for it by the Creator led to the formulation of " natural law. "

Moral action was rooted in the conscience (literally co-knowledge of the divine order of things). In the norms provided by that order it possessed an objective correlate which banished from it the last vestiges of caprice. Since by a free and sinful act man had brought disorder upon the world and mankind, it was the task and duty of the Christian to take his place in the ranks of those fighting for the kingdom of God on earth, to serve in the war against " the prince of this world. "

Classical man's concept of history was a theory of aimless, periodic cycles. In sharp contrast the new man of Christianity had an absolute, transcendental goal, not for himself alone, but as a member of the Christian community in which he had been placed. Augustine's *City of God* developed this thought to its logical conclusion, defining the real meaning of history: universal because directed by a single God to a single goal, history is the struggle between the *Civitas Dei* and the *Civitas terrena*. These " cities " are not simply identical with church and state; they are two mystical communities founded on opposite human attitudes. Essentially, the history of God's kingdom is the unfolding of salvation; historical progress is made through a " *peregrinatio* " or pilgrimage. It is on sacrifice, obedience, and humility that the City of God is built. Lord of its history is God. Everything is completely subordinated to him. Here is no Hegelian God, gradually evolving in and with history; here is history's Lord. His activity in history lies beyond man's disposition; his Providence, which sees through man's intentions and works them into his master plan, is humanly incomprehensible. True history is a never-ending war between belief and unbelief. As long as historical time endures, the realms of light and of darkness are inextricably entangled; their separation will come only with judgment, on the last day.

In this magnificent teleological view of history, men's relationship to one another through the succession of generations was clear, and an order of things firmly anchored in God and directed to him was established. This was a total order from which no part could fail to demand an isolated existence of its own. Even the state received meaning and purpose only as an integral part of that order. In the final analysis, it too was meant to serve universal, other-worldly ideas. There were periods when medieval politics in practice actually " corresponded to a high degree to this demand. "

In the light of theocracy, questions of social and economic life were also explicitly and satisfactorily answered. As Aristotle had taught and Aquinas reiterated, man is by nature a social being. However, man's social impulses are not entirely natural as are those of bees and ants; rather, man's social order must be realized in a manner befitting his rational and true nature; his social order must be realized in ethical endeavor. It is not " historical necessity "—as was taught later—which leads to the perfect society, but only the moral improvement of community life to which all members are obligated.

From the great medieval concept of *ordo* came also the regulations of economic life. The striving for profit too had to obey the basic law of love both of God and of neighbor. Economic goods and their manufacture were not considered ends in themselves; they were never expected to create an earthly paradise. Because in the dimension of eternity all transitory things are but symbols, worldly goods are not to be taken as ultimate full realities. All too easily they confuse man and hamper his pilgrimage. The Christian should trouble himself about earthly possessions only insofar as they are necessary to preserve his life and that of the community. Acquisition for its own sake deteriorates to greedy addiction.

In spite of the definite constraints of the theocratic idea, the independent development of individuals and of peoples was not stifled by gray uniformity. As a result of the decentralization of

the feudal state, life in the provinces bloomed. The state did not
fabricate a mass of indistinguishable human atoms, but an organism
composed of many members, who, though of varying status and
dignity, were all essential to the whole and who strove for the
common good. The Middle Ages adopted the Aristotelian doctrine
of the state as an organism and gave it a religious foundation.

The medieval state provided room for the development of special
social forces, an opportunity which the medieval abundantly used.
From the blending of the Christian idea of community with the
Germanic concept of *comitatus* (allegiance) grew the unique individualism of the medieval world, which left the individual free to
develop as *persona* within the natural framework of the various
communities of family and class, of guild and brotherhood. The
freedom of this restrained individualism of the Middle Ages was
not individualistic in the modern sense, rather it was corporative
freedom. Jakob Burckhardt pointed out that within its framework
a wealth of highly individual personalities could and did flourish;
Dante's magnificent testimony does not stand alone.

Simultaneously, the theocratic ideal protected the freedom of the
citizen from any stifling powers of the state; in the Middle Ages
absolute sovereignty and the omnipotent state were unknown. To
be sure, medieval reality often lagged far behind the medieval ideal,
but even that reality must be credited with binding together all the
conflicting forces of human existence and arching them into one
mighty dome. Herein lies "the ultimate secret of the age and its
greatness." Within its bracing polarity, the Middle Ages engendered
countless personalities who incorporated its great ideal. Among its
emperors and popes it produced "leaders filled with the spirit of
asceticism and renunciation of worldly goods, who at the same time
played the greatest roles in political affairs, doing everything they
could to further the ideals of the heavenly kingdom on earth.
Henry III or Gregory VII—both men succeeded in what is so
essential and yet so rare: in being effective in the world without
succumbing to it. In this sense the Middle Ages found complete
fulfillment in the prodigious figure of a St. Bernard of Clairvaux;
for out of world-fleeing spirituality and the privations of his cloister
cell sprang the most powerful, methodical agitation; yet the tension

was resolved, disciplined by a piety which fused knowledge with devotion. " [1]

Permanent monuments to medieval culture are its *Summa* and its Gothic cathedrals. It is significant that all attempts to revive Gothic architecture have failed. Neo-Gothic structures simply do not have the soul which, for all their austerity, still animates the old Gothic cathedrals. The new buildings lack that vitality which embraces nature and spirit, joy and earnestness, pressing the very demons into its service.

This synthesis of classical, Christian, and Germanic cultures in the one medieval culture was possible largely because the peoples involved were still young and receptive and willingly accepted the Church's role of educator. At that time the various spheres of practical living and intellectual activity were not yet basically independent and hence fitted more easily into a theocratic whole. As they continued to develop, the critical point came at which the people within the orbit of medieval culture had to choose either to remain within the framework of its great unity, or cast off its bonds by an act of self-will.

At the height of the Middle Ages the process which took half a millennium to mature had already begun. This was the formative period for the explosive inner forces which were to shatter the unity of the old world. (Apparently the re-alignment of those forces in equilibrium has been reserved for some unforeseeable, blessed hour.) Whether one welcomes what followed as progress or rejects it as disintegration, it has been in the making since the 14th century, leading by the dynamics of its inner logic to the French Revolution with its theme of revolt and ultimately to the current notion of world revolution. It is vain to belabor the question: Was or was not the course that history followed necessary? At any rate, as far back as the Middle Ages, the individual had begun to disengage himself from the close-knit theocratic order in which he lived. The civilizing influence once asserted on the socio-political and economic spiritual life of the age collapsed before a rising tide of autonomy which demanded uncurbed freedom in every sphere of life.

[1] F. Schnabel, *Deutsche Geschichte im neunzehnten Jahrhundert.* Bd. I, 3 Aufl. (1947), p. 14.

The modern way of life produced types unknown in medieval culture. This was particularly true in Italy. Restless, nefarious adventurers in public, social, and economic life began to assert their self-will, ruthlessly transferring ambition into power over man and nature. Not only the upper classes' traditional sense of *noblesse oblige* but the dignity and self-respect of all classes was replaced by the modern lust for personal fame. Freethinkers and cynics in whom superstition and scurrility were oddly blended became the first unbelievers, although they did not as yet sever their connections with the Church. Dante considered the Epicureans the real infidels of his day. Giovanni Villani says of one of them: " His life was Epicurean, since he believed neither in God, nor in the Saints, but only in bodily pleasure. " [2] The Epicureans drew their belief in a world stripped of its gods from Lucretius. Dante sweepingly consigned all Epicureans to Hell.

Burckhardt has called Emperor Fredrick II the first modern on a throne. Fredrick is the absolute ruler par excellence. His decrees were aimed at the complete annihilation of the feudal state and the transformation of its members into a defenseless, irresolute mass from which the utmost in taxes could be extorted. Out of a people he made an intractable heap of subjects supremely dependent on his bureaucracy. It was the absolute princes who most wantonly trampled upon the theocratic idea of the Middle Ages. They were despots who respected nothing but power, individualists with little patience for individuality other than their own. Burckhardt describes a trait that was characteristic of the tyrants of this period: " The astrological superstitions and the religious unbelief of many tyrants gave in the minds of their contemporaries a peculiar color to this awful and God-forsaken existence. " [3]

Against such a background of unbelief with its pagan concept of the state's omnipotence, Martin Luther stands out sharply as an *homo religiosus*. To be sure, his religious struggle was rooted in the spiritual world of the *via moderna*. On his own lonely path he sought the merciful God. The freedom he described in *The Freedom of the Christian Man* is the uprising of the individual, his

---

[2] J. Burckhardt, *The Civilization of the Renaissance in Italy.* Translated by S. G. C. Middlemore (New York: New American Library, 1960), p. 349.
[3] *Ibid.*, p. 46.

shaking off his fears and worldly dependencies to put his trust in divine grace. Though Luther and Calvin freed the believer from the bonds of Church tradition, the Reformers sought new bonds, new walls to shield man from modern individualism. True, Protestantism destroyed the unity of the ancient Church, but for a long time it held fast to the idea of a unified Christian culture. Indeed, the old Protestant discipline was so strict that it soon came to be considered narrow-minded and doctrinaire.

Here two points must be considered whose unintentional and belated effects led to a profound change. The first is the Reformer's altered concept of God. Luther's aim was to honor God alone. According to Catholic doctrine, in the process of salvation, God effects all things by his grace. In Luther, however, the all-efficaciousness of God is exaggerated. Faced by such a God, man's freedom grows questionable, and—as we shall see later—also man's reality. Luther's private studies led him to adopt not the balanced God concept of the Middle Ages but the Ockhamistic concept of late Scholasticism. Ockham's was a God of absolute sovereignty, almost to the point of pure arbitrariness. He pardons whomsoever he likes and rejects whomsoever he dislikes. According to the classic teaching of the late Middle Ages, God's will, though absolutely independent, yet remains " God's, " that is, identical with his holy and ever benevolent essence. The ultimate and deepest ground of his volition is always his infinite holiness and goodness.

Although Luther too had trouble with the problem of predestination, it was Calvin who allowed this doctrine to slide into a convulsing radicalism that utterly destroyed human freedom. As A. Brandenburg insists in *The Protestant Handbook of Theology,* Luther's idea of the unfree will *(servum arbitrium)* penetrated deep into Protestant theology. One belated consequence of this has been the desperate struggle between Luther's concept of God (which consumes all human freedom and threatens man's personal, individual reality) and modern man's will to intellectual self-preservation. Thus it was to be in the name of human freedom that the German idealist philosophers one day turned on the tyrannical despot-God who robbed them of their freedom and rejected faith in a personal God entirely.

The second point to remember is that from the beginning the

germ of destruction lurked in the new authority of the state over
the churches. Pressed by the political situation in which he found
himself, Luther placed what he considered necessary authority into
the hands of the territorial princes. At first the old Protestant
State came closer to the theocratic concept of the Middle Ages than
many a Renaissance Italian principality. Nowhere was religious
life so thoroughly subordinated to the rule of the princes as in the
State Churches of Germany's northern principalities. There the
prince was " *papa in suis terris* " (Pope in his lands). Once
political and personal worldliness established itself in the courts,
once absolute rulers introduced unbridled political omnipotence, the
incipient danger became acute. Not only did Europe fall apart into
countless absolutistic princedoms whose very existence depended on
violence and cunning, but the one Church fell apart into many
churches, each condemning the others and setting itself up as the
unique saver of souls. In an age of enlightenment, the individual
who had gained his own area of free thought and faith was bound
to protest such claims. As a result of that protest, the God who was
supposed to guarantee the authority of the absolute princes had
to fall.

THE FRENCH REVOLUTION: PIVOT OF THE NEW AGE

In order to gain any real understanding of our own times, we must
go back in history to that event which harrowed the ground for
the epoch in which we live, and show how the intellectual forces it
released shaped the main features of our present world. It is the
French Revolution, whose stirring waves by no means broke on
France's political borders but rolled on, powerful and heady, into
the intellectual life of Germany. For the people of the 19th century
the French Revolution was a European event. In the process of
coming to terms with that event they gained a better understanding
of themselves; above all they attempted to find their place in history

and to clarify their historical mission. For 19th-century man the age he considered contemporary began with the French Revolution. In liberal usage, still largely valid today, it was "the great revolution." Many educated people, particularly several generations of German philosophers, expected from it the dawn of a new world order. Men of such different intellectual stamp as Kant, de Tocqueville, Lorenz von Stein, Fichte, Hegel, and Marx followed its development with the greatest interest. They were convinced that the French Revolution was far more than just another chapter in the history of France; rather it was the beginning of an epochal revolutionizing of the whole modern world. The first stage had been that of political revolution; the next stage, many people were convinced, would continue the revolution on every level. Pessimistic voices, de Tocqueville's for one, were drowned in the chorus of optimistic voices.

Even the mature Kant, who in the cautious wisdom of old age can hardly be expected to share Fichte's enthusiasm for the Revolution, sees it not merely as an historical phenomenon, but as proof of mankind's inherent leaning to progress. Moral advance, says Kant, is part of rational human nature. Such a phenomenon as the French Revolution, he points out in *The Conflict of the Faculties*, will never be forgotten, because it revealed a propensity for improvement in human nature that no political philosopher, however prophetic, foresaw; a propensity which links nature with freedom according to the inner principles of justice. The French Revolution was too great, too tightly interwoven with the interests of mankind, its influence too widespread not to be repeated in fresh attempts by other peoples all over the world whenever conditions allow.

If Kant lets matters rest at mere expectation of repeated, more fruitful revolutions, Fichte and Hegel go much further. Today it is necessary to stress this point if we really want to understand the motivating forces behind German idealism. To many people, German idealism still appears to be what in its day—according to Heinrich Heine—the French thought it was: a kind of mystical, esoteric doctrine, whose secrets were not to be aired before the uninitiated. The French were as convinced of its plumbless profundity as they were of its utter uselessness. They felt that only a country which had renounced all practical attempts to attain its

social and political goals and hence sought an ersatz for them in
the exclusively intellectual realm could consent to such a philosophy.

Fichte's philosophizing was kindled by the theme of the French
Revolution. The young Fichte had no desire to become a mere
scholar. "I want to act, not only to think," he once wrote his
fiancée. Not until he too, stirred by the pathos of revolutionary
ideas, had discovered an approach to man's autonomous freedom
in the philosophy of Kant did the philosophical Eros thus aroused
thrust him onto the road of idealism. The experience of freedom
founded on the Revolution delivered Fichte from the depression
of a vague belief in determinism. In a passionate archdecision, he
joined the ranks of freedom *(Freiheit)*, henceforth to be his watchword. Soon his passion for knowledge, no longer suppressible,
turned to speculation that in the beginning centered entirely on the
political act. The real purpose of all Fichte's philosophical endeavors
was to illuminate his primary theme of human freedom from every
angle, varying it over and over again. His *Prolegomena to Every
Future Metaphysic Which Can Appear As a Science,* in which he
rejects all supernatural revelation and admits revelation of any kind
only as a pedagogic aid that could provide sensual man with an
understanding of moral law, gained him the favor of Kant upon
whose recommendation the work was published in 1792. Overnight
Fichte was famous.

Fichte's freedom did not remain a mere intellectual and moral
postulate; the philosopher of action considered action a socio-
political ideal which it was man's task to realize. In his article
(1793) demanding the return of freedom of thought from the
princes of Europe, Fichte attempted to present the basic demands
of human freedom to the ruling powers of the day. Because of the
current political situation and censorship regulations, Fichte's paper
on the French Revolution appeared without the name of its author
or place of publication. The preface begins: "I am convinced of
the importance of the French Revolution for all mankind." The
Revolution reminds the writer of "a rich painting illustrative of
the exalted text: human rights and human values." In the political
pamphlets of 1793 he passionately demands a speedy end to oppression and servitude. Fichte himself has no wish to be a revolutionary
since he ascribes responsibility for the present embroiled conditions

not only to the oppressors but also to the evils of the existing order. He knows that a mere overthrow of intolerable conditions does not lead to a new order. Nonetheless, he couches his demand for freedom, which he hymns as the heaven-sent palladium of mankind, in the sharpest terms: not even princes may rob men of their freedom. In his demands, above all for freedom of thought, he brands the spiritual power of the papacy as its most formidable opponent, " that dreadful universal monarchy, " which " quashes the last remnant of independence in men. "

Like many of his contemporaries, Fichte saw in the French Revolution the seed of a political renewal which—one hoped—would blossom also in the rest of Europe. Like Kant, he recognized Rousseau as the intellectual spokesman for the new order which should comply to the will of the people as soon as they have become politically articulate. A new day seemed to dawn; the forces of reason would lead to victory over darkness. Fichte's maxim runs: Do not complain, act!

This is the same Fichte who in the winter of 1807-1808 turned to the German nation with his fifth address to convince the Germans of their true mission in the world. He takes great pains to prove that the German race is an indigenous race because it has " remained in the uninterrupted flow of a primitive language which develops itself continuously out of real life. " Because in the German people the original vitality which flows from the mainspring of intellectual life itself is at work, to the Germans falls the task of developing archetypal human conditions, indeed, the creation of " a new life such as has never hitherto existed. We are by no means discussing the mere preservation from decay of those relationships in their present stage. " [4]

Foreign genius may strew flowers on the well-worn paths of the Roman legions and weave a graceful garment for ancient wisdom, but the German spirit—says Fichte—will blaze new trails. The Germans will bring the light of day into the abysmal dark, and hurl intellectual boulders, " out of which future ages will build their

---

[4] J. G. Fichte, *Addresses to the German Nation*. Translated by R. F. Jones and G. H. Turnbull (Chicago and London: The Open Court Publishing Company, 1922), p. 73.

dwellings. " He intimates that " new Titans " have appeared on
the scene, the " earthborn, " who will not storm heaven, but who
will make earth the theater of their gigantic activities.

What the new Titans' deeds are to be, Fichte describes more
concretely in the sixth address: " . . .the latest great and, in a certain
sense, completed achievement of the German people, an achievement
of world-wide importance—the reformation of the Church. " [5] For
Fichte " Christianity, which originated in Asia, " had " in the days
of its corruption become more Asiatic than ever, preaching only
silent resignation and blind faith. " Even for the Romans it had
been something imposed and alien, something they never really
understood or assimilated. On the contrary, Christianity only split
their nature into two ill-fitting halves. Among the Germanic tribes,
Christianity's interest in the soul's salvation had fallen on fertile
soil. The Christian threat of loss of soul had evoked " horror and
loathing. " According to Fichte, Luther was a man of German
earnestness and spirit, who began the liberation movement away
from the papacy because he so strongly feared for his eternal
salvation. The wars he unleashed had as their goal solely " that
they might not again come under the power of the accursed papacy. "

After this first basic liberation, further development was a matter,
Fichte explains, of doing away altogether with a mediator between
God and man, " and of finding the bond of connection in one's
self. " To be sure, for a long time Protestant theology in Germany
had remained enchained, whereas in other countries " this free
thinking, fanned into flame by the brilliant triumph it had achieved,
rose higher and more easily, unfettered by a belief in the supersensuous. " For a long time it was still " far from discovering in
reason (Vernunft) the source of truth which rests upon itself. "
But once the German spirit began to stir independently, it was
expected to abandon its faith in the power of " foreign " authority
and discover " the supersensuous in reason itself, thus creating
for the first time true philosophy by making free thought the
source of independent truth, as it ought to be. " Fichte considers
this task meanwhile " completely solved among us, and philosophy
. . .perfected. " Now the age of complete liberation is to be

[5] *Ibid.*, p. 91.

expected; its prerequisite "the creation in the German fatherland of a new age such as never before existed."

Next Fichte carefully alludes to the French Revolution as an attempt at "the establishment of the perfect state," an attempt which, to be sure, had begun lightly and with ardent daring," but which so deteriorated that the very thought of continuing it was branded a crime and many would have liked to strike it from the records of history. Fichte sees the reason for this failure in the nation's lack of the necessary education for its task. He considers it Germany's mission to provide an education that will assure the success of a freshly launched revolution. "Only the nation that has first actually solved the problem of educating perfect men will also solve the problem of the perfect state." [6]

In the way of a cultural history for a new world, the first step would be to have Christianity de-emphasize respect for external form, which robbed it of its freedom, and to introduce into it the freethinking of antiquity. Though the initiative to this step had come from abroad, it was the Germans who had carried it out. Fichte saw "the second step" which is really the continuation and completion of the first, as the need "to discover in our own selves this religion and with it all wisdom." Because in its thoroughness German philosophy far excels all foreign philosophies, it is the philosophy destined to lay the foundations for the education of the perfect man, whom Fichte discusses at length. It is Germany's task also to implement that education.

Thus in his maturity Fichte still clung to the *Sturm-und-Drang* notions of his youth. His *Addresses to the German Nation* had a far-reaching effect on young Germany; we find his thoughts echoed, often word for word, in the speeches of the Neo-Hegelians.

In much the same way, Friedrich Hegel, the philosopher of the absolute idea, whose idealistic system shaped the thinking of 19th-century German intellectuals (including opponents who had been his former students) saw in the French Revolution not merely a political overthrow but the beginning of an intellectual revolution which he felt himself destined to continue. Even after he had become the official philosopher of the Prussian monarchy, Hegel

[6] *Ibid.*, p. 102.

continued to observe the anniversary of the outbreak of the French Revolution. With (for him) rare exuberance, he celebrated the storming of the Bastille as an event incomparably more glorious than any other in the history of the world. For Hegel the French Revolution represented the demands of justice in a world of injustice, thus proving the power of the human spirit to shape reality according to its own ideas. " The idea of Right asserted its authority all at once, and the old framework of injustice could offer no resistance to its onslaught. A constitution, therefore, was established in harmony with the conception of Right, and on this foundation all future legislation was to be based. Never since the sun stood in the firmament and the planets revolved round it, had it been perceived that man's existence centers in his head, that is to say, in his reason, inspired by which he constructs the world of reality. Anaxagoras had been the first to say that ' nous ' governs the world; but only now had man advanced to recognition of the principle that reason should govern spiritual reality. Accordingly a glorious intellectual dawn was at hand. All rational beings shared in the jubilation of this epoch. Lofty emotions stirred men's minds; a spiritual enthusiasm thrilled through the world, as if the reconciliation between the divine and the secular had just been accomplished. " [7]

It is a misinterpretation of German idealism with its culmination in Hegelian philosophy to ignore if not deny the connection between idealism and revolutionary thought. Yet to this day in many circles Hegel's philosophy is considered a gigantic, purely speculative system which—sprung from the brow of a unique intelligence—was doomed to break down without its master. Thus at Hegel's death in 1831 the questions, what could possibly still come after the absolute philosophy of the Master? Was not all history at an end? must have depressed the Neo-Hegelians to a degree no longer imaginable. Idealism had been a castle in the air which without the dynamics of realization was totally incapable of radiating practical impulses. Hence foreign elements had first to make it dynamic. The Polish Hegelian, Count Cieszkowski, whose *Prolegomena to Historiosophy* was published in Berlin in 1838, is

[7] F. Hegel, *The Philosophy of History* (New York: Dover Publications, Inc., 1956), p. 447.

supposed to have given the cue. Overnight his view of history permeated the appropriate circles and was soon accepted everywhere. Then, impressed by Cieszkowski, the Russian revolutionary Bakunin published his doctrine of revolution, in which he demanded the radical overthrow of the government.

However, this interpretation of German idealism misses its true essence entirely. For although the dynamics of idealism are concealed by speculation, a stubborn will to concrete action permeates the whole philosophy. This will, Hegel proudly insists, does not require inspiration from the outside, certainly not from the Slavs. Its goal is no less than a universal, revolutionary change of existing conditions. The will to action is present in Fichte's philosophy as it is in Hegel's, though as a result of superficial adaptations to the Restoration Period Hegel's thought stands in a peculiar twilight. Outwardly it appears to be trying to render existing conditions in the Prussian State ideologically absolute since it defines the state as God in residence—a phrase that flattered Prussian absolutism while permitting the will to revolution to remain veiled.

The Neo-Hegelians, however, were completely aware of the Master's true intentions. One of them, Karl Marx, saw in the Revolution of 1789 the most significant crossroad in the evolution of humanity, unfolding as it did a maximum of political energy, political power, and political knowledge. Along with Heine and other friends, Marx kept an envious eye on France, which in political practice was far ahead of Germany since so far the Germans had been content to think politically while others acted. Nonetheless, Marx's " Germany has been their theoretical consciousness " was valid. Since the first Revolution had succumbed to the Counterrevolution, it was the Germans' task to take up the cause again with appropriate thoroughness in order to carry out the Revolution " radically. " Who does not hear echoes of Fichte in this? Again and again Marx presses for radical revolution. " It is not *radical* revolution, *universal human* emancipation, which is a Utopian dream for Germany, but rather a partial, *merely* political revolution which leaves the pillars of the building standing. " [8] Marx leaves no one in doubt about what he means by " the pillars of the building. "

[8] K. Marx, *Early Writings*. Translated by T. B. Bottomore (New York: McGraw-Hill Paperbacks), p. 55.

Germany still resembles a fetish-worshipper, a victim " of Christian-Germanic serfdom. " True, Luther in the Reformation had instigated a preliminary religious revolution, but that revolution had yet to be fulfilled by vanquishing " one's own inner priestling, " by man's total emancipation from all religion, a task that falls to philosophy. Much like the young Hegel before him, criticism of the times had led young Marx to criticism of culture, which for him was identical with criticism of religion.

The group of young Neo-Hegelians was powerfully attracted by the Paris of the eighteen thirties and forties, which seethed with new and revolutionary ideas. Saturated with Hegelian and Feuer-bachian thought, Marx arrived there as a political refugee and soon discovered how strongly the unbroken tradition of 1789 still influenced France. His Parisian years (1843-45) were of the greatest importance for the development of his own revolutionary thought, for it was in Paris that he made the acquaintance of the early French Socialists and listened to the communistic demands of Babeuf and his followers. Continuing the " political emancipation, " new revolutions should now bring about the " human emancipation, " in which the relinquishment of the differences between the propertied and the propertyless would be decisive. Among the Neo-Hegelians, to whom also Heinrich Heine belonged, expectation of the "world revolution " was already the great hope.

When the twenty-two-year-old Friedrich Engels went to England in 1842, it was in feverish expectation of the revolution of whose advent he was convinced. Barely arrived in London, he dispatched hastily scribbled contributions to German and Swiss journals. Disdainfully he listened to Carlyle's warnings against the revolution that threatened England and all Great Britain, prophesying a dreadful end if the country did not return to the order of its ancient God. In translating samples of Carlyle's criticism of English society, Engels suppressed the religious core of the author's anxiety. Carlyle concludes his social critique with an appeal to revitalize the worldly regimen with the spirit of religion and to rule Great Britain in accordance with the laws of God. Engels destroyed the heart of Carlyle's conception of God and the world, accusing the rigorous Calvinist, who firmly believed in a personal creative God, of entertaining a vague pantheism, a faith which according to Engels could no longer provide a jejune world with new substance. Rather, he complains, it is religion that has transformed the world into a desert. Into the place of Carlyle's world view steps Feuerbach's image of man, autonomous and proud.

If already for young Marx the theme " French Revolution " had been not only compatible with his views and with those of his radical group but also had actually dominated it, the Revolution's importance for him remained undiminished, in fact deepened by his later, more critical attitude. Obviously it was only because the Revolution had not been well enough prepared in advance, that the Counterrevolution was able to destroy the high hopes and expectations which Marx had placed in continual revolution. Even the July Revolution of 1830 had not completed the great task; it was only one moment in the course of the revolutionary development which aims at a Communistic world revolution. Marx criticizes Robespierre as a bourgeois revolutionary because he still holds fast to private property. Marx demands revolutionary self-confidence, determination to push on to the truly great revolution. His whole concept was upset by disappointment in the Revolution of 1848. To the end of his life, Marx remained a forty-eighter, a beaten but undefeated rebel. His disappointments only strengthened his fundamental idea: the intellectual ground for further radical revolution must first be prepared. All his life he insisted on this. It was the cornerstone of his whole ideology.

As we shall see later, it was clear for Marx that the greatest obstacle to the revolutionaries' much needed self-confidence was religion. Hence his consistent and total rejection of religious forces. This attitude of rejection passed over into Lenin's ideology for the same reasons.

To sum up: if the French Revolution was the prelude to our epoch, it came not as a great historical event loosed by chance like a giant boulder from its foothold and sent crashing down the mountainside, causing tremors palpable to this day. Rather it was the unleashing of a spirit whose dynamic power had been gathering force for over a century. This ideological power with its political consequences developed steadily; it also shaped Marxism, only now, for the first time, unmasking itself completely.

As Hegel pertinently remarked, in the French Revolution (with

Rousseau as mediator) the European spirit gave substance to its own will. Revolutionary leaders are certainly not mere tools of a popular ideology which uses them as a means to an end. Rather they are men who have consciously adopted Communism's philosophical themes, and who publicly, programmatically proclaim them.

PAVING THE WAY FOR THE REVOLUTION

Eleven years before the outbreak of the French Revolution Robespierre made the acquaintance of Rousseau, whom he considered his political and literary mentor. On the eve of his entry on the political scene, Robespierre dedicated his life to Rousseau in a kind of votive offering. A decade later from the tribunal of the Revolution Robespierre promulgated the teachings of the master paying him homage in his famous speech of the 18th of Floreal (May 7), 1794. The high point of the ceremony was the translation of the mortal remains of Jean Jacques Rousseau to the Pantheon. At the Convention Robespierre, his faithful disciple, decreed that the civil religion envisaged by Rousseau now be made the intellectual principle of the Revolution. (Rousseau himself had spoken of the unavoidable revolution but more in fear than in favor.) In the very house in which Rousseau had lived Robespierre prepared the famous speech in which he formally declared the religion of civil humanity described in *Emile* as the state religion. As early as 1788, in one of the public parks of Paris, Marat officially proclaimed Rousseau's *Contrat Social* as the Bible of the Convention. " It is all Rousseau's fault, " Napoleon was to complain later of the French Revolution, as he struggled to destroy its impact. According to Friedrich Sieburg, Rousseau's contribution to the development that led to the Reign of Terror is enormous, far greater than the contribution of any other 18th- century thinker.

The political revolution was preceded by an intellectual revolution (a genuine overthrow of existing ideas) which to this day few appreciate. The French literary historian Paul Hazard has gone far in this little-known field, illustrating the fundamental change between the spirit of the 17th century and that of the 18th with countless examples. This change created such a contrast, the transition was so abrupt, that Hazard calls it a revolution in itself. The " Enlightenment, " which came into being during this period (Hazard concentrates on the years 1680-1715), is not, as one so often thinks of it, primarily a particular set of ideas, but rather a peculiar self-confidence which springs from faith in the power of reason. In a movement started by Descartes a succession of intellectual pundits approached the eternal questions as though they had discovered them for the first time. Friedrich Engels' observation that the great fundamental problems of all philosophy could be posed in their full significance only now that European society had awakened " from the long hibernation of the Christian Middle Ages " is typical of the thinking of the enlightened. These are the fundamental problems of existence and the essence of God, of being and seeming, of the essence of good and evil, of fate and freedom, of the rights of the sovereign, and of the origin of social conditions. Reason, in which enlightened man so proudly puts his faith, is no longer balanced wisdom which establishes connections with the old, sifts truth from falsehood, and longs to further the growth of all truth; it is a critical audacity that declares war on all tradition, dismisses all earlier opinions as prejudices, questions all generally accepted concepts, and takes lofty pleasure in the endless play of critical pro and con.

This new confidence is already proclaimed in the proud self-description: " light " *(la lumière*, indeed, usually in the plural, *les lumières)*, " for it was not a single ray but a sheaf of them which played on the great tracts of darkness that still hung over the earth. The word light was magical for the people of those days and they never tired of repeating it.... How sweet and pleasant they were in the eyes of the sages, these lights which they themselves had kindled! How beautiful, aye, and how strong! How the superstitious, the deceivers, and the wicked shrank from them! At last they were shining forth, emanating from the majestic laws of Reason. They went side by side with philosophy or followed in her train, philosophy that was pressing forward with a giant's strides. Enlightened indeed were the children of the age; and the delectable metaphor reappeared with countless variations. The lights

were torches; they were the lamp which illuminated the way for
men in all they did and thought; they were the dawn of good
augury; they were the sun, constant, steady, unfailing. Mankind
had erred hitherto because they had been plunged into darkness,
because they had lived enveloped in the shadows, in the mists of
ignorance which had hidden the true path from their sight. Their
eyes had been covered with a bandage. Their fathers and their
forefathers had been blind, but they, they would be the Children
of Light. " [9]

The newly discovered human reason bears the features of the
divine *Logos;* it is " the light of the world. " Again man becomes
the measure of all things. In the ensuing struggle the bone of
contention is whether man should continue to believe in God or
refuse to believe; whether he should obey tradition or repudiate it;
whether he should trust the old guides or cast about for new ones.
It became a duel over man's soul which all thinking Europe followed
with suspense, and in which victory inclined ever more unmistakably
toward the side of the new light of reason.

Proud faith in human reason widened to include faith in science
as the child of reason, above all, natural science, which with the
help of mathematics established the laws of nature, thereby paving
the way for a new form of control over nature: modern technology.
Human reason was considered capable of developing from a single
set of concepts a mammoth system embracing everything of fundamental importance. Nothing would be beyond the powers of the
new science. With its help man would be able to compute the
course of the world, to influence and direct it. The old world order
of historical contingency could only be compared with an ancient
city's obscure maze of lanes and alleys; enlightened reason would
raze this ungovernable tangle and excogitate new human habitations
constructed according to the principles of pure reason. Unquestionably the old social order was doomed to perish of its own
contradictions, irregularity, and immorality. On the levelled ruins,
the engineers of humanity would build anew. The scholars and
men of letters believed heart and soul in the omnipotence of reason,
which they equated with nature herself and ultimately venerated as

[9] P. Hazard, *European Thought in the Eighteenth Century* (New Haven:
Yale University Press, 1954), p. 31.

the supreme being. New constitutions, new religions, new social
orders were their brain-children. Russian Bolshevism ventured the
most universal and radical application of this spirit; building on
completely levelled ground, it attempted to create a society that
was rationalistic through and through—a world without God.

D' HOLBACH: GOD ON TRIAL

Representatives of Enlightenment found a strongly rooted faith upon
the scene. Christians, troubled by the attacks of the innovators on
the spiritual bulwark of the existing order, sprang to the defense.
This led to a flowering of " apologetics, " another aspect typical of
the age. But even the apologists were frequently infected by the
spirit of rationalism. They attempted to prove more than was
provable; hence their service to the interests of belief was often
questionable. Hard pressed, the defenders of the Christian God
had to appear before the bar of public opinion, " for proceedings
began the like of which had never been, proceedings against God.
The God of the Protestants was as much involved as the God of
Catholics ... the God who was on trial was the God of the
Christians. " [10]

Bitterness and rancor, the goads of that trial, which Paul Hazard
describes in detail, demanded that God account for his actions.
The charges ran: " The God of the Christians had had all power
in his hands, and he had made ill use of it. In him, man had put
all his trust, and that trust had been abused. . . . Judged by the
light of logic and reason as we understand them, the notion of
Providence did not hang together. " [11]

These charges dating from the period of French Enlightenment
were to be upheld to Lenin's day. They were to become the decisive
reasons for the final rejection of God by the godless, including
present-day atheists. This fact is eloquently documented. The
Communist philosopher Georg Plekhanov, whom Lenin held in

[10] *Ibid.*, p. 46.
[11] *Ibid.*, p. 48.

highest esteem and whose *Essays on the History of Materialism*
are included in the official canon of basic Communist texts, renewed
the charges against God that d'Holbach had raised in the days of
French Enlightenment—and in much the same terms. These essays,
which originally appeared in German (1896), were not published
in Russian until after the October Revolution of 1922. In 1946
the Soviet Military Government of Germany issued a new edition.
The preface calls attention to the book's great value in the war
against God, the clergy, the nobility, and the monarchy.

Eighteenth-century materialistic philosophy was (in this Plekhanov
appraised it correctly) a "revolutionary philosophy." In the
thought of a revolutionary age all so-called truths have an immediate,
utilitarian purpose. The philosophers of the new age set their sights
first of all on dissolving the alliance between morality and religion.
The new morality rehabilitates the flesh in order to establish heaven
here on earth, says d'Holbach, in whom already many of Rousseau's
ideas may be found: Nature in herself is good; it is only the forces
of history that have corrupted man. Hence man must reconstruct
his life according to the laws of reason. In the battle against
religious morality d'Holbach and his school begin by pointing out
that men themselves, without aid from above, are capable of knowing
virtue. Revelation, God's dialogue with man, is superfluous, since
it is in man's nature to distinguish vice and virtue by himself.
Once men possess sufficient reason to be instructed in their duties,
philosophy can supplant theology. In d'Holbach all moral laws
spring from reason, which he identifies with man's eternal nature.
Here is still remnant of faith, whereas later, progressive criticism
manages to erase even the concept of an unchanging nature. When
"Nature"—in some cases "Reason"—is the supreme, immovable
norm, a God who is conceivable only as a cosmic despot becomes
superfluous. D'Holbach directs his protests against human and
divine tyrants alike. Like Lucretius he offers a "*System of Nature,*"
which, incidentally, natural scientists have never taken seriously.
D'Holbach's sole purpose is to utilize the schema of a strictly
physical determinism in order to do away with a personal God,
who as an arbitrary God could only be a disturbing factor. In
all this d'Holbach's thought is heavy with subjectiveness and passion;
he thunders, hurls curses and—revolutionary that he is—dreams

of an Empire of Reason, of universal happiness, and heaven on earth.

Already for d'Holbach religion is a drug, a label which the Neo-Hegelians adopt and which later reappears in Marx's famous " opium of the people. " " Religion, " says d'Holbach, " is the art of inspiring mankind with enthusiasm. It is designed by those who govern to divert men's minds from the evils with which they are overwhelmed. " [12]

For all his praise of reason, d'Holbach never once uses it to test objectively the possibility of God's existence. He is animated not by love of objectivity but by implacable hatred of God. The radical atheism of d'Holbach, who died just before the outbreak of the French Revolution, was not destined to become the world view of its leaders.

If Voltaire takes exception to d'Holbach's views, it is only because he fears that such views might stir up the " vile mob " to independent thought, whereupon embarrassing demands might be made of rich landowners. Once the mob begins to reason, everything is lost, Voltaire warns in his critique of d'Holbach's *Système de la nature* (1780). This is Voltaire's reason for wanting to preserve the faith of the uneducated masses.

In the tragic case of Jean Meslier, a French pastor who in an uneven struggle with the feudal lords fell victim to nihilism, we see to what extent the sinister passions of stifled resentment were the real cause of a furious negation of all existing values and ideals, including faith in God. To this day one cannot read Meslier's testament without shuddering. Springing from a heart laced with gall, the words spit hatred, rancor, and impotent despair. Here is a trumpet call to revolt such as the living Meslier never dared to sound. As a result his conscience accuses him of cowardice and whips him into a frenzy of mockery which he hurls at God and religion. Some historians have questioned the genuineness of the document; others have dismissed Meslier as insane. Today nothing can be proved. Whatever the truth, Voltaire utilized the sorry affair as propaganda; he had five thousand copies of Meslier's pitiful elaborations printed and circulated.

[12] P. T. d'Holbach, *Christianity Unveiled*. Translated by Robertson and Gowan (New York: Columbian Press, 1795), p. 229.

Plekhanov hits the mark when he says that in heavenly matters the French materialists were zealous republicans who guillotined God long before Dr. Guillotin. " They hated him as a personal enemy. A capricious, vengeful, and harsh despot, like the Judaic *Yahweh*, God outraged all their best sentiments both as citizens and as human beings, and they rose in passionate revolt against his harsh domination exactly as though they were the oppressed victims of a worldly power. " [13]   Throughout d'Holbach's polemics, two themes are coupled consistently: protest against worldly tyrants and protest against the divine tyrant. Men are corrupt because they are badly governed. The root of the wrong order of things, says d'Holbach, lies in religion, which bestows divine authority upon sovereigns and proclaims them inviolate. Thus they themselves had to become corrupted and to drag their subjects down into catastrophe with them. Hoodwinked by dishonest priests, rulers were incapable of rising to an attitude of critical, objective reason. Any objective criticism that reared its head the rulers promptly suppressed. Governments are to blame for all misfortunes, d'Holbach insists, certainly those governments that have been misled by religion. Here is indeed the antithesis of Bossuet's religious view of history, in which the inviolability of the ruler stems from authority grounded in religion, for it is precisely the government founded on religious principles which best guarantees good government. From the contrast between these views it is clear that the coming revolution will be directed as much against God as it is against the earthly rulers who rule in his name.

FAITH IN GOD AN " ILLUSION "

The attempts of psychoanalysts to expose faith as an illusion is nothing new. D'Holbach made a similar attempt before the French Revolution. His arguments run: " Man is superstitious because he is fearful; he is fearful because he is ignorant. Since he does not

[13] G. V. Plekhanov, *Essays in the History of Materialism*. Translated by Ralph Fox (London: John Lane the Bodley Head, Ltd., 1943), p. 63.

understand the forces of nature, he imagines nature to be subject to invisible powers on which he too is dependent and which he imagines to be now angry with him, now propitious to him and his kind. " Dispassionate examination of the problem, d'Holbach continues, reveals that God's name on earth is used only to mask men's passions. Self-interest, habit, and public opinion all influence man's so-called religious thinking, which is determined by these to a much larger extent than by religion itself. D'Holbach anticipates Feuerbach's thesis according to which the man who supposedly worships God in reality only worships himself. For d'Holbach this arbitrary God forever jealous for his subjects' adulation is obviously drawn in the image of the princes of this world. Pious illusions are the true source of the countless evils under which men groan.

In the *System of Nature* d'Holbach elaborates at great length on this theme. Man's ignorance of natural causes engendered gods. The chicanery of priests made nightmares of those gods who proceeded to haunt men without bettering them. Thus the priests senselessly terrified man, filling his head with their hideous phantoms, opposing his reason, and preventing him from seeking his happiness. Men's terrors made slaves of those who pretended to desire the best for them. They were instructed to commit crimes supposedly demanded by their gods; they lived in privation because they were taught that the gods had sentenced them to misery; never did they dare to oppose the gods or to shake off their chains because they had been taught that " the sacrifice of man's reason and the humiliation of his soul were sure means to eternal bliss. "

When one considers the conditions that prevailed among the miserably exploited simple folk in the period of French absolutism it is understandable that the resentment was great, and that sympathizers attempted to avenge the wronged against " the tyrants " with psychoanalytical explanations of the existing " order. "

Social conditions under the *ancien régime* closely resembled those in prerevolutionary Russia, which, although officially the feudal system had been abolished, still suffered from the effects of serfdom. Much as Bossuet's theology of history invested French absolutism with the radiance of an inviolable divine institution, the Orthodox Church, degraded to a political instrument, solemnly approved serfdom and the lash. The same resentment which d'Holbach directed against the Church of his day, which was run by worldly bishops from the nobility, boiled in Lenin against the representatives of the czarist regime. Hence he could simply adapt d'Holbach's explanation of faith in God to his needs without having to add a single new thought. Nowhere in Lenin's works do we find a hint that the problem of God was a real one for him. The whole question had been resolved in advance. Even the chance mention of the word " God " was enough to enrage him.

Resentment against the God who failed to run the world decently arouses the image of Prometheus, who takes mankind's fate into his own hands in the attempt to reshape it. The 19th century produced a plethora of ideas, plans, trends, all stemming from the same determination to reconstruct the world and life rationally, according to the great laws of physics. In order to bring about the desired revolutionary reconstruction, knowledge, power, and technology were applied over and over again, each time at a deeper level, until at last the long effort was crowned with success. " Thus it was only the ultimate crowning of this spirit, " says Schnabel, " when Lenin saw as the task demanded of him by his hour of history what he tellingly describes as the need to create a parasite-free mechanism of the highest technical perfection. If the complete rationalization of practical life with all its aims and effects is possible and necessary to men's salvation, science is indeed the supreme power and last resort; then science must become the foundation and prerequisite of all action, and no longer may anything that is done unscientifically ... be countenanced. ... With this, science was allotted the place which as long as men have existed has belonged to religion. Science was the ' new religion, ' enthroned by the enemies of all superstitions and all bonds. Science became her own church with her own believers, dogmas, sects and martyrs, a church that possessed in ' enlightenment ' a powerful instrument of propaganda; that sternly guarded the purity of its doctrines, pulpits and libraries, and that in the French Revolution, as in Russian Bolshevism, dictated which views were acceptable and which were not, regimenting consciences even to the point of the death sentence for heretics. " [14]

[14] F. Schnabel, *Deutsche Geschichte im neunzehnten Jahrhundert.* Bd. I, Die Grundlagen, 3 Aufl. (1947), p. 58 ff.

ATHEISM'S NEW WELTANSCHAUUNG

Again and again the claim is made that the disappearance of faith in God is a logical consequence of the new vision of the world as conceived by Copernicus, Galileo, Kepler and Newton. Above all, runs the argument, increased knowledge of nature has invalidated the qualitative difference between the realms "*terrestria*" and "*coelestia.*" Hence an extramundane heaven in which man can imagine God no longer exists. After the initial successes of the Russian space rocket this view was given its most trivial official expression in the remark that nowhere in heaven did the sputniks come across God. Even serious essays in philosophy insist that new knowledge of the cosmos has essentially weakened the old faith in God.

To this it must be observed that the medieval concept of God contained no specific image of the Deity. Medieval thought was particularly clear on this point: that all images and representations of God are merely anthropomorphic aids which, though indispensible, are under no circumstances to be taken literally. To begin with, the Creator does not exist anywhere in space; he transcends space as he transcends time, hence the reshaping of man's concept of the cosmos does not touch genuine faith.

Furthermore, in the history of thought it is an established fact that the architects of the modern concept of the universe personally not only believed in God and were not the least inclined to draw atheistic conclusions from their discoveries, but on the contrary were inspired by their newly won knowledge to praise God in a new way.

To be sure, although the personal attitude of the pioneers of modern science was basically religious, one consequence of the new methodical approach is that the world can no longer be explained qualitatively and traced back to its true origins. Instead, the new quantitative approach, which enables scientists to discover functional laws, has moved the problem of God outside the realm of the sciences altogether—which by no means implies a denial of God's existence. It is almost exclusively the nonspecialists who incorrectly interpret the research scientists' methodologically correct silence about God as proof of the nonexistence of God.

If and how the problem of God is treated is primarily a matter of personal attitude. In modern times that attitude has taken a turn against a personal God in the belief that this would be of service to the new conception of the world, much as in his day Epicurus believed he was serving the new world image of antiquity. Epicurus used his purely natural explanation of nature for his own, very practical purposes; he was not the least interested in a real explanation of the true causes of natural phenomena.

Similarly in modern times it was Giordano Bruno, not a natural scientist but originally a theologian, who pantheistically deified the universe in accordance with the new concept of the world, supposedly infinite, and who with his pantheism took the initial step toward atheism. Bruno's pantheistic interpretation of the world was opposed by the natural scientists, among others Kepler, who formulated his *Planetary Laws* against Bruno. Again it was not a scientist who was first on the record of Western thought to couple the denial of a personal *Urgrund* or primeval ground of existence with the new discoveries of natural science. The linking of the question of God to natural science in the form of a denial of a personal God came not from the sciences, but from the arts of philosophy and history. Kepler accused Bruno of abusing astronomy and the new concepts of natural science because he understood nothing about such things.

If like Meurers we go through the list of names of the men who in modern times added their voices to the denial of God: d'Holbach, La Mettrie, Vogt, Buechner, Moleschott, Haeckel, Feuerbach, Marx, Nietzsche, we realize that not one of them is an expert in the field of the exact sciences. Among them are two biologists, three doctors, and four who might be called philosophers and writers. Marx was and remained interested in natural science; his friend Engels picked up some scientific knowledge through reading, material that he collected merely for polemic purposes, to support his denial of God. But it is definitely incorrect to claim that disavowal of faith in God is a result of the new scientific conception of the universe.

Typical of the difference between a researcher in the field of the exact sciences and that of the more practical applier of scientific discoveries is the attitude of the mathematician Maupertuis, discoverer of the principle of the least effect. In his *Essai de cosmologie* (1751) he attempted to establish a mathematical proof of the existence of God, which, to be sure, is not without question marks. Maupertuis' exact opposite, the doctor and philosopher La Mettrie, was an outright materialist who sweepingly disclaimed the existence of the soul (*L'homme machine*, 1748). Among the Encyclopedists, Diderot, typically as a writer, was a pantheist and declared atheist. On the other hand, the physicist d'Alembert, originally one of Diderot's collaborators, parted company with him. D'Alembert's formal expression of his belief was guarded, but he held fast to the existence of a highest divine intelligence, which manifests itself in the appropriateness of living organisms; for d'Alembert, the concept of the nonexistence of God always remained an absurdity. From such examples one fact grows clear: the men who paved the way for contemporary atheism were not representatives of the pure sciences, but were above all from the field of the philosophy of history. The thesis that current atheism developed out of the natural sciences of the 17th and 18th centuries is simply false.

VOLTAIRE, PROTAGONIST
OF THE ENLIGHTENMENT

Voltaire is important neither as an originator nor as a consistent representative of Enlightenment's new *Weltanschauung*, but as its chief propagandist. It is almost impossible to overestimate his influence on the age. The salons of the aristocrats and rulers of France were intellectual vacuums; the ideas of the *ancien régime* seemed to be spent, and now only the suction of the *horror vacui* drew men of letters to the drawing rooms and the courts. There the very real misery of the common people and the urgent problems of the day were matters only of hearsay; one knew about them as one knows about conditions in some distant land. The salons had decided that everything would turn out all right, so of course everything would. Hippolyte Taine remarks ironically, " Never was blindness more complete and more voluntary. " He continues sourly, " ...a philosopher with his ideas is as necessary in a drawing room as a chandelier with its lights. He forms a part of the new luxurious system. He is an article of export. Sovereigns amidst their splendor and at the height of their success invite him to their courts to enjoy for once in his life the pleasure of perfect and free discourse. When Voltaire arrives in Prussia, Frederic II is willing to kiss his hand, fawning on him as on a mistress.... [Even after serious quarrels] he cannot dispense with carrying on conversations with him by letter.... It is said with truth of Voltaire that ' he holds the four kings in his hand, ' those of Prussia, Russia, Sweden and Denmark, without mentioning lower cards, the princes, princesses, grand dukes and margraves. The principal role in this society evidently belongs to authors; ...their ways and doings form the subject of gossip; people never weary of paying them homage. " [15]

How powerful Voltaire's influence was on the whole age, we learn from an impressive testimony of the aged Goethe, who on January 3, 1830, on the occasion of a French translation of his *Faust* remarked: " Some singular thoughts occur to me on finding this book translated into a language over which Voltaire was master fifty years ago. You cannot understand my thoughts upon this subject because you can have no idea of the influence which Voltaire and his great contemporaries had over me in my youth, as over the whole civilized world. My biography does not clearly show how powerful was the influence of these men in those years; how difficult it was for me to defend myself against them, to maintain my own ground and true relation to nature. " [16]

Judgments on Voltaire's character and works oscillate between extremes, and understandably, for he certainly was a man of contradictions. His works are an irridescent play of many colors. For a long time he was regarded as a blasphemer, until Alfred

[15] H. A. Taine, *The Origins of Contemporary France.* Translated by John Durand (New York, 1931), p. 283.

[16] J. P. Eckermann, *Conversations with Gœthe in the Last Years of His Life.* Translated by S. M. Fuller (Boston: Hilliard, Gray and Company, 1839), p. 329.

Noyes' *Voltaire* (1939) invited a more just opinion, although at times his apologetics seem to go too far. However this may be, Voltaire unquestionably had also a noble side to him. He hated injustice and fought it passionately. Karl Marx points out the contradictions in Voltaire's nature with the shrewd remark that Voltaire taught atheism in his text and faith in his footnotes, and that people believed the text, not the footnotes. As no other, Voltaire personified the spirit of the Enlightenment. His pen wielded greater influence over the fate of nations than did the statesmen who ruled them. In Voltaire the *Zeitgeist* may be seen at work, molding the age to come. Even Noyes admits: " It is true that, on one side, he was a destroyer. His thoughts, his wit, his ironic smile, were among the elements that destroyed an evil world. They led directly to the French Revolution and much that has followed it in the world of today. " [17] Many will of course object to the idea that Voltaire's powerful weapons were aimed solely at an " evil world. " But in the present context it would be superfluous to quarrel with this.

The French Church sealed its own fate when it made itself a bulwark of the absolute state. Moreover it had become infected with the moral decay of the court. Many an abbé degenerated to a salon-lion of questionable repute and flagrantly paraded his skepticism and immorality. On the other hand, the representatives of a national Church already infected with dry rot were understandably enough hypersensitive to any form of criticism, immediately sensing behind it disbelief, superstition, and atheism. Hence they were prone to harsh, sometimes unjust judgments against the supposed enemy, which only further damaged the reputation of the national Church and incited fresh criticism. On the one hand, the strict censorship practiced by the French Church discouraged frank criticism, and on the other, naturally goaded resentful and daring spirits into pilloring the abuses with elaborate subterfuges as coarse as they were exaggerated. Voltaire was a genius of the literary effect. He was a master of the classical weapons of the oppressed: wit, scorn, and sarcasm, his sharp arrows hitting more precisely, wounding more deeply, avenging more terribly than the often

[17] A. Noyes, *Voltaire* (London: Faber and Faber, Ltd., 1939), p. 2.

cumbersome official powers ever could. The dwarf who wins the laughers over to his side stops the giant in his tracks.

In the ideological crisis brought about by the Enlightenment, faith in the directing of world history by the providence of a personal God was replaced by a secularized belief in autonomous progress. Once again in his *Discours sur l'Histoire Universelle* (1681) Bossuet had renewed St. Augustine's theology of history, tracing the course of events back to Charlemagne. To this Voltaire replied with a " philosophy of history "—the expression comes from him—(*Essai sur les Mœurs et l'Esprit des Nations*, 1756). The tremendous impact of this essay on the mores and spirit of nations was due largely to the fact that it offered enlightened bourgeois circles an historical justification of their own ideals. At the same time it opened fire on dogmatic religion and political contentions as the two great obstacles to progress. The time had come for man himself, by his own reason, to improve the human condition, to make the lot of mankind better and happier.

Voltaire was certainly not an atheist. There is no reason to doubt the earnestness of the written confession of faith in the Catholic Church which the dying Voltaire gave Abbé Gaultier, a true pastor of souls. This belated acknowledgment repudiates ideas which, to judge by his writings, Voltaire had good reason to disavow. His most famous novel, *Candide,* is not really a novel at all but a polemical pamphlet in the guise of a light novel. The world view he mocks here is faith in a good world as reflecting the goodness of its Creator. As the paradigm of this philosophy Voltaire uses Leibniz' best-of-all-possible-worlds optimism which the whole novel satirizes mercilessly. Here is a sample of the intellectual niveau of its ridicule: " ' It is demonstrable, ' said he, ' that things cannot be otherwise than they are; for as all things have been created for some end, they must be necessarily created for the best end. Observe for instance, the nose is formed for spectacles; therefore we wear spectacles. The legs are visibly designed for stockings; accordingly we wear stockings. Stones were made to be hewn and to construct castles; therefore my lord has a magnificent castle, for the greatest baron in the province ought to be the best lodged. Swine were intended to be eaten; therefore we eat pork all the year round. And they who assert that everything is *right,* do not express themselves correctly; they should say that everything is best.' "[18]

The hero of the piece is the doubtful son of a Westphalian baron, a simpleton, (" a young metaphysician ") who in his *naïveté* really believes that everything in the world is for the best. The actual world into which Candide is thrust looks quite different. Its inhabitants are liars, deceivers, perjurers, ingrates, robbers, weaklings, wantons, cowards, enviers, misers, social climbers, murderers, back-biters, wastrels, fanatics, hypocrites, and fools. There is a monstrous amount of evil; everything is topsy-turvy. Possibly, something good exists somewhere, but it is lost in the maze of evils.

In *Candide*, all churchmen, from the monk on up to the pope, are caricatures; all are imputed with the foulest scandals. Candide is arrested by a "familiar of the Inquisition" and led in an auto-da-fé through the streets. "...They marched in procession and listened to a most pathetic sermon, followed by lovely plain-song music. Candide was flogged in time to the music, while the singing went on; the Biscayan and the two men who had not wanted to eat bacon were burned, and Pangloss was hanged, although this is not the custom. "[19]

In the rampant corruption of the world there is but one country, the tiny kingdom of Eldorado, which has preserved its innocence and happiness. There one worships but one God, not three or four. Everyone is a priest. "What! Have you no monks to teach, to dispute, to govern, to intrigue and to burn people who do not agree with them?" In view of the actual evil in the world, one thoughtful person in the novel cannot rid himself of the idea that God has turned the world over to some evil being. "Hitherto I have found only unfortunates in the whole habitable earth, except in Eldorado "; surely the devil has his hand in the game. The entire Church is dragged through the mud. A so-called monk declares: "Jealousy, discord, fury, inhabit the monastery. It is true, I have preached a few bad sermons which bring me in a little money, half of which is stolen from me by the prior; the remainder I spend on girls. " Voltaire anticipates the athestic existentialism of a Sartre. One

[18] J. F. de Voltaire, *Candide*. Translated by Richard Aldington (Garden City, N. Y.: Hanover House, 1959), p. 2.
[19] *Ibid.*, p. 23.

character who does possess worldly goods without being possessed by them is " disgusted with everything he possesses. " Nowhere is there a trace of any positive evaluation of Christianity.

The God of this novel is a deistic, unconvincing figurehead who has left the world to the devil, and Eldorado with its pure worship is a nonexistent dreamland. Here both Church and world are profoundly calumniated and one really cannot blame those so spitefully attacked for branding the author " atheist, " even though a footnote does still mention faith. Here purely destructive tendencies are at work. According to Voltaire disgust and boredom are existential. To inquire into the meaning of existence leads only to useless quarrels. The world—so say the French existentialists—is absurd; this is already Voltaire's view, only Voltaire does not accept the consequences as Sartre does; Voltaire does not yet eradicate God. Instead of taking this ultimate step, Voltaire personally returned to a Creator-God, but other leaders of the Enlightenment did go all the way to the negativistic end. Time and again the Enlighteners chided him for his inconsistency. The remnant of faith that still exists in *Candide* is the faith of diluted deism: God has left the world to the devil. From here it is only a step to revolt against a God who has failed the world and the demand for his elimination.

Friedrich II of Prussia celebrated Voltaire as " the generator of that revolution of the human spirit " which the following centuries were to complete. Immediately after the death of Charles VI of Austria in 1740 Friedrich wrote to Voltaire: " The emperor is dead. . . . His death changes all my peaceful plans, and I suspect that June will see more gunpowder, soldiers, and trenches than dancers and actresses. . . . The moment has come for a complete overthrow of the old political system. The boulder that is to fall upon the idol made of four metals which Nebuchadnezar beheld has torn itself free and will shatter it completely. " [20] Reversing the Biblical image, Friedrich apparently expected the avalanching boulder of new powers to make a shambles of the Holy Roman Empire and with it the ancient Christian view of history.

Karl Loewith in his study, *Meaning in History*, pinpoints Voltaire's place in the process known as the Enlightenment: Voltaire secularized

[20] J. F. de Voltaire, *Œuvres Complètes* (Paris, 1877), Vol, 45, p. 254.

the Christian idea of history's ascent to a transcendent end and established the "irreligion of progress" as a quasi-religion in its stead, "substituting an indefinite and immanent *eschaton* [end] for a definite and transcendent one." [21]

Voltaire considered the Church, which claims to be the authority of the living God among men, to be the most dangerous enemy of the Enlightenment, hence his passionate hatred of her claim. His motto, *Ceterum censeo*, with which he frequently closed his letters, was a battle cry to destroy her: "*Ecrasez l'infame!*" Well-meaning interpreters have declared that Voltaire's "*l'infame*" did not refer to God or Christ or to Catholicism, but only to what Noyes calls "persecuting and privileged orthodoxy." However, Voltaire's polemics unquestionably often went further. By the hundreds he tossed the flaming torches of his brochures into the ancient edifice of church-state culture.

Goethe frequently expressed admiration for Voltaire's *esprit*, in which he found all the literary powers of the French united. But he also recognized the basically negative character of the man's greatness. For all its wit, Voltaire's insolence serves no purpose; nothing can be constructed on it. On the contrary, it causes the greatest damage by depriving men of a needed hold.

Like his abettors, Diderot, d'Alembert, d'Holbach, and Helvetius, Voltaire was out to destroy the old social structure of France with all its prejudices and abuses. He was typical of the self-confident, individualistic, sacrilegious Enlightener who considers everything from the past unworthy of his notice; his spiteful wit holds nothing sacred.

In him burned the lust Nietzsche describes: the sensual pleasure in pulling down everything sanctified by long tradition and publicly dragging it through the mud, thus poking at religion's most sensitive nerve, reverence. With all the refinement of a superior literary education, with his sparkling wit and the elegance of a polished writer he loosed his barbs against religion's most sensitive nerve. Like the vibrations of an earthquake Voltaire's continued hammering weakened the faith in the hearts of almost an entire

---

[21] K. Loewith, *Meaning in History. The Theological Implications of the Philosophy of History* (Chicago: University of Chicago Press, 1949), p. 114.

nation, even though no outward break with religious practices took place.

A veritable lust for ecclesiastical scandal inspired Voltaire to rummage through Church history in the attempt to make the Church responsible for all the human weaknesses and evils which ever existed in the course of her long history. He claimed that her record had nothing to show but an unbroken series of blood baths; that even while she denied guilt for the blood of millions upon her conscience a bored Bishop of Rome reposing on a soft couch allowed his feet to be kissed and fifty castrates to trill to him to beguile away the hours.

In Voltaire's day, men of letters were expected to fill the intellectual vacuum not only with ideas, but preferably with critical, rash, ironic, degrading ideas. The educated vied with one another in their passion for criticism. Among the nobility the rage for scandal was particularly prevalent, probably as a result of idleness. Taine dwells on the subject at length, suggesting that palace gossip provided the cloak needed to hide the sores of one's own conscience, for at court unbridled libertinism was at home. Although Enlightenment was considered an affair of the cultivated, they did not hesitate to use the most unsavory methods to spread new ideas as broadly as possible among the masses. Taine complains, " People dogmatize everywhere. Laughing is as much out of fashion as pantins or bilboquets. Good folk, they have no time to laugh! There is God and the king to be pulled down first; and men and women, one and all, are devoutly employed in the demolition. They think me quite profane for having any belief left.... Do you know who the philosophers are, or what the term means here? In the first place it comprehends almost everybody; and in the next, it means men who avowing war against popery aim, many of them, at a subversion of all religion.... These savants—I beg your pardons, the philosophers—are insupportable, superficial, overbearing and fanatic: they preach incessantly and their avowed doctrine is atheism, you would not believe how openly. " [22] Horace Walpole, who revisited France in 1765, had forebodings of the

---

[22] H. A. Taine, *The Origins of Contemporary France*. Translated by John Durand (New York: Peter Smith, 1931), p. 289.

danger that threatened; he was horrified by the folly of the educated who shamelessly flaunted their ideas to the mob.

Voltaire knew that nothing has such a deadly effect on religion as mockery. It is the surest poison and necessarily mortal. Instead of disproving, he ridiculed. "Ridicule spoils everything, it is my most powerful weapon," he wrote d'Alembert. And no one mastered that weapon as Voltaire did. Anyone whose reverence is suddenly laid low by the cold beam of shameless mockery and who is not mature enough to fight back or to ignore finds the taproot of his religious life severely damaged, often beyond recovery.

One of the most poetic figures of French history is that of Jeanne d'Arc, who rescued France from grave peril. In his *Pucelle,* Voltaire took the most deeply venerated figure of his own people's history and dragged her through the muck of base comedy and obscenity in order to dump the values of faith, virginity, knighthood, honor, monarchy, nobility, morality, and fame into the gutter. When as an old man Voltaire returned to Paris to die, he was hailed frenetically by the mob with cries of, " Vive l'auteur de la *Pucelle!* " While copies of these infamous verses were being circulated in France by the hundred thousands, Friedrich Schiller attempted with his *Maid of Orleans* a chivalrous if not historically correct vindication of Joan's honor. In the preface Schiller directs the following lines squarely at Voltaire:

> " To mock the noble image of mankind
> Mockery wallows in the deepest dust;
> Eternally it wages war on Beauty,
> Believes neither in angel nor in God.
> The world is pleased to blacken radiance,
> To trample the exalted into dust
> It loves to rob the heart of what it treasures
> And warring against error, wound belief. "

Although on the one hand Voltaire aroused public opinion, goading it toward the coming Revolution, " the great bang " which he happily anticipated, on the other hand he hesitated to destroy the belief of the masses in God. For them he demanded a stick-and-carrot God. He approved the dictum in fashion among the sophisticated: if there were no God, one would have to be invented. The divine is necessary, not in order to satisfy any real religious need, but simply because without fear of God, society's moral order would collapse. Thus God is reduced to a moral principle, a mere prop of the social order. In a dialogue between a wise man who pleads for the existence of God and an atheist who denies him, Voltaire gives the victory to the sage. Without God, he answers the atheist, the ties that hold society together would come undone; the masses would become thieves and murderers.

Among the unsolved contradictions of Voltaire's character is the fact that he was a nature worshipper who allowed himself to be deeply impressed by natural phenomena, and who by contemplating, imitating, and revering nature, tried to honor God. But also quite different moods besieged him. Rebellious titan that he was, he set himself up as a creative artist against the gods, making them out to be hostile and despicable powers whom he tried to spite by flaunting his enjoyment of his own creativity. In his opera *Pandora*, for instance, he revives the classical Promethean theme— tailored to fit 18th-century views; he makes Zeus an envious petty tyrant and Prometheus the misunderstood artist and Enlightener victorious over the sinister power of the gods. Voltaire's revolt remained the artistic, never seriously implemented revolt of the individualistic enlightener. Yet it struck an answering chord in the young Goethe. Voltaire, says Alexander Baumgartner in his book on Goethe's youth, is only a "rebellious dancing master"; Goethe is the "real titan," who in gigantic defiance renounces God—if only for a time. For Goethe struggled against Voltaire's influence, overcame it, and to humble himself, publicly retracted his renunciation.

In its attempt to destroy the religious faith of the French people, the Enlightenment was entirely successful. To a large extent, religion succumbed to the blows of enlightened men of letters. Young people boasted of their irreligion, considering this attitude proof of their intellectuality. Saddest of all, even priests and bishops, largely out of fear of the fashionable idols of the Enlighten-ment, failed to parry the blows, and instead publicly flaunted "an enlightened skepticism." In 1722 the Countess of the Palatinate, mother of Philippe d'Orléans, noted that in the whole of Paris there were not more than a hundred people—religious and laity together—who still truly believed.

From year to year the position of priests grew more difficult. They were made the target of general ridicule. In the salons, abbés applied all the arts of apologetics, but these no longer persuaded. Many simply gave up; it was so much easier to howl with the enlightened wolves. In 1753 d'Argenson writes: "The hatred against the priests is carried to extremes. They scarcely show themselves in the streets without being hooted at.... As our nation and our century are quite otherwise enlightened (than in the time of Luther), it will be carried far enough; they will expel the priests, abolish the priesthood, and get rid of all revelation and all mystery.... One dare not speak in behalf of the clergy in social circles; one is scoffed at and regarded as a familiar of the inquisition.... The College of the Jesuits is being deserted.... It has been observed also that, during the carnival in Paris, the number of masks counterfeiting ecclesiastical dress—bishops, abbés, monks and nuns—was never so great. " [23]

Destruction of the old was considered the indispensable prerequisite to the fresh start to be made by the new architects of the nation. The Enlightenment combined a naive overestimation of one's own understanding with a complete misunderstanding of history. While crediting the human mind with the ability to recognize and present the universal, fundamental, and essential, it dismissed all historic events and developments as mere anomalous chance. Thus the Enlightenment attempted by abstraction to distill the essence from all the religions of the world and human history, and rearrange them into only five fundamental principles.

Equipped with pseudo-foundations and ready-made blueprints, the new architects appear on the scene impatient to prove " that every great public structure, religious and moral, and all communities, cannot be otherwise than barbarous and insalubrious since, thus far, they are built up out of bits and pieces, by degrees, and generally by fools and savages, in any event by common masons, who built haphazardly, feeling their way, devoid of principles. *They* are genuine architects and they have principles, that is to say, reason,

[23] *Ibid.*, p. 288.

nature, and the rights of man, all being simple and fruitful principles which everybody can understand, the consequences derived from them sufficing to substitute for the misshapen tenements of the past, the admirable edifice of the future. To irreverent, epicurean, and philanthropic malcontents the temptation is a great one. They readily adopt maxims which seem to conform with their secret wishes; at least they adopt them in theory and in words. The imposing terms of liberty, justice, public good, and man's dignity are so admirable and besides, so vague! What heart can refuse to cherish them, and what intelligence can foretell their innumerable applications? " [24]

ROUSSEAU AND HIS SOCIAL CONTRACT

There was one troublesome rival whom Voltaire, for all his volleys of spiteful wit, was unable to drive from the field. This was the other great forerunner of the French Revolution, Jean Jacques Rousseau. Whereas Voltaire's contribution was primarily destructive (that of the wrecker who clears the ground for a new structure), Rousseau, the constructive lawgiver, was the architect of the Revolution.

Rousseau was fully aware of the crisis in which the French state and society of his day found themselves. He was convinced that the great monarchies could not last very long. He awaited the overthrow, which he considered inevitable, with mixed emotions, half regretting that he would not still be alive to witness the happy revolution that would bring about the changes necessary for progress, half fearful of the storm about to be unleashed. Rousseau makes the atheists, Encyclopedists, and the *ancien régime* responsible for the coming evils, unconscious of the fact that it is his own atheism— which, to be sure, he does not admit—that will give the Revolution its ideological foundation and direction. Basically, Rousseau was

[24] *Ibid.*, pp. 286 ff.

a man in search of religion who suffered from the rootlessness he himself had created and who, as Friedrich Sieburg describes him in his book on Robespierre, " in his weakness. . .sought to recreate on a new plane the order of things he had destroyed, if only to be a support for himself. " [25]

Bewildered, Rousseau was unable to stand on his own feet. An immense existential fear wrung from him such complaints as: " The infatuation with atheism is but a passing fanaticism, a fashion which Fashion herself will destroy again. It is quite evident from the passion with which the masses lend themselves to it, that it is merely a mutiny against the conscience whose gnawing vexes them. This comfortable philosophy of the happy and rich who make this world a paradise cannot last long as the philosophy of the many who are the victims of their passions, and who, lacking happiness in this life, want to find in it at least the hope and comfort which this barbarous doctrine wrenches from them. Men brought up ever since they could walk in an impatient godlessness heightened to fanaticism; in impudent and shameless wildness; youth without discipline; women without manners; peoples without faith; kings without law or any higher power for them to fear hence utterly uncurbed; the conscience-bound sense of duty destroyed; love of country and loyalty to the princes flickered out; ultimately no social constraint other than brute force; one can easily foresee, it seems to me, where all this must lead. . . .   Sooner or later in the blows of Fate that will befall it, [the country] will recognize the fruits of the new doctrine. . . . " [26]

However, Rousseau lacked the fiber for a real elevation of soul to the living God; he was religious without the strength to believe. Rousseau hesitated on the verge of religion, which for him was a fearful abyss from which at last he withdrew, turning in his desperation to a pseudo-religious construct of his own making.   His stifled attempts to attain to prayer without allowing himself to address God are heart-rending. They contain the seed of his whole social doctrine.

[25] F. Sieburg, *Robespierre, The Incorruptible* (New York: Robert M. McBride and Company, 1938), p. 98.
[26] A. Baumgartner, *Geischichte der Welt literatur*, V Die franzosische Literatur (1905), p. 501.

Although Rousseau's joyous yet fearful presentiments of the coming Revolution were fulfilled in a dreadful manner, it would be a fundamental error as well as unjust to attempt to explain the French Revolution simply as the unleashing of a profligate libertinism. On the contrary, the Jacobins were originally a " virtuous band, " who discoursed on nothing more avidly than on the establishment of virtue and the extirpation of vice—all in the name of Rousseau, from whom the Revolution received its new gospel. To be sure, the concepts of virtue and vice had undergone typical changes, with the result that when the new evangel was translated into reality, it proved to be no saving power at all; what it engendered was a faith in the Revolution so fanatical as to lead straight to the gruesome blood bath of the Reign of Terror.

Rousseau's social philosophy made him the political thinker who developed the new conception of the state, the principles of which were faithfully followed by the revolutionaries. Never before had political philosophy played such a decisive role as the regulator of society. Rousseau's conception was regarded not merely as an offshoot of a particular *Weltanschauung,* but as the real center of all self-legislation. Rousseau writes in his *Confessions:* " Of the different works which I had on the stocks, the one which I had long had in my head, at which I worked with the greatest inclination, to which I wished to devote myself all my life, and which, in my own opinion, was to set the seal upon my reputation—was my ' *Institutions Politiques.* ' ...I had come to see that everything was radically connected with politics and that, however one proceeded, no people would be other than the nature of its government. " [27]

Rousseau's *Social Contract* develops no entirely new and original ideas, but his thoroughly monistic view of the state as no longer part of a God-given order is novel. The Rousseauean state rests not on divine law but on the unalloyed self-glorification of man. " Man is born free, but is everywhere in chains. " Thus begins the *Social Contract.* Any kind of fetters contradicts the free nature of man. Never can might make right. There is no such thing as the right of the stronger, the right of conquest, or the powers of violent subjection. Nor is there any power that comes from God, otherwise

[27] *The Confessions of Jean-Jacques Rousseau.* Edited, revised and prefaced by L. C. Crocker (New York: The Pocket Library, 1957), pp. 206-207.

one would have to attribute also diseases to him. Man's original nature is one of freedom, a freedom which may be curtailed only by his free and voluntary partnership in a social contract. The constitution of a society is a " sacred right. " It is the foundation of all rights, which by no means derive from nature with her fixed order but which rest rather on agreement. To renounce one's freedom is to renounce the very condition of man, his rights, and even his duties. Such renunciation is incompatible with the nature of man. The essence of the *Social Contract* is expressed in the formula: " Each of us puts his person and all his power in common under the supreme direction of the general will and, in our corporate capacity, we receive each member as an indivisible part of the whole. " [28] The " general will " represents supreme, completely autonomous sovereignty: " Whoever refuses to obey the general will shall be compelled to do so by the whole body. This means nothing less than that he will be forced to be free. " [29] The sovereignty of the state is inalienable as well as indivisible. Though the individual may err, the " general will " is always right; its goal is the welfare of all. In bowing to the will of the people, man is obeying only himself, not an alien power.

As Sieburg points out, this Utopia of " the general will " as absolute and infallible authority was the tiny seed from which the monstrous growth of the Reign of Terror and the Jacobin dictatorship sprang.

The demand for man's absolute freedom confronted Rousseau with an antinomy to which, with the help of high-sounding phrases, he offers only a theoretical pseudo-solution. Whenever the attempt was made to translate the theory into practice, the destructive results became immediately apparent. For Rousseau's doctrine fails to explain how it will be possible for orderly government to exist if every citizen (in union with all others, yet obeying only himself) remains as free as he was without government. This utopian marvel completely ignores the all-important question: who then will really represent the " general will, " who will interpret it authentically

[28] J. J. Rousseau, *The Social Contract and Discourses*. Translated with an Introduction by G. D. H. Cole (New York: E. P. Dutton and Company, Inc., 1950), Book I, p. 15.

[29] *Ibid.*, p. 18.

and have the authority to implement it? Since the dethronement of God, the liberated, absolute authority in charge requires a concrete representative. He cannot be represented by the sum total of all individuals; the common will cannot equal all the individual wills added together. Even Rousseau knew that. Hence there will always have to be some individual who is aware of his pseudo-mystical vocation to represent the general will, and who on this claim establishes an absolute dictatorship. The general will which Rousseau proclaimed sovereign but for which he named no executor is bound to attract the individual will to power and does so again and again. By inner necessity Rousseau's concept of the state leads to dictatorship, which in turn calls into play the eternal dialectics of revolution and new dictatorship. Thus " permanent revolution " takes root in Rousseau's ideology of the true state.

Once all individuals have surrendered their personal wills to the divine common will, Rousseau continues, what was hitherto " folk " will become a " state collective " that will completely absorb all wills. Since the individual members of a collective can always err in their interpretation of the common will, they are constantly in danger of having their freedom forced upon them by the only legitimate interpreter of the common will. If they resist his power, they must be eradicated from the collective. Fanatical faith in Utopia sets itself the task of correcting the realities of society with crabbed energy, simply destroying those who refuse to be absorbed by the collective. This is precisely what happened—and very soon—in the first state patterned after Rousseau.

In recent times attention has been drawn frequently to the pseudo-religious nature of Rousseau's " new gospel. " Rousseau himself wrote the name of the new deity, " VOLONTE GENERALE " in capital letters, as God himself had been written. The French existentialist Albert Camus underlines sharply the propensity of the *Contrat Social* to be the catechism of the new Religion of Reason. This catechism of a new religion whose God is Reason or Nature as embodied in the common will has the same accents and the same dogmatic manner so typical of catechisms. The attributes of the old God have simply been transferred to the new. The common will is primarily the expression of universal reason, the new God. It is said to be " absolute, " " holy, " " inviolable. " Universal reason demands of its subjects not only legal recognition, but a full confession of faith in the new bourgeois religion. Correct behavior does not suffice. In the bourgeois society every kind of supervision of conscience and the death penalty are justifiable whenever absolute submission to the royal prerogatives of the sovereign people is withheld. " We are witnessing the dawn of a new religion with its martyrs, its ascetics, and its saints. To be able to estimate the influence achieved by this gospel, one must have some idea of the inspired tones of the proclamations of 1789. " [30]

In his portrayal of Robespierre, which reads like a novel despite the fact that only authentic quotations are used and the events are historical, Sieburg masterfully exposes Rousseau's religion as the ersatz that it is. The state in which the people take the place of God is " no more than a profane reflection of the true community of believers. " Sieburg compares Rousseau to a fallen angel, " seeking in his darkened abyss to do God's work over again. " But political dogma is merely " a repetition, an imitation of the Catholic dogma. " Basically, Rousseau's social theory, which was made the program of the Reign of Terror, represents " the outburst of despair of an unbelieving soul thirsting after God. " The Revolution, which had begun under the oriflamme of an autonomous ideal humanity, was to become its own blade-sharp philosophical and historical refutation.

METAPHYSICAL FANATICISM

The events of the French Revolution are intelligible only when we recognize the pseudo-religious nature of its foundations; only these explain among other things the murder of the king. It was not necessary to undergo long years of bloodshed to improve social conditions and change the structure of the state. No; what sharpened the cutting edge of the Revolution was a metaphysical fanaticism.

Louis XVI was definitely not the victim of wildly inflamed masses

[30] A. Camus, *The Rebel.* Translated by Anthony Bower (New York: Vintage Books, 1956), p. 117.

at the outbreak of the Revolution. He was not executed until
January 1793, after a long and detailed trial which revolved round
a matter of principle. In the person of the king a principle was on
trial; it was a principle that was condemned and executed. Unquestionably, the absolutistic *ancien régime* was loaded with sins of
omission and was certainly responsible for the masses' growing
revolt. Particularly reprehensible was the fact that the monarchy's
arbitrary rule claimed the " divine right " of kings to govern.
Thus supreme jurisdiction seemingly legitimized the crassest injustices. And the Church supported the royal claim with blind servility.
It presented the king as one appointed by God to attend to his
temporal affairs; the king was the last resort of the oppressed and
of the victimized.

Against all expectations, the court condemned the king by a
single vote majority. (During the trial Saint-Just, appealing to the
doctrine of Rousseau, testified against the king, and his arguments
influenced the verdict.) The chief argument of the defense was the
still valid inviolability of the king as the representative of divine
justice. The Constitution of 1791 had expressly recognized that
inviolability, which Saint-Just opposed with the divine sovereignty
of the people's will, a will that can be neither summoned before an
ordinary court nor condemned by it. In that historic trial two
interpretations of the transcendent confronted one another. Hence
Camus' observation that Saint-Just's famous speech had " all the
earmarks of a theological treatise. " If the people's will is its own
representative of eternal truth, then monarchy as such is an eternal
crime. Even if individually everyone was willing to forgive the
king, the general will could not. The general will is the new god,
whose spirit hovers over the legislative assembly, and in whose
name the king is condemned to die.

The sentencing of the king was a turning point in history; at
that moment current history began. King Louis' execution, says
Camus in *The Rebel*, is a symbol of the secularization of our history
and of the dematerialization of the God of the Christians. Up to
this point God had had a part in history through the medium of
the kings. But his representative in history was killed, no longer
was king. Hence nothing remained but a semblance of God
relegated to the heaven of principles.

Few historical figures are as controversial as Robespierre. Was he a bloody tyrant or an idealistic statesman? Did he stain the Revolution or was he its pure representative? This much we can say: Robespierre was no vital power-brute who revelled in the spilling of blood. He was a fanatical disciple of Rousseau, the prototype of the modern ideologist, who lived almost the life of an ascetic in order to implement the one idea of the revolutionary world view: the establishment of an earthly paradise. Robespierre pursued this goal until the whole undertaking was stifled in blood, including his own. Never has a political career pursued such a consistently straight line. Anyone reading this man's sermons, lauding an order of things in which all low and brutal passions are curbed, all noble public-spirited impulses stimulated by the law, in which ambition aims only at fame and service to one's country, where the people themselves are the guardians of justice and freedom, would suppose that here a peaceful community of virtue was in the making. But it was precisely the attempt to realize " public virtue " which led straight to the Terror. Virtue is defined as " that which serves the Revolution "; everything " antirevolutionary " is automatically evil and corrupt. In order to attain the paradise for which revolutionaries longed with every fiber of their pseudo-religious faith, all counterrevolutionaries must be annihilated. At the gateway of this paradise there stands the guillotine! Robespierre's rigidly fanatical thinking was incapable of conceiving any other way to the new Eden. The idea of first educating people for freedom was dismissed from the start. " As high priest of his new god, " Robespierre " shrank from nothing. "

" If like politics statesmanship is the art of the possible, if the statesman is a man who weighs possibilities against one another and knows how to select the best, Robespierre was no statesman. Rather he was, " what Sieburg calls, " a derelict priest who practiced Rousseauean religion on the victim, France, and who would have proved his theory by chopping off everyone's head had he not been prevented. " [31]

Robespierre never mingled with the masses. He appeared only before the several hundred members of Paris's Jacobin Club, to

[31] F. Sieburg, *Robespierre, The Incorruptible* (New York: Robert M. McBride and Company, 1938), p. 24.

whom he delivered his long speeches. As the pillars of the Revolution, the Jacobins were never more than a small minority. They considered themselves the new believers engaged in replacing the ancient Christian ritual with the ritual of the Revolution. These rites " smell of the lamp of Enlightenment. They are too absurd to be dishonest, " [32] remarks Crane Brinton. The Jacobins sang chorales, listened to endless sermons, held religious celebrations in which they addressed prayers to " O Liberty. . .chaste daughter of the heavens " and discussed the " miracles " achieved by " holy guillotine. " During the famous celebration of the supreme being, Robespierre's sermon was followed by the burning in effigy of atheism. From the ashes of this puppet produced with much artistry the New Wisdom was to rise. " The devotional language of the Jacobins, their frequent excesses of collective emotion, their conviction of righteousness, their assurance that their opponents are sinners, direct agents of the devil, their intolerance, their desire for martyrdom, their total want of humor—all these are unmistakable signs of the theological temperament, " [33] Brinton continues. (It would have been more correct to say: signs of a pseudo-religious fanaticism.)

Next Brinton points out that only against this theological background does the political theory of the Terror become understandable. The speeches of the revolutionary heroes comprise a regular " Summa, " the Terror's theory of justification. According to Rousseau, freedom does not consist in doing what one wishes to; it consists in performing what is right as determined by the will of the people. The individual may, indeed if necessary, must be forced to exercise such freedom. For whosoever disobeys the general will refuses obedience to his better self, thus proving himself a slave. Hence when society takes draconic measures against a citizen who selfishly follows his own misled will, it is only coercing that citizen to freedom in the Rousseauean sense. For the protection of the virtuous the use of force against the vicious is indispensable. Robespierre himself describes the revolutionary government as the " despotism of freedom against tyranny. "

[32] C. Brinton, *A Decade of Revolution 1789-1799.* Harper Torchbooks, The University Library (New York: Harper and Row, 1934), p. 155.
[33] *Ibid.*, p. 159.

The history of what actually took place unmasks this theory as the illusion of naive self-deception, common enough among the devotees of Rousseau's new religion. Behind its mask of virtue hid the poisonous breed of all human passions, which needed only an excuse to run rampant.

To recall the inner history of the French Revolution is to uncover the taproot from which "unbelief" springs. When unbelief passionately attacks the living, transcendent God who manifests himself in earthly institutions, it seldom contents itself with simple atheism. Instead it invents an ersatz-God in the form of human reason which is supposed to be the ultimate and supreme principle of morality. However, unbelief is not primarily a matter of the understanding, but a matter of revolt. Man flinging off his chains declares himself autonomous, and full of emotional rebellion, demands the rights that have been withheld from him.

The French Revolution was possible only in a society that had inwardly turned away from the Church as a divine institution in the world. According to Taine, there had never been a society inwardly more estranged from Christianity than French society at the time of the great Revolution. That it had come to such a loss of faith was due essentially to the undermining activity of the Enlighteners. Faith in the Church as God's power on earth had been lost. The empty throne in man's heart was easily filled by Rousseau's deified " will of the people. " That was why Rousseau, for all his emotional religiosity, saw Christianity as the strongest opponent of the social spirit as he had formulated it. He went so far as to declare that a community of real Christians would no longer be a human community.

Although the growing spirit of the day mortally injured belief in the living, personal God and contact with him through religion, the existence of the divine was not denied. On the contrary, man was expected to recognize it; belief in a supreme being was required. But the supreme being of the Jacobins was strangely unreal; he had become a principle, an idea which they identified as Nature or Reason.

The results of this changed faith were to become evident with terrible swiftness and clarity. The new religion had been welcomed with boundless enthusiasm. It was expected to bring about a completely new order, a realization of the state both paradisiacal and natural. Men dreamed of a republic on the order of Sparta. The rhetoric of the Latin moralists came back into fashion. In the speeches of the revolutionaries the words " virtue, " " vice, " " corruption " appear over and over again. Although unlimited freedom for all men had been wildly acclaimed, the principle of unlimited oppression of the individual who dared to oppose the general will was soon apparent. In order to achieve the republic of universal innocence where none but the reconciled and the peaceable stroll in gala dress through endless reaches of pastoral landscape, it was necessary to restore what had been ceremoniously abolished; the death sentence. At the beginning of the Revolution Robespierre and Saint-Just had eloquently denounced the death penalty, but when one has vowed allegiance to an absolute principle, for the sake of that principle all opposition must be eradicated. Soon Saint-Just was forced to proclaim: " Either the virtues or the Terror. " Since absolute virtue is impossible, the " Republic of Pardon " to be consistent had to become a Republic of the Guillotine. The religion which identified nature with reason led straight to the senseless spectacle of the guillotine's drop-blade industriously at work until at last it fell upon the elect themselves.

The fruits of the French Revolution are those by which the tree is known. According to a word of Heinrich Weinstock, Rousseau's doctrine of the man-god, like all doctrines on man's natural goodness, was only a variation, albeit the newest and most dangerous one, of the timeless serpent's song: Man, determine yourself the measure of right and wrong and you will be like God! It seems as if Rousseau had been sent to the French to confirm Pascal's prophetic warning that man is neither angel nor beast. To attempt to make him an angel, says Weinstock, only makes a beast of him.

6. The tragic consequences of kantian philosophy

DICHOTOMY BETWEEN VOLITION AND ACT

There is a tragic dichotomy between Kant's will and his work: historically speaking, his work has had a completely different effect from that which he intended. In the preface to the second edition of his *Critique of Pure Reason,* he declared: " I must, therefore, abolish science, in order to make room for faith. " If he wanted merely to remark upon speculative reason's loss of imagined holdings of no real interest for man, he was certainly deceiving himself. The integrity of his gigantic effort cannot be questioned. Kant wanted to give practical morality, the importance of which he was profoundly convinced, an unshakable hold in faith. To do this he considered it necessary first to dispose of metaphysics' so-called proofs of the existence of God. But to a large extent, the world took note only of his work of destruction, either welcoming or deploring it. Kant's penetrating intellectual energy soon established him as *the* authority, and no one dared even attempt to answer his negative criticism with a countercriticism; rather, the " fact " of Kant's annihilation of the proofs of God was simply absorbed unquestioned into the religious consciousness of modern autonomous man.

In a letter, Fichte refers broadly to Kant's " skeptical atheism, " and young Schelling announces triumphantly: "Kant has cleared the decks completely! " Schelling pokes fun at contemporary

" orthodoxy's " attempts to use the moral postulate of God that Kant had recognized as the basis of arguments for the existence of God.   To a better humanity Schelling proclaims freedom of the spirit and refuses to allow man to bewail the loss of his chains any longer.   By " chains " he means only one thing: the presumably objective knowledge of God which Kant has of course long since destroyed.   Later in an annotation to his discourse Karl Marx refers to the " almost notorious. . .proofs of the existence of God " which Hegel " has turned round, that is, distorted in order to defend them. " For Marx they are but " empty tautologies " clearly not worth closer inspection.   Although Kant had labored to give faith in God a new foundation, proclaimers of " the death of God " always refer to Kant for support.   He lives on as the " all-demolisher. "

SIGNIFICANCE OF THE OLD PROOFS OF THE EXISTENCE OF GOD

In the course of the Age of Enlightenment an intellectual revolution took place.   As Paul Hazard notes, the spirit of the age began with an act of humility followed by an act of pride.   That spirit's first proclamation includes a renunciation.   Man admits that he is utterly incapable of grasping the ultimate ground of being, lying as it does in a realm beyond his reach.   Therefore man should have the courage to renounce all attempts to grasp it.   Long enough—runs the argument—have the learned constructed speculative systems, each proudly claiming to be the complete, fundamental, and ultimate order of the universe.   Yet every one of these systems has proved illusory.   Henceforth speculation on that which lies beyond the limits of man's power of reason is to be considered not only a pastime for fools but also a dangerous one.   *Usque huc venies et non procedis amplius!*   This far and no further!   Enlightened reason behaves like a sovereign who, once in power, decides to ignore the provinces he considers too far removed to govern securely. Hence he renounces them in order to establish his rule only over those which are safe. Skeptical pyrrhonism, eternal enemy of thought, is a consequence of all too lofty ambition and disappointed pride, and it leaves only rubble behind it. Wise moderation alone can hold destructive pyrrhonism in check. In Kant's philosophy the spirit of Enlightenment so tellingly analyzed by Hazard plays a decisive role.

Kant, for whom the Enlightenment is man's coming of age, is proud to consider himself an Enlightener. For him it was obvious that the men of past ages had remained under intellectual tutelage because they lacked the courage to break through the darkness with the light of their own reason. The arrogance of the enlightened philosophers was to blame for their insufficient knowledge of the problems of philosophy. Naively they believed that they had discovered the existence of such problems and that they possessed the sole key to their solution.

During the period of the Enlightenment proofs of the existence of God continued to be paraded; indeed, to collect them became a kind of passion. Meanwhile the whole temper of the desire to prove God's existence gradually changed. Rationalism in particular continued to overestimate the powers of human perception.

The recognition that man's knowledge is a tracing back, step by step, from present being to past is gradually lost. Human reason and its concepts is to be considered so exclusively the wellspring of all knowing that reason is thought capable of keeping pace with the very order of existence. Thence the exaggerated importance attached to the conclusion from which one attempts to derive all else. The model for this type of knowledge is the deductive method, which quite one-sidedly is considered the ideal of knowledge in general. With this the meaning of the proofs of God is also distorted. Whereas for medieval philosophers the term " *demonstratio* " meant quite generally to establish the truth of a claim on the basis of objective criteria, for the philosophers of the Enlightenment the ideal was the mathematical proof derived from the establishment of supreme concepts in which all factual information based on the perception of the senses was dismissed with contempt.

Rationalism was not satisfied with a stammering analogous concept of God traced through relationships. Its understanding of " con-

cept " is far more ambitious. It is based on the notion that what
a thing really and actually is lies solely in its inmost being, in its
essence. As a result it accepts as a true concept only that knowledge
of an object which includes its essence. According to rationalism,
the intellect is given real knowledge of an object by an " idea, "
which as an image evokes the essence of that object. Only such
ideas are granted the rank of concepts. Moreover, for the rationalist,
no concept is complete that fails to express the basic characteristics
of that essence. The true concept, then, gives the *Realdefinition* of
its object. The proofs of the existence of God with which Kant
comes to grips are those which bear all the hallmarks of rationalism.
As long as this fact is disregarded it is impossible to understand
Kant's criticism of the proofs. It is the rationalistic view of the
concept which misled rationalists to insist that a concept of God is
valid only when it was composed of all our knowledge of the
existence and attributes of God. The writers of the textbooks Kant
used as the basis for his lectures thought it possible to find a
Realdefinition of God that would conceptually embrace his full
essence. Medieval metaphysics would never have dreamed of making
such demands on a concept of God.

Christian Wolff, the great rationalistic systematizer who between
1703 and 1753 filled 67 volumes with the philosophies of everything
possible, neatly stored it all in flawless, homogenous definitions
which he packed and sealed in boxes from which nothing could
spill or escape His concept of truth was already rationalistic.
Everything is true that contains no contradictions within itself. For
Wolff clarity is the hallmark of truth, obscurity the hallmark of
error. Knowledge of a thing is pure when its concept contains
nothing mystifying or contradictory. It is less important that a
concept agree with the facts about an object one seeks to understand
than that the steps leading to that concept be strictly logical. For
Wolff thought had to conform above all not to reality but to logic.
The criterion of truth is not reality but logical correctness, the
strictness with which conclusions are drawn, and the flawlessness
of the derivation.

When such a concept of truth is applied to the metaphysicians'
knowledge of God, that knowledge is doomed. For with the
medievals the will to know sets its sights on divine reality, which

lies far beyond the tangible. Concepts of the divine necessarily remain full of dark, enigmatic, unresolved contradictions, for as Nicholas Cusanus pointed out, God is, after all, the "*coincidentia oppositorum.*" The rationalist, for whom everything is completely clear, no longer has an eye for such things. True, Wolff proved the existence of God with great zeal. He was always a believer in positive religion and fought all his life against Spinoza, Locke and Bayle. He protested against English freethinking and French deism, materialism, and skepticism. He died praying; nonetheless, as Hazard points out, Wolff's thought was no longer fundamentally Christian. What he really believed in was reason. For him even God was only a creation of human reason. It is in this sense that Christian Wolff's successors are pleased to interpret him. "The God of the Christians had all power and he had made ill use of it. In him man had put all his trust, and that trust had been abused. . . . Judged by the light of logic and reason as we understand them, his idea of Providence did not hang together." [1]

Because the process of human thought cannot begin replete with ideas from which everything possible can be developed, the rationalistic approach was bound to provoke empiricism as its critic and opponent. Equally one-sided, empiricism considers sensible experience as its sole source of knowledge and firmly rejects the possibility that a spiritual-intellectual interpretation of such experience might illuminate the ground of being.

KANT'S INTELLECTUAL REVOLUTION

Coming originally from rationalism, but his faith in it shaken by the criticism of the empiricists, Kant felt the necessity of finding some sort of agreement between the mutually incompatible opposites. Both spring from the soil of the Enlightenment. Kant tried to reach agreement between them by completely breaking away from

[1] P. Hazard, *European Thought in the Eighteenth Century. From Montesquieu to Lessing* (New Haven: Yale University Press, 1954), p. 48.

the old metaphysics, a revolutionary break which, *de facto*, rationalism had already made but which Kant elevated to a principle and
intrepidly set about pushing to its ultimate conclusion. " Hitherto
it has been assumed that all our knowledge must conform to objects.
But all attempts to extend our knowledge of objects by establishing
something in regard to them a priori, by means of concepts, have,
on this assumption, ended in failure. We must therefore make trial
whether we may not have more success in the tasks of metaphysics
if we suppose that objects must conform to our knowledge. This
would agree better with what is desired, namely, that it should be
possible to have knowledge of objects a priori, determining something
in regard to them prior to their being given. " [2] The circumstances
in this case, Kant continues, resemble those confronting Copernicus,
who not making any headway in the explanation of the movements
of the heavenly bodies when he supposed the whole firmament
turned round the spectator, wondered whether the opposite supposition might answer better: if, for instance, he left the spectator
himself to turn and the stars at rest.

Even this famous Copernican revolution does not yet break completely with the original intention of retrospection, which is to
direct the attention to things in themselves. For Kant the order
of being and things *(das Ding an sich)*, remains an immovable
reality which precedes thought. The attempt now to solve the
problem of knowledge by placing the reality after the thought, no
longer shaping the thought to fit the reality after the manner of
Copernicus and in so doing to invoke Copernicus is, to say the least,
unfortunate. Copernicus' revolution was in exactly the opposite
direction! Before Copernicus, the movements of astral bodies had
been gauged by information supplied by human vision; what Copernicus did was to liberate knowledge from the subjective limitations
of the human eye by applying a method of thought which coincided
with objective reality. Instead of taking a similar step from the
subjective limitations of discernment to a greater objectivity, the
Kantian revolution was a step *away* from objective or thing-
structured thought to the subjective limitations of knowing.

With this, Kant cleft human knowledge forever in two. For—

---

[2] I. Kant, *Critique of Pure Reason*. Translated by Norman Kemp Smith
(London: Macmillan and Co., Limited, 1933), p. 22.

Kant himself mentions this repeatedly—man's natural desire to grasp reality *as it is* is ineradicable. Solely with this intent does all our intellectual effort have direction and meaning. Not even Kant could escape the mind's tug in this natural direction, for when he examines the structure of human knowledge, he too has no other wish than to trace it back, step by step, intellectually; he does not attempt to set the direction of reality by precept. Never does Kant abandon the discovery that it is the very nature of human understanding to reconstruct the grounds of reality intellectually, because only such knowledge can provide a basis for human action.

By only half completing Copernicus' revolutionary turn in the field of philosophy Kant split man's world into a phenomenal half of mere appearances and a noumenal half of things existing in themselves, leaving between the two a gulf so deep and wide that only intellectual gangplanks precariously connect them. He himself utilizes them often enough because not even he could shift the natural inclination of man's striving for knowledge and force it into a subjective direction.

Once the gulf between the world of appearances and the world of reality had been cleft, Kant really did not need to waste another word on the old proofs of the existence of God. But he had become too involved with them to be able to abandon them lightly. Hence the tragic dichotomy between his revolutionary intellectual attitude and his natural inclination to solve the ultimate problems of existence. It is a moving thing to follow this struggle through its various phases, reaching as it does into the last days of his life and to see Kant, broken by the marasmus of old age, scribble weakly into the chaotic jumble of his notebook: " A plurality of gods is as unthinkable as a plurality of universes...only one God and one universe; both ideas are necessarily dependent on one another. *Ens summum, summa intelligentia, summum bonum.* .... God, the being that from the beginning has established the laws of nature and of freedom, is God...not only the supreme being, but because supremely holy, the mind's highest good. *Ens summum, summa intelligentia, summum bonum.* The mere idea of God is proof of his existence. .... The concept of God is simultaneously the concept of an obligatory *subject* outside myself. A being for whom all human duties are simultaneously his commandments. .... He must be capable of everything because he wills everything that duty demands. He is supreme in power. As a being with rights, he is a living God in the quality of a person. " [3]

In the preface to his dynamic early work *Allgemeine Natur-geschichte und Theorie des Himmels* (1755) in which Kant undertakes the ingenious task of presenting a theory of heaven along with a history of the development of the universe from original chaos according to strict mechanical laws, he says: " I did not plan this undertaking before I could assure myself that my religious duties had been attended to. My eagerness was doubled when I saw the fog in which monsters had once seemed to hide gradually clear with every step, and with its dispersion, the glory of the supreme being break forth in divine brilliance. " [4] This work was the matrix of the famous Kant-Laplace Theory.

There is a characteristic reversal of this attitude in Laplace. When in 1812 he sent his *Mechanics of Heaven* to Napoleon in Witebsk, the work was accompanied by the arrogant comment that his system rendered the hypothesis of a God superfluous. Over Kant's writing lies the transfiguring breath of profound reverence and admiration of divine wisdom and power. To the end of his days Kant emphatically rejected all pantheistic blurring of the concept of God. For him God is always the supreme, self-existent, perfectly self-sufficient, absolute, infinite, reasonable, understanding, personal, holy being. In the last analysis, the only question round which all his thinking turns is that of the knowability of the real existence of this being.

In the treatise, *The Only Possible Evidence for a Demonstration of the Existence of God* (1763), the Kant of the pre-critical period had applied himself specifically to the problem of the proofs of God and had taken the equivalent of a rational basic position. Even the preface contains several significant ideas. There he declares that our most important knowledge (the conviction that God really exists) is certain knowledge, quite independent of any metaphysical inquiry. " Providence certainly did not intend that the knowledge so necessary to our bliss should rest upon hair-

---

[3] I. Kant, *Opus posthumum*, Hg, v. A Buchenau. Erste Haelfte, (1936), pp. 11-17.
[4] I. Kant, *Werke*, Ak. Ausgabe I, pp. 221 f.

splitting sophistries, but rather that it would be passed on by natural common sense, which, when not confused by false art, is sufficient to lead us straight to the true and the profitable. " Common sense is perfectly sure of itself. It need not venture out into " the bottomless depths of metaphysics, that sinister ocean without lighthouse or shore. "

Nonetheless Kant undertakes to lay the logical foundations for a rigorous demonstration of God's existence. To do this he considers it necessary to reject the old arguments and to establish new foolproof ones. At the end of his inquiry he returns, characteristically, to the ideas expressed in the preface. He repeats, " Seek the proof herein, and if you do not seem to find it, turn from this untrodden footpath to the wide highway of human reason. It is absolutely necessary to convince oneself of the existence of God; it is not so necessary to be able to demonstrate it. "

Although Kant invariably speaks of the teleological argument with deep respect, recognizing in the purposeful conduct of the world and in its appropriate arrangement and fittings a convincing indication of the existence of a divine intelligence that directs all things to an ultimate goal; although in his *Critique of Pure Reason* he demands respect for the teleological argument as being the oldest, clearest, and most suitable for ordinary human understanding; although he admits that knowledge of the evident suitability of nature's furnishings augments faith in a supreme cause " to the point of irresistible conviction, " he will not concede that this or any other a posteriori proof based on experience has the stringency of a mathematical formula. For him a demonstration of " geometrical rigor " is possible only on the basis of a priori data. Kant is convinced that his treatise on the existence of God offers a " perfect a priori proof " substantiated by the argument that the negation of God would imply the impossibility of anything either actual or potential existing at all. For possibilities exist only in that the actual exists, in which they are united as direct or indirect realities. But even this proof of God as the necessary ground of possibility Kant discards later in his *Critique of Pure Reason* with the remark that the idea of a totality of reality is a purely transcendental idea. By mere poetic fabrication (in other words, by hypostatizing the concept) this idea was made God.

KANT'S CRITICISM OF THE PROOFS OF THE EXISTENCE OF GOD

In the *Critique of Pure Reason* Kant deems it necessary to clear away with finality all hitherto existing proofs of God's existence. He recognizes only three arguments as worthy of serious attention: the ontological, the cosmological, and the teleological arguments. It is typical of his rationalistic attitude that Kant considers the ontological proof, which the medieval thinkers had rejected, the fundamental proof to which the other proofs are ultimately directed. For this reason he begins his criticism with the ontological proof. He justly attacks the notion that from the idea of the absolutely necessary or most real essence one may infer its actual existence.

" The concept of a supreme being is in many respects a very useful idea; but just because it is a mere idea, it is altogether incapable, by itself alone, of enlarging our knowledge in regard to what exists. . .since the criterion of the possibility of synthetic knowledge is never to be looked for save in experience, to which the object of an idea cannot belong, the connection of all real properties in a thing is a synthesis, the possibility of which we are unable to determine a priori. And thus the celebrated Leibniz is far from having succeeded in what he plumed himself on achieving—the comprehension a priori of the possibility of this sublime ideal being.

" The attempt to establish the existence of a supreme being by means of the famous ontological argument of Descartes is therefore merely so much labor and effort lost; we can no more extend our stock of [theoretical] insight by mere ideas, than a merchant can better his position by adding a few noughts to his cash account. " [5]

After criticizing the ontological proof, Kant dispatches the cosmological. Here the argument runs that from the finite, accidental data of existence it is possible to infer a self-existent, necessary being—an *ens a se* as the Schoolmen called it. It would have to have existed of itself from the beginning by the power of its own

---

[5] I. Kant, *Critique of Pure Reason.* Translated by Norman Kemp Smith (London: Macmillan and Co., Limited, 1933), p. 506.

essence. It would not have *become*. This proof, which Leibniz termed the *argumentum a contingentia mundi*, Kant formulated as follows:

" If anything exists, an absolutely necessary being must also exist. Now I, at least, exist. Therefore an absolutely necessary being exists.... The proof then proceeds as follows: The necessary being can be determined in one way only, that is, by one out of each possible pair of opposed predicates.... Now there is only one possible concept which determines a thing completely *a priori*, namely, the concept of *ens realissimum*. The concept of the *ens realissimum* is therefore the only concept through which a necessary being can be thought. In other words, a supreme being necessarily exists. " [6]

As Bernhard Jansen illustrates in his book on the religious philosophy of Kant, it is important to examine Kant's criticism of this proof closely, for " seldom has a philosopher of Kant's stature criticized more uncritically and with more sophistry than the Sage of Koenigsburg does here. " Kant declares: " In this cosmological argument there are so many sophistical propositions that speculative reason seems to have exerted all its dialectical skill to produce a transcendent illusion of the most extreme nature.... In order that it might rest on firm foundations, it bases its conclusions on experience, thus appearing to be completely distinct from the ontological argument which is based entirely on pure, a priori conceptions. But this experience helps reason only one step further—to the existence of a necessary being. The properties of that being cannot be learned from experience, hence reason abandons it altogether and pursues its inquiries in the sphere of pure concepts, where it hopes to discover what the properties of an absolutely necessary being should be.... Hence it is really only the ontological argument which figures in the so-called cosmological proof and which constitutes its whole strength. " [7]

The rationalistic misunderstanding in these arguments is evident. On the one hand it is conceded that the existence of a necessary being may be concluded from experience, yet on the other hand

[6] *Ibid.*, pp. 508 f.
[7] I. Kant, *Werke*, Vol. II, p, 538.

Kant assures us later that absolute necessity is a being deductible by mere concepts. From the contingency of actual things, the cosmological proof infers a self-existent being as their primary cause. If things which are indeed accidental exist not in themselves, but as things that have come into existence, they must have been brought into existence by some being that does exist in itself; in other words, by some uncreated, essential being. There is no question but that the existence of the necessary being is proved by facts of the experience and not derived from mere concepts.

Once the existence of such a being has been proved, it is possible and necessary to proceed to the question of appropriate attributes. When this is done with impeccable logic, nothing can be said against it. There can be absolutely no talk of a relapse into the ontological proof with its attempt to prove the existence of God by mere concepts. By no means must a complete concept of the object of knowledge exist before one may discuss knowledge at all. Prehistoric stone tools and weapons discovered in caves give sure knowledge of Stone Age man's existence, even though a complete skeleton, which would testify to his actual shape and form, has never been found. Similarly, when exploring creation, it is enough to discover tracks which are clear evidence of God's presence, even though they do not suffice for a complete conception of him.

Kant sees a further presumption on the part of the cosmological proof in its application of the principle of causality to include things outside the range of the senses, whereas it is meant to be used only to assimilate sensual impressions intellectually. Here Kant is misled by the immanentization of intellectual principles; his thinking here is inconsistent.

The whole point of our questioning is directed at the ground of existence. We are forced not only by an inborn need to examine that ground but also by objective knowledge itself. Our conclusions as to the existence of such a ground are being constantly corroborated by experience, each time deepening our conviction that we do well to delve to the bottom of outward appearances. But even when our conclusion (that the ground of an object must exist) cannot be verified by experience, it is valid to apply the following principles: first, everything that exists must have a cause, either in itself or in something else; second, everything coming into existence must have a cause, not only in the sense of subjective truth, but also in that of objective truth.

There is a long-standing reservation regarding Kant's objection: namely, the invalidity of his prohibition of the existence of a cause simply because that cause is not perceptible. The groundlessness of Kant's objection is exemplified by the interesting history of the discovery of the planet Neptune. In the year 1781 Herschel had discovered the seventh great planet, Uranus, and had charted its orbit. In 1815 it had been observed that Uranus deviated somewhat from that orbit. Twenty-seven years later from the manner of this deviation, Leverrier concluded the existence of another, as yet unobserved planet which he concluded must be diverting Uranus. Soon after the arrival of Leverrier's computation at the Berlin Observatory, Galle actually discovered the new planet only half a degree from its computed position. Leverrier had calculated the position of the hypothetical planet Neptune mathematically, and his conclusion was accepted as valid, a validity soon proved by actual observation. Even if for some reason Neptune had remained invisible, Leverrier's conclusion would have been accepted.

By analogy then, Kant's objections to proofs based on the purposeful behavior of things is invalid. All his life Kant himself was profoundly impressed by the intrinsic purposefulness of things, above all, of living things, recognizing in that purposefulness an essential characteristic of the animate as distinct from the inanimate. Nonetheless, in his critical period Kant suddenly veered round to the position of conceding the purposefulness of nature only as an evaluating or " regulative principle " and not as a " constitutive principle " directly applicable to the thing itself. He grants that the cosmological proof points to a world architect but insists that this is not, without further examination, to be equated with God. Before Kant philosophers had had the same reservations. Nonetheless, once the existence of a world architect has been demonstrated, objective reason can very well continue to the conclusion that ultimately that architect must be God, without falling back—as Kant accuses it of doing—upon the ontological argument.

Kant's persistent differentiation between constitutive and regulative principles drove a fateful wedge into human thought causing a split which could not fail to produce revolutionary results. On the one hand he speaks of metaphysics as a natural inclination of the indestructible " dialectical appearance " of the God-idea; of man's necessary commitment to that idea rather than of mere possible acknowledgment of it. On the other hand Kant claims that man is constantly duped by this idea since its validity can never be demonstrated. However, Kant never dreamed of contesting every kind of knowledge of God. He wanted only to establish a new critical foundation for that knowledge. In the process, he advanced classical philosophy a step further by recognizing the attributes of the divine by analogy. Taking Kant's principles on the idea of the absolute in the *Critique of Pure Reason* as the point of departure and developing them logically in accordance with Kant's own points of application, W. Brugger has demonstrated that the existence of the absolute follows by logical necessity.

KANT'S ESTABLISHMENT
OF FAITH ON MORALITY

Convinced that the day of the theoretical proofs of God was over, Kant decided that ethics should be founded on the metaphysics of voluntarism, above all on the postulate of the existence of a supreme being. Thus he led religion back to a question of morals and reduced religiousness to morality. Here again there is a sharp cleavage: for Kant the essence of morality was autonomy, total independence from external laws, above all from divine laws. Unquestionably Kant was filled with the rigorous moral spirit of the true Prussian, but his will to unqualified arbitrariness and independence from religious motives was pronounced. His categorical imperative, the absolute command to moral behavior transports the human soul directly to the realm of the intelligible, unlocking the door to the inner life that remains closed to theoretical considerations. Whereas the empirical world of phenomena is necessarily determined by mechanical causality, the freedom of moral action reigns over the world of the spirit. Since logical thought is already engaged in the workings of the phenomenological world, Kant establishes morality on a-logical emotion. The *Critique of Practical Reason* takes as its point of departure the unconditional validity of the categorical imperative. It founds its absolute nature, which is obligatory for all rational beings, on the independent autonomous self. To be sure the result is a purely formal ethic. Since all constitutive, material determination is dependent on experience, which never conveys universally valid insights, only the formal and typical can be an object of philosophical examination. This formality clings to the subject insofar as it is the expression of human reason and participates in it. The universal applicability of moral action flows from autonomous human reason. Thus moral action, the autonomous ideal of the Enlightenment, finds fulfillment.

According to Kant's *Critique of Practical Reason* the basic formula of true morality runs: " Act as if the maxim of thy will were to become, by thy adopting it, a universal law of nature " (Semple translation). An act has moral value only when its motive is worthy of becoming a law for all reasonable beings. Respect for such law should be man's sole motivation. It is the duty of the individual to express the idea of humanity in himself and in others as perfectly as possible. The personality that determines itself in freedom has absolute supreme value. The moral law is valid for all reasonable beings. The moral law is the direct expression of a higher intelligible sphere intrinsic to reality. It does not belong solely to the outside world perceptible to the senses.

Time and again Kant equates freedom with autonomy; for him freedom is always understood in the sense of the Enlightenment: man as his own sovereign. The moral law, then, is the law that rules the world of all reasonable beings, placing man on an equal footing with God. " It is thus not limited to human beings but extends to all finite beings having reason and will; indeed it includes the infinite being as the supreme intelligence. " [8]

As Jansen points out, nowhere in Kant's works do we find a trace of any struggle with a religious problem which had to be resolved before the full fruit of his notion of autonomy could be plucked. Rather for Kant autonomy as independence from all constitutive

[8] I. Kant, *Critique of Pure Reason and Others Works on the Theory of Ethics*. Translated by Thomas Abbot (Longmans, Green), p. 38.

motivation comes first and is the most important, most universal
of all. From the beginning of his *Critique of Practical Reason*
it is a fixed concept. Kant's exclusion of divine authority is only
one instance of the subordination which is autonomy's due. He
discusses this at length in all its various formulations long before
God is even mentioned. Autonomy is the expression of the unconditional self-will. It implies the dethronement of the living, theistic
God, leaving room only for a deistic God as a finishing touch to
the world idea. Such a God no longer has any vital, personal
influence on the world.

As Kant terms it, the ultimate task of the moral will is the
realization of the highest goal, which includes absolute holiness
and supreme happiness. Since in this life neither is realizable
because of the inherent dissension between sensuality and reason,
the soul must continue to exist after death, attempting to draw
closer to the Ideal by gradually perfecting itself. Because no
natural, necessary relation between holiness and happiness exists
Kant postulates a supreme, omnipotent, and holy being who establishes this relation. In other words, the relation is demanded for
man's sake in order that he might attain to his ultimate happiness.
The God we have here is a mere *deus ex machina* who no longer
has the slightest personal contact with his creature and whose only
task is to provide him with ultimate bliss.

On the basis of this a priori concept of autonomy religion is
stripped of its unique value. There is no longer a logical place
for religion in the critical system. All religious acts are expected
merely to serve the demands of moral convictions. The existence
of independent religious acts with an intrinsic value of their own
is denied. With uncompromising logic Kant rejects all positive
manifestations of religion, particularly those of revelation. Christianity is an idea of religion, and to the extent that religion is founded
on reason it must be natural.

Although at the apogee of the intelligible world God remains
king, it is as a king whose real existence can only be postulated,
not established. With this the stage is set for the type of as-if
speculation that Vaihinger was to develop later in his theory of
fiction. In any case man's relation to a personal God is severed.

Kant insisted that as a motivation for a moral act the desire to please the supreme being was an undignified, servile attitude unworthy of man. With outright contempt he scores this " pathological " urge in man, painting it as black as possible so that against its darkness respect for autonomous law might shine the more purely. He declares expressly: There are no particular duties to God. " The one true religion comprises nothing but laws, that is, those practical principles of whose unconditioned necessity we can become aware, and which we therefore recognize as revealed through pure reason (not empirically). " [9] Religious acts of reverence and service to God are not merely worthless but positively dangerous to morality. Everything that surpasses the moral life is " mere religious illusion and pseudo-service of God. "

Kant's friends speak reverently of his honest belief in God during the last years of his life. " Faith in a supreme being...pervaded Kant's thinking, and though he admitted that he was as incapable as any other human being of comprehending the incomprehensible, and that his faith in God was grounded not in any insight of reason but in the striving for holiness demanded by reason, he clung to this faith tenaciously.... Kant was neither an atheist nor a materialist.... How often and with what genuine delight...[he] poured out his heart over God's wisdom, goodness, power. Not only could such converse not fail to convince everyone that Kant believed in a God...it would have transformed even an unbeliever into a believer. " [10]

Kant's closest friend, the theologian Borowski, says: " We owe Kant our most fervent thanks for tying our moral faith here on earth so tightly to God. " But neither Borowski's theology nor his friendship was able to change Kant's stand or move him to participate in religious services, or utter a word of prayer on his deathbed. Christian Wolff still managed to die praying, but Kant, even in the face of death, refused to pray. He was laid to rest in the Cathedral at Koenigsburg, which living, he never set foot in, although as Rector of the University it was his duty to attend the services there.

In view of these facts it is idle to argue whether or for how

[9] I. Kant, *Religion Within the Limits of Reason Alone* (New York: Harper and Brothers, 1900) Part II, p. 156.

[10] R. B. Jachmann, *Immanuel Kant geschildert in Briefen an einen Freund* (Elfter Brief, 1804), pp. 115 f.

long Kant believed in the reality of God, whether and from what point God had for him declined to a mere assumption or philosophical norm useful in the practice of the art of living.   Over Kant's faith in God lies the shadow of a tragic, irreconcilable dichotomy. Though he labored hard and honestly to give faith a new foundation, he contradicted his own efforts to do so by his unquestioning acceptance of the sacred dogma of human reason as an absolute. Hence he failed.   Only this explains his strangely long-lived influence.   Objectively Kant's ethics are much closer to the traditional ethics founded on the Christian idea of God than are modern value ethics.   Even his notion of autonomy can be applied to God.   But the young intellectuals who grab so greedily at Kantian thought come away only with the parole " autonomy and freedom, " into which Kant's critical disposal of the old proofs of God fits nicely.   For generations the authoritative aspect of Kant's thought seemed so absolute that only a few independent minds succeeded in extricating themselves from it.   Ortega y Gasset's comment is thought-provoking.   " For ten years I lived within the structure of Kant's thought.   I inhaled it like air.   Kant was at once my home and my prison. . . .   It cost me a great effort to escape from the Kantian prison and its all-pervading influence. . . .   The intellectual world is full of unwitting disciples of Kant who will always remain his followers because they are unaware of their allegiance to him. Today these incurable Kantians are the greatest impediment to progress; they are the only reactionaries who really are obstructionists. " [11]

---

[11] J. Ortega y Gasset (translated from the German edition) *Buch des Betrachters* (1952), pp. 141 f.

7. *The philosophical revolution of german idealism*

THE FAR-REACHING EFFECTS OF THE FRENCH REVOLUTION

" ...who will deny that his heart was lifted up,
That his breast freer, with purer pulse-beat throbbed
As he caught the new sun's early radiance,
Heard tell of rights held common to all men,
Of glowing Freedom, worthy Equality! "

With these words, which Goethe puts into the mouth of the old judge of the refugees in *Hermann and Dorothea*, he vividly portrays the initial impact of the French Revolution upon wide circles in Germany. The new ideas particularly inflamed German intellectual life, offering philosophical thought a parole which German thinkers with typical thoroughness pushed to its ultimate conclusions. It was Fichte who gave the development of that thought its impetus. The new ideas from France had made a deep impression on his young spirit, unleashing a storm of enthusiasm which was to become the mainspring of his whole philosophy. He was quick to pin the hopes of all mankind on the French Revolution. In the year 1793, fired by the conviction that he had solved the problem of the state founded on freedom, he published two studies on legal philosophy which clearly reflect the influence of the revolutionary upheaval then taking place. In them he affirms without qualification the people's right to change their form of government, directly referring to Rousseau's conception of the sovereignty of man in society. Fichte champions the view that there is nothing on which a society can legally found its sovereignty save on a contract between its members. Later, somewhat sobered by the opposition which his thesis aroused, Fichte modified his initial youthful enthusiasm for the French Revolution, but the basic theme of his ideological thinking remained unchanged.

FICHTE AND THE CONCEPT OF FREEDOM

Freedom! It was not only Fichte's political thought that was affected; the catchword of the French Revolution spurred him to construct a whole philosophical system. Deliberately he makes the concept of freedom its starting point. In a letter to Baggesen he explains: "My system is the first based on freedom. Just as that nation [France] tears off man's outward chains, my system frees him from the shackles of things in themselves, from outside influences, and with its very first principle establishes man as an independent being. During the years in which the Revolution was struggling for political freedom with physical force, this system was being born of the spiritual conflict within me fed by all my deep-rooted prejudices and fostered by the Revolution. Its values were what lifted me higher in order that I might grasp them. It was while I was writing about the Revolution that as a kind of reward the first inklings and presentiments of this system came to me."[1]

Rousseau and Lessing had impressed Fichte deeply. The annihilating criticism of the believer's conception of the church and of Christendom which Fichte had been taught by the theological polemics of Lessing and the doctrine of autonomy as preached by Kant had been decisive factors in Fichte's intellectual life. Once the notion of an absolutely autonomous ego fully dawned on him,

[1] J. G. Fichte, *Briefwechsel* (Krit. Gesamtausg. v. H, Schulz, 2 Bde. Leipzig, 1923), I, pp. 449 f.

he no longer hesitated. As he himself often admitted, this was the prior decision of his philosophy of the self- and world-positing ego.

"The law of freedom in our breast" by which the original, unaltered form of the self becomes conscious—in other words, "the pure ego" which is simultaneously the moral law—becomes for Fichte the "ultimate ground" of all truth and certainty. Instead of broadly expanding, as does the thought of Hegel and Schelling, Fichte bores straight down into the problem of the existence of a free ego. All acts radiate from action like spokes from an invisible hub. Action is absolute, never to be objectified inwardness; action is not existence but life. For the idealist the only thing that is positive is freedom. Freedom means choice, self-possession. For Fichte the term freethinker is high praise: it means one who makes just and dutiful use of the freedom within him. This conception necessarily changes man's relation to God. To be sure, Fichte does mention God, but he expressly denies any creaturely dependence on the Creator. Though a divine spark glows in the human breast, man is not God's property.

For Fichte the whole question of God was determined by the question of freedom. As a student, before becoming acquainted with Kantian philosophy, he had been a determinist. Thought through to its natural conclusion, the notion of God as the absolute seemed to leave no room for human freedom, for if divine freedom is the absolute, if it is the factor that determines the world and history, then man's self-determination is necessarily nil. That is why the young Fichte had called himself an "intellectual fatalist." To one caught in this deterministic impasse, Kant's doctrine of the freedom of autonomous man had a liberating ring, and Fichte greeted it enthusiastically. In his revolutionary years, he pinned his hopes for the future of mankind on the vital forward thrust of the human spirit toward a new consciousness of self. When he attacked a church, it was not because he took exception to its particular doctrine, but because he objected to churches on principle. In brief, Fichte fiercely rejected any authoritative faith or church established on authoritative faith. The mere existence of a church disturbed him deeply, and his ego protested, determined to belong unconditionally to none but itself. To submit to any church as "judge in God's stead" and to accept its teachings contradicted

Fichte's whole conception of intellectual freedom. This explains his own highly typical brand of so-called Christianity: Jesus as the founder of a humanitarian religion, Luther as the destroyer of the church as the deputy of God, Kant as the perfecter of the philosophy of freedom—these three are the great guardian spirits of Fichte's Christianity of Freedom.

Fichte's lectures on the theory of knowledge in the summer of 1794 closed with a dithyramb on the dignity of man. Though Fichte took Kant's practical philosophy as a starting point, he soon outdistanced it, practical reason becoming in his hands the principle of a speculative world view. For Kant human dignity rests on man's autonomy, by which he means essentially man's independence from the mechanism of nature. Man is above *nature*. For Fichte's concept of freedom this is not enough. According to him man's dignity consists in his being in a sense creator of the world—at any rate its lord. Autonomy proves to be the law that rules the entire world; man's freedom becomes the theoretical determining principle of the world. It is precisely this extending of freedom to a world principle that is the real essence of German idealism. To be sure this essence was given concrete expression in several different forms, all of which developed from the same root. In the sovereignty of the ego, that is in man's autonomy, lies his dignity, and by " man " Fichte means primarily the individual, not the genus.

Fichte takes the synthesizing power of human thought that he finds in Kant and exalts it to the creative function of knowing. He sees the ego as the guarantee that hand in hand with the individual's growing culture also universal culture will progress. With these assumptions—man as lord of nature and the ego as lord of time and death, man usurps attributes hitherto considered divine. Fichte insists: the ego exists eternally and of its own strength. No one can curtail its activities.

Fichte completes the metaphysical revolt begun by the Enlightenment by turning it into a metaphysical revolution, thereby inverting the old faith in God to its exact opposite. Whereas the old faith rested on the conviction that the existence of the world and of man is an accidental, posited existence whose being and existence testify to a divine Positor, Fichte brands such convictions " confused philosophy." He insists that the attempt to trace the world and its forms back to a divine intelligence is total nonsense; questions of this kind should never have been raised. A world which existed in itself would be absolute. According to Fichte's logic, the world exists only as the reflection of our own inner activity, that is to say, thought. Because the world does not exist in itself, one cannot ask to know its ground. According to the laws of reason, the world is nothing but the reasonable expression of our own interior acts become tangible, or the materialized stuff of duty. The ground of the supersensual or transcendental world lies in me. I find myself free of all influences from the sensible world. I am as it were absolute, a power far above the sensible. The moral order is the divine within us. It is formed by right doing. This is man's only possible confession of faith.

"That living and operative moral order is itself God; we need no other God, and we can understand no other. Reason has no call to quit the moral order of the world, conclude a Founder on the strength of the founded, or to assume a special being as the world's cause; unwarped reason certainly does not draw any such conclusion or assume any such special being; only a philosophy that misconstrues itself makes this mistake." [2] For Fichte a God with his own, other than human existence is self-contradiction, mere classroom prattle which he feels it his duty to silence.

Once I decide to obey the law of reason, "I *am* immortal, imperishable, eternal; I do not *become* these. The metaphysical world is not a remote world of the future, it exists now. It cannot be more real in one respect than it is in others. Even after myriads of life-spans it would be no more actual than it is at this moment. Other modes of my sensible existence are future modes, but they are as far from being my real life as is its present mode. With that decision [to obey reason], I lay hold of eternity, now stripping myself of this life of dust and of any other sensible life which might lie ahead to place myself high above them all. I myself become the sole wellspring of all my being and appearances; henceforth I possess life in myself, unconditioned by anything

---

[2] J. G. Fichte, "Ueber den Grund unsere Glaubens an eine Goettliche Weltregierung," *Werke*, ed. Medicus, Bd. III, p. 130.

outside me. My will which I and no other fit into the world order is the source of true life and of eternity. " [3]

Man, eternal through himself and by his own strength. With this thesis Fichte reaches the apogee of his thought, where he dares to apply the Biblical attributes of God to men. For one awakened to such consciousness of self, a thousand years are as a day. With this step, everything less than human, everything bestial, barbarous, including the anguish of death seem to have been overcome. Even in the darkness of the barbarian, human majesty and divinity lie hidden and will sometime in the course of history step forth. Death becomes a bagatelle, more, it is remolded and idealized. It can do nothing, says Fichte, but enlarge our field of activity; it cannot alter our plans or goals by one iota.

Every moment of his existence man lays hold of something new outside himself and drags it into his circle of activity, so continuing until everything has been consumed. Then comes joy, supreme, overwhelming joy: the joy in one's self. Bliss in and through the self—here is the antithesis of the *visio beatifica* of the Christian who expects bliss from God, the source of all being. All that is left of the transcendental God is the " transcendental law in a transcendental world. "

The mystique of the infinite ego flows from the Promethean choice of self to a role of exalted heroism. By his own self-possessing will, man defies the onslaught of finitude, placing himself forever beyond the reach of time. " Boldly I lift my face to the threatening mountains of stone and to the raging waterfall and to the clouds crackling in a sea of flame, and I say: I am eternal, and I defy your power! Crash down upon me, all of you, and you, earth and heaven! Mingle in wild tumult you elements all! foam and toss, in your rage annihilate the last mote of this body I call mine;—my will alone with its unshakable design will soar boldly, coldly over the ruins of the universe, for I have forged my destiny, which is more lasting than you. It is eternal, and I too am eternal. " [4] Unconcerned, the Prometheus in Fichte oversteps the limits of logic. If his vision cannot be proved, what of it? The will from which it flows is the will which compels destiny.

[3] *Ibid.*, p. 152.
[4] J. G. Fichte, *Die Bestimmung des Gelehrten,* ed. Medicus, Bd. I, pp. 250 f.

The accusation of atheism which forced Fichte to relinquish his chair at the University of Jena was not groundless. He of course rejected it, attempting in his written defense to present himself as the intellectual believer, his opponents as the real atheists, the completely godless makers of an unredeeming idol. He describes their concept of God as crudely primitive, coarsely sensual, and infinitely inferior to his own spiritual and refined one. Besides, he stresses the principle of moral law so heavily that it is practically hypostasized to a new God. " I accept the law of such a spiritual world, accept the fact that my will does not exist, nor that of any finite being, nor the will of all finite beings together; I accept that under which my will and the will of all finite beings stands. Neither I nor any finite and hence in any way sensible being can even conceive of the consequences of a pure will, or of the nature of those consequences, since the essence of our finiteness is precisely its inability to comprehend these. . . . There is nothing truly real, lasting, intransient in me save these two things: the voice of my conscience and my free obedience. Through the first the spiritual world stoops down and embraces me as one of its members; through the second, I lift myself up into the spiritual world, seize it and participate in it. It is that infinite will, however, which mediates between that world and me, for it is itself the source both of that world and of my being. " [5]

Fichte's version of man's autonomy perfected the notion of the Enlightenment, which had elevated reason to its God and attempted to shape the world according to the laws of reason alone. From the standpoint of this highest value Fichte categorically pronounces judgment: that which is unreasonable and against freedom is sinful and immoral, regardless of where one believes to have discovered it. The fear of God and reverence for the unknown Godhead inspired by nature's terrors are rejected by Fichte as the bugaboo of ancient religions. No longer fear of God but reverence for one's own law—much as in Goethe—is the primary attribute on which true morality is founded. Far from critizing the prevailing lack of fear of God, Fichte considers it an asset to be encouraged. The will to absolute human freedom cannot coexist with absolute divine freedom.

[5] J. G. Fichte, *Die Bestimmung des Menschen.* Nach: Hirsch, pp. 153-155.

Hence Fichte passionately combats the idea of the world's and of man's createdness; he rejects the acceptance of a creation as " the absolutely fundamental error of all false metaphysics and religious doctrine. ... " Only Jews and infidels, Fichte continues, allowed finite things to proceed from a divine being as primal Cause " by an act of absolute arbitrariness. " He describes the positing of a creation " as the first criterion of the falseness of a religious doctrine. "

In Fichte one finds expressed, though only sporadically and incipiently, the leitmotif of that 19th- century thought which turns its back on faith. For one thing we find already in Fichte the idea which Ludwig Feuerbach is to develop later: that for true religion mankind is the true God. From the notion of autonomy Fichte concludes that man is politically free and independent of any supreme authority. Fichte completely misses the reality of evil. For him nothing that bears a human countenance can be sinful or rejected. Fichte's metaphysical faith in freedom is completely foreign to any gospel of expiation and reconciliation. These remain in the realm of the historical, which for the believer in reason is without interest. Only the metaphysical beatifies, not the historical.

If these basic ideas of the founder of German idealism long continued to have an important influence on other thinkers it is because Fichte himself spent his whole intellectual energy trying to control the paradoxes which sprang from his views. Although he never mastered those paradoxes, he himself gradually returned to a personal God utterly different from all earthly beings, a God whom man can address and who hears. Finally Fichte turns to " the Father of souls, " to him who is different from the finite not in degree but in kind, to the Father understood best by childlike simplicity.

The breaking out of the order of the ancient belief; Promethean self-reliance; stubborn, passionate rejection of a living God as the Creator of the world; the search for a center of the self but simultaneous shrinking from the hard consequences of such a center when found; backtracking along dialectically torturous paths to a kind of faith, if only in eternal principles that are fundamentally unattainable—these are to become the characteristics of all idealistic thought as they were of that of its founder.

The atmosphere of the entire age was loaded with such ideas. Seized upon in a state of confusing intoxication, they clamor for expression, thus contributing to the establishment of a new era. Fundamentally the direction of German idealism is inward. What Kant achieves on a theoretical basis: the establishment of the transcendental subject (in reality the human ego) as the center of his system, becomes the signal for humanity "to try with all its strength to find its center." In the process, the reality of God, the center of the old world, is diminished to a supreme but merely regulative idea. No longer does man seek his center outside himself, in the world and in a transcendent God; he seeks it in himself, in the depths of his soul, for which the attribute "infinite" is demanded back from God. Ever since Kant, man bears within himself the "sun" of a conscience. He believes the Supreme Being to be active within him, relating the self, "*autos*" to the "*nomos.*" Man is aware of the beginning of an endless process within him, a process of monstrous dynamism and tension from which divine sparks flash. Here is "creative man," convinced that the springs of life gush forth within him, that his life flows on the one hand creatively with God into the world and on the other hand with the world to God. Thus God is drawn into man and into the world. God is the spark, the "*Seelenfunklein,*" in man awakened to wholeness. God is absolute only in the totality of the relative and eternal, only through time.

THE PROMETHEAN SYMBOL AND GOETHE

When in 1800 Fichte rejected the "old arbitrary God" as incompatible with his new philosophy, proclaiming instead a religion answerable only to the inner law of the self, he chose as its symbol the mythical figure of Prometheus. Obviously under the influence of the dramatic fragment, *Prometheus* and the ode of the same name which Goethe had written in 1793, Fichte describes the Titan as one who "conscious of his good and just deed. . .laughs, unafraid, to see the ruins of the world crash down upon him."

The new thought stirred men's spirits powerfully; simultaneously in many quarters the same mythical figure was revived. Shaftesbury had proclaimed the poet another creator, the true Prometheus under Jupiter, so Prometheus was used again and again as the symbol of the poet-genius who considers himself equal to the Gods. Somehow for the proud era of genius the symbol of the Titan seemed to be the only appropriate one; the *spiritus creator* which the reverent Middle Ages hymned now becomes " *l'esprit créateur* " of the genius divinely fired to Titanic deed. Prometheus symbolizes the genius' claim not to God-given creative powers but to a creativity that is entirely his own. Divinity is *his*. He insists on being his own *origo*, the true source of his own achievement. Even when such exaggeration tragically splits his whole being, he insists that a power all his own, equal to that of God, is at work in him.

According to Goethe's own account, it was his awakening consciousness of self as a creative poet which simultaneously awakened his determination to belong to no one but himself, to reject everything not his own, and to found his whole existence solely on the strength of his own nature. Goethe cut the ancient Titan garb to his own size. The revolt of his *Prometheus* far surpasses that of the *Prometheus* of Aeschylus. Loudly trumpeting his own accomplishments, Goethe's Titan feels himself not only equal to God but superior to Heaven's Highest, for whom everything is effortless. Defiantly Prometheus mocks him.

Better known than Goethe's dramatic fragment *Prometheus* is his ode. Here garbed in classical mythology, Prometheus renounces a God who needs tithes and " the breath of prayers " to preserve his majesty. Though in all this Goethe very likely was considerably influenced by Voltaire, it was Goethe's own " titanism, " as his friends called it, which gave the ancient theme new life and power. When Prometheus, intoxicated by his own creative powers, turns his back on Zeus and proudly, rebelliously exalts himself to a cosmic *demiurge*, it is not only the voice of Johann W. Goethe we hear remonstrating but that of a broad current in the thought stream of his day.

> Curtain the face of your heaven, Zeus,
> With steaming clouds.

A boy beheading thistles,
Try your strength
On oak and soaring mountain peak.
This though, this earth of mine
You must not touch,
Nor my hut which you did not build,
Nor my hearth
Whose friendly glow
You envy me!

I know nothing more niggardly
Under the sun than you, gods,
Miserably sucking
Your majesty
From mortals' alms
And the breath of prayers.
You would starve
Were not children and beggars
Ever hopeful fools.

When I was a child,
Not knowing in nor out,
I often turned my troubled gaze
To the sun, as though above it were
An ear to listen to my plea,
A heart, like mine
To pity one sore-pressed.

Who helped me
Against the Titan's insolence?
Who rescued me from death,
From slavery?
Have you not done it all yourself,
Holy, glowing heart,
That young and good was tricked
Into giving thanks to the sleeping
" Rescuer " up there?

I honor you, what for?
Have you ever stilled the pain
Of the heavy-burdened?

Have you ever dried the tears
Of the fearful ones?
Was it not all-powerful Time
That forged my manhood
And eternal Fate,
My lord and yours?

Do you really suppose
That I should hate my life,
Flee to the deserts
Because not all
Dream-blossoms ripened?

Here I sit shaping men in my image,
A race that is like myself,
To suffer, to weep,
To enjoy and rejoice,
And to ignore you
As I do!

In this poem the spirit of the age found valid expression. The sharp ear of the twenty-four-year-old Goethe, finely attuned to the many-tongued chorus of voices, caught and identified them with his own intoxicating awareness of genius. So masterfully did he capture the features of the dawning epoch in a perfect symbol, that those who later attempted to do the same invoked that symbol again and again.

Six years later Goethe expressly abjured this revolt and called men back " within human limits, for no mortal should measure himself with the gods. " Nonetheless, Goethe remained the son of a secularized, de-Christianized and de-sanctified age and never quite succeeded in breaking the *hybris* he himself warned against. He did struggle against the spirit of revolt that he had caught from Voltaire. But even in Goethe's old age man in the strength of his own inmost being remains demiurge. For the poet the axis of the world, round which all things must turn, remains shifted from God to man. As an old man Goethe still admits: " I was always conscious of the mythological point at which Prometheus appears; this was to become a lively fixed idea. "

In one scene in *Faust* there is a wonderfully vivid portrayal of the clash of the new intellectual world with the old faith in God. Gretchen asks Faust if he believes in God. She asks because her heart, which is anchored in God, senses in Faust a totally different attitude. His reply is as ambiguous as her question is candid. The plain question receives no plain answer but new questions, in which the point is shifted from the objective to the subjective or psychological, from God the reality to a mere emotion in man. Nominalistically, the reality for which the word stands is devitalized so that the whole weight is shifted to the purely subjective. " Feeling is all; names are but sound and smoke. "

God is allowed to remain. However, God and faith in God are no longer powers in themselves. They have become useful means to an end: the cultivation of human personality. Goethe tells us that basically it doesn't matter what one believes; all that is important is *that* one believes. For him monotheism, polytheism, and pantheism are all equally justifiable forms of faith. They can easily substitute for one another whenever it is convenient to have them do so.

In Goethe's aesthetic world view, beauty has been exalted to an absolute, autonomous value. For Goethe the final product of ever advancing nature is the beautiful human being. Placed at the apex of nature, man imagines himself to *be* nature. The beautiful human being incorporates all that is splendid, all that is venerable, all that is worthy of love in himself, thus exalting man above himself. In Goethe's essay on Winckelmann, which we have cited here, one sentence plays slyly on the doctrine of the Incarnation. The addition of a single letter is enough to distort the meaning completely. In the sentence: " God became man for our sake, in order to raise man to God " (zu Gott) Goethe writes, " in order to raise man to a God " (zum Gott) thus giving a modern twist to the Biblical Christ as *Viator*, the Way. With this, *religio*, the re-tying or reestablishing of the bond between God and man, is reduced to a purely human concern. Although the vocabulary of faith remains, God as *the* reality is dethroned.

Goethe's aesthetic humanism anxiously shied away from the elemental religious experience which shatters a man's illusion that beauty suffices. Face to face with the " *mysterium tremendum,* " man suddenly becomes aware of beauty's impotence. In order to protect man's aesthetic self-sufficiency, certain experiences, above all the experience of death, must be kept at a distance and aesthetically falsified. Art is accorded the task of transfiguring the ugly and of making the unbearable bearable.

However, the figure of Goethe can never be fixed in any formula. He remained a *Werdender,* one in a constant state of becoming, and he underwent important metamorphoses again and again. The political events unleashed by the French Revolution, particularly in the period of the Napoleonic Wars, exposed the values of the humanistic world view as neither broad enough nor strong enough. Events forced Goethe to measure them by the yardstick of world history. In the process, he recalled his early preoccupation with the Old Testament. As a youth he had been particularly attracted to Moses, of whom he writes: his is " a language of souls, and from the depths of the divine, his tongue flashes life and light. " In order to resist the forces of violent change, in order not to succumb to chaos as the ultimate power on earth, Goethe looked about him for a higher order that would embrace all laws and all values. He tried to reorient himself from the Books of Moses, which he carefully explored for their permanent value. We have taken as the motto of this book the classical words of the answer he found: " The real, the deepest, the sole theme of the world and of history, to which all other themes are subordinate, is the conflict of belief and unbelief.

All epochs in which faith rules, whatsoever the form, are radiant epochs, uplifting and fruitful for those who live in and after them. All epochs in which unbelief celebrates its miserable victory, whatsoever the form, even when they boast moments of seeming brilliance, disappear forever because no one willingly burdens himself with the knowledge of barrenness.

THE PROTESTANT SEMINARY OF TUEBINGEN

The whole phenomenon of German idealism is comprehensible only through a knowledge of its history: it originated as a revolt against the dominant Christian faith of the day. The revolt began at a Protestant seminary, the famous *Tuebinger Stift*, when three young intellectuals pledged mutual help in their search for a new solution to the religious problem. Hegel, Schelling, and Hoelderlin, one day to be leaders of the new intellectual forces swiftly coming to the fore, spent two decisive student years together at Tuebingen. Part of the time they even shared the same room. Suddenly, into the peaceful atmosphere of a patriarchal tradition that bound the seminarians to a moral life, highly inflammatory matter was tossed. Through Strasbourg the ideas of the French Revolution reached Tuebingen. In 1791, Schelling, Hegel, and Hoelderlin set up a liberty tree on the outskirts of the city.

The spirit of the Enlightenment with its criticism of the historical foundations of Christianity and of social conditions marched practically unchallenged into Germany. No higher spirituality stepped forward to intercept it. Close behind followed the new image of man as inspired by Kant and first embodied by Fichte, his originally nebulous features gradually growing clearer and more recognizable. Imaginations soared. The *Stift's* young theology students were deeply stirred by the impact of the French Revolution. (We have already mentioned Hegel's practice, even while a philosopher of the Prussian State, of solemnly celebrating the anniversary of the outbreak of the Revolution.) The realization that social conditions do not necessarily have to be accepted but can be improved by courageous action; the parole of freedom from the chains of slavery; demands for an end to man's tutelage—all this took on feverish proportions among the students, inflaming apocalyptical hopes of a spiritual self-liberation that would lead to mankind's permanent bliss, to a veritable kingdom of God on earth. Schiller's "*In tyrannos!*" was enough to render all *Stift* authorities "tyrants" and perfect targets for the general rebelliousness.

The haziness of revolutionary ideas was matched only by their astonishing efficaciousness. A secret conspiracy was reported in which at least Hegel and Schelling definitely participated. Eclectic young minds groped their way through the phenomena of the day, appropriating everything they could find that seemed to clarify the situation and further the cause of freedom. Rousseau's extolling of the inalienable rights of human nature, Voltaire's mockery of

revealed religion, Lessing's historical criticism of tradition, Kant's
rejection of the classical proofs of the existence of God—these were
ideas which the revolutionary spirit clutched at greedily. A number
of students inwardly turned away from Christianity; several refused
to participate in the grace recited at meals. Zeltner describes the
special enthusiasm that quickens Hegel's and Hoelderlin's correspondence with Schelling, five years their junior, left behind at
Tuebingen. The letters are still vibrant with faith in the future—a
faith, for all the writers' rebellion against the seminary's schooling
and discipline, expressed in Biblical metaphor: " May God's kingdom
come, and not find us with hands lying idle in our laps! " Thus
Hegel closes a letter to Schelling in 1795, the same letter which
also suggests that " ' Reason and Freedom ' remain our watchword. "
Next to Kant's agnosticism it is the fundamental idea of his
Critique of Practical Reason, according to which reason educates
the free moral character to become its own lawgiver, which makes
the deepest impression. In these letters the notion of moral autonomy
mingles with ideas of political maturity, fanning the friends'
enthusiasm for their avowed cooperation toward a better future.

One appropriate expression of their *Weltanschauung* seemed to
be contained in the doctrine of the unity of all existence as proclaimed
by pantheistic thought since the 17th century. " The discovery of
Spinoza...was of particular significance to the trio, " Zeltner continues. " The Heraclitean ' *Hen kai pan* ' (one and all) in which
Lessing sums up the doctrine of pantheism becomes their much
trumpeted password, and Spinoza's ' *Deus sive natura* ' (God or
Nature), above all for Schelling, the underlying theme of their
thought. " Here is a frank monism rooted in the emotional rejection
of, indeed hostility to, current theology: above all, to faith in a
personal God.

With a violence culminating in satire Schelling attacks established
theology. Using philosophy as his weapon, he combats " the nonsense of the theologians. Kant has done away with all that "—only
the theologians haven't noticed it. With Fichte, Schelling passionately strikes out against " the old superstition, not only of positive but
also of so-called natural religion. " Kant had left at least the God
of moral postulates, God as the guarantor of eternal justice. Now
he too must go! With this, " that hated, personal Being up there

in heaven" is laid low. According to Schelling it is "high time to proclaim the freedom of the mind to superior mankind and no longer permit men to mourn the loss of their shackles." These shackles are none other than the supposedly objective knowledge of God, which Kant had long since destroyed. It is only a matter of recognizing them as shackles. For the weakness of reason consists not in its craving for such knowledge but in the conviction that it is incapable of getting along without an objective God and without an absolute, objective world.

In other words, the will to arrive at an objective God is interpreted as "weakness" and dismissed from the start. It is important to examine the affective root of this rejection of the old faith in God. It is not rejection resulting from an intellectual examination of the facts of the world, as was the case of the medieval proofs of the existence of God. It was not that now, thanks to a better or more thorough examination of those facts, the opposite conclusion had been reached. At the root of Schelling's attitude—even that of the young Schelling—is what has been described as "monstrous vainglory." In his *Epicurean Credo of Heinz Widerporsten* Schelling clearly acknowledges the omnipotence of man. In a famous dream Franz von Baader beheld Schelling as Hegel's successor to the chair of philosophy at the University of Berlin. Schelling appeared "like an Oriental god doffing with innumerable arms innumerable hats from his own innumerable heads.... Schelling, above all, the young and the middle-aged Schelling, can do everything. He can do everything because he knows everything. God and man are one and the same."[6]

BELATED RETURN TO GOD

In the last analysis, the systems which spring from the new attitude of self-reliance are based on a priori monism. Yet all the philoso-

[6] F. Heer, *Hegel* (1955), p. 20.

phers of such systems recoiled from the unbelief to which they logically led. They wanted to remain religious and with increasing age tried to return to the God they had deserted.

We have already mentioned Kant's *Opus Posthumum,* which was published in full only a few decades ago. Throughout these very rough notes which monotonously return over and over again to certain patterns of thought, God is the chief concern. Obviously Kant's whole thinking in his later years was deeply involved with the problem of God. On the first page he refers to God as " the Supreme Being, who knows all things, " To him as holy being to whom no comparative, no superlative can apply; there can be only One. " [7] By the concept of God one means " a person, that is, an intelligent being who first of all possesses rights; secondly, without being bound himself by duties, binds all other intelligent beings by the duties he commands. " [8] Repeatedly God is described as " *Ens summum,* " " *summa Intelligentia,* " " *summum bonum,* " much as pre-Kantian classical philosophy and theology had described him. " By the concept of God transcendental philosophy understands an essence of the greatest possible existence in regard to all active qualities and free from all sense impressions (reality) ; for all true purposes, One who is also according to human understanding, human judgment, and human reason, the supreme being. " [9] Of course, such statements should not be interpreted, as they frequently have been, simply as the aging Kant's return to his starting point, as a disavowal of his critical position. For one thing, the maze of thought is too unclear. Moreover, at that stage, Kant was no longer able to extricate himself from his critical conclusions. They keep reasserting themselves. For instance in the following: " There is something in the way of a moral practical reason which like divine commandments contains the principle of all man's duties, without there being, therefore, a special substance outside man that may be taken for granted. " [10] A final dichotomy is here, a contradiction which to the very end Kant vainly but with all his strength endeavored to master.

[7] I. Kant, *Opus Posthumum,* a. a. O., p. 3.
[8] *Ibid.,* p. 10.
[9] *Ibid.,* p. 13.
[10] *Ibid.,* p. 17.

Years ago, in a kind of stroll through modern philosophy entitled *The Old-age Wisdom of Modern Philosophers,* Max Ettlinger demonstrated that many important modern philosophers undergo a change of attitude in old age. Almost universally, the wisdom of age leads men to revoke their extreme protests against faith and to attempt to reconcile themselves to it again. Fichte's own son, J. H. Fichte, in a paper which critically tests the foundations of Idealism, (and which is still not nearly as well known as it deserves to be) paves the way for a clear faith in God. J. H. Fichte points out that above all Hegel's philosophy with its equating of God and world really is a cancellation of God that no dialectical mediation can justify, a cancellation which naturally disrupts man's religious-ethical movement toward God.

8.   *The dialectical philosophy of Hegel*

HEGEL'S FUNDAMENTAL RELIGIOUS DECISION

Through the argument for dialectical materialism runs a strange contradiction: it simply equates every form of idealism with religion, thereby damning it; yet that same dialectical materialism proudly acknowledges as its intellectual forebear the philosopher whose philosophy is considered the fulfillment of idealism.   In Lenin this contradiction is already clearly visible.

With his usual thoroughness Lenin himself studied Hegel's philosophy as the indispensible foundation of Marxism.   Later as dictator he demanded a solid knowledge of Hegel from all Communist intellectuals even while violently condemning every form of idealism. It is too easy to pass over this contradiction with the remark that dialectical materialism is interested only in the dialectical *method* of Hegel (which, incidentally, Marx had to revise entirely).   Such a crude presentation is far more apt to obscure the connections that really exist than to discover them.

Hegel's far-reaching influence by no means ended with the destruction of idealistic philosophy in the generation after the Master.   On the contrary, though altered, it is still very much alive, and its influence on current intellectual problems remains powerful. Hegelian philosophy is such a self-willed and sweeping innovation, that to come to grips with it intelligently it is always necessary to return to the beginning.   To be sure, such a discussion cannot proceed in the manner that is usual with philosophies that accept the principle of contradiction as the basis of existence and thought. Hegel's principle of dialectics nips in the bud every attempt at genuine confrontation and criticism.   His system presents a well rounded, self-contained unit throughout which a primary judgment is operative.   For from the philosophical viewpoint, Hegel's dialectic is what Richard Kroner calls a revolutionary act, "since it revolutionized all areas of philosophy, leaving no thought unturned." When we seriously examine the positions so far taken to the logical and ontological principles of the Hegelian system, we come away with the dubious impression that here no real dialogue ever took place.   Instead, one standpoint was simply set up against another. There is certainly no getting at Hegel this way, for dialectical exchange is the soul of his system.   More attention should be paid to Hegel's opening remark in the first *Systematic Program of German Idealism* (which appeared in the early summer of 1796) to the effect that henceforth all metaphysics will fall to morality.

The only way criticism can avoid talking round the whole problem of dialectical materialism rather than tackling it is to leave the system as a whole, and to pull out from under it one by one the primary judgments on which it stands.   These will most likely prove to be of a religious nature because until he was thirty, Hegel was a theologian.   So far, however, the fact of Hegel's religious background has not been used to full advantage.   Twice in almost identical words in his aphorisms of the Jena period he asserts that, "for the public" philosophy is an ersatz for lost religion. As we shall see later, not only for the public but for Hegel himself, philosophy was a substitute for lost religion.   But in his case can one really speak of a lost religion?   Has not the whole of Christianity with all its teachings been taken care of by his system?   It certainly is—in all the ambiguousness of the phrase.

Since Herman Nohl's publication of *Hegel's Early Theological Writings* (1907) and the previously mentioned documents on Hegel's development by Johannes Hoffmeister, we are in a much better position to understand Hegel's fundamental religious decision and to follow its development to a solid intellectual system.   Moreover, this material has already been interpreted in a series of studies and its main ideas illuminated.   Although these studies approach Hegel from completely different angles, their findings converge on the important points. From the masses of intellectual raw material with which young Hegel struggled comes the amorphous literary style which bespeaks its many unconscious and unresolved contradictions; one can observe patterns of thought slowly crystallize, sometimes after years of rumbling ferment. From these patterns emerge the guidelines for a first tentative program.

The first of young Hegel's deeply formative experiences came from his family and religion. Religion was the strongest force in his upbringing and it remained influential also in the decisions of the nature man. Characteristically, *Early Theological Writings* begins: " Religion is one of the most important concerns of our lives.... Already as children we are taught to stammer prayers to the godhead...when we mature, preoccupation with religion fills a good part of our lives. " [1] In the process of attaining intellectual maturity Hegel was confronted by the personal need to come to grips with the powers of religion, which until then were his merely by heritage. To be sure, his *Early Theological Writings* are not really a profession of his own religious development. Nonetheless, as Asveld points out, beneath the general considerations the sharp ear can detect an undertone of deep resentment against the Christian Church that is soon to become the constant accompaniment of Hegel's religious judgments.

From various hints we can safely guess that from early youth and well into maturity Hegel suffered from a profound and perfectly natural resentment that was fed by unfortunate clashes with paternal and school authority. During the years at the *Tuebinger Stift* he was constantly reading Rousseau in the hope, as a former classmate reports, " of thus ridding himself of certain prejudices and tacit assumptions " or, as Hegel himself puts it, of " shaking off his chains. " He also took particular pleasure in the Book of Job because of its natural and unrestricted language. Hegel considers God's " primary right over us, " in view of which we owe him " the duty of our obedience, " a kind of coercion from which one can

---

[1] *Hegels Theologische Jugendschriften.* Edited by H. Nohl (1907), p. 3. See Translator's Note of *The Phenomenology of Mind* (Macmillan, 1955). Nohl printed in footnotes passages written, then deleted by Hegel. These are not included in the English edition.

never escape. The "positive religion" to which the Christian finds himself coerced is necessarily accompanied by the loss of intellectual freedom. "This is the point from which all belief or unbelief in a positive religion takes its departure...one may be unconscious of this fact, yet it remains the cause of all servility or refractariness."[2] A positive religion, such as the Christian religion, claims to be founded on historical facts, on the "Word of God decreed to men in historical time and demanding acceptance in the obedience of faith." However, in the spirit of the Enlightenment, Hegel rejects on principle the historical argument, which claims "that a particular (for instance, the Christian) religion is such a God-given religion." Once we acknowledge our "servitude," we renounce our "right to demand intrinsic reasons that can stand on their own reasonableness."

According to Hegel church authority weighs so heavily on its members that it suppresses "even such doubts as spring from our understanding and reason." Church doctrines "are armed with all the terrors of the imagination"; they "are capable of paralyzing all the powers of the soul." Because the teachers of the church are simultaneously its officials they are (in Hegel's eyes an annihilating accusation) mere "servants...not masters, not lawgivers but those obedient to a foreign will."

SELF-LIBERATION FROM THE FEAR OF SIN

One can only interpret Hegel's drive to freedom as self-liberation from an ominous burden. The grave danger which Hegel was convinced threatened him proved to be Lutheran Christianity's anguished doctrine of sin. According to this doctrine, man, corrupted by original sin, has lost his freedom and can reassure himself only through faith in a merciful God. Ephraim too sees liberation from Christian fear as the goal of all Hegel's striving. This goal he pursues at all costs oblivious of the contradictions that result.

[2] *Hegels Theologische Jugendschriften*, p. 234.

Basically it was "fear of fear" which prompted Hegel to oppose his ideal of freedom to the idea of a personal God who rewards and punishes, a God who as the supreme value demands unconditional love from man, his creature, and who threatens "to punish disobedience with everlasting punishment." Who would not react to ever newly aroused fear of unworthiness by flying to the means of grace proffered by the very doctrine which makes these terrors known to us—who would not in that moment of fearful catastrophe in which he not only takes leave of everything he ever held dear, but in which he knows that within minutes or hours he will behold no longer the brightness of this sun "but of the Judge's throne before which his eternal fate will be decided—who would not in that moment of dreadful expectancy arm himself with all available accoutrements of solace?" For Hegel the "torments of hell" are "religious excesses of the imagination... outbursts of the sorest, most anguished despair, which disturb man's faculties and often cause permanent damage." On the other hand, Hegel knows "that the expectation of reward and punishment in another world...is based on reason's practical need to 'establish' the connection between this and another life, and that this doctrine has been a major point of all religions." [3]

The fear of God which the Bible praises as "the beginning of wisdom," which Aeschylus, Plato, and the great teachers of Christianity considered prerequisite to man's conscious attempt to lead a moral and fully human life, apparently had such a terrifying and pathogenic effect on young Hegel that it caused him to discard all faith in a personal God.

In Hegel's *Early Theological Writings* we find Nietzsche's main argument against Christianity: that to be a religion of salvation it had to frighten man, to make and keep him sick so that he is always in need of divine medicine. First it disquieted the conscience so that later "it could rescue the disquieted conscience." Thus countless misunderstandings about man's inclinations and impulses came into being, so that "instead of rich emotions we have jaded emotionalism and empty talk." Pluck, confidence, and self-respect were shattered, to be replaced by "false humility and a spiritual

---

[3] *Ibid.*, p. 55.

pride constantly preoccupied with itself and its impulses and forever prattling about its feelings, victories, and frightening temptations. " Hegel even claims that religious handbooks were obviously written not to impart a knowledge of religion but only to create certain states of soul. It is all so confused that " anyone who examines these things by daylight and with sound eyes must be embarrassed. " Admittedly, the grossest abuses were beginning to die down, but an enormous amount of this spirit still remained. Just as excessive authority in the rearing of children only causes disobedience and sullen stubbornness, a religion too that " ties a man eternally to its apron strings " is " more likely to cause bitterness. "

When Hegel speaks of bitterness against church authority, he certainly speaks from painful experience. His own bitterness was so deep that in his radical efforts to free himself from it he sacrificed the main tenets of Christianity. Understandably enough young Hegel's growing urge to freedom was further stimulated by the catchword of the times, " Revolution! "

The ideas of the French Revolution thundered across the border into Germany inflaming university students everywhere. That those at the *Tuebinger Stift* were no exception we know from documents written by their contemporaries. A political club was founded at the *Stift;* French newspapers were subscribed to. Soon even feuds arose. Hegel is reported to have been one of the wildest champions of liberty: " As long as the sun has stood in the firmament and the planets have circled round it, nothing like it has ever been seen! " Step by step Hegel proceeded to make the idea of liberty the " basic element, " indeed, the " sole stuff " of his philosophy.

REVOLUTIONARY PHILOSOPHY

The amazement of former classmates of Hegel at his sudden fame in the field of philosophy despite the lack of talent he exhibited at school is revealing. It confirms that it was not a natural interest in speculative thought that made Hegel a philosopher, but the practical need to liberate himself from " chains. " Joachim Ritter observes: " The event that was the focal point of all Hegel's philosophizing. . .was the French Revolution, and there is no second philosophy that is so much and so completely a philosophy of revolution as Hegel's. " [4]

Initial enthusiasm for the French Revolution was dampened by the Terror, which obviously also was a part of the Revolution, as were the political events known collectively as " the Restoration. " But these in no way diminished the fervor of Hegel's espousal of the Revolution. To the end of his life he stuck unequivocally to his position. In his opinion, it was through the French Revolution that political liberty, that is to say, human rights, and with them man's opportunity for self-realization, first became the principle and the goal of society and of the state. He was convinced that any legal and constitutional order of the future would have to take as its point of departure the Revolution's universal principle of liberty which Hegel accepted as " absolutely consistent with his conviction that the permanent substance of world history was attaining political self-realization through the Revolution in spite of the ' impotent resistance ' of the Restoration. The Restoration was fundamentally wrong to the extent that it undertook to restore institutions and positive rights that conflict with the principle of the rights and liberties for all established by the Revolution. " When it is not restoration but revolution that is the principle of history the preservation of obsolete rights and privileges becomes the real danger, the great cleaver of the present, which must be overcome in a new unity.

The first great revolution succumbed to a counterrevolution only because it had not gone deep enough, Hegel continues. Hence the basic need to develop a theory of revolution that would be conducive to realization through action. This is the problem that is to become decisive in Left-Hegelian thought and that both Heine and Marx are convinced is fundamental. Thence Marx's claims that thorough Germany cannot revolt without revolting thoroughly, and that the emancipation of the German is the emancipation of mankind. The head of this emancipation, Marx declares, is philosophy.

[4] J. Ritter, *Hegel und die Franzoesische Revolution* (1957), p. 24.

Hegel's revolutionary will to freedom so permeated his thought that it continued to activate his philosophy even in its mature form.   Hegelian philosophy is and remains quite literally a philosophy of revolution; revolution is its point of departure and its sustenance.   Nothing is more characteristic of Hegel's development than the positive stand he takes to revolution, a stand that determines his growth from beginning to end.   It was this that stamped the religious experience of Hegel's youth.   With this radical application of revolution as a world view Hegel could not help but interpret " positive Christianity " with its faith in a personal God as the true enemy.   Even at the high point of his life the struggle with traditional Christianity remained in the foreground, a struggle in which Hegel received essential support from liberal rationalistic theology's methods of reinterpretation, and from the idea of autonomy in Kant's practical philosophy.   True, Hegel rejected the essential tenets of true Christianity, but he did not simply negate them, he reinterpreted them in a monistic fashion.   During his year-long attempts at such reinterpretation, the main lines of his own system became increasingly clear.   Hegel's notion of morally liberated man's independence from God, his proud refusal to depend on grace, his possession of an incontestable claim to bliss through obedience to the moral law—this is the basis of Hegel's struggle against Christianity.

When Hegel calls the Christian religion with its faith in a personal God unnatural, he is appealing to a much invoked principle of Enlightened thought, " human nature. "   To what he considers " the theological prejudice " (the notion of man's inborn corruptibility) Hegel opposes " the indestructible goodness of human nature. "   With the philosophers of the Enlightenment he distinguishes " natural religion, " of which there can be only one since human nature is but one, from " positive religions, " all of which are unnatural accretions of natural religion.   In the process he changes Enlightenment's concept of the one universal human nature so radically as to render the old definition invalid.   In Hegel's *Early Theological Writings* we read: " The concept of human nature no longer suffices; freedom of the will must become the sole criterion. "   This change in Hegel's attitude is due to the influence of Kant.   For Kant's " autonomy of the will, " on which alone true morality should stand, Hegel substitutes Enlightenment's principle of nature. He even goes much further than Kant and polemicizes increasingly against him. Kant always remained aware of the danger to man from the deep-rooted evil within him and recognized only a damaged human freedom. He firmly believed in " the awful majesty of God " which transcends human morality and he therefore attempted to disquiet men's consciences for their own good, whereas Hegel, in an attempt to quiet them, recast Kant's thought into a tool with which to break what he considered the chains of religious and church tutelage. Through Hegel's endorsement of the moral impera- tive rings pride in man's self-established freedom. He no longer sees the connection that Kant saw between " our lower degree as creatures " and " moral necessity. " In his emphasis on freedom Hegel practically ignores the possibility that through lack of moral responsibility man can miss the good, that both he and his works can become evil. So convinced is Hegel of the fundamental goodness of human nature that for him it is self-understood that man is capable of preserving his goodness unaided. Hegel entirely over- looks the fact that human freedom includes also the freedom to sin. For him freedom is a positive absolute value that knows no evil. That is why he is also convinced that religious freedom needs to be protected only from external dangers.

Hegel aims his polemics above all against Kant's concept of duty, which he considers a kind of " servitude under a law of its own. " He speaks condescendingly of " the coercion of Kantian virtue. " So long as law and justice remain superior instances with the power to curtail man's freedom, Hegel complains, the supremacy of life is not yet guaranteed, hence no " return to life " is possible. A man's destiny is a totality which naturally corrects itself. After a period of disorder and fragmentation it is quite capable of returning to order and wholeness. With his concept the notion of " the bad conscience " disappears.

Hegel sees the essence of the beautiful soul in its complete self- centeredness whereas subjugation to any external power whatsoever is the mark of ugliness. Although " the beautiful soul cannot live without sinning, " invariably it returns " through love to its beauty. " By love Hegel means essentially self-love or love of one's own fate.

He interprets also God's love monistically: "To love God is to feel oneself part of life's infinitude. " [5]

From this standpoint Hegel discards objective religion, granting validity only to subjective religion. "What virtuous men must have is subjective religion; their objective religion can be of any kind; it matters little. " [6]

Man's ego becomes its own lawmaker and judge: "What man may well call his ego, that which is beyond the reach of the grave and decay, can determine its own self-earned reward; it is capable of judging itself. It proclaims itself as reason, whose laws are sufficient unto themselves and whom no other authority on earth or in heaven can supply with any other norm of judgment. " [7] Thus every kind of service to God, which is an acknowledgment of a personal God, is dismissed as fundamentally servile and ugly. Hegel proclaims this opinion repeatedly. It is the reason why he rejects Judaic religion in the harshest terms. Ultimately in Hegel the reality of an absolute, self-contained and self-existent God fades to an immanent idea of the infinite.

Hegel draws the consequences for Christianity with unmistakable clarity. In his opinion the Christian has been talked into believing that his corrupted being is incompatible with the idea of holiness, which therefore must be attributed only to a distant Being. The Christian's "degradation of human nature" does not permit us to recognize ourselves in virtuous men. Now, however, after long depriving himself of virtues he attributed solely to divinity, autonomous man has the right and duty to demand them back, among others the virtue of holiness. "Although there have been some attempts—at least theoretically—to claim the treasures squandered on heaven and to make them man's property once more, this task has been reserved primarily for our own day. But when will man have the strength to validate his claim and take possession? " [8] This certainly sounds as though Hegel were calling for disciples with the courage to carry out the great liberation by Titanic action. Can the Left Hegelians be blamed for overstepping the limits laid

[5] F. Hegel, *Early Theological Writings* (New York: Macmillan Co., 1955), p. 247.
[6] *Hegels Theologische Jugendschriften*, p. 10.
[7] *Ibid.*, p. 89.
[8] F. Hegel, *Early Theological Writings*, p. 159.

down elsewhere by the Master because they felt the time had come to shift from the intellectually completed revolution to its political and social realization? How can anyone still claim that a real break separates Hegel from Feuerbach, Nietzsche, and Marx?

The prevailing interpretation of the Christian history of salvation is also based on the new revolutionary philosophy. Thus for Hegel faith in Christ becomes " faith in a personified ideal. " Religious faith is even described as a " lack of confidence in the notion that reason is absolute, perfect in itself, and that its infinite idea must be created by reason free from any foreign admixture. " The principle of the immanence of reason leads inevitably to the conclusion that the wills of God and man are mutually exclusive: " two autonomous wills, two substances cannot exist. God and man must be one, " Hegel states unequivocally in *Early Theological Writings,* and a paper entitled *The Life of Jesus* opens with the programmatic words: " Pure boundless reason is itself the Godhead. "

Hegel's crass rejection of a personal God is reflected in his deprecating remarks about the God of the Old Testament, whom he calls " a demon of hate. " Hegel describes the essence of the Jewish religion as total lack of love. Judaism is the exact opposite of the religion of humanitarianism; it is a religion born of misery for misery; hence Jewish history was to become " the most unholy frenzy, the wildest fanaticism. "

In Hegel's *Fragment of the System of 1800* the process of reducing God to a mere idea is perfected and brought to a close. In the concept of religion which is presented here God no longer appears at all. " Life as the infinite existence of the living " has replaced him. According to Hegel religion is that which exalts man from finite existence to infinite.

Hegel explains that it was possible for Christianity to be accepted and to spread in the Roman Empire only because the people of that time were " supremely corrupt and of the profoundest moral impotency. " They thirsted for blind obedience. Today the time has come " to acknowledge joyfully as our own creation what is rightfully ours and to make it our own: the beauty of human nature, which we ourselves have implanted in men by shielding them from

all the loathsomeness of which nature is capable." [9]   Today
" Christians are right back where the Jews once were. What was
characteristic of the Jewish religion, namely, subjection to the law
from which Christians had once ardently hoped to escape, is again
to be found in the Christian Church " [10] for " the Christian religion
preaches a moral law that exists outside ourselves. ... "

" FATE " INSTEAD OF GOD

For Hegel " fate " or " destiny " takes over the regimen of the
world in the stead of the deposed personal God; Greek fatalism is
idealized to a brilliant harmony. Hegel does not yet suspect that
the ultimate consequences of fatalism lead to the absolute opposite
of the absolute human freedom he demands and thereby abrogates
it. The first *Systematic Program of German Idealism* written in
the spring of 1796 clearly expresses Hegel's basic notion of the
absolutely free ego. " The initial idea is naturally the concept *of
myself* as an absolutely free being. Together with the free self-
conscious being a whole *world* emerges out of nothingness—the only
true and conceivable creation out of nothingness. "

Equally clear is the demand for radical revolution: " Overthrow
of all sham belief, persecution of the priesthood—lately feigning
reason—through reason itself. Absolute freedom of all who have
the spiritual world within them and who ought not to seek God
and immortality *outside* themselves. " Hegel concludes with a hymn
of ardent eschatological faith in the ultimate goal: " Then everlasting
concord will reign among us. ... Then universal freedom and spiritual equality will prevail! " These are the new glad tidings. " A
heaven-sent higher spirit must establish this new religion among us;
this will be mankind's last and greatest achievement. " [11]

Obviously Hegel himself feels called to establish this ultimate

[9] *Hegels Theologische Jugendschriften*, p. 71.
[10] F. Hegel, *Early Theological Writings*, p. 139.
[11] J. Hoffmeister, *Dokumente zu Hegels Entwicklung* (1936), p. 219.

religion of absolute freedom. Jesus Christ was only an enthusiastic " dreamer, " though he too strove at least part of the time, for the great goal of freedom. " Jesus' existence was one of separation from the world and flight from the world into heaven. " For this reason Hegel was convinced that his philosophy should replace the religion of Jesus. Later Nietzsche spoke openly of his own vocation to be the founder of a new religion that would perfect what Jesus " the dreamer " had not been able to perfect.

The new religion of absolute freedom completely changes man's position in the world. By its own inner consistency such freedom leads to the exact opposite: to the determining of man's position by a world process. Once objective moral law has been consumed by the immanence of the absolutely free ego, moral evil loses the absolute earnestness of offence and the nature of " sin. " Sin becomes merely a partial and temporary disloyalty to the self and to the intrinsic wholeness of life, which as such tends to press for new union. Relative evil assumes the task of quickening the flow of becoming. Thus personal " history, " until now a history of the individual's decision for or against God made in the presence of God and hence a decision of absolute importance, fades away. The life of the individual dwindles to a more or less noteworthy but basically substitutable medium for the great process of world history in which the absolute spirit of the world comes into its own. In this notion of the relativity of morality lies the germ of the Hegelian dialectic which unmistakably proclaims itself in Hegel's early writings and which he later broadens to include man and the world. Thus irreconcilable opposites are seemingly reconciled.

In Kant the placating of the conscience was only a side effect of man's infinitely moral effort. Consciousness of the impossibility of ever living a life that is entirely just in the sight of God held the conscience with its awareness of the personal responsibility involved in every act tightly spanned and sensitive. In Hegelian thought with its removal of the polarity of good and evil, personal history ceases to exist. Thus extreme individualism calls its own opposite upon the scene. It is as though true dialectics avenged themselves for being forced to oscillate between unrealistic extremes.

Although the " process " of world history unfolds in a dialectical back and forth, it moves stubbornly and irresistibly towards its goal of absolute self-consciousness. With this, authentic history, in which free beings freely participate, degenerates to a mere "process," even though according to Hegel's optimistic enlightened faith it leads to the apogee of fulfillment. No longer is the world reluctant raw material for duty. Instead, rational ideas are automatically consummated by the unwinding of history.

HEGEL'S PERFECTION OF IDEALISM

In *Faith and Knowledge,* which appeared in 1802, Hegel attempts to complete and strengthen the incomplete and in some respects decadent idealism of Kant, Jacobi, and Fichte. This publication with its unmistakable bias has to this day received too little attention. Hegel's aim is to give his philosophy the last word on what he calls the old antagonism between reason and faith. The then current forms of idealism, as formulated by Kant, Jacobi, Fichte, had partly but not entirely resolved that antagonism. To be sure, positive religion had been assimilated by philosophy. No one any longer spoke of reason as "the handmaid of religion." On the contrary, Hegel observes, philosophy has invincibly asserted "her absolute autonomy," so that even discussion with positive religion on "miracles and so forth, is now considered something outmoded and obscure." Not even Kant had any luck with his attempt to reinstate what remained of positive religion. Yet the subjection of religion was never total. Imperceptibly the vanquished regained authority over the victor. Therefore Hegel was determined to do away entirely with the "bastard" of a religion of Enlightenment in order that reason alone might hold sway.

The fact that reason still considered religion something positive although not idealistic was for Hegel proof of the decline of reason, which thus admitted the existence of a better, transcendental world "in a faith outside and beyond reason itself." This is precisely what had taken place in the philosophies of Kant, Jacobi, and Fichte ("to the degradation of philosophy," which thus again became the handmaid of religion.) According to these philosophers, the absolute is something that transcends reason. This Hegel decries. He shifts the absolute, placing it within the bounds of reason. As long as Enlightenment considers the eternal possible " only in the beyond, " the victory of Enlightenment is only half a victory. Since agnosticism had hitherto renounced attainment of the absolute because of the limitations of reason, only the subjectivity of desire and intuition remained to conjure up illusions of the infinite. This is why the prevailing idealistic philosophies are inadequate and must be replaced by a totally idealistic philosophy. This is the next step, which the *Weltgeist* is about to take. That World Spirit's great principle, simultaneously " the principle of the north and—religiously speaking—of Protestantism " is subjectivism. As long as religion objectified itself it remained bound to superstition and evil. By its " flight from the finite " *(Flucht aus dem Endlichen)* religion objectified its own ideas, thereby degrading ideals to mere fantasies. Thus religion fell victim to an " unreal game. "

When the time came, " infinite longings. . .made their peace with existence " and plunged into the empirical world. The fixed point of departure is " the empirical subject and that to which it is reconciled, the ordinary world which it thus dares to trust and surrender itself to without sin. " What Hegel criticizes as a basic lack in previous idealistic philosophies is that they permit " the absolute opposition of the finite and the infinite to remain. " In those philosophies " the purely abstract has not yet been attained, the concept of the infinite has not yet been clearly posited. " Whereas pre-Hegelian philosophers still held to the principle of contradiction which hindered them from equating the finite with an absolute (to be sought beyond the world), the whole purpose of Hegel's dialectical philosophy was to eliminate the principle of contradiction and to incorporate contradiction into his system. According to Hegel, an absolute philosophy of concepts is possible only when for the concept " the empirical is simultaneously an absolute something and an absolute nothing. " Hegel is convinced that by such absolute immanence the tortuous longing of man's better nature for a transcendent absolute may be overcome. Hitherto our better nature, tormented by such limitedness or by absolute contradiction, expressed itself in longing and in attempts to believe in a beyond, that is to say, beyond that limitedness. It was not possible to exalt one's self, to attain to absolute self-content " in the clear and desireless realm of reason itself. "

Previous idealistic philosophy, Hegel points out, portrayed man with a melancholy smile on his lips, yet gods exalted above longing and melancholy were not permitted. In this philosophy man " bears inextricably deep in his flesh the arrow of absolute opposites. " However touchingly the resources of sentimental art may portray human longing, such works are but " sops for reality. " People who are inwardly so divided are like bats, " which are neither bird nor beast and belong neither to earth nor to heaven. " Sentimental, transcendent beauty " is not without ugliness, such morality not wihout weakness and meanness, such understanding not without triteness; as for the happiness and unhappiness involved, the former is not without baseness, the latter not without fear and cowardice, both not without despicableness. " [12]

Unquestionably, here lie the roots of the doctrine that later Nietzsche was to formulate and that has been echoed and re-echoed ever since: Brothers, stay true to earth! With it the longing for fulfillment and bliss in the beyond is deprecated and becomes something inferior. As long as the finite posits a relationship to the infinite, " this infinite is itself not the true [infinite] since it is incapable of consuming the finite. " This is what absolute idealistic philosophy aims at: in it " the finite and the infinite are One in the Idea, hence finiteness—to the extent that it possesses of and in itself truth and reality—disappears. The only thing that exists in itself is the abstract concept. " [13]

It is only in this closed circle of the world-in-itself that Hegel sees idealism perfected; his fundamental criticism of the philosophies of Kant, Jacobi, and Fichte is based on this concept. For the purpose of this book it suffices to present briefly the main points of Hegel's criticism of Kant.

Hegel concedes that Kant's is a philosophy of critical idealism because it makes " unity of reflection supreme, " but he criticizes Kant's philosophy for treating the most exalted idea that it produced

[12] F. Hegel, *Saemtl. Werke*, ed. Glockner, I Bd. (1958), p. 292.
[13] *Ibid.*, p. 285.

as "hairsplitting" or an unnatural schoolboy trick of culling reality out of concepts and setting up the resultant philosophy as a postulate. Consequently Kantian philosophy remains locked in opposites. Because that philosophy "declares finite knowledge as the only possible knowledge...it relapses into absolute finiteness and subjectivity."

In view of this Hegel demands a philosophy of absolute identity, the sole idea of which is "the absolute of opposites. And this absolute identity is...the only true reality." For Hegel only such a philosophy of absolute identity is idealism. His philosophy takes as its point of departure the principle "of the truly necessary, absolute, original identity" and is thus compelled to that dialectic which adopts contradiction as the fundamental law of being and of thinking. With this, empirical consciousness is endowed with reason itself as the true *an sich*. In Kant "absolute dualism remains; it has not yet been suspended." Kant still distinguishes man's finite thought from the "primary intuitive understanding of a God." In Kantian philosophy antinomies such as freedom and necessity remain. The absolute thought of Hegel insists on clearing out these contradictions. For him "reason should at the same time have absolute reality," an idea which supposedly "suspends all opposition between freedom and necessity." Thus infinite thought becomes absolute reality or the absolute identity of thought and existence.

Without going into each of Hegel's arguments in detail, let us call attention here to one result of Hegelian thought, a result which Hegel himself saw clearly. Where his conception is taken seriously, the historical process of absolute thought and becoming completely absorbs the individual with his freedom, kneading him into the collective historical process. The individual revolts against this in what Fichte calls aversion and horror. Sharply Hegel castigates such revolt: "What monstrous arrogance, what insane presumption of the ego to dread, despise, and bewail the idea of being one with the universe, the idea that eternal nature acts in you; you despise, dread, and bewail the resolve to submit yourself to the eternal laws of nature and her strict and holy necessity; to despair at not being free, free from nature's eternal laws and strict necessity; to believe that such obedience would make man unspeaka-

bly wretched—this requires the basest view of nature, a view devoid
of all reason, a view to which the absolute identity of subject and
object is totally unknown, a view the principle of which is absolute
nonidentity. " [14]   Hegel's philosophizing, a kind of absolute and
revolutionary *Weltanschauung*, began with the will to liberate man
from the personal tyrant-God and to demand absolute freedom for
man. Yet his absolute philosophy of reason ends with man's far
more radical enslavement. No amount of strong language against his
opponents could hinder one of Hegel's own students from becoming
his sharpest critic and from taking the despised and rejected
category, individualness, *(" Einzelnheit")* seriously again. That
student was Sören Kierkegaard.

At the end of his essay, *Faith and Knowledge*, Hegel discusses
unequivocally where " this whole revolution in philosophy " is
leading. This philosophy of absolute identity of being and thinking
must continue on its way, simply ignoring as one ignores a temporary difficulty, " the infinite pain " on which the religion of the
modern age is based—" the feeling that God himself is dead. "
However, as a part of this philosophy with its " concept of absolute
freedom " is man's tragic dichotomy, " the absolute suffering " of
a " speculative Good Friday, " unavoidable consequence of the
harshness of man's godlessness.

What Hegel touches on in *Faith and Knowledge* he develops
in *Phenomenology of Mind*. In this work certain hints—usually
misunderstood—become intelligible only in the context of Hegel's
intellectual development, which we have attempted to sketch. For
Hegel faith in the personal, transcendant God of revealed religion
is still the faith of an " unhappy self-consciousness. " The figures
of a preliminary spirituality " crowd expectantly round the cradle
of the spirit to be born as consciousness "; the pain and longing
of the unhappy consciousness, which grips everyone, is " both
common center and common birthpang. Its oneness is that of the
pure concept, which includes the waiting figures as its moments. " [15]
This growth must pass through pain, which expresses itself in the

---

[14] *Ibid.*, p. 417 f.
[15] F. Hegel, *Phaenomenologie des Geistes, Werke*, ed. Glockner, II Bd.
(1951), p. 574.

harsh word that God has died. "This death, then, is his birth as spirit."

In this Hegel hints at the death of a divine mediator, necessary if the spirit is to possess itself on a higher plane. What dies is not self-consciousness as such; rather "its particularness fades away in its generalness." And again, "The voluntary death of the mediator is the cancellation of his...particular self-existence... [which] has now become general consciousness." [16] The so-called death of the concept is simultaneously the death of the abstraction of divine being that is not posited as self. This is the painful sensation of the unhappy self-consciousness, the feeling that God himself has died. This is the harsh expression of the inmost self's knowledge of its oneness, the return of the consciousness to the deep night of the ego, an ego that no longer differentiates or knows anything outside itself." [17]

Allusions to "the death of God" are to be found also in other works of Hegel. For him "God's death" is a necessary moment in the process of the absolute spirit's becoming conscious of itself. As long as man believes in a personal transcendent God his self-consciousness will be split and unhappy. According to Hegel this disastrous dichotomy can be overcome only by man's complete identification of himself with God. In the process, the old God dies.

As we have seen, Hegel's intellectual revolution began with the fundamental religious decision he made against a personal God. The principle of dialectics made possible the suspension of Christian faith (instead of the radical denial of God which logically follows) by positing the philosophy of a World Spirit coming into its own in the world process; God is not simply cancelled, he is "only" radically reinterpreted. No longer is there a God who transcends time and space, all becoming and all sin; no absolute, divine opposite for man awakened to himself as person. God is identical with the world. Never complete, he is forever in the process of becoming. Only at the completion of the world process will absolute thought *(das absolute Denken)* have come entirely into its own. The dialectic between finite and infinite is annulled. Noetically

[16] *Ibid.*, p. 597.
[17] *Ibid.*, p. 598.

and ontically God and man are posited as one; human thought becomes the stage for infinite thought; only in man does the absolute attain self-consciousness. God and man are one and the same since God " is " God only to the extent that he attains consciousness of himself in man.

A further consequence of this oneness of God and man is that the world's becoming is identified with the self-becoming of the absolute spirit. Thus the infinite Creator becomes finite, while the creature is divinized. Titan-fashion, says Erich Przywara, Hegel with his identity of opposites usurps the very ground of God by laying hand on the inner rhythm of divine life.

We must leave it to the direct disciples of Hegel, to Bauer, Marx, Heine and Feuerbach. They read and understood their Hegel better than the generation that followed them. They recognized in his philosophy of absolute identity of thought and being the most radical closing of the world upon itself, and the foundations for an atheism which they needed only to translate into simpler language for popular consumption. Logically developing Hegel's implications, Eric Voegelin remarks openly: " Systematized thought necessitates deicide; and vice versa, thought is systematized to commit deicide. " [18] Feuerbach did not have to abandon an idealism that he equated with religion in order to formulate his atheism. Rather the unbroken continuity of thought is so fundamental that the taproot of the whole lore of " the death of God " lies right here.

Hegel's own students considered the Master's ambiguous dialectical treatment of faith in God not only a self-contradiction, but also a cowardly conformity to the Restoration, which younger and bolder spirits should courageously ignore. Meanwhile Hegel himself apparently recoiled from the ultimate consequences of his thought. He had no wish to be an atheist and he refused to be a pantheist; in his last years he even considered it necessary to help much debilitated faith back on its feet by lecturing on the proofs of the existence of God. But even in this attempt he did not budge an inch from his basic idealistic position; hence his efforts were quite different from the medieval proofs, which attempted to lead the

---

[18] E. Voegelin, *Wissenschaft, Politik, und Gnosis* (1959), p. 83.

reality of the world and man to an ultimate, all-sustaining Ground.

As we have already pointed out, in Hegel's *Early Theological Writings* he declares that the most pressing task of the day is to demand back, " at least in theory, " the treasures man has squandered on heaven. Somewhat doubtfully he adds: " But what age will have the strength to enforce this right and take possession? " Hegel's disciples considered themselves called to this titanic undertaking.

9. *Hegel as the " Fate " of religion*

BRUNO BAUER'S PATH FROM THEOLOGIAN TO ATHEIST

Confronted with a choice between Schleiermacher and Neander on the one hand, and Hegel on the other, Bruno Bauer, a young student of Protestant Theology at the University of Berlin, chose Hegel as his master. For a time, Hegel (who died in 1831) and Schleiermacher held chairs together at the University. Each attracted enthusiastic devotees. However, the two masters were mutually exclusive. Complete surrender to the one meant remoteness from the other, for Schleiermacher could not have been more different from Hegel, both as a personality and as a scholar. Schleiermacher's appeal to the emotions was a world away from Hegel's determined will to solve the metaphysical enigma of the universe; Schleiermacher's religion seemed to dissolve in subjectiveness. We have Bauer's own testimony that he decided against joining Schleiermacher and Neander because as a follower of the positivist theological direction, he was not satisfied by them. Hegel attracted him because his novel system of thought seemed to give new foundations to the old religious truths which, denied or supplanted by new truths, were beginning to totter.

Upon Hegel's death Bauer considered it his vocation to carry out the work of strengthening the foundations of Christian faith by reinforcing them with the Hegelian system. Even in Hegel's lifetime several of his followers had assumed a more conservative attitude toward the Christian religion than Hegel's own. Hegel himself was not against having his system considered the long sought reconciliation between theology and philosophy. In the years following his death this interpretation of his system predominated.

On Easter 1834 the barely twenty-five-year-old Bauer was made licentiate of theology at the University of Berlin. The very next year, the appearance of a book at the *Tuebinger Stift* by David Friedrich Strauss entitled *The Life of Jesus, Critically Revised* split the university's Hegelians into two camps. Strauss himself labeled the conservative Hegelians the "Hegelian Right." It was the intention of this group, which had assimilated his principles, methods, and conclusions, to further "the genuine Hegel."

However, because of their Christian attitude, which they made a point of stressing, they omitted many of Hegel's remarks against the Jews and against Revelation. Above all, they attempted to justify anew the religion of the Old Testament, which Hegel's disparaging comparisons with Greek and Roman religions had devaluated. As an enthusiastic member of this group of Hegelians, Bauer had contributed articles to the *Journal for Speculative Theology* (1836-38) and had written a two-volume work, *The Religion of the Old Testament*. In these early writings of his, whenever Bauer went further than Hegel, his thinking was shared by all the other members of the "Hegelian Right."

Young Bauer differed clearly from his philosophical master in that for Bauer religion was not merely a process of subjective thought which relates itself to God, but equally a relationship in which God relates himself to the subjective mind. The God who created man before all time set history a specific goal, that of ever greater union with the subjective spirit. To be sure, Bauer's God departs from the Christian God inasmuch as he does not transcend time and space but rather is drawn into time, undergoing himself a process of development toward ever greater perfection until the divine spirit becomes one with the subjective spirit hitherto outside it. But precisely this inclusion of the absolute divine spirit in the immanent development of the world had to shatter the concept of the Lord of history, just as it had to relativate the absoluteness of Christianity, which Bauer originally accepted. Was not Christianity after all merely the apogee of man's conception of the divine, a high point beyond which evolution toward pure thought continually pressed?

Certain facts could not escape Bauer's attention for long; the fact that herewith all religion is brought to the point of ambiguous, equivocal annulment; that in Hegel's system all theology ultimately dissolves in philosophy; that the transcendent becomes the immanent; that the endless " evolution of the absolute spirit " must eventually force every type of Christianity into its exact dialectical opposite. Bauer was much too passionate a champion of the principle of criticism not to see through the sophistry of the Hegelian Right's apologetics.

His first challenging criticism in the form of a letter to the right-wing Hegelian, Hengstenberg, made Bauer's position at the University so difficult that in the fall of 1837 he was forced to exchange his lectureship for one at Bonn. However, by this time the conviction at which he had arrived, namely, that the dissolution and negation of the entire world of finite consciousness must be so penetrating and total that not an atom would remain untouched, was bound to attract negative attention. People were disturbed, even though Bauer took pains to reassure them that this dissolution would not damage Christianity; that on the contrary, only from the basis of total dissolution could the fullness of Christian truth radiate. The mistrust with which Bauer was received at Bonn and the consequent isolation forced upon him only hardened his attitude and led him to a determined stand diametrically opposed to the attitude of his previous assumptions, as he himself confides in a letter to his brother Edgar. Furthermore, Bauer's intense preoccupation with Hegel's philosophy of religion for a new edition on which he and Marheineke were working opened his eyes to Hegel's real and fundamental attitude beneath the touched-up version of the Right Hegelians.

As a consequence of Bauer's critical exposure of the Gospels as human makeshift, (which he begins with a critique of St. John and continues with a critique of the Synoptics), the rigid, inspirational concept of an absolute, transcendent and unchanging God who uses men as mere tools collapses, and with it, for Bauer, the whole concept of a personal Lord of the universe.

It is understandable that the dialectical about-face of this Right

Hegelian turned critical should drive Bauer into the arms of the
"younger Hegelian pack." Thus Bruno Bauer's religious decision
becomes more than a purely personal affair; it is typical of the
religious decision of Left Hegelians in general, and its effects
continued, ultimately bearing fruit in the atheism of Nietzche.

To the Left Hegelians, who were largely writers and journalists,
Bauer seemed a professional theologian. He possessed a thorough
knowledge of Hegel. He was personally deeply involved in the
decision which confronted the young intellectuals of his day as a
result of their choice of Hegelian philosophy. For Bauer the
religious issue was a profoundly disturbing problem with which
he wrestled passionately, albeit his passion was a flame which
negativistic criticism reduced to a heavily smoking flicker. Furthermore Bauer became addicted to the special debauchery of the cynic,
temple-desecration, which made his position on the theological
faculty at Bonn increasingly untenable. Finally, as the result of
a cynical *mardi gras* prank he was suspended. Bauer's tendency
to the negative might well have been augmented by resentment
over the loss of his lectureship. In addition his acquaintance with
Karl Marx drove him in a more radical direction. Bauer announced
in a letter to his "esteemed friend," Marx, his defense of his
position, "which is meant to settle the religious question with
finality and to take the present reactionaries by surprise." In this
self-termed "so very extreme" paper he tries to prove "that religion
is the hell of philanthropy and God the provost of that hell." [1]

Bauer's gradually solidifying philosophy may be summed up as
follows: "Divine power definitely does not exist. We have no
proof that such power ever interceded in the cause of history; at
any rate the existence of the transcendent would only curtail the
freedom of human self-consciousness. Hence explanations of all
spiritual phenomena, also religious phenomena, should be stated
purely and simply in human terms. In religion we are dealing
with a splitting of the self-consciousness, for in the religious
experience the *essential* certainty of the self-consciousness confronts
the consciousness as a new power, in other words: in the religious
experience a man empties himself of self. Thus every religion

---

[1] B. Bauer - anonym), *Die Posaune des juengsten Gerichts ueber Hegel den
Atheisten und Antichristen* (Leipzig, 1841).

merely testifies to the level which men had attained when that
religion flourished and it bears the stamp of the human spirit at
that time. At present the human spirit is developing steadily
upward...Christianity is undeniably the fulfillment of religion, but
religion is not absolute fulfillment; rather it is something to be
overcome.... The deepest and most dreadful alienation of the
self-consciousness as it occurs in Christianity (despite the fact that
of all religions Christianity comes closest to the truth), should teach
us to cherish truth, which is the freedom that consists in the ego's
knowing itself to be all things, including universal power. " [2]

After this " self-liberation, " Bauer was consumed by a violent
hatred of theologians, or in his own words, of " the " theologian.
Toward the end of Volume II of his work on the Synoptic Gospels
he insults all theologians. Bauer was to infect Nietzsche with his
almost hysterical emotionalism regarding them.

In this frame of mind, Bauer felt the need to settle accounts also
with Hegel, his philosophical master. Bauer was more familiar
than anyone with the story of Hegel's intellectual development, and
he knew Hegel's philosophy of religion intimately from years of
careful study. By a kind of inner necessity, disappointment had
turned the love and respect of the former disciple into hate. He
now felt impelled to demask Hegel. And indeed, Bauer's critique
ruthlessly tracks Hegel's intellectual motives to their hidden lair;
certainly no more thorough critique of his philosophy and religious
attitude has ever been written. To be sure, like all criticism born
of love-hate, Bauer's is one-sided and occasionally overshoots the
mark. In his interpretation of passages from Hegel certain details
are incorrect. But that Bauer's critique of Hegel presents the
decisive points with brutal clarity cannot be denied.

Bauer now set to work on a full-scale denunciation of Hegel,
as he himself describes it in a letter to his brother. His article
entitled *Theological Impertinances* which appeared in *The German
Yearbook* trembles with rage. Here prevailing Christian religion
is described as pure baseness and shamelessness since it denies the
fundamental duties of human nature: morality, freedom, and reason,
which are blindly sacrificed to faith. No wonder " the madman

---

[2] M. Kegel, *Bruno Bauer und seine Theorien ueber die Entstehung des
Christentums* (Abh. z, ihrer Gesch. 6. Heft, 1908), pp. 41 ff.

is terrified by reason, the inhuman being by humaneness!" But man's self-consciousness will establish its kingdom on this earth; to it belongs the future; it laughs to scorn faith's impotent attempts to prolong its dominion.

Bauer's critique of Hegel is contained in two papers, the first of which is harshly entitled, *The Trump of Doom on Hegel the Atheist and Antichrist.* The second, *Hegel's Doctrine of Art and Religion from the Standpoint of Faith,* goes even further in its denunciations. In the second article the religious decision treated in the first with tragic earnestness becomes an ironic force.

Unfortunately Bauer's *Trump* remained unknown, hence ineffective. In Prussia it was forbidden and was considered a purely ironical document not meant to be taken seriously. It was pointed out that all Bauer had really done was to play the Pietist, whose supposedly offended religious fervor had assembled all the passages in Hegel directed against Christianity and religion in order to condemn them. With this, the matter was dismissed. No judgment could be more false. Anything but a hastily scribbled pamphlet, Bauer's paper testifies to an exhaustive study of Hegel. For all its passion and at times fanatical exaggeration, it is thorough.

The opening passage on the duty of every man of good will to testify courageously to the power and truth of faith cannot simply be dismissed as derisive irony. Faith actually was Bauer's point of departure, which he originally took with deadly seriousness. When we consider that Bauer's early development passed through extreme contradictions which naturally left their mark on him although his character remained basically unchanged, it becomes clear that of all his works *The Trump* comes closest to being a document of honest wrestling with faith, whereas from this point on, the negative, disintegrating element in his criticism unquestionably takes over. Moreover, Bauer introduced a wealth of Biblical quotations with such adroitness that the whole paper gives the impression of a religious prophet's wrathful, flaming judgment.

We must not forget that this was an age enamored of dialectical irony; it loved to juggle with extremes, and it is often impossible to say where seriousness ends and irony begins. Precisely the exaggerated pathos of the fire and brimstone threats permits one to question the earnestness of the writer's indignation. On the other hand, perhaps he himself no longer quite knew how much of the rhetoric was sincere and to what extent he was already attracted by the other extreme and felt the need to shout down temptation. Although in this regard Bauer's *Trump of Doom* is suspect, this is no reason to reject his criticism of Hegel where it hits the mark. For over Hegel's philosophy of religion lie the thick veils of his dialectical thought made the thicker by his difficult language, so that many and serious efforts have not succeeded in lifting those veils and revealing what lies beneath. What Bauer has provided is a genuine psychoanalysis of Hegel's religious attitude. He uncovers the really effective underlying motives that led Hegel to his characteristic, fundamental decision as expressed in his philosophical system. One point stands out with astonishing clarity: the decisive importance of emotional and moral influences in the founding of Hegel's *Weltanschauung*, a point that is usually denied or dismissed as an unfair insinuation.

We must limit ourselves here to a few of Bauer's basic criticisms of Hegel. Bauer is among the first to appreciate " that Hegel considers the French Revolution, this product of an atheistic philosophy, history's greatest event. . .the redemption of mankind, and the deed by which philosophy has completely proved her vocation to dominate the world. " [3] Hegel " envies the French nation ' for the blood bath of her Revolution ' by which she ' has liberated herself from many established customs which the human spirit has outgrown as a child outgrows its shoes. Useless as such customs were, they had hampered her as they still hamper others. ' In Hegel's opinion these senseless fetters still weigh upon the German people, and all possible means must be taken to relieve them of their burden. ' However, Fatherland, princes, constitution, and so on do not seem to be the right levers with which to uplift the German people; the question arises, what would happen were religion to be attacked? Certainly nothing is more to be feared than this. The leaders are isolated from the people; they do not understand each other, and what the former are capable of this age has pretty well demonstrated. ' " [4]

Bauer continues: " Was this then the intention that he pursued

[3] B. Bauer, *Posaune*, ed. Loewith, p. 173.
[4] B. Bauer, *Hegels Lehre von der Rel. und Kunst*, p. 69.

with extraordinary consistency and energy all his life? As regards religion, did he desire to seize the Germans and lead them to 'the blood bath of the Revolution'? ... He thought like the French atheists, who likewise did not begin immediately with an attack on the established forms of government, but who, as one of their dogged enemies expresses it, chose religion as their hate's first victim in order to overthrow the throne more surely once religion had been removed. Enviously Hegel read the proclamation of the French people declaring Voltaire to be 'the first cause of that great Revolution which has struck all Europe with terror,' announcing that Voltaire has overthrown despotism's most dreaded defense, the forces of religion; for had he not broken their yoke, it would have been impossible to break the yoke of the tyrants. How Hegel would have loved to experience 'that happy moment' in which, like Lamettrie, he could cry, ' Philosophy has triumphed!' ' " [5]

Repeatedly Bauer mentions Voltaire's powerful influence on Hegel. After leaving the university young Hegel's favorite reading had been Voltaire's works. But although Hegel adopted the substance of his French master's teaching, he did not adopt Voltaire's tone of impudent self-confidence, knowing that this is no way to tempt " the stolid German people. " Hence the German philosopher expresses the same thing more cautiously, slyly, and elegantly. " With the calmness and steadiness of the German phlegm, he knew how to take the glowing hatred against Scripture and everything divine which he had received from his French master, and give it more solid foundations. " [6]

In the stand he takes against the Old Testament Hegel uses the same arguments as Voltaire. He attacks it first from the moral side, stressing as did Voltaire David's " countless atrocities, the gruesome acts of Samuel, " the abuses of the men of God in order to excuse human crimes. " After indicting religion on the grounds of immorality, he makes it even more difficult to defend her by saddling her with the further crime of being the enemy of art and beauty. " [7] Hegel's *Early Theological Writings* are heavy with the tendency to degrade the Old Testament and its history of salvation

[5] *Ibid.*, pp. 69 f.
[6] *Ibid.*, p. 71.
[7] *Ibid.*, p. 70.

in order to project in its place as the supreme ideal the Greek cult of the beautiful.

In tones of sharpest indignation Bauer decries Hegel as the German Voltaire whose aim is to expose Scripture as a lie. But the very sharpness of the indignation makes one suspicious. Is **Bauer** serious? Originally he probably was. But *les extrêmes se touchent,* and Bauer really does, himself, fall victim to the fascination of the other extreme, a lust for destructive criticism for which nothing remains sacred; he exalts criticism to a principle.

Bruno Bauer does not stop at the revelation of the basic motives of Hegel's philosophizing. He goes on to criticize the whole Hegelian system in the sharpest terms, first and foremost, Hegel's philosophy of religion.

If Hegel, says Bauer, prepared the downfall of religion (meaning above all, the Christian religion, which he considered an outgrown stage in the development of the human spirit), he hid his destructiveness behind a double veil. " With the critical blade of faith, " Bauer proposes " to cut that veil away. " The older Hegelians had not had the courage to penetrate to the danger point of Hegel's dialectic. They clung to the words of the Master. " Very often, countless times, practically on every page of his book on the philosophy of religion, Hegel mentions God, and invariably one gains the impression that he means the living God, who before the world began was the sole reality, who as the Three-in-one existed before the creation of the universe, and who revealed his love of men in Jesus Christ. " [8] However, it is not difficult to lift this outermost veil. " It falls of its own accord once we have demonstrated that the second veil, over the heart of the system, destroys itself by the negative dialectic of its own principle. This second veil consists in considering religion a substantial relationship, or the dialectic in which the individual spirit succumbs to the power of the Universal Spirit (often referred to as substance or Absolute Idea) surrendering its own particular individuality in order to share in the unity of that Absolute Idea.

" This is the more dangerous illusion, to which, accordingly, the stronger spirits have abandoned themselves, the illusion of pantheism.

[8] B. Bauer, *Posaune,* ed. Loewith, p. 150.

Even more dangerous than this illusion is the thing itself, which is at once evident to the trained eye that makes a real effort to see: namely, that conception of religion which considers the religious relationship to be no more than an inner relationship of the self-conscious to itself, and which holds that all those powers which as substance or Absolute Idea seem to be distinguishable from the self-conscious are in short nothing but personal impulses or objective moments of the religious imagination.

" This is the terrible, terrifying, all piety-and-all-religion-destroying fruit of the system. He who eats of this fruit is dead to God, for he considers God dead; he who eats this fruit falls deeper than Eve who ate of the apple and seduced Adam to do likewise. For Adam ate in the hope of becoming like God, whereas the follower of this system lacks even this, albeit sinful, pride. He no longer wishes to be like God; he desires only to flatter his ego and to achieve and enjoy the blasphemous infiniteness, freedom, and self-sufficiency of the self-consciousness. This philosophy desires no God or gods as the heathens do; it desires only man, only the self-consciousness; for it everything is proud self-consciousness. " [9]

It is impossible to trace Bauer's criticism of Hegel's religious philosophy in more detail here. The tragedy is that Bauer himself succumbed to the fascination of Hegel's ideology.

Bauer exerted a decisive influence on Friedrich Nietzsche. Nietzsche was much closer to Bauer than the rare references to his name in Nietzsche's work lead one to believe. But it was precisely because Nietzsche owed so much to Bauer that he avoided naming him. As a staff member of *The International Monthly* (which opened publication in 1882 with an introductory article by Bruno Bauer) reports, Friedrich Nietzche had been persuaded to become a contributor. For Nietzsche, Bauer was primarily a critic of theology, and as Ernst Benz points out, it is his criticism of the history of Christianity that Nietzsche adopted. In Bauer's *Christianity Discovered* we find a whole string of surprising analogies to those ideas popularly attributed to Nietzsche and developed in his criticism of Christianity, *The Will to Power* and *The Antichrist*.

[9] *Ibid.*, p. 151.

Nietzsche followed Bauer's literary development closely and Bauer was one of Nietzsche's most avid readers as we see from his letters. At a time when Nietzsche's books were largely ignored, Bruno Bauer proclaimed their author's fame, evidence enough of how kindred these two spirits were.

HEINRICH HEINE:
THE UNSUCCESSFUL PROCLAMATION
OF THE DEATH OF GOD

Under the title *The Great God Pan*, Plutarch recounts a mysterious tale which has been interpreted and reinterpreted for two thousand years. Eusebius of Caesarea, who got it from Plutarch's *De Defectu Oraculorum*, put a Christian interpretation on it in his treatise *Praeparatio Evangelica*. * The story goes that while on a voyage to Italy the Egyptian pilot Thamous, sailing past the Paxos Islands near Corfu, heard a voice thrice commanding him to go to Palodes in Epirus and there proclaim the death of the great Pan. As Thamous, arrived in Palodes, obediently announced his tidings, lamentations as though of many voices could be heard. The disturbing event was reported to the Emperor Tiberius.

Heinrich Heine used this saga to proclaim " the death of God " which Hegel had only darkly intimated. During his Berlin student days Heine had been attracted by the personality of Hegel, who at that time was at the height of his fame. By education Heine possessed a vital personal faith formed largely by the Jewish Bible. An early natural spirituality in which God was the beginning and end of all his thought prevented Heine from being blinded by the intellectual grandeur of the admired Master's conception of the world. Heine regarded Hegel as the intellectual giant of his age, as a man for whom creation held no mysteries; however, instinctively he felt that the elaborate intricacy of the Master's language screened something that Hegel dared not submit to his public. Thus Heine found himself forced to question the Master on the ultimate mystery.

Heine's personal acquaintance with Hegel, writes Lukacs, enabled

± *Translator's Note:* See G. A. Gerard's *The Death of the Great God Pan.*

him to draw a sharp line "between Hegel's exoteric proclamation
of religion as absolute spirit and the esoteric doctrine of his
atheism." Heine was the first critic to do so. He explains Hegel's
consistently divided and ambiguous attitude to religion as his
outward adaptation to the political conditions then prevalent in
Germany. Hegel had to conceal his real intentions from the masses
behind exoteric doctrine. Heine claims to have stood "behind the
Master as he composed the music of atheism in extremely ambiguous, florid lines so that none could decipher them—I saw how he
sometimes looked round, anxiously, fearful that he might be
understood.... Once, as I became impatient over his 'Everything
that exists is reasonable,' he smiled curiously and remarked that
one might also say 'Everything that is reasonable must exist'....
Thus somewhat belatedly I began to see why in his *Philosophy of
History* he had claimed that Christianity was a step forward because
it proclaimed a God who had died, whereas the heathen gods knew
nothing of any death. What progress, then, when the god never
existed at all! " [10]

The decisive question that young Heine put to Hegel was the
question of a personal God. Heine had never experienced "any
great enthusiasm" for the rest of philosophy. "I was never an
abstract thinker, and I accepted the synthesis of Hegel's doctrine
without examination because its conclusions flattered my vanity.
I was young and arrogant, and it flattered me to hear from Hegel
that it was not the God residing in heaven who was the good Lord,
as my grandmother had taught me, but I myself here on earth.
This foolish vanity by no means corrupted me; it inspired me to
the point of heroism. During that period my display of magnanimi-
ty and self-sacrifice certainly overshadowed the highest and most
brilliant deeds of those virtuous Philistines who obeyed only the
moral law, for was not I myself now the living moral law and
wellspring of all justice and all authority? " [11]

Heine's own numerous anecdotes of his association with Hegel
clearly reveal that this encounter shook the faith in a personal
God which had been his since childhood. Unquestionably Hegel
exercised an extensive and lasting influence on Heine, whose entire

---

[10] H. Heine, *Werke*, Ausg. Elster, Bd. IV, pp. 148 f.
[11] H. Heine, *Werke*, Ausg. Friedemann, Bd. XV, pp. 44 f.

thought was profoundly affected by the philosopher, however much
Heine might later protest and rebel against him.   Heine's chance
remark to Lassalle that he had understood nothing of Hegel cannot
be taken seriously; Heine was thoroughly acquainted with Hegelian
philosophy.   This is clear from what he says in his *Confessions*
about the two years he spent translating Hegel's intellectual system
into French.   In the process he realized how easy it is to misun-
derstand what one has uncritically accepted in the way of dialectical
formulas.   The attempt to translate these into another language puts
one's own understanding to the test.   " The translator must know
exactly what he has to say, and the most bashful concept is forced
to drop its mystical garments and show itself in all its nakedness. "
With great effort Heine succeeded " in mastering the prudish stuff
and in presenting the most abstract passages as popularly as
possible. "   To be sure, by the time the manuscript was completed
Heine had advanced so far beyond the Hegelian standpoint that
the sight of the finished work filled him with a strange dread, and
he threw it into the fire.

Heine joined the group of young Left Hegelians and became a
friend of Ruge, Feuerbach, Marx, Bruno Bauer, and others.   Osten-
tatiously he declared himself an atheist.   Although basically Ruge
shared Heine's opinion that it was from Hegel that true liberation
from the ancient yoke and terrible burden of servility imposed by
church and state had come, Ruge objected at first to Heine's
facetious manner, only later to change his judgment and praise
Heine as " the freest German after Goethe. "

Convinced that he had a special mission to accomplish in Paris,
Heine transferred there.   In his farewell letters he mentions " succumbing to a new religion and expecting to receive. . .ordination
as a priest in Paris. "   Heine felt it his mission to prepare France
intellectually for the great revolution which he was convinced was
at hand by unlocking for Frenchmen German idealism's true
revolutionary message, which the French considered a mystical
doctrine whose secret must remain closed to the uninitiated.   The
French were as certain of the plumbless profundity of the Hegelian
system as they were of its utter uselessness.   Only a nation that
has renounced all practical social and political aims and that seeks
to compensate for these in the realm of the intellect could afford such

a philosophy. Compared with the German dreamer, the Frenchman was very much aware of his superiority as a man of action; his was the leadership of Europe; hence he could without envy leave to others the painstaking elaboration of intellectual detours. Many educated liberal groups in Germany shared much the same conviction; they accepted the superiority of the French in practical and political life and allotted the domains of philosophy and poetry to the Germans.

Heine too was originally of the opinion that France was politically far ahead of Germany, who could do nothing better than to catch up with the democratic methods of her western neighbor. Thus he felt that destiny intended him to provide the French with a summary of German speculation, thereby compensating France with the treasures of German philosophy and poetry. Gradually, however, and quite unintentionally, Heine's goal assumes a political dimension. He tries to make it clear to the French that German philosophy is by no means a purely theoretical and mystical affair, but a typically German, thorough, intellectual preparation for a revolution that will attain its great goal, whereas the French Revolution failed because of lack of methodical preparation. Hence he purposely stresses the revolutionary nature of German philosophy. In the introduction to a political pamphlet he writes: " One has only to compare the history of the French Revolution with the history of German philosophy to believe that the French, who had so many real tasks that required them to stay awake, had asked the Germans meanwhile to sleep for them and to dream, and that our German philosophy was nothing but the dream of the French Revolution. Thus we made the break with tradition and with the powers that be in the intellectual field as the French did in the social; our philosophical Jacobins flocked to the *Critique of Pure Reason,* accepting as valid only what survived that criticism. Kant was our Robespierre—later came Fichte with his ego, the Napoleon of philosophy...his dictatorship of thought, his sovereign will, ...his despotic, terrifyingly lonely idealism. The flowers of life that had survived the Kantian guillotine, or had bloomed after it unnoticed, now cried out under Fichte's logical footsteps. The counterrevolution broke out, and with Schelling in command, the past...was acknowledged again...until Hegel, the Orléans of philosophy, mobilized a new regiment.... In brief, we successfully completed philosophy's great circle and it is only natural that we now turn to politics. " [12]

For Heine political leaders are nothing but the "handymen of the intellectuals. " Accordingly, Robespierre was the bloody hand that carried out what the philosopher Rousseau had conceived. Analogously, Heine sees the philosophers of German idealism as the intellectual trail blazers of a political revolution. According to him, this intellectual revolution began with Kant's *Critique of Pure Reason*. He styles Kant the executioner who with the blade of his criticism beheaded belief in God. The French succeeded in killing only a king; under Robespierre a " supreme being " continued to exist. Under Immanuel Kant, " that great destroyer in the realm of thought, " the terror far exceeds that of Robespierre. Because by Kant's critical norms we can know nothing about God, God therefore is "nothing but a fiction. " Above Kant's criticism of the proofs of the existence of God one could write the Dantesque word, " All hope abandon, ye who enter in. " Heine claims that compared with *The Critique of Pure Reason* with its destruction of the fundamental notion of God, Kant's further works play no role at all. Though his *Critique of Practical Reason* attempts " to revive the corpse of deism killed by theoretical reason " with " the magic wand " of a moral postulate, it cannot be taken seriously but only as a concession to those not yet ready for the new idea. Thus " the Lord of the world swims unproven in his blood. Ever since, deism has faded into the realm of speculative reason, though it may take centuries for the sad news of its death to become general knowledge. " [13]

Heine too sees Fichte entirely in the light of intellectual preparation for the Revolution. Later he develops the chance comparison of Fichte with Napoleon: both " represent the great inexorable ego in which thought and act are one, and the colossal edifices which both succeeded in constructing testify to a colossal will.... Fichte's philosophical ego conformed perfectly with his uncompromising, obdurate, iron nature. " [14]

[12] *Ibid.*, Bd. XI, p. 153.
[13] *Ibid.*, Bd. IX, pp. 234-247.
[14] *Ibid.*, Bd. IX, pp. 251 f.

In the initial exuberance of youth, Heine continues, Fichte openly flaunted his atheism, in those days a stance which was bound to be poorly received. With offensive harshness Fichte declared God to be a mere phantasm; he treated him ironically; he denied God's existence because to exist is a concept possible only to a sensual being. Fichte's " God " has no existence; he is only another name for the cosmic law. In the resultant war over Fichte's atheism, what " the ministerial, accommodating, hush-hushing Goethe " really deplored was the fact that Fichte had spoken openly of things that should be mentioned only in traditionally veiled terms.

" He does not criticize the thought, but only the wording. Although, as I have already mentioned, in the German intellectual world it was an open secret that since Kant deism was dead, still, this was not to be shouted from the housetops. Goethe was as little a deist as Fichte; he was a pantheist. . . . ' The great pagan ' is what Goethe is being called in Germany. " [15]

Heine knew of course, that Fichte did not remain true to his atheism but returned to a veiled Christianity. The man who had climbed heaven on the ladder of idealism and grabbed for the emptied throne of God ultimately had returned to belief in a personal, living God, though in his stubbornness he never found the courage to admit his conversion. " Fichte died early enough to prevent his defection from his own philosophy from becoming all too blatant. " [16]

However, it is the philosopher Schelling whom Heine charges with the most ignominious " apostasy. " The man who had once advocated pantheism more boldly than anyone in Germany, who had preached loudest the sacredness of nature and the restoration of man's divine rights, " this man has become a turncoat to his own doctrine; he has deserted the altar which he himself consecrated; he has crawled back into the pen of bygone faith, he. . .preaches a transcendent personal God. " [17]

Though like Kant and Fichte the early Schelling represents " one of the great phases in our philosophical revolution, " the later

[15] *Ibid.*, p. 258.
[16] *Ibid.*, p. 272.
[17] *Ibid.*, p. 271.

Schelling presents " a pathetic picture of fallen grandeur. " Schelling is a victim of the counterrevolution. Into his place steps " the great Hegel, Germany's greatest philosopher since Leibniz. " Heine sincerely believes his claim that Hegel has completed the philosophic revolution. " Hegel has closed the great circle. " In the domain of the mind, he continues, Hegel was sovereign. We have Hegel to thank for the perfection of pantheism. Although pantheism is only a shame-faced atheism intended to shield the educated from the reproach of godlessness, this ersatz for religion does give the devotee a proud sense of heaven-high superiority as compared with the mass of naive believers. Nor does pantheism simply lead to indifferentism and amoralism. God becomes the great Law of Progress in Nature which stimulates men to self-sacrificing efforts to advance. God manifests himself in the things, movements, and acts of history.

Yet Heine does not spare even Hegel the accusation of cowardly conformity and adaptation to the powers that be. What Schelling did in Catholic Munich, Hegel undertakes in Protestant Berlin: he attempts to rescue sinking Christianity from complete shipwreck by incorporating into his system a kind of allegorical reinterpretation of the whole of Protestant dogma.

It was the group of Left Hegelians, intimates of Heine, who took the revolutionary ideas of pantheism seriously. Under their influence Hegel, " with his almost ridiculously sober mien, " reminds Heine of " a setting hen " brooding " on fateful eggs. . .to tell the truth, I rarely understood him, it was only through later reflections of my own that I came to understand his words. I believe he really did not want to be understood, hence his overly involved presentation. " [18] With his demonstration of the revolutionary nature of German philosophy, Heine hoped to place it not only on an equal footing with French philosophy but also to prove it superior. Exactly like the French, the Germans too aim at revolution. But because Germans are a " methodical people, " they are superior to Frenchmen, who, intellectually unprepared for the great Revolution, had to pay a high price for their lesson; the first Revolution succumbed to the counterrevolution. The methodical Germans

[18] *Ibid.*, Bd. XV, pp. 42 f.

must begin with the Reformation, then advance to philosophy, and " only after perfecting it, proceed to political revolution. "

It is a mistake to believe that after Hegel's death the question: " What could still come after the absolute philosophy of the Master— was not all history at an end? " had lain oppressively on the spirits of the Left Hegelians until the Slavs had given the cue with their revolution of action.

Much like Fichte, Heine had once declared that for a philosophy that has run its full course the shift to political action is natural. Therefore, he warns, the German revolution will not be milder or gentler because preceded by Kantian criticism, Fichtean idealism, and natural philosophy. " It is through these doctrines that the forces of revolution have developed; they are only waiting for the day when they can break out and fill the earth with wonder and dread. " Ancient Germanic pantheism has been resurrected and has shattered the one restraining talisman, the cross of Christianity; now the rage of destruction can break out anew in all its old savagery. The revolution of thought has already taken place; the revolution of the act must follow. " The thought precedes the act as lightning precedes thunder. " Compared with what is in the making in Germany, the French Revolution will seem like a harmless idyll.

As the man of freedom in the circle of young Left Hegelians Heine felt it to be not only justifiable but morally necessary to clear their philosophy of Hegelian ambiguity and openly proclaim the death of God. Thus he anticipated Nietzsche's proclamation. This theme of the dying and death of God appears in many and various forms. In the poet's vivid imagination images taken from the pagan twilight of the gods intermingle with images of the death on Calvary. Heine's poem on this theme, *Goetterdaemmerung*, closes:

> " And a savage yell clangs through the universe,
> Its pillars crumble, earth and heaven totter,
> Fall; the old primeval night prevails. "

At this stage Heine flings to the winds the remaining inhibitions of his youthful piety and reverence, and carried away, depicts the death of God with blasphemous frivolity.

In Volume II of his *On the History of Religion and Philosophy
in Germany* Heine again refers to " this catastrophe of deism. "
He writes: " A strange dread, a mysterious reverence prevents us
from writing further. Our breast is filled with a terrible pity.
Here is the ancient Jehovah himself preparing for death. We have
known him well, from his birth in Egypt on. . .we watched as he
gradually. . .spiritualized himself: first whimpering gentle bliss;
then gradually maturing to a tender loving father, a univeral
friend, a world benefactor, a philanthropist. Nothing availed him.
Do you hear the tinkle of the bell? On your kness, they are
carrying the last sacraments to a dying God. " [19]

At the same time, Heine is profoundly aware of the consequent
loss. " There is no more pity, no paternal kindness, no future
reward for present self-restraint. The soul's immortality is at its
last gasp—this is its death rattle. " [20] These are words very similar
to those Nietzsche will use later. Also Heine's vision of the " selfgods, " men who have lost all idea of the divine, anticipates
Nietzsche's superman. Although Heine prophesies that the tidings
of God's death will take centuries to be universally known, only
a few decades later Nietzsche will write that the greatest news, the
news that " God is dead, " is beginning to cast its shadow over
Europe. Most people do not yet suspect what has happened, or
know what demolition and destruction lie ahead, now that the
foundations of man's life have collapsed.

Heine's will to radical revolution made him incapable of seeing
anything in the leading German philosophers' return to belief but
cowardly fear of their own daring. Even pantheism is really only
a timidly veiled atheism. For Heine, as for the whole coterie of
young Hegelian friends, clear, openly avowed atheism is a prerequisite of revolution. Hence the Left Hegelians' new slogan:
Religion is intellectual opium! From the viewpoint of literary
history, it was probably Feuerbach who in his Bayle Book of 1838
first mentioned the opiate of religious fear. In 1839 Heine declared:
" Heaven was invented for people who no longer expect anything
from earth. . . . Hail this invention! Hail to the religion that
poured into mankind's bitter chalice a few sweet, narcotic drops,

[19] *Ibid.*, Bd. IX, pp. 234 f.
[20] *Ibid.*, Bd. IX, pp. 246 f.

spiritual opium, drops of love, hope, and faith. " [21]   Though the
first recorded remark of the kind comes from Feuerbach, it is
nonetheless probable that the opium label was first applied to
religion (possibly in some passing remark to the group) by Heine,
the man of the witty *bon mot*. In all events, this is where the source
of Karl Marx's definition of religion as the opiate of the people is
to be sought; Marx was a friend of Heine.

As early as 1841, Bruno Bauer had used similar expressions,
mentioning religion's narcotic effects and describing the sottishness
or wild destructiveness of those addicted to religion.

However, in the midst of his efforts to spur pantheism into full-
fledged atheism, Heine suddenly stops short, apparently alarmed
by certain dubious experiences. What hitherto only the educated
had been permitted to intimate in discreet pantheistic guise is now
being openly proclaimed by Communist activists. Heine came to
know one of these personally, Wilhelm Weitling. He writes of
him: "This Weitling, now missing, was, by the way, a man of
talent; he was full of ideas, and his book, *The Guarantees of
Society*, was long the catechism of the German Communists. In
Germany the number of Communists has increased enormously in
the last few years, and across the Ruhr, the Communist Party is
without doubt one of the most powerful. The hard core of this
army of disbelievers is made up of journeymen who are perhaps
not particularly well disciplined, but who in questions of doctrine
are extraordinarily well versed. By and large, it is the German
artisans who confess the crassest atheism; they are, so to speak,
damned to pay homage to this desolate negation if they do not
wish to contradict their principles and thus become totally impotent.
These cohorts of destruction, these sappers whose axes threaten the
whole structure of society are far superior to the revolutionary
levellers in other lands because of the terrible consistency of their
doctrine; for, as Polonius would say, there is method in their
madness. " [22]   In this later "confession," fear of a sovereign mob
capable of annihilating all culture in a bloody revolution is already
evident. The thought strikes Heine with terror.

Heine's Epicurean dream of liberation from fear of the gods

----

[21] *Ibid.*, Bd. XIV, p. 108.
[22] *Ibid.*, Bd. XV, p. 42.

did not last long. The vision of the coming superman, who would inherit the emptied throne of God turned out to be one more illusion of youthful genius. A matured and sobered Heine came to see the blows dealt him by life as evidence of his being in the grip of a personal God. Thus he arrived at the great turning point of his life, and it does Heine honor that he had the courage to openly admit his conversion. In the preface to the second edition of his essay *On the History of Religion and Philosophy in Germany* he writes: " I confess without reservation that everything in this book concerned with the great problem of the question of God is as false as it was ill considered. Equally ill considered and false is the claim which I echoed, that the theory of deism had received its death sentence, and that deism today barely ekes out an existence in the world of appearances. No; it is not true that reason's destruction of the proofs of the existence of God as we have known them since Anselm of Canterbury put an end to the existence of God himself. Deism lives, it is vitally alive; it is not dead, and the last thing capable of killing it is the newest German philosophy. " [23]

Although there was a period in Heine's life when " only unbelievers could still doubt [my] divinity, " after the loss of money and health, " there was a serious hitch " in [my] godliness, ..." like many another down-at-the-heel god of that revolutionary period, I too was forced to abdicate ignominiously and return to mortal existence. This was also the wisest thing I could do. I returned to the common fold of God's creatures. . . . " [24]

When in the fall of 1847 the archeologist Ferdinand Meyer paid a sick-call on the half paralyzed Heine, he found a picture of misery. Withal, the invalid wore an expression of such cheerful peace that the visitor wondered where such peace and contentment could come from. " They came from a source I hardly expected to find in the atheist Heine, who earlier had even made boast of his atheism. They sprang from a pure, unshakable faith in a God who after our death rewards good and punishes evil, and from the firm conviction that this just and gentle Father does not count or punish as sins the mistakes sincerely repented of during life. . . . This man laid low in his best years by paralysis announced with

[23] *Ibid.*, Bd. **IX**, pp. 164 f.
[24] *Ibid.*, Bd. XV, pp. 45 f.

the greatest calm, almost smilingly, that he knew perfectly well that he would never leave his sickbed again and that he waited hourly for death to rescue him. I was profoundly shaken when Heine, motionless save for the slight movement of his lips, said in a clear strong voice: 'Believe me, my friend, for Heinrich Heine tells you this on his deathbed after years of mature consideration: after having weighed everything that all nations have ever said or written on the subject, I have arrived at the certainty that there is a God who is the judge of our acts; that our souls are immortal; and that there is a beyond in which good is rewarded, evil punished.... Knowing that my condition is incurable, had I not this belief, I should have put an end to my miserable existence long ago.... There are fools who after a lifetime in the clutches of error once proclaimed by them in word and deed no longer have the courage to admit that they could err so long; as for me, I admit it openly; it was blasphemous error that imprisoned me so long. Now I see clearly, and anyone who knows me, seeing me, will testify that I speak as I do not because I am depressed or intimidated, but at a time when my intellectual powers are unimpaired and as clear as ever.' " [25]

In the literary productions of his last years, Heine repeatedly and unconditionally admitted his religious transformation. Thus in the epilogue to *Romanzero* (1851): "I have made peace with my Maker, much to the dismay of my enlightened friends, who reproach me for this backsliding into the old 'superstition', as they like to call my homecoming to God. (Others, in their intolerance, have expressed it even more sharply.) The entire high clergy of atheism has pronounced its anathema over me, and there are fanatic priestlings of unbelief who would like to span me on the rack that I might revoke my heresies.... Yes, like the prodigal son, I have returned to God after a long period of tending the swine with the Hegelians. Was it misery that drove me back? Possibly a less miserable impulse. Homesickness for heaven overcame me and drove me on through forests and gorges, across dialectic's most dizzying mountain passes. On the way I met the God of the pantheists, but he was of no use to me. This poor

[25] *Gespraeche mit Heine*, Gesammelt und herausgegeben von H. H. Houben, pp. 704-707.

chimera ingrown with the world that imprisons it gapes at one, willess and impotent. For to have a will, one must be a person. . . . If one wants a God capable of helping—and after all that is the main thing—one must accept also his personality, his transcendence, and his holy attributes, all-goodness, all-wisdom, all-justice and so forth. . . . I said the God of the pantheists, but I cannot avoid pointing out that basically, he is no God at all, just as pantheists are really only timid atheists, less afraid of the reality than of the shadow that it casts on the wall: the epithet ' atheist. ' Moreover, during the Restoration, most pantheists in Germany played the same fifteen-year-old comedy with the good Lord that the constitutional Royalists here in France (largely Republicans at heart) played with the monarchy. "

It was characteristic of Heine's return to faith in God that he considered himself faced with the alternatives of religion of philosophy, of choosing " between the revealed dogma of faith and the ultimate consequences of thought, between the absolute God of the Bible and atheism. " [26] Apparently for him, thought and its consequences were still on the side of atheism. Nevertheless in another passage, Heine says clearly that consideration of his own experience was what led him back to faith. It was certainly not philosophical arguments that led him to God. Rather, it was his encounter with God in the Bible that profoundly impressed him and stirred his vital faith in a personal God. This explains why Heine's concept of God is vividly anthropomorphic, as yet philosophically unclarified. It was during this period of his religious conversion that Heine threw his manuscript on Hegelian philosophy into the fire. Asked by his brother Gustav during a visit after a twenty-year separation, whether he had become a " prayer-sister " he replied: " No, I have become a prayer-brother, and I pray daily to the good Lord that he imbue you, dear brother, with more political sense. "

Although in the converted Heine the old mocker never died, Heine took his conversion to a personal God with unquestionable earnestness, as many of his bedside visitors attest. His appraisal of atheism, whether outright or camouflaged as it is in pantheism, comes straight from the Bible, whose clarity on this point leaves

[26] H. Heine, *Werke*, Bd. II, pp. 266 f.

nothing to be desired. Heine names pride the real, affective root
of unbelief and reminds the " godless selfgods, " the Left Hegelians,
of Genesis' story of the first couple's fall.   Right at the beginning
of the Bible " stands the story of the forbidden tree in Paradise and
of the serpent, that little *Privatdozent*, who several thousand years
before the birth of Hegel, held forth on Hegelian philosophy.   This
bluestocking without feet ingeniously demonstrated how the absolute
exists in the identity of being and knowing; how through knowledge
man becomes God, or—what amounts to the same thing—how in
man, God attains to full knowledge of himself.   But this formulation
is not nearly as clear as the original words: ' If you eat of the Tree
of Knowledge, you will be like God! ' " [27]

LUDWIG FEUERBACH AND
THE SHIFT FROM IDEALISM TO ATHEISM

The ambiguity of Hegelian dialectics in regard to religion, which
made it possible to interpret Hegel in the old conservative sense
as well as in the new, revolutionary sense, caused a crisis in the
generation that followed Hegel.   His students, particularly those
who had penetrated most deeply into his thought, felt themselves
forced, for the sake of consistency, to go further than the Master.

When Ludwig Feuerbach went to Heidelberg to study theology
in order to become a Protestant minister, this was not only in
deference to his father's wishes, but because his Protestant upbringing had stimulated his own interest in the subject.   " God was
my first thought, " he declares.   Caught up into the *Zeitgeist* of the
students' revolt against the reactionary forces of the country (in
Erlangen his own brothers were playing a leading role in a widespread secret organization) and infuriated by the feudal police-state
which severely punished his brothers, Ludwig could hardly be
spared a difficult inner conflict: Could he really serve the spiritual

---

[27] *Ibid.*, Bd. xv, p. 49.

power that was encouraging the State to put down the revolutionary student body's struggle for freedom with police methods? " In an exceedingly torn, unhappy and undecided frame of mind " Feuerbach enrolled at the University of Berlin. Already he felt the conflict between philosophy and religion and the necessity " of sacrificing either philosophy to theology or theology to philosophy. "

His anxiously anticipated meeting with Hegel was the turning point of Feuerbach's life. Hegel became his " second father, " Berlin his " spiritual birthplace. " In Hegel Feuerbach was to experience " what a teacher is. " To Hegel alone he continued to feel deeply indebted even when his criticism of Hegel forced him to a more radical position than Hegel's own. Feuerbach's relation to Hegel was " more intimate and influential " than to any other of his professors; he knew him personally and attended his lectures " for two whole years. " Under Hegel's influence theology came to seem a stage in man's intellectual development that was now outgrown. Feuerbach now entered into what he called a new life with " a liberating sense of well-being " at having escaped " the clutches of the dirty clerics. " His dissertation was on the fundamental idea of Hegelian philosophy, " on reason, the one, the universal, the infinite, " just as he had lectured while a *Privatdozent* at Erlangen on Hegelian idealism. In his dissertation Feuerbach developed the central concept of idealism: reason is the supreme metaphysical principle, the *Urgrund* or primal cause of all things, the " all-embracing, universal, true abode of all things and subjects. " The divine attributes of unity, universality, and infinitude are transferred without question to Reason, the new God.

By 1830 Feuerbach, determined to take a radical position to what he considered Hegel's provokingly conservative standpoint on Christianity, had gone much further than Hegel. Hegel still considered Christianity the absolute religion and attempted to reconcile religion with reason. Feuerbach formulated this concept in his paper, *Reflections on Death and Immortality with a Theological-Satirical Supplement.* In the dedication he personally declares to Hegel that according to the principles of panlogistical idealism, Christianity cannot be considered an absolute religion; that rather, as a result of those principles, the traditional modes of interpreting time, death, the here and the hereafter, the ego, the individual. . .God, and so forth...were truly destroyed. In *Thoughts on Death and Immortality* Feurebach demands that the pillar of Christian theology, the traditional *Weltanschauung* with its faith in personal immortality and clearly dualistic world view, be overcome by a monistic concentration on the here and now. This paper's revolutionary tendency is heightened by the accompanying doggerel, which according to Theodor Kolde, chronicler of the University of Erlangen, consisted in "recklessly impudent, even base attacks on Christianity, Pietism, and rationalism manifestly intended to expose conditions at Erlangen." In these verses theology is called the spiritual police of the absolute state. With them Feuerbach gives the storm signal to revolution; he is the first of the Hegelian Left to break away from those of his contemporaries who go back "to the old... attempting to restore it in its unaltered form...as though the rivers of blood had thundered through past centuries in vain. However, history teaches that when something is on the verge of complete destruction it pulls itself up one last time as though to begin its completed course all over again." [28] With this Feuerbach becomes one of the first to approve and passionately further the revolutionary tendency in Hegel's system disguised as it was under the mantel of Hegelian conservatism. He demanded that "philosophy emigrate from Christianity," and called for a new "religion of action," for undivided concentration on the here below, for the formation of "efficient, spiritually and physically sound people," in other words, people fit and willing to assume the task of revolutionizing life. After the collapse of his academic plans for the future, Feuerbach looked longingly to the Paris of the July Revolution where he knew Heinrich Heine and other freedom-loving German writers already at work on the ideological preparation for the Revolution of 1848. However, his plans to emigrate were never carried out.

Feuerbach's aim was "the pure Hegel." He defended Hegel as his master against the attacks of Schelling and welcomed a publication of Bayer's that was supposed to have restored the original meaning of the concept of freedom. It is from this stand too that Feuerbach's development of the Hegelian attitude toward outright

---

[28] L. Feuerbach, *Saemtliche Werke*, hg. von O, Wigand, 1846-1866, Bd. III, p. 9.

atheism is to be regarded. What Kant, Fichte, and Hegel had begun in the way of developing a philosophy in which freedom of thought and freedom of residence are the supreme law, Feuerbach felt it his duty to continue because he considered their efforts inadequate.

Even as the Pole, Cieskowski, dissatisfied with the conservatism of Hegelian philosophy, demanded its revolutionary continuation, Feuerbach accused Hegel of being infected by the spirit that had led to the destruction of philosophy and thereby to the revival both in theory and in practice of ancient superstition. In brief, he made Hegel responsible for the barbarity of the present world.

According to Feuerbach, all recent philosophy was characterized by the contradiction between theoretical knowledge and practical behavior, between seeming theology and factual atheism. For him the history of his day is a period of illusion and untruth, of half-heartedness and illusion, indecision and immorality. Because of its " indecisive half-heartedness and lack of character. . .the super-human and supernatural essence of ancient Christianity still haunts the minds of men—at least as a ghost. " [29] With his ambiguous dialectics Hegel seemed after all to have reconciled absolute contradictions. However, in the long run the existence of such contradictions was intolerable. Both orthodoxy and heterodoxy based their claims on Hegel. Thus it is understandable that Feuerbach considered it his historical mission to erase " this most rotten stain, the stain of our present history. " He sees this not only as his right, but as his vocation and duty. Only he " who has the courage to see through his religious feelings and needs is a truly moral person. He who is the lackey of his religious emotions deserves also to be treated politically no better than a lackey. He who crosses free thought with religious sentiments is an enemy of the Enlightenment and of freedom. Hence it is a moral necessity, man's sacred duty, to put dark obscurantist religion completely under the control of reason, and the greater the conflict between the conceptions, feelings, and interests of religion and other conceptions, feelings and interests, the more reason to exert such rational control. At present the need for this is very great, which

[29] L. Feuerbach, *Das Wesen des Christentums*, hg. von W. Schuffenhauer (1956), Bd. I, p. 6.

no one can deny who is not, himself, entangled in that conflict. " [30]
Again and again Feuerbach stresses the close link between religious
and political liberation. He is convinced that the destruction of
religion is a historical turning point, the decisive step in the
liberation of mankind.

In all this the real question is the question of the absolute,
personal God of the universe. " Either no God or an absolute
God, like the God of the ancient faith! There is but one true God
worthy of adoration—the immediate, autonomous, self-speaking,
self-illuminating, self-thundering, self-lightening God of the Old
Testament. Either this God or no God! " [31] At first Feuerbach's
attack is directed against falsification of the ancient concept of
God. Against all pantheistic blendings, Feuerbach clearly underlines the difference between God and man—to be sure, in order
to reject God. The great question of the possible existence of God
is already solved; " the question, " says Feuerbach, " whether God
exists or does not exist had a place in the 17th and 18th centuries,
but it no longer has one in the 19th. " Accordingly faith can only
be error. Hegel must be criticized for not saying this clearly.
This is the point with which Feuerbach's fundamental criticism
of Hegel begins; he accuses him of wearing an " ambiguous aura
of mysticism. " Hegel's equivocal retaining of the Christian articles
of faith, whose meaning he has falsified, is a consequence of this
mystical attitude. In reality, philosophy and Christianity belong
to two heterogenous spheres; they are different from each other
not only formally but substantially. Any compromise between them
is a " *concordia discors* " against which " one must protest in the
name of philosophy as well as in that of religion. All religious
speculation is vanity and lies—lies about reason and lies about
faith. " [32] Thus Feuerbach sets out on the road to criticism of
Hegel not on a basis of objective and speculative arguments but
on the basis of moral considerations.

In this Feuerbach met with the hearty approval of his fellow
critics. In 1843 Friedrich Engels declared completely in Feuerbach's

[30] L. Feuerbach, *Werke*, hg. von Bolin u. Jodl, Bd. I, pp. 252 ff.

[31] *Ibid.*, Bd. IX, p. 295.

[32] L. Feuerbach, *Werke*, hg. von Wigand, Bd. I, pp, 80 ff.

vein, " The essence of theology, particularly in our times, is mediation between and whitewashing of absolute opposites. Even the
most logical Christian cannot completely emancipate himself from
the assumption of the times; he bears in him premises whose
development could lead to atheism. From these comes that type of
theology which...permeates our whole life with its inner untruth
and hypocrisy. " [33] Such statements explain Ruge's enthusiasm over
Feuerbach's " world-moving step " which " with unrouged truth
demasks Christian and philosophical hypocrisy. " The tendency
to atheism existed also in other young Hegelians. Bruno Bauer
and Karl Marx entertained the prospect of dropping the " religious
cloak " from their views and openly confessing their atheism. They
planned the publication of an *Archive for Atheists* which was to
be even more radical than the *German Yearbooks* of Arnold Ruge.
Ruge depicted the ideological position of 1841 with the words:
" Bruno Bauer (and Marx)...and Feuerbach have already reached
the summit and planted the flag of atheism and mortality; God,
religion, and immortality are hereby deposed, and the philosophers'
Republic, Man, and the new gods of Man proclaimed. " [34]

Feuerbach clearly defines the crux of this religious struggle as
" positive religion " with its belief in God as absolute personality,
its philosophical recognition of God, and its reconciliation of philosophy with Christianity; for Feuerbach here lies " the specific
evil of the present day, which establishes itself in the field of
philosophy. "

God's existence cannot be proved, " therefore " there is no God.
Since for Feuerbach this so-called unshakable fact stands (albeit
heavy with fallacy, and on very shaky ground) the only possibility
that remains is to give a psychological explanation for people's
stubborn insistence on faith. Until now criticism of the knowledge
of God seems to have completely blocked the way to true knowledge
of God. As a result Feuerbach considers God unreal and feels it
his duty to expose the religious relation between man and God as
a misunderstanding and illusion. By so doing Feuerbach only
shifts the weight of an evaluation at which Hegel already hinted

[33] Marx-Engels-Lenin-Stalin, *Zur deutschen Geschichte*, Bd. II, p. 89.
[34] A. Ruge, *Briefwechsel und Tagebuchblaetten*, hg. von Nerrlich (1866),
Bd. I, p. 23.

when he spoke of the idealistic consciousness' intoxication with its own infinite ego. It is what Feuerbach calls drunken speculation that makes man God in order that man may enter into a relation with this "God" as with a supreme personal being. Just as drunkenness causes people to see double, "drunken speculation" too leads to double vision and the splitting of one's own self, which in the simplicity of the consciousness is really one. Thus the image of God is nothing more than the drunkard's doubled image of himself, a self-deceit, and it is the task of philosophy to bring men back to sobriety. To be sure, Feuerbach does not mean simply to reject all religions. He wishes only to show man what he considers the true object of religion, man himself. "By bringing theology down to anthropology, I am really elevating anthropology to theology, just as Christianity by lowering God to man, raised man to God—albeit once again to a remote, transcendent, fantastic God, "Feuerbach explains in his Preface to *The Essence of Christianity*. Once the misunderstanding has been clarified, man's task is to become his own God, "*Der Mensch ist dem Menschen Gott.*" Man is the supreme being for man—this is the substance of the new anthropology, which now takes the place once occupied by religion and theology. With realistic sobriety man as the supreme value, taking his religious meaning upon himself, should replace the old illusion.

Because of the dissolution of idealistic reason, which Feuerbach considers an unrealistic abstraction no longer capable of fulfilling its original purpose, he abandons it and exalts man to the new principle of his philosophy. For Feuerbach man is the most real being of all, true *ens realissimum*. In order to make "theology" (the myth of God in which all the longings of man's heart are given form) understandable, Feuerbach employs the Hegelian interpretation of renunciation, by which he means that for the sake of an illusion man has robbed himself of things essential to him: the reason, love, will power, and perfection of which his absolute essence consists.

It is a fundamental misunderstanding of his own viewpoint when Feuerbach refers to his philosophical position as "materialism." What he really means is epistomological realism, the recognition of objective rather than subjective reality. Chance remarks of his

indicate that he harshly rejected true materialism. Critically Feuerbach turned upon the so-called proofs of the spirit's dependence
on matter; only what is itself of the nature of matter, he points
out, can be dependent on matter. Thought is " *toto genre* different
from matter, consequently determined only by itself. " *The Essence
of Christianity* begins completely antimaterialistically with its
development of the thesis that it is through religion that man differs
essentially from the animal. Animals have no religion. Religion
distinguishes man as man. Whereas animals have merely sensual
consciousness with powers of perception, for man a double life is
possible. On the strength of thought and speech man is capable
of existing in and unto himself, something no animal can do. It
was not until a truly consistent materialism developed that this
thesis had to be rejected, in order that all essences might be
described as basically materialistic.

Feuerbach's materialism, then, is the rejection of a so-called
idealism which creates its own world. " Unconditionally I reject
absolute, nonmaterialistic speculation with its self-discontent—the
kind of speculation that creates its own objects. There is a heaven-
wide difference between myself and those philosophers who pluck
out their eyes in order to think better; I need my senses to think,
my eyes above all; I base my thinking on material things, which
we can assimilate only by means of our senses; I do not create the
object from the thought but the other way round, the thought from
the object; an object is that which exists solely outside the mind.
Only in the field of practical philosophy am I an idealist. For me
the idea is merely faith in the historical future, in the victory of
truth and virtue; for me the idea has only political and moral
significance. In the field of genuine theoretical philosophy my
position is the exact opposite of that of the Hegelians: I accept
only realism as valid, which is materialism in the above-mentioned
sense. " In this programmatic declaration in the preface of the
second edition of his *Essence of Christianity*, Feuerbach unequivocally identifies realism with materialism. How far the consequences
of such materialism extend, consequences which do not exist in the
concept realism, we need not discuss here. It was only with
reference to English and French conceptions of materialism that
Feuerbach's realism, that is, recognition of an ultimate reality,

was narrowed to mean recognition only of material things—in other words, a materialism limited to matter.

A revolutionary development of the Hegelian system had been long overdue. This accounts for the impact that Feuerbach's main work, *The Essence of Christianity*, had. As Engels puts it, with one blow Feuerbach "pulverized the existing contradiction by unhesitatingly reinstating materialism. Nature exists independently of philosophy; nature is the foundation on which we men, ourselves products of nature, grow; aside from man and nature nothing exists, and the higher beings created by our religious fancy are only fantastic reflections of our own essence. The ban was broken; the system was blasted to pieces and discarded; the contradiction as something that existed only in the imagination was resolved. One must have personally experienced the liberating effect of this book to have any idea of it. The enthusiasm was universal. For a while we were all Feuerbachians. How enthusiastically Marx greeted the new conception and how greatly—for all his critical reservations—he was influenced by it, one can read in *The Holy Family*." [35]

For Marx the criticism of religion had now been completed and the road was clear for revolutionary action. "Criticism of religion is prerequisite to all criticism." Feuerbach is to be thanked for this. Marx adds the final touch: "Criticism of religion ends with the doctrine that man is the supreme being for man, in other words, with the categorical imperative to overthrow all conditions that keep man a degraded, enslaved, deserted, despised being." [36] Along the path Feuerbach had smoothed Marx and Engels strode ahead to the construction of an ideology of social revolution. Both shared the conviction, unshakable as a dogma, that atheism must provide the basis for man's ultimate emancipation.

Yet Feuerbach's criticism of religion was not quite the end of the critical process. It was Max Stirner who took the final step in his book *The Individual and His Property* (1845). In spite of Stirner's criticism of Feuerbach, Feuerbach acknowledged Stirner as "the greatest genius, the most liberated writer I have ever met." Stirner

---

[35] F. Engels, *Feuerbach und der Ausgang der klassischen deutschen Philosophie* (Neuausg, 1946), p. 136.
[36] K. Marx-F. Engels, *Die Heilige Familie*, p. 20.

takes the final step and destroys the remaining semblance of the
trancendent in the supposedly eternal idea of man. " Although the
stress was finally being laid on man or mankind, it was again the idea
that was being eternalized: Man does not die! One believed now at
last to have found the reality of that idea: Man is the ego of history,
of world history; it is he, this ideal, that develops, that is, that
realizes itself in history. " [37] Stirner considers this a last remnant
of the transcendent; as long as it remains, Christianity's " enchanted
circle " is not broken. As long as a single valid idea remains
higher than the actual, individual man, " Christianity still remains. "
Stirner's purpose is to destroy, utterly, that transcendence and to
place man as he is completely on his own. " I am my own power,
and I am that power when I know myself to be unique. In its
uniqueness the self returns to the creative void from which it was
born. Any higher being over me, be it God or man, weakens my
sense of uniqueness and fades only in the sun of that awareness. " [38]
Here at last revolutionary Russian Messianism finds perfect atheism
and can proceed to the task of putting it to work.

THE RELIGIOUS DECISION OF KARL MARX

The burgeoning revolutionary spirit proceeeds logically from
Feuerbach to Marx. Moses Hess, a Rhenish merchant's son, who
as author of a book on the philosophy of Communism enjoyed
a certain prestige among intellectuals, hailed Karl Marx as the
greatest living philosopher. He wrote, " Marx is Rousseau, Voltaire, D'Holbach, Lessing, Heine, and Hegel all rolled into one. "
To the extent that Marxism is understandable only as a heritage
of these men's doctrines, Hess's evaluation of Marx is valid.

Marx did not adopt the atheism of Feuerbach; Marx already
was an atheist. Since opinions on the origin of his atheism conflict
and frequently ignore the highly personal religious decision behind

---

[37] M. Stirner, *Der Einziger und sein Eigentum*, Ausg. Reclam, p. 5.
[38] *Ibid.*, p. 429.

his atheism, it is important to examine Marx's attitude toward religion more closely.

Born in Treves in 1818 as the son of a Jewish lawyer, Karl Marx grew up in an intellectual world completely different from that of his classmates at the *Gymnasium*. The other boys came largely from solid, middle class, Catholic families, and many of them planned to study for the priesthood. As a Jewish Protestant whose liberal-minded father had converted to Christianity mainly for the social advantages entailed, young Marx found himself an outsider everywhere. For although both parents came from highly respected rabbinical families, Karl's father had made a complete break with Mosaic Law and the Talmud. As his granddaughter Eleanor writes, " He was permeated by 18th- century French thought in matters of religion, science, and art. " [39]   Hence young Karl could hardly expect to find an atmosphere conducive to religion in his own home. Instead his father read aloud passages from the writers he most esteemed: Voltaire, Rousseau, and Racine. The boy had little in common with his classmates and it was no wonder that he made few friends. " He was simultaneously liked and hated—liked because he was always ready for pranks, hated because of the ease with which he. . .lampooned his enemies. " [40]

The term paper assigned young Marx in his religion class has been preserved. It was praised by his instructor for its " powerful, fresh, and original style " but criticized for lack of depth. Obviously the essence of Christianity escaped young Marx; today it is impossible to say to what extent this was due to the liberal education he received at home.

Also preserved is Marx's *Abitur* thesis, *Meditations of a Young Man on the Choice of a Profession*. This is unquestionably more than a clever exercise in style; it contains the germs of significant, original ideas. Of course it must be taken into consideration that, like any other student interested in good grades, Marx naturally tried to make a favorable impression. In this paper he writes that the Deity has given men the task of ennobling themselves and mankind; however, it is the right and privilege of the individual

[39] E. Marx, " Karl Marx, " *Karl Marx als Denker, Mensch und Revolutionaire* (1928), p. 27.
[40] *Ibid*.

to see to it that the choice of a profession is not left to chance. The individual is responsible for giving this problem his most earnest consideration, otherwise he runs the risk of ultimately ruining his life. " Every man has a goal that is great, at least to him, if his deepest convictions, his heart's inmost voice call it so. For the Deity never leaves mortals totally without guidance; he speaks softly but unmistakably. " [41] In this decision of his life young Marx was aware of the dangers. He knew how easily the inner voice is drowned; how prone a man is to illusions that cause him to fling himself passionately at a goal supposedly indicated by the Godhead. Hence the need for sober self-examination and the duty to test inspirations in order to be sure that " what we hold to be a summons of the Deity is not really self-deception. " The youth was conscious of his ambition to outshine others and knew that ambition leads to no true satisfaction. The resulting disappointment often causes one to " bear a grudge against the Deity and to curse humanity. " The recurrence of this theme of the choice of a true vocation which is a calling from on high that is easily lost in the clamor of siren voices from within is evidence that young Marx was aware that in the major decision of his life he was being addressed by a personal God.

A few years later he succumbed to the siren voices he had warned against. In a letter to his father (Berlin, November 10, 1837) Karl Marx gives a frank account of his development. He knows that he has reached a turning point in life, which he considers " an intellectual activity that expresses itself in knowledge, art, and personal experience. " Love has unlocked a new world for him which he tries to capture in lyrical poetry. Marx's view of the world at this time is purely idealistic. " My love, remote as the beyond, has become my heaven, my art. All reality blurs, and the blurred knows no limitations; reality has no hold on the present, which dissolves in vague emotions; nothing seems natural, everything moonshine, the complete opposite of what is really there. " [42]

Love was succeeded by philosophy, which, he hoped, would bring clarity in this chaotic period of *Sturm und Drang*. The study of

[41] K. Marx, *Fruehe Schriften*, I Band. Hrsg. v. H. J. Lieber und P. Furth (1962), p. 1.
[42] *Ibid.*, p. 8.

matter alternated with readings in metaphysics. Several poems
from this period, especially one strongly reminiscent of Goethe's
Prometheus, reflect the deep inner struggle that was taking place.

It has the following text:

Prayer of Despair (Prometheus)

Has my God wrecked everything I had,
Rolled it away in the yoke and curse of Fate?
Am I to lose all, all his worlds?
One would remain—revenge remains to me!

Proudly on myself I will avenge me
Against that being lording it on high.
My strength be a patchwork of my weaknesses,
Even my virtues unrewarded be!

I will build myself a towering throne,
Cold and immense its back against the sky;
May its bulwark superhuman horror,
And its marshal darkest suffering be!

You who lift sound eyes to gaze at it,
Recoil as grey and dumb as death!
Happiness, go dig yourself a grave
Under the impact of that chilling breath.

Rebound from my soaring iron structure,
Envious lightning bolts from him on high.
Were he to breach my walls, batter my halls,
Eternity would rebuild—defiantly!

Young Marx was fascinated by the symbol of Prometheus, much
as Fichte and Goethe had been before him. Goethe confesses that
for him the Titan remained a fixed idea even in old age. Characteristically also the youthful Nietzsche's first poetic efforts revolve
round the same figure. Young Marx's poem goes much further
than the Promethean poem of Goethe, which was inspired by a
passing rebelliousness against the deity. Marx not only revolts but
defiantly plans to construct a rival throne for himself. Here it is

not merely a matter of giving poetic form to a momentary mood
but rather of expressing a permanent attitude. This is evident
from further poems of Marx in which he lauds his single-handed
victory over heaven. One poem that reveals his notion of God is
in reality a high prayer to Marx's own greatness:

> Like the very gods I dare to roam
> Victorious through their ruined realms,
> My every word is act and flame,
> My breast and the Creator's are the same!

In this poem, *Thoughts on God,* the relationship between man and
the transcendent is annulled. Its theme is the poet's own Godlikeness and divine creativity. Marx wrestled " through many nights "
before he could write: " A curtain has fallen, my holy of holies
has been torn to shreds, and new gods must be enthroned. "
Stimulated by Kantian and Fichtian idealism, Marx began " to
search out the idea within reality itself. If the gods once dwelt
above the earth, now they have become its center. " [43]   Marx was
dissatisfied with Hegelian philosophy because he did not really
understand it. He was nonetheless dominated by its basic notion,
which he attempts to develop in his first essay on philosophy,
" *A philosophical-dialectical development of the godhead and its
manifestations as an independent concept, as religion, nature, and
history.* My last sentence was the beginning of the Hegelian
system. " [44]   In order to clarify this new thought complex, which
cost him endless effort, Marx studied Schelling. A casual remark
in Marx's writings of this period is significant. " This my favorite
offspring " that is, the new notion of an evolution of the idea of
God, " false siren that it is, carries me in its arms over to the
enemy. " Here again is prophetic self-appraisal.

Further on we find another significant account of Marx's reaction
to what he calls succumbing to the current philosophy. " I was
so angry that for days I could not think at all...ran about like
a madman in the garden along the Spree's dirty water ' that washes
souls and dilutes tea, ' even joined a hunting party with my host;

[43] *Ibid.,* p. 13.
[44] *Ibid.,* p. 14.

next I rushed off to Berlin where I felt like hugging every beggar I met. " [45]   In what he calls " a rankling rage "...at being forced to make an idol of an opinion that was hateful to him, Marx grew ill.   Recovering, he burned everything he had written " in the illusion that then I could forget the whole matter. "

As we learn from a letter to his father, it was during this crisis that Karl Marx became acquainted with the philosophy of Hegel and the Young Hegelians.   He soon found himself in their *Doktorklub*. " Many controversial opinions were aired in the debates here, and I " shackled myself ever more closely to the current world view which I had hoped to escape.   But all that had once been resonant in me now fell silent; I was caught in a veritable rage of irony— natural enough after so much negativeness. "

Here again it is important to note every word Marx uses to describe his reactions, which are surprising.   He had hoped to escape the prevailing philosophy and had instead fallen victim to it. As a result the better voices of his own heart were struck dumb. The shock was followed by the will to avenge his loss.   This Marx attempted by means of cynicism, a sure sign of unhappiness and discontent.   Hostility and sarcasm are the ego's way of rejecting the direction decided upon and of constantly reiterating that rejection.   At the close of the same letter Marx again mentions that his " heart, shouted down by the aggressive clamor of the warring mind, seems to have erred. "

Once made, the decision hardens; the sarcasm remains and becomes an essential part of Karl Marx.   It is accompanied by an impatient fanaticism that simply refuses to listen to voices like those rejected once and for all.   Ever more wholeheartedly Marx settles into his chosen role of a 19th century Prometheus.   It is not by chance that the frontispiece of the first volume of the completed collection of the joint works of Marx and Engels represents Marx as Prometheus in chains.   The picture reappears in the new East German edition published in 1957, this time with the caption, *Prometheus Bound*, an allegorical reference to the interdiction of the *Rheinische Zeitung*. *

Already in the preface to Marx's doctor's dissertation there are

[45] *Ibid.*, p. 15.
* The short-lived leftist newspaper of which Marx was editor.

hints of the cutting fanaticism and haughty self-confidence that later were to harden into a permanent attitude, ultimately to that of the notion of Karl Marx as indistinguishable from the Godhead. The dissertation is on the difference between the Democritean and the Epicurean philosophies of nature, in itself a scientific theme; but Marx's development of it was anything but scientific. He chose the subject himself and worked on it alone. He submitted the completed dissertation to the University of Jena, where he had never studied. It was accepted, and on April 15, 1841, Karl Marx received his Ph.D.

The Preface contains a condescending remark about the " primitive designation " of the work as a dissertation. Marx is convinced that he has solved a hitherto unsolved problem of Greek philosophical history and has thereby rehabilitated Epicurus, succeeding where Gassendi had failed. Gassendi, Marx concedes, did cause the interdiction to be revoked which had been placed on Epicurus by the early Church and the Middle Ages, the " Age of consummate Unreason. " Gassendi had attempted in vain " to accommodate pagan science to his Catholic conscience and Epicurus to the Church. "

Sarcastically Marx rejects Plutarch's invitation to review philosophy before the forum of religion. Marx quotes a passage from Hume about the affront that it is to philosophy, the sovereignty of which should be universally recognized, to be constantly made to answer for the consequences of its teachings and forced to defend itself before every art or science that happens to take offense. This is like a king being accused of high treason by his subjects! To the quotation from Hume, Marx adds his private creed. Solemnly invoking Epicurus and the *Prometheus* of Aeschylus, Marx writes, " As long as one drop of blood still pulses in the world-conquering, utterly free heart of philosophy she will continue to proclaim with Epicurus: Not he who despises the gods of the masses is godless, but he who clings to the notions of the masses about the gods! Philosophy makes no secret of her convictions. Prometheus' avowal, ' In one word, I detest all gods ' is philosophy's avowal, her own dictum against all gods, heavenly and earthly, who do not accept human self-consciousness as the supreme Deity beside which there shall be no other. To those sad March hares who rejoice in philosophy's present loss of bourgeois prestige, she can only say in Prometheus' words to Hermes; 'Understand this: I would not change my painful plight, on any terms, for your servile humility.' Prometheus is the most illustrious saint and martyr on the calendar of philosophers." [46]

It is not the science of nature in the philosophies of Democritus and Epicurus which really interests Marx but rather "the perfect construct of the consciousness" which he thinks he has discovered in the later Greek philosophers. He is particularly attracted to Epicurus, of whom he writes approvingly, "in his descriptions of the various natural phenomena he proceeds with a boundless nonchalance." Epicurus was interested only "in the *ataraxia* of the self-consciousness...not in the knowledge of nature for its own sake." Marx considers Epicurus the embodiment of "quiet of mind and of that independence which draws its wisdom *ex principio interno*." Marx continues: Veneration of the heavenly bodies was a cult to which all Greek philosophers subscribed. Herein we see an expression of the Greek spirit, which was still on a lower level of self-consciousness. "Hence in worshipping the heavenly bodies Greek philosophers were in reality worshipping themselves." Against this conception of religion, which all the Greeks shared, Epicurus had protested. He shifted the center of human life back to men, and in so doing led them to a higher form of self-consciousness. "Thus Epicurus censures those who believe that men have any need of heaven." In other words, "the autonomy and freedom of the self-consciousness is the principle of Epicurean philosophy". [47] For this reason Marx praises Epicurus as "the greatest of Greek enlighteners," one justly lauded by Lucretius as the first Greek to defy the gods and vanquish men's fear of the gods.

With this interpretation of Epicurus Marx revived the classical atheism of antiquity even before Feuerbach aroused his enthusiasm. Chronologically, interest in an atheism which stresses the revolutionary rejection of a personal universal God precedes Marx's interest in economic and social problems. The claim that it was Marx's materialism which led him to atheism is invalid. For Marx any explanation of the world from the standpoint of objective

[46] K. Marx, *Dissertation*, pp. 21 f.
[47] *Ibid.*

principles was of secondary importance, a matter on which like Epicurus he offered no particular opinion. The decisive principle of the Marxian *Weltanschauung* is the "perfect construct of the consciousness," which is by no means materialistic.

The *Dissertation* in the form in which it was presented was intended as a first step toward clarification of Marx's own world view. Obviously further chapters were to follow. The book was never completed, but fragments of it have been preserved which are important enough to indicate the direction which the *Dissertation* would have taken had it been developed.

In *Notes on the Dissertation* Marx attempts once again to preserve what he calls his "faith in the absoluteness" of the Hegelian system. For already voices could be heard among the Left Hegelians interpreting "this or that stipulation in Hegel's system as accommodation, in a word, morally." At this stage Marx still resists the tendency to deprecate Hegel, calling it lack of conscience "to accuse the Master of hidden motives." But the Left Hegelians state their suspicions in no uncertain terms. In what is supposed to be an epic poem Friedrich Engels depicts Danton, Voltaire, and Hegel in hell. They have gathered round Satan, just returned from earth, where he has been helping the freethinkers and atheists in their battle against belief.

> " And Hegel, whose mouth until this moment grimness locked,
> Suddenly rose up giant high and spoke:
> ' I consecrated all my life to Science,
> Preached atheism with my whole strength;
> I placed Self-Consciousness upon her throne,
> Convinced I had already conquered God. ' "

Gradually Marx's resistance to the criticism of Hegel flags. He begins to regard what he had once called "this unphilosophical change" in many young Hegelians as "a phenomenon which invariably accompanies the transition from discipline to freedom." Now that Hegel has brought theoretical philosophy to unsurpassed perfection, the time has come for a shift to practice. Philosophy must have a universal historical impact. "She must cast her eyes behind her, which is to say, now that she has the courage to go out and create a world, she must stop theorizing. " Like Prometheus who stole fire from heaven in order to build houses for men and better their lot on earth, philosophy when it comes down to earth turns against the historical world it finds; this is precisely what Hegelian philosophy is doing today. " [48]

The question: Can man live at all by a total philosophy? has not been solved by the " abysmally inadequate attempts " of many philosophers since Hegel, Marx continues. Rather a great political struggle is in sight. " Titanic are the times that follow on the heels of a philosophy that is complete in itself.... Unhappy iron ages are these, for their gods have died and their new goddess still seems as strange as an uncanny Fate which is either all light or all darkness. " [49] In Marx no definite program of the tasks to be achieved precedes his titanic will to action. For him as for others the French Revolution of 1789 was the most important turning point in the development of mankind, and since the Revolution has succumbed to the Counterrevolution, the challenge of the hour is to take up the cause once more. Intermittently Marx worked on an outline for a new kind of history of the French Revolution which was to serve as the authoritative textbook for the coming revolution.

In a special section of *Notes on the Dissertation* Marx listed certain ideas under the heading " Reason and the Proofs of God. " In these he plays up the younger Schelling against the older. " The time has come, " he writes, " to proclaim freedom of thought to superior mankind and no longer permit men to mourn the loss of their chains. " The proofs of God as reviewed one last time by the age of Hegel, Marx continues, were " turned upside down, that is, rejected in order to justify them " in a new synthesis. Such " empty tautologies " prove nothing but the existence of a self-consciousness that is essentially human. In the last analysis it is only a matter of the autonomy of the absolutely free being.

This is to be the spirit of all Marx's polemics with their typically 18th-century arguments, most of which are not sufficiently interesting to go into here.

[48] K. Marx, *Aufzeichnungen zur Dissertation*, p. 102.
[49] *Ibid.*, p. 104.

The year in which the *Dissertation* was completed, 1841, Feuerbach's major work, *The Essence of Christianity*, was published. This book strengthened the position which Marx had already won for himself. *The Holy Family*, a joint Marx-Engels publication, contains Marx's high praise of Feuerbach for having cleared away all the old intellectual impediments and returned man to his true place at the center of existence. Marx agrees with Feuerbach that essentially the critique of religion is finished. Marx does not go back to the subject in his old age because he considers the matter settled. More discussion would be only a waste of breath.

In December 1841, a new censorship regulation proscribed " frivolous and hostile criticism of the Christian religion. " This, writes Marx, is the equivalent of a proscription on all criticism, " for religion can only be attacked in a hostile or frivolous manner, a third does not exist. " [50] With a group of friends Marx planned to publish a journal, *Archive of Atheism*. The reaction of the Left Hegelians to this project is expressed in a letter to Arnold Ruge: " Dr. Marx, Dr. Bauer, and L. Feuerbach have become associate publishers of a theological-philosophical journal; may all the angels flock to the old Lord God's assistance and he have mercy on himself, for those three will certainly toss him out of heaven and hang a lawsuit on him to boot. Marx is accusing Christianity of being the most immoral of religions; incidentally, though a wild revolutionary, he has one of the keenest minds I know. " [51]

OPIUM OF THE PEOPLE

The notion barely suggested in the *Dissertation*—namely, that criticism of religion is the foundation on which the man who has attained to consciousness of self can begin to shape his own destiny through revolutionary action—Marx develops with unmistakable clarity in his *Contribution to the Critique of Hegel's Philosophy of*

[50] K. Marx, F. Engels, *Werke* Hist.-krit. Gesamtausgabe, I, 1, 2, pp. 261 f.
[51] *Ibid.*, Siehe " Briefe, " A. Ruge.

Right. It is in this work that Marx scornfully labels religion the
" opium of the people. " Religion prevents the masses from awakening to the self-consciousness necessary for revolution. Because
of the historical importance of these arguments, they should be
examined in some detail. Marx writes: " For Germany, the *criticism
of religion* has been largely completed; and the criticism of religion
is the premise of all criticism.

" The *profane* existence of error is compromised once its *celestial,
oratio pro aris et focis* has been refuted. Man, who has found in
the fantastic reality of heaven, where he sought a supernatural
being, only his own reflection, will no longer be tempted to find
only the *semblance* of himself—a nonhuman being—where he
seeks and must seek his true reality.

" The basis of irreligious criticism is this: *man makes religion;*
religion does not make man. Religion is indeed man's self-consciousness and self-awareness so long as he has not found himself
or has lost himself again. But *man* is not an abstract being,
squatting outside the world. Man is *the human world,* the state,
society. This state, this society, produce religion which is an
inverted world consciousness, because they are an *inverted world.*
Religion is the general theory of this world, its encyclopedic compendium, its logic in popular form, its spiritual *point d'honneur,*
its enthusiasm, its moral sanction, its solemn complement, its general
basis of consolation and justification. It is *the fantastic realization*
of the human being inasmuch as the *human being* possesses no true
reality. The struggle against religion is, therefore, indirectly a
struggle against *that world* whose spiritual *aroma* is religion.

" *Religious* suffering is at the same time an *expression* of real
suffering and a *protest* against real suffering. Religion is the sigh
of the oppressed creature, the sentiment of a heartless world, and
the soul of soulless conditions. It is the *opium* of the people.

" The abolition of religion as the *illusory* happiness of men,
is a demand for their *real* happiness. The call to abandon their
illusions about their condition is a *call to abandon a condition
which requires illusions.* The criticism of religion is, therefore,
the embryonic criticism of this vale of tears of which religion is
the *halo.*

" Criticism has plucked the imaginary flowers from the chain, not in order that man shall bear the chain without caprice or consolation but so that he shall cast off the chain and pluck the living flower. The criticism of religion disillusions man so that he will think, act and fashion his reality as a man who has lost his illusions and regained his reason; so that he will revolve about himself as his own true sun. Religion is only the illusory sun about which man revolves so long as he does not revolve about himself.

" It is the *task of history*, therefore, once the *other-world of truth* has vanished, to establish the *truth of this world*. The immediate *task of philosophy*, which is in the service of history, is to unmask human self-alienation in its *secular form* now that it has been unmasked in its *sacred form*. Thus the criticism of heaven is transformed into the criticism of earth, the *criticism of religion* into the *criticism of law*, and the *criticism of theology* into the *criticism of politics.* " [52]

The criticism of religion " ends with the doctrine that *man is the supreme being for man*. It ends, therefore, with the *categorical imperative to overthrow all those conditions* in which man is an abased, enslaved, abandoned, contemptible being.... " [53] According to Marx, Germany's revolutionary history began with Luther. However, Protestantism liberated man only from external religiosity; the struggle of the layman " against his own internal priest " has only begun. Only through the proletarian revolution can " the total loss of humanity " become again " a total redemption of humanity. "

Marx concludes: " In Germany *no* type of enslavement can be abolished unless *all* enslavement is destroyed. Germany, which likes to get to the bottom of things, can only make a revolution which upsets *the whole order* of things. The *emancipation of Germany* will be an *emancipation of man*. Philosophy is the *head* of this emancipation and the proletariat is its *heart*. Philosophy can only be realized by the abolition of the proletariat, and the proletariat can only be abolished by the realization of philosophy. " [54] When

[52] K. Marx, *Early Writings*. Translated by T. B. Bottomore (New York: McGraw-Hill, 1964), pp. 43-44.

[53] *Ibid.*, p. 52.

[54] *Ibid.*, p. 59.

all inner requirements have been met with, the "Gallic cock will sound the Germanic resurrection."

All his life Marx upheld these notions, according to which atheism is by no means a mere superstructure or chance garment which may be removed without essentially changing Marxism itself. As Jean Lacroix comments in his study on atheism in *Documents* (1934), atheism is "an absolutely essential ingredient of Marxism."

Much like contemporary atheistic existentialists, Marx confronts men with a choice between man's freedom and God's existence. For Marx the concept of freedom is closely connected with his particular philosophy of work, according to which man is the demiurge of the world, of man, and of society. Marx says: Since it is only through his struggle with nature that a man becomes a human being, man cannot have been created by someone else, by God. Thus atheism reverses the positive definition of a man as a workman who by his works changes the world and wins his humanity. Human freedom becomes absolute freedom with its absolute self-sufficiency. Only so long as a man has not yet awakened to full awareness of freedom can he believe that he has been created by another being. Once the full significance of freedom, (which Marx calls the eternal aristocracy of human nature), has dawned on a man, his choice has already fallen—for himself and against God. The more human a man becomes, the more he is inclined to peel off the religious husks of his dream-wrapped past. In all Marx's works, his late works included, we find the same basic theme: the more religious a man is, the less human; the more human, the less religious. Atheism has entered into a unique partnership with what Marx calls the practical life.

Here again we see that modern atheism is not a product of speculation. It is not as though reason upon reaching maturity had submitted the ancient problem of the existence of God to critical examination and reached a negative conclusion. Nineteenth-century atheism no longer posed the question of the existence of God, which was considered settled. For modern atheists everything revolves round the question of man and his humanity. A man eliminates God in order to take full possession of his own greatness, of which faith in God deprives him. When God is overthrown an obstacle to one's own freedom is removed.

In Marxism there is a *Frageverbot* on certain questions right from the start; interdiction takes the place of discussion. The question of origins, of primordeal man, and of nature in the true sense of the word is arbitrarily dismissed or covered over by a façade of sophistry. This is why Eric Voegelin calls Marx "a speculative gnostic" and "intellectual swindler."

A logical line runs from Hegel to full-fledged atheism. Bruno Bauer, who as both the publisher and editor of a journal for speculative theology originally represented Hegelian orthodoxy, later tore off Hegel's mask. In the guise of an orthodox Pietist and armed with countless Biblical and Hegelian quotations Bauer demonstrated that by no means were the young Left Hegelians to be considered the first atheists, but rather their " Father," whose atheism had flourished under cover of a philosophical justification of Christian dogma. " Oh the unhappy wretches who allowed themselves to be deceived by whispers that the subject of religion, as of philosophy, was eternal truth in all its objectivity; that it was God and nothing but God and the definition of God. Poor things, in their eargerness to hear that religion and philosophy coincided, they imagined they could keep their God and accept that religion is the self-consciousness of the absolute spirit. " [55]   For all its Christian wrappings, Hegel's interpretation of religion aimed at the destruction of religion. His more gullible students tried to interpret this as a kind of pantheism; actually it is a definite atheism which substitutes the human self-consciousness for God. To such godless consciousness, Bauer continues, Hegel accords the attributes of the divine. Well-meaning souls fail to see through his devilish ruse and recognize him as the revolutionary that he is. Actually he is more of a revolutionary than all his followers put together, for Hegel " completely abrogates all substantial relationships. "

---

[55] B. Bauer, *Die Posaune des juengsten Gerichts ueber Hegel den Atheisten und Antichristen* (1841).

ARTHUR SCHOPENHAUER:
FIRST AVOWED ATHEIST

Even for so willful a thinker as Arthur Schopenhauer Kant's critique
of the proofs of God had all the finality of an unshakable fact.
Otto Linder writes that Schopenhauer considered the *absolutum*
of the cosmological proofs so annihilated by Kant that he, Schopenhauer, had found only its "mortal remains." Indeed, he even goes
so far as to remark, "When the stench of a corpse fills my nostrils
I become indignant. " [56]   Although Kant's critique had given so-
called "speculative theology" the *coup de grâce*, Kant had tried
to lessen the shock by offering "a palliative"; but Schopenhauer
refuses to take Kant's founding of faith on a moral postulate
seriously.

Schopenhauer is stingingly critical of the philosophers of his
day, whom he accuses of lacking the courage to admit to the State
authorities what has happened. Instead the professors of philosophy
make long equivocal speeches to gratify the government's desire
to have the philosophy halls turn out good Christians and sedulous
churchgoers. Schopenhauer bitterly resented and hated the professors who, he insists, kowtow to official demands for Christianity
against their real convictions. Thus for him Fichte is "at bottom
a mere sophist, not a true philosopher. " Penalized after his initial
attempt to ignore the doctrine of the established church, Fichte
had taken the hint, and upon receiving a teaching post in Berlin,
"he most obligingly transformed the absolute ego into the good
Lord. "

In the sharpest possible terms Schopenhauer attacked "that
philosophy professor Hegel, " whom he accused of coining the
expression "absolute religion" in order to cloak his true intentions.
Above all Schopenhauer felt the need to denounce the pantheism
of the day as a purely academic camouflage for atheism. Some
of the philosophers haven't even the courage for pantheism! "It
is most amusing to watch the philosophers ogle with pantheism as

[56] A. Schopenhauer, "Fragmente zur Geschichte der Philosophie, " *Saemtliche Werke*, hg. v. M. Frischeisen-Koehler, Bd. VI, p. 143.

with a forbidden fruit they haven't the spunk to pick. " [57]   Schopenhauer's pertinent criticism of pantheism is that it really does not
mean a thing; it merely identifies the world with God, thus enriching
the language by a superfluous synonym for the word " world. "
In reality, Schopenhauer continues, pantheism makes sense only
when it has been preceded by theism.   For only when one begins
with God, in other words, when one has a God with whom one is
familiar, can one ultimately " identify him with the world in order
to eliminate him in a respectable manner. "   Instead of taking the
world as the starting point and accounting for it impartially, one
started with God as an accepted fact.   Only when one no longer
knew what to do with God was it necessary for " the world " to
assume God's role.   This was the origin of pantheism. [58]   Basically
then, pantheism is only " a masked negation " of God.

Although Schopenhauer frankly professes atheism, his atheism
is of quite a different kind from that of the Left Hegelians.
Schopenhauer does not aim at the destruction of religion and
religious practices among those who truly believe.   His purpose
is merely to provide a new (atheistic) " religion " for those who,
following the intellectual trend of the times, have abandoned religion.
Schopenhauer's atheism is unrelated to materialism.   On the contrary, by its very nature it must ultimately conflict with materialism.
Schopenhauer holds that by destroying the foundations of theism
with his critique of religion, Kant cleared the way for a completely
different and much more profound explanation of existence.

Schopenhauer has very personal reasons for his rejection of
theism as faith in a personal God of the universe.   For him the
idea of Arthur Schopenhauer as a personally created being face
to face with a universal and personal God is intolerable.   As a
result of philosophical and Indian studies Schopenhauer feels that
his " head has grown incapable of supporting such a notion. "
For him theism has lain like an Alp on the intellectual—above all
on the philosophical efforts of the whole Christian era, blocking
the achievements of progress or causing them to be neglected.   In
the field of philosophy, he says, Kant has really put an end to
" this Jewish theism. "   For Schopenhauer the idea of faith in a

[57] *Ibid.*, Bd. VII, p. 96.
[58] *Ibid.*

personal God is intolerable because he considers the coexistence of
divine freedom with human freedom an impossibility. For him
the concept of freedom is inseparable from the concept of origins.
" For to be a being created by another yet *free* in will and in deed
is something that can be said with words but not reached by thought.
Namely, he who called that being into existence created also the
essence, i.e. all the characteristics of that being which he posited
as part of him. For one cannot create without creating something:
a particular being exactly and wholly determined by his characteristics from which all that being's words and actions flow. These
are but the interplay of his posited characteristics, which require
only some impetus from without in order to be set in motion.
As a man *is,* so must he act. Guilt or praiseworthiness properly
belong not to a man's acts but to his essence and existence. Hence
theism is incompatible with the responsibility of a moral being
because in theism responsibility always falls back on the Creator
of that being, where its center of gravity lies. With the concept
of moral freedom men have attempted to construct a bridge between
irreconcilable theism and the moral freedom of the human being,
but invariably the bridge collapses. *Free* being must also be
original being. If our will is *free* it is also original being *(das
Urwesen),* and vice versa. " [59]

Thus Schopenhauer's atheism joins the chorus of denial of God
on the strength of the rationalistic argument of the irreconcilability
of human and divine freedom, without succeeding in attaining true
freedom for man.

[59] A. Schopenhauer, *Werke,* Bd. VII, pp. 215 ff.

10. *The death of God*

NIETZSCHE AS PROPHET

Against the background of growing atheism and steadily diminishing consciousness of the reality of God Hegelian philosophy struck Nietzsche as little more than a final stop on the way to honest atheism. Hegel had made one last effort to rescue foundering Christianity with his philosophy of the absolute *logos,* a philosophy in which history is considered the gradual coming to self-consciousness of unconditional genius, and religion the imperfect self-presentation of that genius. To Nietzsche, says Karl Loewith, this "equivocal union of theology and philosophy, of religion and atheism, of Christianity and paganism at the zenith of metaphysics" seemed only a vain attempt to check the triumphal march of atheism. Nietzsche writes, "...the decay of the belief in the Christian God, the victory of scientific atheism,—is a universal European event, in which all races are to have their share of service and honor. On the contrary, it has to be ascribed precisely to the Germans —those with whom Schopenhauer was contemporary,—that they delayed this victory of atheism longest, and endangered it most. Hegel especially was its retarder par excellence, in virtue of the grandiose attempt which he made to persuade us of the divinity of existence, with the help at the very last of our sixth sense, 'the historical sense.' As philosopher, Schopenhauer was the *first* avowed and inflexible atheist we Germans have had: his hostility to Hegel had here its background. The nondivinity of existence was regarded by him as something understood, palpable, indisputable; he always lost his philosophical composure and got into a passion when he saw anyone hesitate and beat about the bush here. It is at this point that his thorough uprightness of character comes in: unconditional, honest atheism is precisely the *preliminary condition* for his raising the problem, as a final and hardwon victory of the European conscience, as the most prolific act of two thousand years' discipline to truth, which in the end no longer tolerates the *lie* of the belief in a God. " [1]

As early as 1840 Feuerbach had proclaimed the need for a change; he was the first to demand a " definitely non-Christian philosophy. " Outstripping the " pious atheism " of Feuerbach, who still accepted the divine essence of man, Nietzsche now takes over from Schopenhauer the task of forcing a crisis and an ultimate decision for atheism, which meanwhile had become legal. " It was atheism that led me to Schopenhauer. " Nietzsche considers it his vocation to write the concluding chapter on the decline of Christianity, whose highly spiritual God history has already disproved.

Across Europe Nietzsche sounds the tocsin to awaken the sleepers oblivious of the approaching disaster. Theirs is a dangerous slumber. Already the sinister breath of the thaw wind has blown the ice so thin that it barely holds. Soon no one will be able to walk on it. Christianity has grown hollow, its substance is gone. Or again, Christianity on its deathbed has fallen into gentle moralizing. What remains of it is not so much God, freedom, immortality; as kindness, decency, and the belief that somehow in the end kindness and decency will prevail. It is " the euthanasia of Christianity. "

The time is past, Nietzsche continues, in which nature could be considered " proof of the goodness and care of a God " and history interpreted " in honor of a divine reason, as a constant testimony to a moral order and final purpose in the world "; in which personal experiences might be explained as " pious men have long enough explained them, as if everything were a dispensation or

---

[1] F. Nietzsche, *Joyful Wisdom* (New York: Frederick Unger Publishing Co., 1960), pp. 307-308.

intimation of Providence, something planned and sent on behalf of
the salvation of the soul; all that is now *past,* it has conscience
against it, it is regarded by all the more acute consciences as
disreputable and dishonourable, as mendaciousness, feminism, weakness, and cowardice,—by virtue of this severity, if by anything,
we are *good* Europeans, the heirs of Europe's longest and bravest
self-conquest. " [2]

Nietzsche accepted the mandate to become the prophet of his age
and proclaim the tidings of the death of God for the following
reasons: first, because Schopenhauer and the first apostles of
materialism to openly attack Christian faith in God as an illusion
born of fear and trickery had met with little success; second,
because in all too many people reverence for their sacred past was
still alive and they dared not admit the change that had taken
place. Passionately and in prophetic stance Nietzsche flung across
Europe the tidings that its ancient God was dead, a proclamation
that raised and continues to raise a thousand echoes.

Nietzsche was well aware of the far-reaching effects that his
message would have. He does not belong to those shallow thinkers
who proclaim unbelief with naive triumph, little suspecting what
terrible disenchantment must follow their cheers. Nietzsche knows
that belief in God is the spiritual foundation of European culture,
that when the sun of faith sets, the whole world grows dark.
Thus Nietzsche is the prophet of an unprecedented eclipse and
darkness. On the horizon of the age he discerns the coming
ravages of atheism, ineluctable consequences of the disintegration
of faith.

" The most important of more recent events—that ' God is dead, '
that the belief in the Christian God has become unworthy of belief—
already begins to cast its first shadows over Europe. To the few
at least whose eye, whose *suspecting* glance, is strong enough and
subtle enough for this drama, some sun seems to have set, some
old, profound confidence seems to have changed into doubt: our
old world must seem to them daily more darksome, distrustful,
strange and ' old. ' In the main, however, one may say that the
event itself is far too great, too remote, too much beyond most

[2] *Ibid.*, p. 308.

people's power of apprehension, for one to suppose that so much as the report of it could have *reached* them; not to speak of many who already knew *what* had taken place, and what must all collapse now that this belief had been undermined,—because so much was built upon it, so much rested on it, and had become one with it: for example, our entire European morality.   This lengthy, vast and uninterrupted process of crumbling, destruction, ruin and overthrow which is now imminent: who has realized it sufficiently today to have to stand up as the teacher and herald of such a tremendous logic of terror, as the prophet of a period of gloom and eclipse, the like of which has probably never taken place on earth before? ... " [3]

The unbelievers of Nietzsche's day are like careless children who have committed some misdeed without quite knowing what it is.   Although they deny God, they have not the faintest notion of the consequences of their denial.   Thus in the eyes of his contemporaries Nietzsche with his tidings of the death of God is mad.

" The Madman.—Have you ever heard of the madman who on a bright morning lighted a lantern and ran to the market-place calling out unceasingly: ' I seek God!   I seek God! '—As there were many people standing about who did not believe in God, he caused a great deal of amusement.   Why! is he lost? said one. Has he strayed away like a child? said another.   Or does he keep himself hidden?   Is he afraid of us?   Has he taken a sea-voyage? Has he emigrated?—the people cried out laughingly, all in a hubbub.   The insane man jumped into their midst and transfixed them with his glances.   ' Where is God gone? ' he called out. ' I mean to tell you!   We *have killed him*, —you and I.   We are all his murderers!   But how have we done it?   How were we able to drink up the sea?   Who gave us the sponge to wipe away the whole horizon?   What did we do when we loosened this earth from its sun?   Whither does it now move?   Whither do we move? Away from all suns?   Do we not dash on unceasingly?   Backwards, sideways, forwards, in all directions?   Is there still an above and below?   Do we not stray, as through infinite nothingness?   Does

[3] *Ibid.*, p. 275.

not empty space breathe upon us? Has it not become colder? Does not night come on continually, darker and darker? Shall we not have to light lanterns in the morning? Do we not hear the noise of the gravediggers who are burying God? Do we not smell the divine putrefaction?—for even Gods putrefy! God is dead! God remains dead! And we have killed him! How shall we console ourselves, the most murderous of all murderers? The holiest and the mightiest that the world has hitherto possessed has bled to death under our knife,—who will wipe the blood from us? With what water could we cleanse ourselves? What lustrums, what sacred games shall we have to devise? Is not the magnitude of this deed too great for us? Shall we not ourselves have to become gods, merely to seem worthy of it? There never was a greater event,—and on account of it, all who are born after us belong to a higher history than any history hitherto! ' —Here the madman was silent and looked again at his hearers; they also were silent and looked at him in surprise. At last he threw his lantern on the ground, so that it broke in pieces and was extinguished. ' I come too early, ' he then said, ' I am not yet at the right time. This prodigious event is still on its way, and is traveling,—it has not yet reached men's ears. Lightning and thunder need time, the light of the stars needs time, deeds need time, even after they are done, to be seen and heard. This deed is as yet further from them than the farthest star,—*and yet they have done it*'—It is further stated that the madman made his way into different churches on the same day, and there intoned his *Requiem aeternam deo*. When led out and called to account, he always gave the reply: ' What are these churches now, if they are not the tombs and monuments of God? ' " [4]

Nietzsche's proclamation of the death of God was taken as the starting point for two important intellectual movements. One, the Godless Movement, invoked Nietzsche as its crown witness and intellectual father. But Nietzsche proclaims not only, God is dead!—but also, Long live Superman! Superman, then, is to be the ersatz for the dead transcendent God. He is the new God here below. The second movement furthered Nietzsche's attempt to

[4] *Ibid.*, pp. 167-169.

immanentize the divine; its disciples, Rilke and Stefan George, dream of a mankind whose bliss and fulfillment are to be found not in the hereafter but here. They cancel the honesty of Nietzsche's proclamation of the dead God when they apply the word "God" both to human becoming and to the heroic humanizing earthly power of man while emphasizing their rejection of Christian faith in God. The new God is no eternal, immutable, primal Cause of all becoming, but becoming itself. Thus, says Friedrich Koch, "God grows and matures with the growing and maturing culture of man. In man God awakens to life; man delivers blind, mute God from the trammels of the cosmos.... From the viewpoint of intellectual history, the image of the becoming godhead is a secular process. It is part of that process which ever since the Enlightenment has penetrated the domain of the religious: the immanentization of everything transcendent. " [5]

RELIGIOUS BECOMING

Nietzsche's painful passage through the torments of doubt in his childhood faith gradually shapes that philosophical individualistic basic attitude out of which atheism must grow. Referring to his own atheism Nietzsche says in his last autobiographical essay, *Ecce homo,* which he wrote only a few months before the beginning of his final illness, and which because of its uncritical exaggeration has always caused embarrassment: " I know atheism not at all as a consequence, still less as an occurrence: with me it is an instinct. " And again, " God, the immortality of the soul, redemption, the beyond—mere notions on which I wasted no time or attention, not even as a child. " [6] Such words suggest that Nietzsche was deficient in some integrant; that he lacked, so to speak, the sense of religion. It sounds as though he had never had an inner relation to the Christian articles of faith. It is sufficiently clear today to what

[5] F. Koch, *Rilkes Studen Buch—ein Akt deutschen Glaubens* (1943), pp. 25, 18.

[6] F. Nietzsche, *Ecce homo,* VIII, p. 332.

extent the later Nietzsche, by this time manic-depressive, falsified the picture of his own development. In absolute contradiction to this late self-testimony stands the opinion of a woman to whom Nietzsche was long bound by a deep love, Lou Andras-Salomé.

Mrs. Salomé has left a sensitive study of the intellectual Nietzsche in which she says that his deepest side is the religious and that any serious study of Nietzsche would have to be above all a study in religious psychology.

Nietzsche's own early notes testify against his later ones. That the war which broke out in Nietzsche's soul before he was twenty was primarily a religious war is evident from his famous poem, *To an Unknown God.*

In this prayer—for that is what it really is—the young man in his loneliness reverently raises his hands to God to whom he has consecrated his altars, imploring that should he ever stray from God, God might always call him back. The youth pauses at the crossroads still undecided which road to take. The dynamic of his inner cleavage drives him away from God and pulls him back. Already he feels himself one of " the apostates' throng "; he struggles against the snare God has laid for him even while proclaiming his readiness to serve God.

> Once more before I go my way,
> Before I fix my gaze ahead,
> I lift my trembling hands to thee
> To whom in solitude I pray.
> To thee in my heart's depth
> Sacred altars reverently
> I consecrate,
> Imploring that thy voice should keep
> Summoning me; altars whereon
> The words glow: TO AN UNKNOWN GOD.
> His I am, though to this hour
> I trot with the apostates' throng.
> I am his! I feel his net,
> Still fight its closing in on me;
> Were I to flee,
> I would return to serve him yet.

I will to know thee, unknown one!
Thou deep into my soul reaching,
Storm swift through my life sweeping,
Unknowable, like-to-me one,
I would know, *Lord, I would serve thee!*

The poem is vibrant with profound religious emotion. The *mysterium fascinosum* has thrilled the soul of the young man. His awakening can' be postponed no longer. Henceforth this life must revolve round God whether it decides for or against him. It remains chained to God though it strains to break away. It is no longer possible to be neutral or unconcerned. A personal decision must follow, either the " yes " of love of God or the " no " of hate. There is no third possibility.

Nietzsche decides against God. His sister, the embodiment of traditional piety, implores him to abandon the new path. But he rejects " stuffy German parlor-happiness " and the weak impotent faith of his female guardians. He longs for what he considers the virility of going his own way with all its dangers; he wants to explore on his own. He writes his sister, " If you want peace of mind and happiness, then believe; if you want to be a disciple of truth, explore. What counts is the main goal. " For Nietzsche belief is the quiet harbor; unbelief the dangerous, hence beckoning sea.

CAUSES OF UNBELIEF

Even in the young Nietzsche's writings the solid intellectual block posed by transcendental idealism, which Nietzsche adopted from Kant and Schopenhauer, is clearly evident. Thus the possibility of penetrating to divine reality by way of reflection on the world and experience is blocked from the start. Behind faith there cannot exist, independent of the human subject, a divine beyond, the effects of which reach into the here and now. All his life Nietzsche remained under the spell of epistemological skepticism, so from the beginning he failed to pose the question of the transcendental reality of God: Is there behind faith a transcendental God, a divine reality that can be reached by knowledge and faith? Nowhere do we find the slightest evidence that Nietzsche was ever troubled by the need of some First Cause to explain the world and himself. Not once do we see him assembling and weighing objective pros and cons concerning the existence of a divine reality as a basis for some personal decision. The closest Nietzsche comes to it is in an unfinished essay, *Teleology Since Kant—the Teleological Proof of the Existence of God*, which "even Voltaire considered invincible." But Nietzsche never gets far enough to be able to evaluate for himself the "yes" and "no" of faith. He leaped to a conclusion before he began: "The appropriateness of the organic, the regularity of the inorganic—these have been imposed upon nature by our understanding." A page or so later he writes: "It is of great practical value to rid ourselves of teleology. All that is needed is to reject the concept of a higher intelligence; then we are content." He openly admits the aim of his proofs, which is to destroy teleology. Nietzsche had no idea that leading physiologists of his day like Johannes Mueller, K. von Baer, Edward Pflueger considered teleology a scientifically demonstrable fact, and that by intellectual elaboration of that fact had proved the existence of a higher intelligence. Nietzsche was equally unaware of the conclusions reached by Trendelenburg and young Fichte and of their victory over epistemological idealism, a victory which cleared the road to an authentic beyond. (Nietzsche did jot down a note to read Trendelenburg's *Examination of Logic*.) From the fundamental philosophical position that Nietzsche had already assumed it was impossible for him to see these developments in perspective. For him faith was always no more than the result of desires projected into the world beyond. His arguments against faith approach the problem solely from the question: Is such projection of mood and desire justifiable?

In his book on the legacy of Nietzsche, Friedrich Wuerzbach says: "For Nietzsche the notion that for millennia men have worshipped errors as truths was an indisputable fact." Nietzsche himself insists, "A nation that has kept its faith in itself also has its own God in whom it honors the conditions through which it became great; in other words, its own virtues. It projects the joy it takes in itself and its sense of power in a being whom it can thank for that joy and power.... One is thankful for one's self: for this one needs a God. " [7]

Later he writes, " All the beauty and sublimity with which we have invested real and imagined things I will show to be the property and product of man and this should be his most beautiful apology. Man as poet, as thinker, as god, as love, as power. Oh, the royal liberality with which man enriches things in order to impoverish himself and make himself wretched! Hitherto this has been his greatest selflessness, that be admired and worshipped and knew how to conceal from himself that it was *he* who had created all he admired. " [8]

How was it possible that a man like Nietzsche could dismiss the grave problem of the reality of God from the start, that he could fail to seriously pose the question: could faith in God be more than a projection of man's desires and needs? Here we touch on a mystery that can never be fully solved, the mystery of a man's most personal decision. One can of course point out that agnostic skepticism had impressed Nietzsche so profoundly that he no longer saw the possibility of any other solution. But how can this happen to a philosopher of " open horizons " who always and on principle keeps all roads, left or right, up or down, passable? That in Nietzsche's case extremely personal prior decisions set the course of his thought is suggested by words of his from a very early period. At sixteen Nietzsche writes in his diary, " whenever one speaks openly against religion people impudently suppose that not one's reason but one's passions dictate what he believes. " And in Nietzsche's posthumous papers we find: " To criticize anything based on reverence there must exist on the part of the critic a certain insolent, brutal, even shameless attitude.... Such immoralists should be forgiven for constantly playing the martyrs to the truth; the fact is that it was not the urge to truth but the spirit of destruction, wanton skepticism, and lust for adventure which led them to negate. " [9]

[7] Nietzsches Werke werden nach der Kroenerschen Klassiker-ausgabe (I bis VIII und der Gross-oktavausgabe IX bis XX zitiert).
[8] F. Nietzsche, *Werke*, Klassikerausgabe, IX, p. 120.
[9] F. Wuerzbach, *Das Vermaechtnis Nietzsches* (1940), p. 118.

Even intellectual decisions that seem to be matters of objective, impersonal understanding easily succumb to the temptations that rise from the intangible depths of the instincts and beckon siren-like. Youth is instinctively tempted to rebel against the firmly established order of its given world, to smash it to pieces and create autonomously a new world of its own, a counterworld.

At fourteen Nietzsche dramatized this temptation in poetry; his hero is the mythical Prometheus who in his pride rebelled against the gods. Here the most deeply personal theme of Nietzsche's whole life stirs, and he struggles to express it in poem and drama. Through the childish outline for the drama sounds the already passionate theme of his later *Zarathustra:* " My proud spirit cannot bear that the gods. . .should wield the scepter. . . . Take courage, heart, for now a fraud must be revealed: Whether he ruler be or merely an illusion. " The final act was to depict " the end of Zeus, foreknown by Prometheus. " Zeus is to be overthrown by Prometheus personally, whereas the Germanic gods are destroyed by the forces of nature. As Heimsoeth points out, " Here twilight of the gods strives to become overthrow of the gods. Nietzsche pits the freedom of titanic and prophetic man—' my freedom, my joy, my pride '—against ' the boundless power of God' or more specifically, against man's ' predestination ' by the Christian God. This is the inflammatory theme. " [10] Hermann Nohl writes, " False radicalism, which is forever bewitched by extremes, is nothing but a kind of retardedness; Nietzsche's work reveals a whole range of characteristics that experts are inclined to explain in the light of the illness that broke out at the end of Nietzsche's life, characteristics which in reality reflect certain intellectual patterns of Nietzsche's youth that he never outgrew; in this respect Nietzsche never really matured. " [11]

In that almost instinctive rebelliousness which permits no questioning of the metaphysical first place one holds in the scheme of things, which not only refuses to place its trust in existence but bars the whole conception of existence as a gift and of man's life as meaningful—these notions are the result of the cramp of self-

[10] H. Heimsoeth, " Des jungen Nietzsches Weg zur Philosophie, " in *Neve Beitraege deutschen Forschung*, hg. v. Fidder, 1943), p. 154.
[11] H. Nohl, *Charakter und Schicksal*, 2. Auflage (1940), p. 160.

deification which simply dismisses reasons as of secondary importance. Hence Nietzsche's attitude can never be explained by reasons.
Apparently Nietzsche too succumbed to the demonic attraction
that lies in the enjoyment of power, a power that revels in the
destruction of all that has long been considered unassailable and
worthy of deep reverence. This is what draws him to what he
calls "the ranks of the blasphemers." It is Nietzsche's ambition
to run the whole gamut of the modern soul, including its night
side; to explore its every fold and cranny; to experience consciously
and fully the antithesis of a religious soul; to become acquainted
with the devil and know God from the devil's perspective.

To be sure, with the razing of faith the foundation of values
on which faith stands also collapses; nihilism threatens to engulf
everything, including the blasphemer. With this, man, the wanderer, loses sight of every goal, every path; he gazes into the night
of madness. "I stand still, suddenly I am tired. The road ahead
seems to drop steeply; in a flash the abyss is all about me.
I am loath to look down. Behind me tower the mountains.
Trembling, I grope for a hold. What? Has everything turned to
stone and precipice? This shrub—it breaks to pieces in my hand,
and sallow leaves and scraggly roots trickle downwards. I shiver
and close my eyes—where am I? I peer into a purple night; it
looks at me and beckons." [12]

DIONYSIAN LIFE

The will to live fights against submersion in night; it tries to over-
leap the void to a new world. Unceasingly the liberated spirit
contends with the shades of the world it has rejected, which
attempt to lure it back. It presents itself first of all in the form
of Dionysian ecstasy. Here a new path seems to open to "the
womb of being."

[12] F. Nietzsche, *Werke*, XII, p. 223.

In a supposedly classical philological study, *The Birth of Tragedy from the Spirit of Music*, young Nietzsche for the first time conceives the notion of Dionysian life as a substitute for God.

This life reveals itself to him through the world of the Olympians. "Nothing in these deities reminds us of asceticism, high intellect, or duty: we are confronted by luxuriant, triumphant *existence*, which deifies the good and bad indifferently." [13] Here man's urge to harmony, or rather the individual with his personal measure of possibilities realizes oneness with nature by ecstatically plunging into the self-forgetfulness of Dionysian transport. Lyric poet and musician are fundamentally the same artist, "become wholly identified with the original Oneness, its pain and contradiction." Not as *knowers* are we fused with that essential spirit; only through the creative act of genius does the mysterious fusion "with the primal architect of the cosmos" take place. Now the individual "is at once subject and object, poet, actor, and audience."

Thus existence and with it the world as a purely aesthetic phenomenon is eternally justified. The Greek satyr is the prototype of man, expression of his highest and strongest aspirations, of the enthusiast ravished by the nearness of the god. "The satyr is symbol of the sexual omnipotence of nature, which the Greek was accustomed to view with reverent wonder." [14]

Here is the god of pantheism, the cosmos, life, nature as godhead, ecstasy that redeems by annihilating the individual so that he may merge with primeval Oneness.

Dionysian art hymns the eternal bliss of existence. We can face the horror of the individual existence without allowing it to turn us to stone because metaphysical solace is ours for the taking. "For a brief moment we become, ourselves, the primal Being, and we experience its insatiable hunger for existence...we become one with the immense lust for life and are made aware of the eternity and indestructibility of that lust." [15]

In these passages Nietzsche reveals the real motive behind the

---

[13] F. Nietzsche, *The Birth of Tragedy* (New York: Doubleday and Company, Inc.), p. 29.
[14] *Ibid.*, p. 52.
[15] *Ibid.*, pp. 102-103.

longing for ecstasy as it is found all through the history of religion as well as is in certain artists (Baudelaire for one) whenever ecstasy exercises its uncanny power.

When a man realizes the unfathomableness of his life and tastes of his mortality, the demonic cleavage and unreality of life become suddenly oppressive and he is happy to plunge into the whirlpool of ecstasy in order to escape from his inner voices. For a while the *daemon* of ecstasy can delude him into believing he really has escaped from himself, that he has burst the cocoon of his ego. The borderline between the ego and the world seems to dissolve; the individual is carried away on the lifestream of the All. As such ecstasy consists in the maelstrom of all passions, naturally the most accessible are the most readily inflamed, above all the sexual passions, so that often everything revolves round sex and eroticism. In these the Dionysian adept seems to rent the veil of the cosmos. In sensual passion he seems to attain true ecstasy, to break free from the bonds of the ego. We know from the history of religion, which abounds in cults of the sexual organs, that sexual orgies often lead to pseudo-religion and pseudo-mysticism.

The Attic interpretation of Dionysian life as ecstasy, the state natural to Pan and to pantheism, has been accepted and developed by Ludwig Klages. In Nietzsche it is gradually replaced by a new interpretation. Nietzsche personally never succeeded in shattering "the glass walls" of individuality, in breaking out of the cell of self and becoming submerged in the tides of Dionysian transport. Only in the experience of music, particularly in the intoxicating, rich tonality of Wagnerian music, was he able to attain briefly to the longed for submersion of self—until the falseness of that music dawned on him and he turned passionately against it.

The real significance of Nietzsche's disappointment in Wagner was that Wagner opened his eyes to the spuriousness of such ecstasy and enabled him to overcome and sublimate his whole conception of ecstasy as the essence of Dionysian life. Only at great cost to his nerves was Nietzsche able to nurse the illusion of exalted and blissful moments, a strain that naturally had profound repercussions. "People who know moments of exaltation and ecstasy, who after squandering their nervous energy easily fall into the opposite extreme of hopelessness and despair, are prone to regard as their supreme moments those in which they are truly 'themselves,' their wretched and despairing moments those in which they are 'beside themselves.' Such people resent their environment, world, age. For them ecstasy is the only life in which they can be truly themselves. Everything else, whether intellectual, moral, religious, or aesthetic, they consider inimical to life. Mankind has these drunken enthusiasts to thank for many evils." [16]

THE WILL TO POWER

In the process of clarification Nietzsche's basic concept, " Dionysian life, " is transformed from vital ecstasy to the will to power. All life presses beyond itself, avid not only for survival but for conquest. All processes of the subconscious as of the conscious mind tend toward the acquisition of power. Here lies the root of all impulses. Even religion, Nietzsche insists, was born of the priests' will to power. Indeed the whole world, the inorganic included, strains for power.

"Do you know what the world is to me? Shall I show it you in my looking-glass? The world: a monstrous force without beginning, without end, a solid iron bulk whose energy remains constant, is never spent, only transformed, inestimably huge in its entirety, a household without expenditures or losses but likewise without increase or gain, bounded by nothingness as by a frontier, nothing uncontrolled, nothing wasted, nothing endlessly extended, rather as a specific force consigned to a specific place, and not a space 'void' anywhere but as vitality everywhere, as the interplay of powers and sources of power simultaneously one and many, piling up here even as they diminish there, an ocean of raging, flooding, ever shifting forces with mammoth intervals of return, an ebb and flow of forms, from the simplest to the most complex, from the stillest, stiffest, coldest, to the most ardent, wildest, self-contra-

[16] F. Nietzsche, *Werke*, IV, p. 245.

dictory, and back again from complexity to simplicity, from the interplay of contradictions to the lust of acquiescence...affirming itself, blessing itself as a becoming, an ever returning that knows no satiety, no surfeit, no lassitude:—this my Dionysian world that eternally creates and eternally destroys itself, this mysterious world of dual lusts, this my 'Beyond Good and Evil' with no goal unless in the circle's joy there lies an involuntary goal, unless a ring is well disposed towards itself,—would you have a name for this world? An answer to all your riddles? A light also for you, you strongest, staunchest, most clandestine midnight ones? This world is the will to power—and nothing else! And you yourselves are this will to power—and nothing else! " [17]

The cosmic *Urwille* has no goal outside itself, hence strictly speaking it is not the will to power but the will as power. This will seeks only its own pleasure by overpowering and appropriating all that is outside itself, by imposing its own forms, by assimilating and exploiting. For Nietzsche this will to power is the unquestionable, fundamental fact and cardinal value of the world. From this standpoint he lets fly his arrows at faith, which since it contradicts his view can only be an illusion and a lie. Any faith in God is necessarily a formidable obstacle to the will's striving for the absolute realization of its own power. Faith denies, cripples, and kills the will to power; hence God is a debilitating force which perverts and corrupts man. Out of cowardice man fails to claim what he senses to be overwhelming power as his own, attributing it instead to a divine Person: "...when the sense of power seizes and overwhelms a man, as it does in the case of all great passions, a doubt stirs in him concerning himself. He dares not consider himself the cause of this astonishing sensation but posits a stronger person a Godhead, as the cause. *In summa:* the origin of religion lies in the strange and extreme sensations of power which take one by surprise. Much as the sick man one of whose limbs feels unaccountably heavy and strange concludes that someone must be sitting on it, the ingenuous *homo religiosus* feels himself to be several people. " [18]

Man, says Nietzsche, has never dared to give himself credit for

[17] F. Nietzsche, *Werke*, ed. Beck, XVI, pp. 401 f.
[18] F. Wuerzbach, *Das Vermaechtnis Nietzsches* (1940), p. 120.

the marvelous and dynamic moments of his life. Religion is an abortive offspring of doubt. It denies the unity of the person, thus splitting man into two parts. Religion calls everything pitiful and weak " man, " everything wonderful and strong " God. " It despises the natural, glorifies the unnatural. " The concept ' God ' represents a turning away from life, a criticism, even a contempt of life. "

This basic argument against faith is presented with many variations. Once it is faith in Providence which cripples the will and reason; then it is the democratic equality of all souls before God which threatens the species with ruin; or again the moral laws that spring from faith pervert life's natural instincts.

Worst of all, the idea of God makes man in the role of creator impossible. Nietzsche knows thought only as creativity. For him the supreme joy would be to create a whole world out of himself. The only happiness lies in the reason. Reason is the sole ray of light in a shoreless and answerless night. But by reason Nietzsche means reason the artist. Only through the efforts of creative reason is the world really created. Hence titanic ambition stirs, demiurgic tasks beckon. Because faith resists man's will to ultimate, absolute autonomy, faith must go. In *Zarathustra* we find the true reason for the rejection of faith:

" God is a conjecture; but I desire that your conjectures should not reach beyond your creative will. Could you *create* a god? Then do not speak to me of any gods. But you could well create the overman. . . .

" God is a conjecture; but I desire that your conjecture should be limited by what is thinkable. Could you *think* a god? But this is what the will to truth should mean to you: that everything be changed into what is thinkable for man, visible for man, feelable by man. You should think through your own senses to their consequences.

" And what you have called world, that shall be created only by you: your reason, your image, your will, your love shall thus be realized. And verily, for your own bliss, you lovers of knowledge.

" And how would you bear life without this hope, you lovers of knowledge? You could not have been born either into the incomprehensible or into the irrational.

"But let me reveal my heart to you entirely, my friends: *if* there were gods, how could I endure not to be a god! *Hence* there are no gods. Though I drew this conclusion, now it draws me.

"God is a conjecture; but who could drain all the agony of this conjecture without dying? Shall his faith be taken away from the creator, and from the eagle his soaring to eagle heights?" [19]

A page later Nietzsche tersely sums up his whole attitude toward religion: "What could one create if gods existed?" He could hardly make himself more clear. The unquestioned a priori of Nietzsche's thought is his own absolutely sovereign individuality. To think is to create; man alone is the measure of man. For Nietzsche there is no such thing as the intellectual recreating and comprehending of a non-ego. Only one question concerning God interests Nietzsche: Can one *create* a God? Because God as the creative source of all being runs counter to Nietzsche's individualism, God must fall, for "Shall the creative man be robbed of his faith?" No other creative principle can coexist with the absolute, creative ego.

HYBRIS

As Nietzsche's life unwinds it becomes more and more evident that the ultimate reason for his rejection of faith lies in his attitude of inordinate pride, the *hybris* of Greek tragedy. The attitude proper to human reason is that of humble receptivity to truth, which must be pursued long and ardently before it reveals itself. The subject in search of truth must subordinate himself to the data of truth. This basic and normal order of procedure is reversed and destroyed when the subject attempts to subordinate truth to his human ego, which claims for itself the right to posit truths. By so doing the arrogant ego becomes the source of all being and

[19] *The Portable Nietzsche*, selected and translated by Walter Kaufmann (New York: The Viking Press, 1954), pp. 197-198.

value. It does not pride itself on its achievements and values as compared with those of others for it no longer seriously compares itself with others; it considers itself on an entirely different plane. Everything connected with such an ego is held to be superior to everything that has no part in it. Stepping out of the actual order of the world, the arrogant ego exalts itself, investing itself with the radiance of the absolute. Everything that does not belong to it must be kept at an absolute distance, even God. Inevitably, true arrogance refuses to recognize the supremacy of God.

Nietzsche's consciousness of uniqueness was unconditional. Mrs. Ida Overbeck, who understood and appreciated Nietzsche's interior life better than almost anyone, writes in her memoirs, " The normal person, no matter how gifted, is inclined to seek the company of others. Nietzsche hated normal people because his inability to be normal himself condemned him to a uniqueness that was absolute. Conscious of the terrible strain this cost him, he exalted himself above everyone normal.... What would Nietzsche have done had he ever met his equal? Probably killed him or himself, he could not have borne it! " [20]

In *Zarathustra* Nietzsche himself writes, " A new pride my ego taught me, and this I teach men: no longer to bury one's head in the sand of heavenly things, but to bear it freely, an earthly head, which creates a meaning for the earth. " [21]

For Nietzsche to live in this attitude of defiance, which became second nature to him, was to live with the torments of Lucifer. From this private hell where he was martyred simultaneously by ice and by fire he still bore witness to heaven, which he never could forget. *Nitimur in vetitum,* here was indeed the agonizing lure of the unattainable. " Even by classical Greek standards, " Nietzsche writes, " our whole modern existence appears to be nothing but *hybris* and godlessness....*Hybris* our attitude toward God....*Hybris* our attitude toward ourselves, for we experiment on ourselves... what do we still care about the well-being of our souls! " [22] Arrogance takes pride even in its own hell; it looks down on what it

[20] C. A. Bernoulli, *Franz Overbeck and Friedrich Nietzsche, Eine Freundschaft* (1908), I, pp. 250 f.
[21] *The Portable Nietzsche,* selected and translated by Walter Kaufmann (New York: The Viking Press, 1954), p. 142.
[22] F. Nietzsche, *Werke,* VII, p. 416.

considers the stuffy and befogged world of the healthy and the sound. Of the arrogant man Nietzsche writes, " Disdainfully he recalls what were once his dearest and noblest dreams; whatever the cost in bitterness of soul, he enjoys invoking his disdain, as it were from the bottom of hell. . . . " We find ourselves in a veritable cramp of arrogance. "

Nonetheless, or perhaps for this reason, " All the gods are dead; now it is our will that overman live. " Thus at high noon spoke Zarathustra. Nietzsche's great hope and expectation lie in the superman. * When man's soul no longer flows into the sea of God, but like a mountain stream is dammed up to spread to an ever widening lake, perhaps then, when man has cut himself off from God he will find the strength to rise to the heights of the super- human. Even if this means plunging the world into unprecedented night, even though earth were to be convulsed, and man, the very ground beneath his feet giving way, were to fall into a void with neither up nor down—after all these things, Nietzsche passionately insists, superman * will come. In order to hasten the realization of that coming Nietzsche was prepared for Dionysian self-sacrifice.

DOCTRINE OF THE ETERNAL RECURRENCE OF THE SAME EVENTS

With the sunset of faith in God all human goals topple; man's eternal homesickness cries vainly for home. The aimlessness of a wandering without end threatens to destroy the wanderer, whom it leads into the purple night of madness. In heroic self-conquest man is meant to overcome and affirm the vanity of life, his unshak- able faith in terrestrial existence in its entirety transcending and redeeming his nostalgia for heaven. This faith has been baptized in the name of Dionysus. The everlasting quest for the ultimate

* *Translator's Note:* Since Shaw's translation of the word *Uebermensch* has irreplaceable connotations, in English the use of " superman " in addition to Walter Kaufmann's " overman " cannot always be avoided for the sake of consistency.

goal and point of rest becomes the endless perigrination of an eternal circling. Thus the finiteness of the world is exalted to a divinity. Man must affirm—and totally—this world alone. No least part of it may he in any way deny. Christianity's concentration on a goal that lies beyond life makes a man single-minded. All his efforts tend toward that goal, which repeated reminders of the inevitability of death help to keep fresh and urgent. A man's progress toward his transcendent goal is the measure of his earthly fulfillment.

In the world that is Nietzsche's countercreation this close relation between life and afterlife is abrogated by his doctrine of the eternal recurrence of the same, which slams shut once and forever the door to another world. This world becomes a closed cosmos complete in itself; no longer does a single signpost point beyond it. A God-proof earthly existence seals itself off from the transcendent, the last chink offer a glimpse of the beyond is sealed.

The concept of an eternally cycling world history which feeds on itself and regularly returns to itself is of Babylonian origin. It was renewed by the Pythagoreans and appears in pre-Socratic thought, where Nietzsche discovered it. He was profoundly impressed by it. Even in his early period he saw in the notion the possibility of abrogating what he calls the monstrous fortuitousness of causes, which propel historical events by a necessity as unalterable as the orbit of a star. At first Nietzsche only tentatively weighs the idea of an eternal recurrence of events. But like a demon the notion hunts him down in his loneliness and whispers in his ear: "This life as you now live it and have lived it you must live again and countless times over; nothing about it will ever be new, yet every pain and every pleasure and every thought and sigh and all the unspeakably small and great moments of your life must return again and again for you, all exactly in the same order—even as this spider must come again, and this moonlight between the trees, and this moment, and I myself. The everlasting hourglass of existence will be turned upside down over and over again—and you with it, dust mote from the dust that you are." [23]

[23] *Ibid.*, V, pp. 265 f.

The notion of the eternal recurrence comes to Nietzsche just as he has exhausted the entire cycle of values and *desiderata* hitherto important to him, when he has recognized their questionableness and reached the point of radical nihilism. At that moment it comes as a saving revelation, thrilling in its novelty, exciting as a newly discovered continent that only he who is overman may tread. Like one imparting an overwhelming mystery, with hushed voice and all the outward signs of dread Nietzsche reports his discovery of the doctrine to Overbeck and Lou Salomé. No longer does Nietzsche feel isolated in historical existence; he is a creator for mankind. In him, the great cycle is " back again at high noon, " at the point where man stands equidistant " from animal and overman. "

Out of the ocean of Nietzsche's sufferings this revelation suddenly looms in front of him like a great island mountain. The thought takes complete possession of him; it is the alpha and omega of his philosophy of the glorification and deification of the world by which eternity is transferred to *this* life. Nietzsche cannot wait to proclaim his discovery in all its decisive power and with all its divisive effects to men. All the great affirmers of life who have outgrown their humanity and are on the way to superhumanity can submit themselves to its test. Are they strong enough to affirm life and bear the seal of eternity on everything they do and suffer or will they attempt to flee from life and in reality be crushed by it? Through life those worthy of life will become supermen. Man must find the strength to assent indiscriminately to everything, to all pain and inexplicableness, to all chance, to all existence in its depth and breadth. Man the dispenser of blessings must enthrone everything that exists in a heaven of its own. Once all intermediate stages of good and evil have been dispelled everything becomes its own justification. Then each thing, every chance incident becomes its own god and no longer needs any other.

Nietzsche refers to his theory of recurrence and its effect surreptitiously by innuendo. To the stranger he speaks of a thought " which has dawned on me like a star " and which, for such is the nature of light, " would shine on you and on all men. " With this thought the real and complete antithesis of faith in God has been found, for only in the cyclic process of the universe does the world

and its history rest entirely in itself, becoming an existence with
no need of any other. "He who does not believe in the cyclic
process of the All must believe in an arbitrary God. " [24] Since
of the two possibilities one has completely ceased to exist, only the
alternative remains. This thought is to exalt affirmation of this
world to unsurpassable heights; hence Nietzsche's claim that it
"contains more than all the religions which despise this life as
something transient. " It is "the religion of religions. "

The doctrine of eternal recurrence is the test of the truth of
Nietzsche's philosophy. Can it withstand critical analysis? And
existentially, is man's living that doctrine really capable of making
him the superman who without inner conflict can represent the
self-made counterpart to the "dead God? "

The first point to be made is that Nietzsche himself strongly
felt the need to demonstrate his basic ideas on physical facts, and
with this in mind even considered resuming his studies in natural
science. However, he never got any further than a few inadequate
attempts to confirm his hypothesis scientifically. Actually it is
refutable by simple mathematics, and for this reason has never
been accepted in scientific circles. Another and more significant
fact is that this key and cornerstone of Nietzsche's construct has very
feeble philosophical consequences.

When tested for existential authenticity it quickly reveals a
gaping inner crack that causes it to split apart. On the one hand
the recurrence doctrine is meant to be a new "ethical emphasis"
that provides human existence, which has become purposeless, with
a new goal above and beyond itself. With the establishment of this
ideal goal for the man capable of willing it, Christian belief in
immortality is replaced by the will to self-immortalization. On the
other hand the unbroken recurrence of the same events is meant to
have the compulsion of an immutable physical process that *can*
unfold only one way and no other. Between these two forms of the
doctrine: recurrence as atheistic religion and recurrence as physical
metaphysics, gapes an unbridgeable chasm.

Because modern man no longer knows where he stands, because
all the goals toward which he might have planned his life have

[24] *Ibid.*, **XII**, p. 57.

collapsed, it is essential that he have a new orientation altogether; this Nietzsche believes his recurrence doctrine provides. Long enough, he insists, men have labored under the mistaken notion that they had a goal if only they could find it. In reality, they had always given themselves that goal and now on their own authority they should give themselves a new one. For it is time for men to outgrow mere manhood and become lords of the earth, supermen. This summons to superhuman courage, this supreme challenge to man rests on his inherent and unconditional responsibility for living every instant of his life in such a way that he will eternally desire its recurrence. The model of such an autonomous, highly developed man is Zarathustra. Our affirmation of life as ever-lastingly recurrent will give a new moral earnestness to our lives and provide a new form of immortality. " The ability to bear our immortality—that would be the supreme achievement. " Conse-quently Nietzsche's doctrine is above all an ersatz for belief in immortality. The stirring religious power of Christian belief in immortality with its clear commands, Thou shalt...has its parallel in Zarathustra's sermons, save of course that here the " I will " of man's autonomous decree is substituted. " Were thou to com-prehend the thought of thoughts it would transform thee. In all that you do, the question ' Is it so that I would desire to do this countless times? ' has the greatest weight. " [25]

But precisely this ethical significance which Nietzsche attributes to the recurrence theory is cancelled by the cosmological aspect of his teaching. For on the law of unyielding physical necessity man's will is shattered from the start, indeed it becomes meaningless. If everything must of its own inescapable inner necessity return as it already has returned innumerable times, if Sirius, if the spider, if the fleeting thought must return just as they are in this moment, if a man's life is no more than an hourglass ever and again turned upside down, such necessity must counteract every summons to a higher level of existence. Not in his own life but only in the poetic symbol of Zarathustra did Nietzsche succeed in reconciling the divergent halves of his recurrence doctrine. As Loewith points out in his book on the Nietzschean philosophy of the eternal recurrence,

[25] *Ibid.*, XVI, pp. 64 f.

Nietzsche and his philosophy broke down in the attempt to retie the severed existence of modern man to the eternal law of the cyclic world. The terrible " solution " of the problem of Nietzsche himself, namely his insanity, is in keeping with the essential absurdity of the problematic in his doctrine.

Amor fati! Love thy fate—this is Nietzsche's ultimate answer to the enigma of life. Elementary to his philosophy is rejection of the existing world as of the existing self in order that the unrestrained, utterly free spirit may choose its own being. Actually this premise is not really feasible; it only leads Nietzsche's thought to the absolute opposite of freedom: to enslavement by the existent and the unchangeable which must unroll mechanically in man, for whom freedom of choice no longer exists. Nietzsche himself says that it is and remains, " an absurd idea to suppose that one can freely choose one's own being, even one's own thus-and-so being. Back of this lurks the demand that there exist a being which has hindered a self-deprecating creature like myself from coming into existence. It is absurd to feel oneself an argument against God. " [26] Only a " fateless absolute freedom of will, " says Nietzsche, " could make man God...the mere principle of Fate makes man a robot. " [27] At eighteen Nietzsche knew this; the mature Nietzsche got no further. Man finds himself between what Nietzsche calls two *Automaten,* between two mechanical processes, one the process of an immutably unwinding Fate and the other of a being that has created itself out of nothing. Man is free either to accept his own nature and to develop its potential meaning or to miss that meaning, even to deny and reject it. But he cannot do what Nietzsche demanded: he cannot combine automat and God in one person, himself.

Man's becoming and self-fulfillment can take place only in the unequivocal movement toward a future in which the fulfilling of a mere possibility can become a reality. In the process all that has been achieved and has taken place must be stored in the memory in order that one may advance in the direction of the chosen goal. But if everything is broken off before that goal is reached, and man in a circle of becoming is brought back again and again to the same

[26] *Ibid.,* XVI, p. 409.
[27] F. Nietzsche, *Jugendschriften,* p. 69.

point of imperfection, the desired goal, superman, remains an unrealizable and senseless illusion. Then man really is, as Nietzsche himself in a moment of insight pointed out, like a tree seen in delirium which nowhere sinks its roots into the earth. "In the human being all superhumanity appears as sickness and insanity." [28]

Contingency is the law also for the person who tries to get away from himself in order to make a new countercreation. Although a man is not consulted on the matter of his nature, his " accidental " existence remains with all its daily plagues, frustrations, sufferings, uglinesses, shortcomings, and personal failures to which Nietzsche was especially sensitive. The law of one's own being remains, summoning and obliging man to perfect his allotted potentialities. Desperately as Nietzsche tries to transcend this law, to sacrifice his actual self in order to create overman, he cannot jump over his own shadow, and in the attempt to do so he breaks. " O, then give me madness, you heavenly ones! Madness so that at last I may believe in myself. ... Doubt is consuming me, I have slain the law and the law terrifies me as a corpse terrifies a living man; if I am *not* more than the law, I am the most depraved of men." [29]

Lastly, Nietzsche too believes in the given task of a man's life, in his mission, which can only be surmised little by little in the course of unfolding his talents to meet the demands of his particular existence, and which grows clear only in the course of his development. Nietzsche is aware of a task which in prospect can be known only like the letters of foreign words, but which in retrospect become a complete and meaningful communication. Thus ultimately one is enabled to read the message that was written on the wall and to interpret one's life as a philosophical experiment. Only by varying the essentially unchanging motif of his life can a man simultaneously possess himself and fulfill his mission on earth, which is to recognize and accomplish the task allotted him by destiny. Setting aside the question of the correct recognition and actual performance of that task, the mere existence of the need to recognize it is indication enough that a man's life is not arbitrary. Rather it is something planned and traceable through the fine mesh of talents, circumstances, and challenges. In other words it is a

[28] F. Nietzsche, *Werke*, XII, p. 361.
[29] *Ibid.*, p. 215.

predestined task, a concept that is impossible without the existence
of a predestiner.

Nietzsche longed to be the inexhaustible source of his own
riches, and in the attempt to be so he dug deep into his own
substance. He condemned himself to drink his own blood without
ever being able to quench his thirst. Lou Salomé writes "He
suffered so deeply from life that the certainty of its eternal recurrence must have filled him with dread. The quintessence of the
recurrence doctrine with its apotheosis of life which Nietzsche
later developed stands in such drastic contrast to his own tormented
experience that it suggests an uncanny mask." [30] Even during
Nietzsche's sojourn at Basel, where he was surrounded by friends
and filled with enthusiasm for Wagner and where he tasted the
success of his first book, *The Birth of Tragedy*, he suffered from the
terrible loneliness of the last philosopher. In his Oedipus fragment
he writes: "I call myself the last philosopher, for I am the last
human being. No one speaks with me save myself and my voice
reaches me like that of a dying man! Beloved voice, give me an
hour with you, my last memory of all human happiness; through
you I cheat loneliness *(Einsamkeit,* onesomeness) and deceive
myself into manifoldness and love. For my heart resists the belief
that love is dead, it cannot bear the horror of the loneliest of
all lonelinesses and forces me to speak as though I were two." [31]

For Nietzsche the most difficult test, the crisis of his life was the
loss of a personal God and God of history, the acceptance in his
place of a demonically arbitrary Fate. "Namely now for the
first time the thought of a personal Providence confronts us in all
its moving power." Nietzsche overcomes this "temptation" with
all the resoluteness of which he is capable, forcing from himself
heroic affirmation of the darkness of Fate. "*Amor fati:* henceforth
be this my love!" Love—of chaos, of darkness, of the inscrutable,
of all the impersonalness of Fate! Here is but the faceless It of
monstrous forces churning within themselves, at best the bestial
grimace of the will to power rushing to take form, trampling and
devouring everything in its path. Still Nietzsche tries to love it,

---

[30] L. Andreas-Salomé, *Friedrich Nietzsche in seinen Werken* (1894), s. sp.,
pp. 39, 41.
[31] F. Wuerzbach, *Das Vermaechtnis Nietzsches*, p. 372.

to give it his "Yes!" But just as in the beginning men could
only dread, never love the impersonalness of Fate, could merely
march with courageous determination into the fateful night, so also
Nietzsche's convulsive affirmation of Fate is unable to stifle his
soul's deepest dread. Love in the true sense is possible only
toward a person or toward that which comes from a person.
Fate is the antithesis of everything personal. Thus in Nietzsche
the nausea grows, and he writes to Lou Salomé: "Even now to
accept life costs me a supreme effort."

INCURABLE DICHOTOMY

Nietzsche's inexhaustible restlessness drove him constantly beyond
himself, an insatiable thirst for love drew him toward the God he
had spurned. His books and letters are full of examples of this
unrest. Masterfully Nietzsche depicts man's longing for God as the
shadow that clings to Zarathustra's heels, never allowing him to
find peace. If Zarathustra is an idealized self-portrait of Nietzsche,
the shadow that dogs Zarathustra's footsteps is the real self which
Nietzsche was never able to shake off. God never ceases to pursue
him, as though in answer to the prayer of Nietzsche's youth,
"that thy voice shall keep summoning me."
  Space allows only a few of the many proofs of the
incurable dichotomy in Nietzsche's unbelief. One of the most
obvious is reported in the memoirs of Nietzsche's intimate friend,
Mrs. Overbeck, who once confided to Nietzsche that the Christian
religion gave her no comfort or sense of fulfillment, that for her,
faith in God had too little substance. "Moved, he replied: 'You
say that only to comfort me. Never give up the thought of God!
It is yours unconsciously, for as you are and as I always—and in
this instant—find you, your whole life is dominated by one great
thought, which is the idea of God.' He swallowed with difficulty.
His features, for a while all distorted, took on the hue of stone.
'I have given him up. I want to create something new. I will

not, dare not turn back. I shall be destroyed by my passions which toss me about here and there. I am constantly falling apart, but I don't care!' These were his own words in the fall of 1882. Nietzsche has honored us with such frankness! You can imagine what a burden this is to me and how I respected and still respect him." [32] From the depths of utter loneliness Nietzsche's unsatisfied will to love complains. In a letter dated 1885 he writes, "For all who have some kind of 'God' for company the loneliness *I* know could never exist. My life now consists in the wish that it were otherwise with things than the way I understand them and in the longing that someone would make *my* truths incredible for me."

There are soul-shaking confessions in *Zarathustra*, particularly in Part IV. Once Zarathustra comes upon an old magician writhing on the ground in a convulsion of woe. He symbolizes the real Nietzsche as contrasted to Zarathustra, the ideal Nietzsche.

" Who warms me, who loves me still? " the old magician cries,
" Give hot hands!
Give a heart as glowing coals!
Stretched out, shuddering,
Like something half dead whose feet one warms—
Shaken, alas, by unknown fevers,
Shivering with piercing icy frost-arrows,
Hunted by thee, O thought!
Unnamable, shrouded, terrible one!
Thou hunter behind clouds!
Struck down by thy lightning bolt,
Thou mocking eye that stares at me from the dark:
Thus I lie
Writhing, twisting, tormented
With all eternal tortures,
Hit
By thee, cruelest hunter,
Thou unknown *god*!

Hit deeper!
Hit once more yet!

[32] C. A. Bernoulli, *Franz Overbeck and Friedrich Nietzsche, Eine Freundschaft* (1908), I, pp. 250 f.

Drive a stake through and break this heart!
Why this torture
With blunt-toothed arrows?
Why dost thou stare again,
Not yet weary of human agony,
With gods' lightning eyes that delight in suffering?
Thou wouldst not kill,
Only torture, torture?
Why torture *me*,
Delighted by suffering, thou unknown god?

In vain!   Pierce on,
Cruelest thorn!   No,
No dog—only thy game am I,
Cruelest hunter!
Thy proudest prisoner,
Thou robber behind clouds!
Speak at last!
What wouldst thou, waylayer, from *me*?
Thou lightning-shrouded one!   Unknown one!   Speak,
What wilt thou, unknown—god?

What?   Ransom?
Why wilt thou ransom?
Demand much!   Thus my pride advises.
And make thy speech short!   That my other pride advises.

Hah, hah!
Me thou wilt have?   Me?
Me—entirely?

Away!
He himself fled,
My last, only companion,
My great enemy,
My unknown,
My hangman-god.

No!   Do come back
With all thy tortures!
To the last of all that are lonely,

Oh, come back!
All my tear-streams run
Their course to thee;
And my heart's final flame—
Flares up for thee!
Oh, come back,
My unknown god! My *pain*! My last—happiness! " *

Anyone who reads these lines attentively must realize that their elemental power and passion can only stem from agonizingly personal experience. The ravaged ground of the man's soul cries out to God even as the self in its egocentricity spurns him.

Another time Zarathustra tries in vain to shake off his shadow, which complains to him: "What would be left to me? A heart tired and insolent; an unsteady will: flap-wings, a broken backbone. This search for *my* home: O Zarathustra, you know it well, this seeking was *my* visitation with all its afflictions, it is consuming me. 'Where is—*my* home?' Ask and seek and when I sought I found it not. O eternal Everywhere, o eternal Nowhere, o eternal—in vain! "

The most heart-rending confession of an individualism lived to its ultimate consequences is probably the poem *Among Birds of Prey*. Zarathustra, only recently the bold hunter of God, has caught himself in his own net and become his own prey. Digging into himself, he scoops his grave out of his own substance until nothing is left but a corpse! He who was recently so proud, who sought to know himself, lies one with his own grave, the knower and hangman of himself. He has become a dying man poisoned by the serpent's venom because he has crawled into the paradise of the old serpent and succumbed to the tempting voice: "You will become like God! "

" Why did you tempt yourself
Into the paradise of the old serpent?
Why did you creep into yourself,
Into yourself, your self?

* *Translator's Note:* From the Walter Kaufmann translation.

> Moribund now,
> Poisoned by serpent's venom. "

In Genesis' so-called mythical image of man sick and dying of the venom of sin Nietzsche reveals the profoundest meaning of his acts: *mysterium iniquitatis*. How often this account of the Fall at the beginning of the Bible has struck modern readers as a mere myth no longer to be taken seriously! For Nietzsche it is no myth, it is a terrible reality, a tragic event that has actually happened, and not only to him. Here lies the true collective guilt of modern man, who refuses to accept and trust the given conditions of the world. Distrust has made arrogant defiance the foundation of the modern attitude in order that man might create a counterworld of his own. Nietzsche stands at the end of a long row of rebellious generations and consistently lived out to the end what his predecessors bequeathed him. He had to break on that heritage, but in his breaking he testifies to the God he has rejected but cannot escape. In the tragedy of Friedrich Nietzsche modern man may realize in fear and trembling that he has been tricked by the old serpent's perennial temptation to become like God. Thus involuntarily Nietzsche becomes the penitential preacher of the age for all who know how to listen. Karl Jaspers concludes his comprehensive appraisal of Nietzschean philosophy with the observation that Nietzsche's nihilistic transcendence of existence does not bring him peace. Hence his so-called godlessness is really the mounting unrest of a search for God that perhaps no longer understands itself.

Nietzsche took the supreme risk; his life and thought was an experiment on himself to see whether and how far man can live without God. Since Nietzsche immolated himself in order to complete that experiment it is now up to us who succeed him to draw the consequences of that experiment's negative result. It is not our task to judge to what extent Nietzsche is responsible for the collective guilt of modern man and to what extent he is a victim of the modern age. Human insight can never penetrate the depths of such an ultrapersonal decision. Our business is to set about the task of honestly trying to find the way back to the paradise we have lost.

With the pity and dread inspired by great tragedy, we witness

Nietzsche's end. He labored titanically to move the pillars of existence until at last the vanity of his effort struck back at him, and his own existence was thrust out of plumb, *ver-rueckt,* mad. Nietzsche had to leave this ground of reality completely to become the initiate of his god Dionysus, indeed to become one with him, which he considered "the highest kind of existence." And actually at the end, his madness was just such a state of ecstasy. The scribbled notes from this period are still an irreplaceable essential of his work. From that point on Nietzsche really believed he had become the god Dionysus, even as he also signed himself "the Crucified One." He imagined himself to be Everyman, all the dead and all the living. Creation and history lie in his hands. Thus Nietzsche forces reality to retreat—if only in the delusion of mental derangement. Reality had to be completely submerged in night before the circle of Nietzsche's hallucinations could close and he could take the stance of the "successor of the dead God."

11. *The atheism of Russia*

SINGULARITY OF THE RUSSIAN PEOPLE

The decline of faith in large areas of the Occident has often been compared with the setting of the sun. Even as the sun goes down at the equator quite differently from the way it does in the temperate zone, the sunset of faith too is different in the East and in the West. In the tropics, where right up to the moment of setting, the sun floods the earth with light, the sinking of the sun beneath the horizon results in an abrupt change. In a matter of minutes there is complete darkness. In more northern zones sunsets are frequently accompanied by a magnificent show of color in whose afterglow activity may continue unhindered for a long time. In the West the process of centuries of development gradually gave atheism form and power so that the old foundations of Western culture were slowly undermined. But because the adjoining bulwarks of faith, namely Christian culture and Christian civilization still held, one was deceived into supposing that these could continue indefinitely on their own strength. By contrast, the East seized the gospel of nihilistic atheism with unparalleled radicalism and swiftly hammered the old world to pieces in order to construct a new world in its place, a world without God.

The difference between the decline of faith in East and West has deep roots in the uniqueness of Russian history and in certain characteristics of the Russian people. Over the history of Russia hangs the fateful star of her inability to create out of her various races a national culture such as was created in the countries of Western Europe, a culture which provides a certain stability and coherence. On the other hand a millennium of profound religious experience left its imprint on the Russian people, even though Russian Christianity was directed primarily toward the other world and gave scant impulse to the shaping of this. Thus for a long time Russia lacked an identity of her own. As Vladimir Weidle points out, the only kind of identity that Russia knows is the kind " which growth in the same soil lends to its crops, not the sense of identity which springs from an inheritance that has been continually fostered and enriched from generation to generation, from century to century. " A hundred years ago the Russian philosopher of religion and history, Chadaev, spoke of the cultural cargo of Europe as something he missed in his own country. Alexander Herzen, one of the intellectual precursors of Marxism, saw in this lack of a coherent Russian culture a guarantee for the success of his Messianic mission. Belinski, who paved the way for revolutionary atheism in Russia, once exclaimed, "Boundless is the breadth of Russia, tremendous her youthful vitality, limitless her power—and her soul, trembling with ecstasy at the thought of her high destiny, grows faint. " [1] Unsteadied by any established rhythm, with no centuries of traditional culture to guide it, yet already awakened to religious consciousness, the Russian soul ardently embraced Western atheism as the joyful new gospel, and despite enormous difficulties put it to the test.

Let us waive the question as to the correctness of the theory of some historians that the first Russian state was founded by foreign traders and adventurers. Certainly the Russian people were accustomed to regarding the czars and their entourages with awe as well as with a certain reserve. For the simple *muzhik* they were foreigners whose language and customs were not his own. Even much later no natural link connected the ruling class with the broad undifferentiated mass of the people. The State was always a burden to the people, who in turn relayed the pressure to the individual.

[1] B. Schultze, *Belinskij*, p. 77.

Over the Russian peasant hangs the tragedy of landlessness. To this day he has not succeeded in making the land he tills his own; hence he has never learned to work it with unstinted care and love. Under the lash he gave it only what he absolutely had to. There was no escaping the leaden fate which hung over him. As Fedor Stepun remarks in his book on Bolshevism and Christianity, the Russian country estate did not teach the peasant an ethos of work. Generally speaking the Russian has never had the salutary discipline of working responsibly on his own. Responsible work presents problems that demand solutions; it broadens a man's horizons by requiring him to fit his work into the economics of the whole. Moreover, with few exceptions the Russian peasant had no schooling. For centuries the absolutistic State denied him a share in education.

Thus the peasants could neither develop their creative powers nor cultivate their personality. The State remained indifferent to them, especially after its illegal seizure of the land. It is impossible, says Masaryk, for any Westerner to imagine the oppression of the old serfdom. As late as 1833 the Russian landlord could sell his serfs at will, severing family ties as mercilessly as death. His serfs were a kind of currency for the estate owner; at cards he could wager so and so many " souls, " or he could select this or that serf as a present for his mistress. " The picture of serfdom we get from the accounts of the best writers is shocking. Anyone who reads the older Russian literature attentively will find a background of moral and social decay everywhere. " [2]

Not until centuries after the Baltic Provinces had succeeded in emancipating the serfs was serfdom abolished in Russia herself. The so-called Emancipation Act of 1861 was intended by the Czar and his advisors to pacify the people and to bring about a more just distribution of the land. But the liberation was only a half-hearted measure and consequently unsuccessful. The landlords retained too much land, the peasants got too little. Above all, they still had no freedom of movement. Despite their new status as freemen, as debtors (often they were obliged to pay installments

---

[2] T. Masaryk, *Russland und Europa. Zur russischen Geschichts- und Religionsphilosophie.* Soziologische Skizzen. 2 Bde. 1913. E. Briem, *Kommunismus und Religion in der Sowjetunion. Ein Ideenkampf (1948)*, p. 56.

for years to come on the acres promised them) they remained for all practical purposes the slaves of the landlords. It was not long before riots broke out in the country, now led not only by the educated and the noble as they had been in the past, but by the peasants themselves, sometimes even by peasant women.

THE ORTHODOX CHURCH

All experts on old Russia stress the high degree to which the spiritual power of Christianity permeated and formed the Russian people. For almost a thousand years—in 988 it became the state religion—Christianity has been the most powerful spiritual force in Russia; " for the peasants until well into the twentieth century, for the upper classes as a whole until the time of Peter the Great, and even later for the overwhelming majority of them" (Klaus Mehnert).

Whereas in western Europe intellectual and spiritual life coincided to a large degree only during the Middle Ages; whereas in modern western Europe the layman declared himself to be of age, demanded his religious autonomy, and created his own secular culture, in Russia medieval conditions survived well into the last century, although influences from the secularized West began to make themselves felt as early as the 18th century.

There is no doubt that as a religious and moral force the Orthodox Church succeeded in imbuing the Russian soul with such reverence and interiority that these became second nature to it. During the same period, through the influence of traditional Eastern Christianity, Russian thought developed quite differently from that of Western Europe. Russia never knew the typically Western conflict between faith and knowledge. Never was the one elevated to a leading principle over the other. The whole idea of emancipation from " blind faith " was foreign to the Russian, for whom the mind always remained religiously disposed. The intellectual acrobatics which employ a whole battery of rationalistic concepts and systematize purely logical themes was unknown to Eastern thought, which Stepun describes as " never more, but also never less than the logical transcription of religious feelings and experiences. It was never autonomous but always theonomous thinking. " Because the theology held by Orthodox Christianity was not attacked and never needed to be defended, Orthodox belief was never really conscious of its own foundations; it never came to a conceptual formulation of faith, and neither apologetics nor dogma were developed to the degree that they were in the West.

When the intellectual aspect of a church fails to cultivate self-criticism and a sense of moderation, its religious aspect inclines toward overzealousness and fanaticism. Much as the Orthodox Church did for the soul of the Russian people, it offered few solutions to their earthly problems and did little to encourage badly needed reforms. Today, after a long and often difficult struggle for objectivity, many Russian experts in the philosophy of religion agree to the existence of certain fundamental deficiencies in the Orthodox Church which render her incapable of understanding the demands of the time. These deficiencies are rooted in the specialness of her claim to be orthodox, that is, the true believing church.

After the severing of the Eastern Church from Rome and eventually of the Russian Church from Byzantium, Moscow came to consider itself " the Third Rome " and the pillar of orthodoxy on earth. At the beginning of the 16th century the monk Filofei (Philotheus) declared in an outburst of prophetic self-assurance that all the Christian kingdoms of the world had fallen, either through their own heresy or by the conquest of infidels. Consequently their spiritual heritage had passed over to the only truly Christian ruler who remained, the Grand Duke of Moscow. " As foretold by the Prophets, the empires of Christendom have crumbled; in their place stands alone the Empire of our Sovereign, namely the Russian Empire. For the First and Second Rome have fallen, but the Third Rome stands, and a fourth there will not be. " [3] Here lies the root of the Russian consciousness of mission, its Messianism, which was secularized in the 19th century

[3] G. Bergenkopf, *Welterloesung ein geschichtlicher Traum Russland* (1962), pp. 174 f.

and in secularized form became the activating force behind Bolshevism.

The shortcomings of the Orthodox Church dawned suddenly and
painfully on Vladimir Soloviev in the midst of a spirited comparison of the Orthodox Church with the Catholic Church of the
West, which he rejected and was engaged in attacking. In sharp
contrast to Western cultures with their development of the human
personality, the Eastern attitude in general is based on man's
subordination to a superhuman principle. The earmarks of its
ethical ideal are humility and complete subjugation to higher
powers. " It is easy to see the temptations of these virtues:
servility, rigidity, and apathy. Loyalty to tradition and to the
past are inclined to lead to complete isolation and stagnation in all
areas. In the social and political fields the spirit of Eastern
peoples often takes the form of a patriarchal despotism that finds
its purest expression in theocracy...man's powers are subordinated
to the point where they have only a passive significance.

The contrasting virtues of Westerners: independence and energy,
like their vices: personal pride, arbitrariness, and belligerency,
spring from a self-will which insists on having its own way and
which frequently leads to a personality cult.

Although schism was the greatest evil for all Christendom,
according to Soloviev, it was the Orthodox Church which suffered
most from its fateful consequences. Because of the attitude peculiar
to her the Eastern Church failed to recognize her earthly mission.
She even denied the existence of such a mission, thereby robbing
herself of all social and political effectiveness. For the Byzantines
Christianity was something complete, closed; it was divine truth
in the safekeeping of Church tradition, a treasure to be guarded
and stubbornly preserved. It was enough that divine truth simply
exist, ready for pious veneration, dialectical interpretation, and
mystical contemplation. The best forces of Christianity spent
themselves in the cloisters contemplating divine truth; as a result
its application was neglected. Little effort was made to interpret
current problems in the light of Christian truth or to make its
influence felt in political and social life. The Orthodox hierarchy
declined the task of molding a truly Christian society. Thus religion
could be neither a fortifying vital force for the present nor a

pledge or seed for the future. " Byzantine piety, " says Soloviev, " forgot that the true God is a God of the living and it sought the Living One among the dead. " Such one-sidedness with its over-emphasis on the dead letter was bound to lead to the distortion of tradition and to universal narrowness. This alone explains how such ritualistic bagatelles as the regulations for priests' beards and tonsures, the pros and cons of the Sunday fast, and whether the sign of the cross should be made with two fingers or three could become matters of heated controversy.

The Russian schism was but a fruit of the Byzantine offshoot which had separated itself from the unity of Christendom. In that fruit local custom elevated to a universal tradition was declared sacrosanct and obligatory, thereby perpetuating the substitution of accidental forms. The Muscovite soon found himself heir to an eternal truth which is meant to permeate all life by temporal, Orthodox faith, in which the inalienable essence was often usurped by the most trivial details of Church tradition. Imperceptibly the influence of fanatically conservative sectarians, the Old Believers *, replaced true universal Christian faith, and a once vital unity became rigid uniformity. It was the realization of this change that opened Soloviev's eyes to the real difference between the Christian East and the Christian West: namely, that in spite of its many short-comings, essentially in the Western conception of Christianity the church of God is responsible for the application of divine truths to human society, a task which to be properly achieved requires the joint effort of all Christian forces under the direction of a central authority. This is the view held primarily by the Roman Catholic Church. The passivity of the Orthodox Church in regard to the problems and pressing needs of the time left her in no position to point the way to needed reforms.

Unfortunately the breadth and farsightedness of Soloviev's criti-cism was rare even among outstanding Russian philosophers of religion. Moreover, Dostoevski mistook the actual State Church (whose limitations deprived her of the required strength and ability to meet the need of the hour) for the ideal " universal

* *Translator's Note:* The Old Believers were members of a large and extremely conservative sect which protested against changes in the Orthodox Church.

church of all peoples " and the goal of Russian socialism for which all Russians unconsciously longed. To be sure, the heart of the Russian people belonged to their Church, but even this loyalty was unbalanced. To a large extent it was a loyalty to the letter of the past which refused to countenance any new vitality.

The piety of the simple Russian people should be neither idealized nor underestimated. Popular faith may have been often superficial, superstitious, and formal, but it is utterly untrue that the Russian people " are profoundly atheistic by nature, " as Belinski once claimed in an emotional outburst. Nor are they as Gogol, Dostoevski, and many Slavophiles insisted—" the most religious people on earth, a people of matchless Messianic significance. " There is indeed a " Holy Russia " of unique spiritual tradition. Its noblest blossoms are to be found in *staretz,* cult, and icon, and in the unshakable faith of simple men and women. For all the cultivation of a timeless mysticism in the monasteries and among the people (stirringly testified to in the famous *Tales of a Russian Pilgrim*) the efforts of the most estimable members of the Russian priesthood were concentrated almost entirely on preserving the purity of the Byzantine heritage. By rejecting any kind of change whatsoever, conservatism, the ruling force in the Russian Church, extended its vigilance also over the errors and changes that had crept in unnoticed.

RELIGIOUS CRISES

The religious crisis in Russia during the 17th century gave strange testimony to the Church's hardening in the mold of her forms, a process that was the antithesis of the Western Reformation with its active pulling away from the old Church and its arbitrary setting of new courses. In Russia the Christian soul rebelled in the name of tradition and sacred custom against the efforts of the supreme ecclesiastical authority to eradicate certain errors and abuses. Vainly Patriarch Nikon (+ 1681) warred against the deterioration of the Greek heritage in the Church, demanding the return to former purity. Although initially victorious, in the end the Patriarch was forced to submit to the opposition of the Old Believers. He died in exile.

The opposition smoldered on for centuries, ever quick to flare up in fresh revolt. " Later with the universal introduction of the new rites, resistance to them became a psychosis. The Old Believers flocked together, and when compelled to participate in the new rites, set themselves on fire rather than submit. There were cases in which several thousand persons simultaneously burned themselves to death in protest. " [4]

The Old Believers became a kind of preserve for vague religious longings and apocalyptical expectations. For them Patriarch Nikon's renovations were apostasy; by accepting them the Muscovite Church was abandoning her mission to preserve for the world the purity of the only true faith until the apocalyptical return of Christ. Even as the First Rome had fallen away from the true faith in 1054 and the Second Rome in 1439, in 1666 through Nikon the Third Rome and last empire of Orthodoxy, which was meant to stand until the end of time, also began to totter. History could not know a Fourth Rome. Hence for the Old Believers perseverance in the historical, Muscovite, " pre-Nikonian " reality combined with chiliastic expectations of the kingdom of God that was to succeed the Third Rome (Sarkisyanz).

The roots of Russian spirituality reached deep into the old " orthodox, " that is to say, true religion, the only spiritual force that united all Russians, even as it simultaneously divided them. The masses drew their strength and support from their religion, and the stubbornness of their resistance to change is understandable, particularly when the changes in question were as drastic as those of Peter the Great, whose reforms have been described as a revolution from above. Stamped by Western Enlightenment, the new culture which Czar Peter established was pragmatic and jejune; it lacked Christian warmth. The transfer of the capital from Moscow to St. Petersburg made Russians painfully aware of the new spirit of change.

[4] J. Chrysostomus, *Die religioesen Kraefte*, p. 122.

Under Peter the Great three important changes in the Church were instigated: the patriarchate was abolished, Church administration was reorganized along the lines of the Protestant Church, and the Holy Synod was established as the administrative organ. The general procurators of the Synod were appointed by the Czar. For two hundred years the procurators ruled the Russian Orthodox Church, which they soon managed to subject to the State. They share with the State the responsibility for the widespread debilitation of the creative forces within the Church. Thus it came to a "mummification of the Church" (Stepun) that was more dangerous than her secularization. The once lively religious spirit was replaced by bureaucracy with its formalistic, impersonal stamp so inimical to human warmth and vigor.

Under the influence of French Enlightenment the Church became a secularized institution which, completely subjugated by the State, could be used by the State for its own purposes. This heaped fresh fuel on the old smoldering rebellion in the Russian soul. At the same time religious expectations departed further and further from the ground of earthly reality. Hope centered on the creation of a "New Jerusalem" in which the whole of life was to be a divine liturgy. The more the authorities obstructed attempts at a true reformation of this world in the Christian sense, the more the people turned away from the real world, losing themselves in vain longings for the coming of a temporal paradise. This reaction is what Florovski calls "the characteristic temptation of the Russian soul," temptation to the mystical escapism of the Old Believers. Also Turgenyev writes: "When left to himself the Russian always becomes an Old Believer."

Thus the popular image of the czar became increasingly controversial and divided, a division that in the long run was bound to have fateful consequences. For the Orthodox Church the Czar was surrounded by an aura of the divine; for the people he was unapproachable, hence their inclination to take him for the heaven-sent representative of *pravda,* if not to exalt him to a Saviour. Even Belinski, who died in 1848 and who is celebrated today as the Father of Revolutionary Ideology, still shared in the popular faith in the czar as the vital fountainhead of supreme power from which everything men cherish flows. Without the czar, writes Belinski, there would be no holiness for the saint. " Our freedom rests upon the czar because our new civilization comes from him, our culture stems from him, as does our very life "; he considers this reason enough " for permanent and unconditional subordination to the will of the czar as though to the will of Providence itself.

Each new czar was welcomed by the people with boundless acclaim; from each " salvation " was expected. The " czaristic *charisma* " is an integral part of the old Russian world view in which the czar was the bearer of *pravda*. Accordingly he considered himself the infallible head of the Church. As worded in the statute of 1716 for the Imperial Army, " the czar is the autocratic monarch who needs to account for his actions to no one, since as Christian sovereign he has the power and authority to rule his countries and provinces according to his will and judgment. "

Under the constraint of czarist autocracy, no sense of fundamental personal rights was able to develop and no doctrine of natural human rights ever flourished in Russia. For Russian autocrats justice was never more than laws laid down by anointed sovereigns which the Church zealously confirmed. The concept fundamental to Greek and Christian natural law (according to which every human being possesses inalienable rights which even the state must respect) was never developed in Russian thought. Just as the believer before his God empties himself of self, the subject before his sovereign abrogates his personality. As a result the Orthodox Church almost had to be lacking in that will to resist the state which in the West had been generated by frequent clashes between churches and states.

EXPECTATIONS OF PRAVDA

Pravda! This much used intrinsically Russian concept is so iridescent that it cannot be translated into a single word, truth for example. For in the intellectual and spiritual life of Russia truth as an isolated value or abstraction distinct from life and action never played the role that it plays in the West; the East has known neither a scientific world view constructed in accordance with its own laws nor a pedantic science of philosophy and theology. Through a process of intellectual differentiation which took place in the West, part values with laws of their own separated themselves from the wholeness of life. After violent disputes the natural sciences and theoretical disciplines, independent middle-class morality, and various churches and confessions finally arrived at a kind of truce and mutual toleration in which resistance to one another stimulated in each a lively awareness of its own essence. Politics and the entire field of education and culture detached themselves from the unified religious foundations of life and created their own forms, much as art with its demand to be practiced for its own sake emancipated itself. With the cutting off of many areas of life a widely branched system of intellectual forces was created which distributed intellectual energies.

In Russia it was quite different. Stepun points out that because of her characteristic attitude toward life as a totality, Russia had to deny the principle of autonomous values. As a result her spiritual powers in all their vehemence streamed undivided into a single river bed. That power was all the more elemental because it found no natural outlet for its energy. Like water that has been dammed, it mounted precariously. To be sure, the masses were infinitely passive and long-suffering. But as the number of individuals stirred by the intellectual awakening grew, as ever more hopes for *pravda* among the masses were dashed, a new energy began to make itself felt, the energy of indignation.

By virtue of the undifferentiated wholeness of Russian spiritual life the word *pravda* stands for the collective value of truth, justice, and salvation. In the concept of *pravda* faith in the prototype of a moral order for this world is kept alive. All Russia's spiritual striving, in her popular piety as well as in the thought of her intellectuals, circles round the realization of *pravda*. The weakness of this idea lies in its renunciation of pure science. From the first, the Muscovite Empire rejected the study of the sciences for their own sake. As Sarkisyanz expresses it, "The concept of truth contained in the word *pravda* does not suggest knowledge in the sense of awareness of reality. More in the traditional, religious sense it points almost ontologically to the concrete foundations of being which man has deserted and to which he is trying to return. " [5]

The popular notion of *pravda* did not differentiate between the fields of religion, social justice, and politics. For the bondman the division of society into peasants, landlords, and czar was the God-given order of things over which the czar ruled supreme in the name of God. Just as natural phenomena came straight from the hand of God, so the classes of society came from the czar. Precisely because the hoped-for deliverance was not specialized according to the various spheres of life, the czar could be appealed to again and again as the Messiah who—also religiously speaking—was to bring salvation to suffering mankind.

Nonetheless, hopes for *pravda,* whose advent was considered imminent, focussed on tangible things. This world and this earth were to be transformed and transfigured. For one thing, earth was to return her dead, because the resurrection of the dead was to signal the arrival of *pravda.* It was precisely this concrete, tangible Messianism which, quickened by revolutionary currents, merged with Bolshevism's communistic expectations and shaped the dream of paradise on earth. The striving for *pravda* was a feature common to both ideals, to the old conservative ideal and to the revolutionary. Its origin is to be sought in religious tradition. Despite the haziness of its aims the longing for *pravda* in Bolshevistic ideology was to give it unprecedented political force.

In the vague nostalgia for *pravda* there is an element of puerile enthusiasm which lacks the virility and courage to hew existence with the hard cutting edge of solid deeds, losing itself instead in ardent daydreams. This tendency was bound to weaken the Russian spirit which, as Kirejevski points out, " strove to unite all the separate aspects of the soul in one great power, to find that inner point of concentration where thought, feeling, and will, where the conscience, the true...the just, and the merciful are fused into a vital whole, and man's nature is restored to its pristine undivided-ness.

[5] E. Sarkisyanz, *Russland und der Messianismus des Orients. Sendungs-bewusstsein u. pol. Chiliasmus des Ostens* (1955), p. 16.

To the extent that Messianic yearning endowed the czar with superhuman attributes, disappointed hopes in the czar were bound to turn into a profound rebelliousness. During the Petersburg era with its Western rationalistic reforms, its creation of a bureaucratic state and a bureaucratic Church, disappointment in the czar steadily spread. It became increasingly clear that the czar was not the expected Messiah who was to establish the New Jerusalem; that he was not the long-awaited pillar of justice who would allot to each the acres he had been denied. Once it became obvious that the nation " had turned away from the old traditional piety, " it did not take long for the Old Believers to brand the czar " antichrist. " The epithet was considered particularly fitting for Peter the Great. With Peter's reforms not only the official church but the entire political and social system came under fire from the Old Believers. On the other hand the separation of the Old Believers from the Orthodox Church sorely weakened the Church and hastened her complete subjugation by the State. Thus the measures of Peter I became the ideological focal point of popular resistance. In the opinion of experts the dynamics of this tension passed from the movement of the Old Believers to the intelligentsia, who prepared the way for the Bolshevik Revolution.

CHILIASTIC MOVEMENTS

In the eyes of the Old Believers the legitimate church as an earthly establishment had ceased to exist. Hence from 1666 on, a growing chiliastic or apocalyptic mood began to spread among the Old Believers. At first the end of the world was prophesied for the year 1669: thereafter the deadline was postponed as often as the world's failure to end made a change necessary, just as under similar circumstances it had been postponed earlier in Russia and elsewhere. But when the kingdom of God on earth that was to liberate men from the rule of the antichrist repeatedly failed to appear, the Old Believers resorted to desperate measures. In the decades following 1670 acts of self-immolation by fire took an unheard-of toll. Between 1660 and 1690 more than 20,000 persons were reported to have burned themselves to death and ever new outbursts of religious fanaticism added to the number of living torches and self-crucifixions.

Throughout the 19th century the movement of the Old Believers spread, as did many other religious movements. By 1907, besides fifteen million members of other sects, there were an estimated ten million Old Believers, who carried far more weight than their number might suggest. For the Old Believers were highly esteemed by the Orthodox masses, who shared many of their views and who often remained in the Orthodox Church only because they feared the compulsory measures of the State. There are Russian scholars who claim that had religious liberty existed the peasant masses would have all gone over to the Old Believers. As early as 1850 the Slavophile, Ivan Aksakov, expressed the fear that Russia would soon be rent in two, that the official church with the government and nobility would stand alone while the rest of Russia turned to the religion of the Old Believers.

Many religious fanatics still sought the vanished kingdom of God on earth, a kingdom which though hidden *must* exist somewhere. This was the leitmotif of innumerable eternally wandering pilgrims. However, the more stubborn fanatics held that since Nikon, the Orthodox Church on earth had ceased to exist. In the apocalyptical and eschatological expectations of the day there were clear intimations of an incipient communism. The Old Believers aspired to the radical dissolution of all earthly bonds: of the State, of society, of the family, and of private property. Since God had created all things for all men in common, the word " mine " was obviously created by the devil. Logically, the next step was condemnation of the existing class society.

By the true law of dialectics, where two extremes exist, their fringes are inclined to overlap. This law is not, as metaphysical exaggeration led men to suppose, a material law but rather a law of the spiritual life and its reality. Disappointed over and over again, the extreme religious expectations of the people were bound, ultimately, to merge with nihilism. In the religious fanaticism of the sects it actually did come to a denial of God that was indi-

genous and completely independent of atheistic influences from the
West. A hymn composed in 1885 by the Nietovzy Sect, commonly
referred to as " the priestless ones " and reputed to be inimical to the
State, declared:

> " There is no deliverance in this world,
> No, the lie reigns supreme;
> Only death can bring liberation.
> There is no God in this world,
> Countless its delusions;
> Only death can bring liberation.
> There is no life in this world ...
> Only death can bring liberation. "

The fever of apocalyptical hopes in the imminent arrival of the
long overdue divine kingdom necessarily led to disenchantment, and
no imaginable disappointment wounds more deeply than the disappointment of ardent religious hopes. Understandably, disillusionment can cause radical spiritual energy to veer round to radical
denial. Full of rebellion, the disillusioned believer rejects the
realities of sober truth. He refuses to live any longer in such
a frightful world. Incensed, he flings himself into an orgy of denial.
There is nothing behind this world—absolutely nothing! Impotently
he kicks against the traces. He clenches his fist and curses the God
who has duped him. Out of protest he declares God to be a figment
of the imagination and he abrogates him. Ha! God doesn't even
exist! The radical refusal to accept life as it is leads logically
to self-immolation. Where genuine faith possesses the heroism of the
martyr's self-sacrifice, nihilism embraces self-destruction as a protest
that springs from religious disappointment. The true disciple of
nihilism does not hesitate to sacrifice his life to the great goal of
revolutionary destruction.

According to the oldest Russian annals, the empire founded
on *pravda* had been the great ideal. Ivan III is referred to as the
Czar of *Pravda*. Sixteenth-century chroniclers describe the Muscovite Empire as the Kingdom of *Pravda* on earth. At each coronation
the newly crowned czar was wildly hailed as the Messianic Bringer
of *Pravda*. But invariably the actual policies of the sovereign
proved disappointing. Above all, the rationalistic internal policy of
the enlightened czars of the Petersburg period so constantly dashed

the hopes of the people that the last great Revolution may well be defined, as Ammann has defined it, as " the consequence of a development within the social and economic framework of Russia that misfired. "

For a long time, despite the injustice of actual conditions, a large segment of the Russian people nourished a secret yearning for *pravda,* which though vanished from the earth, remained for safekeeping in the soul of the czar. In the famous poem by the royalist Tiutschev, written in 1867, we read:

> Although it has fled from the face of earth,
> *Pravda* has one refuge still—in the soul of the Czar.
> Who has not heard the solemn word
> That century passes on to century?
> Age without a soul, of wrathful mind,
> On the open square, in the chamber, on the throne,
> Everywhere you have become the enemy of *pravda*!
> Nonetheless, one august refuge,
> One sacred altar remains to *pravda.*
> It is thy soul, our true-believing Czar!

Since *pravda* had vanished, it had to be sought. Even a special word existed for this quest, the equivalent of " the search for *pravda.* " As late as the middle of the 19th century it was not uncommon to meet peasants on the road who were prepared to wander through the whole world in search of the missing *pravda.* Dostoevski pondered at length on how to satisfy the longing for *pravda,* and how the people might learn to recognize *pravda* when they saw it. He asked himself: How are the people to be persuaded that *pravda* is not yet dead in our land; how might its banner be flown again?

Despite many disappointments the people's faith in the czaristic charisma survived into the 20th century. At the beginning of World War I it flared up one last time. In his remarkable memoirs the French ambassador to the court of St. Petersburg describes the Muscovites' " insane enthusiasm for their czar. " Paléologue had not expected to find such " deep-rooted fetishism in the Muscovite soul. " For on Blood Sunday, 1905, that fetishism had suffered a terrible blow. The Orthodox priest Gapon had headed a procession of the faithful bearing icons and pictures of the Czar to the palace in the hope of contacting the invisible Czar through whom *pravda* was to be returned to Russian soil. Gapon's word was: We must go to the Czar. The Czar is *pravda*. Beside the Czar there is no *pravda*. But the procession was never to reach the Czar; it was scattered by the gunfire of the palace guards, leaving many dead in the street. What decades of revolutionary and Marxist propaganda had not been able to achieve Bloody Sunday achieved. For a large segment of the population faith in the Czar as the charismatic bearer of *pravda* was dead. That evening Gapon proclaimed that with the slaying of the people faith in the Czar had also been slain. Gapon wrote the Czar: bloodshed has dissolved the bond between the sovereign and his people; now the bloody terrors of the coming revolution can no longer be stayed.

After the Revolution of 1905 the Czar made certain concessions to the Church and to the religious denominations. In the name of freedom of conscience the once forbidden transfer of faith from Orthodoxy to another belief was permitted, and the non-Orthodox denominations were generally treated with more tolerance. But the Czar did not keep his promise to convoke a General *Sobor* or church assembly. Thus the long demanded reforms were never undertaken and many believers were disappointed and estranged. The leading ecclesiastical representatives and administrators still servilely supported policies of the Czar that were hated by the people. The Synod condemned all expression of revolt and damned as blasphemous all enemies of the Church who dared to protest against the anointed Czar. Almost nothing was done to correct the weaknesses within the Church. Things seethed among the lower clergy, who suffered from social and economic discrimination and who were often treated despotically by the bishops (most of whom belonged to a monastic elite). Many seminarians turned their backs on the Church and joined the ranks of the revolutionaries.

The complete domination of the Orthodox Church by the Russian State eventually led to an abject dependence on the good graces of the government. With the ascendency of Rasputin the worldly powers that controlled the Church grew increasingly oppressive, the bishop's dependency ever more degrading. This "*staretz,*" who belonged to a sect that mingled ritual with unbridled debauchery, was an unholy caricature of a true "holy man." He exerted a pseudomystical influence on the imperial couple, especially upon the Czarina over whom he had hypnotic power. Through her Rasputin gained so much influence over the Orthodox hierarchy that conditions within the Church were soon totally deranged. The so-called secret of this dissolute peasant's influence over his sovereigns was common knowledge; the ensuing scandals were discussed in parliament and described at length in the press, inflicting the gravest damage to the prestige of the Church. Through the Czarina Rasputin commanded the government. He simply forced the discharge of the bishops who opposed him and replaced them with puppets of his own choice.

By the time the Bolshevist storm broke over the Orthodox Church, it had completely discredited itself as a tool of czarism. Throughout Russian history the rallying motto of the princes of the Church had been: For Faith, Czar, and Fatherland! When Nicholas II fell there was profound bewilderment. At the news of his murder the Archbishop of Novgorod is said to have declared: "There is no Czar, there is no Church!"

Under such circumstances it is understandable that after the initial confusion the reaction of the Orthodox Church was political. In 1918 the Russian Church fought the Soviet regime as its mortal enemy and attempted to overthrow it. Moreover, struggles within the Church, especially between the lower clergy and the bishops over attemps to break the crippling lethargy of the Church by reforms, were unavoidable. The Soviet regime retaliated in its own way and with its own methods. But its reaction to Church politics in Russia was the result of a particular situation and should not be considered an integral part of the general war on religion, which is one cardinal doctrine of the Bolshevist program that has never been abandoned.

THE INTELLIGENTSIA
AS PILLARS OF THE REVOLUTION

Fed by ever more disappointed hopes, the stream of revolutionary forces that would one day sweep away the old order swelled steadily. By the beginning of the 19th century it was already an imposing river. This was the century in which Russia was to witness the reversal from exaggerated expectations of *pravda* to a nihilistic and revolutionary ideology. The trend was furthered by a small group of young people who proudly referred to themselves as " the intellectuals. " The great mass of the people was incapable of giving the general discontent forceful direction; defenseless, helpless, passive, they simply waited. Thus a mere handful of intellectuals whom the masses had originally rejected became the power that set the radical spiritual and political revolution in motion.

Forbidden to emigrate to the tempting freedom of the West, these intellectuals were a type that was new in Russia. Cut off from the rest of the people, prevented from participating in any fruitful activity, their heads forever full of dreams of an ideal future, they developed a rebellious attitude and were quick to revolt against every injustice. They grew to a kind of militant order that despite the absence of a written statute knew its own, who were scattered over the length and breadth of Russia. In a kind of tacit agreement and by acts which no one really organized the intellectuals warred against the authorities. They were hated by some, passionately loved by others. The intellectuals completely rejected Russia's past even as they rejected her present; they preferred to concentrate on a future which they knew would have to be won by violence. Their credo was very simple: We alone are human beings; to us belong the injured and humiliated. All the trouble comes from the system and its bad governments. Only the Revolution can bring salvation. Because of their lack of roots anywhere in Russia's social structure the " intelligentsia " were regarded with suspicion by the authorities, a fact which only served to isolate the student revolutionaries and to make them more fanatical.

The word " intelligentsia " was coined in 1860 by a little known novelist named Bobrikin and has been used loosely ever since. By no means were all intellectuals in 19th-century Russia revolutionaries. There were many respected and highly successful figures in the intellectual fields—scientists, theologians, writers—who were not the kind of persons generally suggested by the word " intelligentsia. "

At least originally the term intelligentsia meant the young intellectuals caught in the ideological and spiritual crisis which set in between 1830 and 1840, a crisis traceable to the spread of German idealism in Russia. Idealist philosophy has been described in terms of three generations: of its largely aristocratic " fathers, " its utilitarian " sons, " and its radical " grandsons. " The intelligentsia claimed to represent the conscience of Russia. Although sketchily organized, it was highly influential and for decades brought intellectual pressure to bear on autocracy. " Moreover, when the collapse of the old order came, one faction of the intelligentsia was able to exploit the furies of peasant and worker anarchy to the extent of assuming absolute power over all classes more ' real ' than it, before being dissolved in the conditions created by its own success. " [6]

As early as the first half of the 19th century, especially after the Decembrist Uprising, czarism badly damaged its own prestige by its brutal persecution of all whom it considered its enemies. During the reactionary reign of Nicholas I (1825-1855) the country was ruled by a narrow-minded administration that was petty, pedantic, corrupt, and dull.

Significantly, the small group out of which Russia's revolutionary ideology grew originally consisted almost exclusively of the sons of nobles. They came from rich families and were not burdened by the obligations of work and personal achievement. Their parents did not hold administrative posts, and no amount of lavish entertainment or dissipation could disguise the emptiness and beredom of their homes, where they lived by the labor of their serfs as a matter of course. In the libraries of the country nobles the philosophers

---

[6] M. Malia, " What is Intelligentsia? " in: R. Pipes, *The Russian Intelligentsia* (New York: Columbia University Press, 1961), p. 4.

of the French Enlightenment enjoyed priority. They were considered the acme of Western culture.

Alexander Herzen was typical of many of his class and generation.
Intellectually gifted, he grew up in a wealthy home with little
regard for the responsibilities of wealth. His French tutor boasted
of having been among those who sentenced Louis XVI. After the
Decembrist Uprising he seems to have molded the boy's spirit
solely for a revolutionary future in which unrestrained genius
would be the paramount value. Consequently the religious instruction that the fourteen-year-old received left few traces.

In 1847 Herzen, an enthusiastic admirer of revolutionary France
and brimming with great expectations, rushed off to Paris. He
could hardly wait to visit Port-Royal and the Bastille. But he was
profoundly disappointed by the people and the political conditions
that he found in Paris. The French impressed him as hopeless
Philistines. After their brief revolutionary delirium they failed
to mold French life according to the spirit of the Revolution. A
disappointed Westerner, Herzen returned to Russia, land without
Philistines.

Young men of Herzen's background were utterly unprepared for
the unspeakable difficulties involved in rectifying injustices and
improving conditions through personal effort and achievement.
Lack of sustaining encouragement from the world and of a sense of
obligation toward the world kept them puerile enthusiasts to the
end of their lives. They were unmoved by the misery around
them, and although they proudly called themselves intellectuals,
they lacked the strength and perseverance to study the philosophical
systems that they hastily rifled for ideas. Not one member of the
intelligentsia can be called a serious philosopher. These young
people were half-educated Utopians, dreamers, preachers, and journalists. Herzen's philosophical journalism paved the way for much
intellectual irresponsibility in Russia.

NIHILISM

The rigidly authoritarian system under Czar Nicholas evoked a nihilism that spread like an epidemic over the entire country. It met with no firm resistance by the Orthodox Church, largely because of the devastating theological illiteracy of the upper classes. Intellectually unsure of themselves, even seminarians frequently became the spearheads of the new spirit from the West that was finding wide acceptance. In the past the study of philosophy had leaned heavily on German textbooks. Almost all the philosophers of German idealism had been former theologians whose philosophies were protests against the theology of the day. Something analogous occurred in Russia, where German idealism swiftly gained influence. The first generation of Russian idealists, for example all the disciples of Schelling at the universities, came from the theological schools. Furthermore, after 1840 these schools were so permeated with Hegelian thought that many students gave up the study of theology altogether. In the judgment of Peter Scheibert, author and expert on the ideology of the Revolution, Hegel's most enthusiastic disciples were to be found in Russia. Here too idealistic philosophy, only half understood, became the substitute for neglected theology and religion.

Further evidence of the inadequacy of the philosophy and scientific theology of Eastern Christianity was the fact that the Orthodox Church proved helpless against the shifting tides of Western Protestant theology. As a result, criticism by liberal Protestant theologians caused a profound religious skepticism. Thus not only did Orthodox theology fail to exercise the needed influence on secular education but it also shared the blame for the revolt of many young seminarians against the rigid system it had helped create. It was former seminarians who initiated the movement of apostates demanding the inner freedom to accept the new which they felt the theological schools were withholding from them and introducing a note of radical negation into the ranks of the generation just coming of age.

Nihilism was an inexhaustible subject of discussion in the circles of dissatisfied students, foundering intellectuals, and cultivated idlers. It set the mood of a declassed bourgeoisie, becoming, despite its lack of any genuine substance, the fashion of the times. Nihilism was the doctrine of the half-educated who were interested only in proving that nothing can be proved. In endless debates the art of debate made Feuerbach's and Stirner's denial of the intellectual world its own.

Things finally reached the point described by Dostoevski in *The Possessed:* "Nihilism has appeared among us because we are all nihilists. It is only the strangeness of its new form that frightens us. . . . The consternation and concern of the wise who attempt to discover where nihilists come from is amusing. Nihilists come from nowhere but have been with us, in us, and among us all along." Speaking of the effects of nihilism Dostoevski remarks, "Nihilism may be compared with the schism in our Church. Yes, but the schism was very useful to us." Its usefulness consisted in forcing one to study the problems of the day intensively, to get to the bottom of things. For the intellectually alert a new dimension was unfolding that made superficialities no longer acceptable. What was needed could be found only deep within existence; only by getting to the root of things would it be possible to outlive nihilism. This was the need that inspired Dostoevski's work.

The third Department of the Chancery of His Imperial Majesty has left us a terse summary of nihilism: "Russian nihilism unites within itself administrative and social order. It does not recognize government."

Nihilism alone, phenomenon of a tired negativistic disintegration that it is, would never have had the strength to launch a revolution; largely secularized, it lacked the vital *élan* of the eschatological expectation of an earthly *pravda* with its dynamic will to radical absoluteness. Those who swept the masses along with them were a mere handful of professional revolutionaries, a few hundred young men and women. (It was an exception when the total number of party members exceeded two or three thousand.) These were driven by an intoxicating, "mystically" exaggerated, originally Christian, now long since secularized ideal. In spite of their efforts to win the masses, the revolutionaries were at first rejected by them. But as the idealized image of the czar faded, as the general discontent and demoralization caused by the Japanese defeat spread, the revolutionaries gradually succeeded in gaining the influence over the masses that was needed for victory.

It must not be forgotten that also the Russian revolutionary came from a Christian background, that he belonged to a people imbued with a basically sound, not yet disintegrated Christian ethos. Ideologically he had to wrestle with the ghost of his Christian conscience, often until he had convinced himself that he should bear the terrible martyrdom of mortal sin with its spiritual death and should sacrifice his own salvation for the great goal. It was the radicalness of the revolutionary, his unhesitating willingness to stake body and soul that made the relatively infinitesimal group of revolutionaries the dreaded power in the realm against which an enormous police apparatus could not prevail.

In the beginning the revolutionaries fought for a holy cause. " Power is the original sin. The Czar has surrendered to the Evil One. No more awful blasphemy can be imagined than his claim to be the Lord's Anointed with power over the Church! " Hence revolt must restore the outraged rights of man, return dignity to life, and serve ultimate truth. Here is revolution as a moral principle. The struggle for freedom was to be carried out with clean hands; should it demand the murder of the Czar this would be unpardonable but necessary, a sin that would demand the expiation of voluntary death by hanging. . . . According to this fervent conviction, it was God's will that a man be prepared to sin and die for his love of the people. This was the attitude with which the revolutionaries set to work, the challenge with which they managed to recruit many of the best youth of the land. They organized conspiracies, taught terror, indoctrinated the masses with the philosophy of the Enlightenment; they quoted Scripture, pointed to the Commandments and to the real purpose of human life which is to sacrifice everything for one's neighbor, demanding nothing for one's self; indeed to lose oneself entirely in one's convictions, fearing neither the Siberian *katorga* nor life imprisonment, neither the dungeons of the fortress Peter and Paul nor banishment to the tundras of the north.

It is unlikely that it ever would have come to principles of amoral radicalism had not ideas from the West crept in, ideas that were received with the impassioned enthusiasm of a new revelation.

In the intoxicated welcome accorded German idealism only a very few concepts were really understood and eagerly accepted: above all, the autonomy and sovereignty of man, who was now to be no longer subject to the law, but sovereign over it. The Feuerbachian substitution of man himself for the ancient God implied the need to reject the old sovereignty of the law, as did Stirner's autocratic solipsism. Under the impact of these ideas such questions arose as whether or not unatoned murder is justifiable: in other words, is man his own autocratic lawgiver, or does there exist a living God who has forbidden murder once and for all under any circumstances? This is the problem with which Dostoevski's Raskolnikov wrestles.

IDEAS FROM THE WEST

Feelingly the young intellectuals called the sufferings of the people to their attention and to that of the whole world. Finding no solution to the social problem in their own spiritual world because of the theological ignorance that prevailed in Russian society, the intellectuals hearkened westward. Uncritically and with the passionate faith usually accorded divine revelation they embraced every idea that presented itself as the latest truth.

Nineteenth-century Russia was only beginning to stir intellectually and she reached first of all for German ideology, gulping down certain of its notions and feverishly attempting to apply them, often in exaggerated form. So strong was German influence that one may well speak of the Germanization of Russia. Actually the process had begun with Peter the Great's quiet colonization by German educators, administrators, and officers. This was followed by systematic Germanization under Nicholas I. The first university in Russia, founded in 1750, was German. The great stars of German philosophy, already beginning to pale in Germany, blazed anew in Russia. Even clear symptoms of intellectual and spiritual exhaustion were hailed ecstatically by young Russian enthusiasts as gospel truths. In the excitement Western ideas were adopted as they appeared, indiscriminately. Fichte, Oken, Schelling, and Hegel seemed to promise the ultimate solution to all the world's problems. Their uncritical Russian disciples made no attempt to further the development of a world view. In their opinion all that was needed was to popularize the new thought and speedily put it into practice. In this will to practical application the Russians considered themselves superior to the Germans, for had these not caught themselves in the intellectual nets of their own weaving where they remained, unable to extricate themselves and proceed to the decisive deed? Thus Germans remained behind in the realm of pure thought. Now, however, the era of action was at hand.

In 1836 the pistol shot of Chadaev's *Philosophical Letter* shattered the graveyard stillness of Nicholas I's reign. It raised the question of the Empire's providential destiny. With the publication of the *Philosophical Letter* Russian intellectuals as a class began to be conscious of their special mission. Regardless of background they knew that in an age of absolute bureaucracy their only chance lay in the future and that they must prepare themselves for the task of guiding the destiny of the people. Through their faith in the Enlightenment as a means to improve the world flowed a strong current of rationalistic confidence in the power of human reason much like that which dominated the West since the 18th century.

Even the abstract theories of Hegel's system fired the boundless enthusiasm of Russian youth. Nothing is more revealing than the effects of Hegel on Belinski, whose portrait up to the eve of the Revolution gave a room the stamp of an intellectual. Coming from a vague idealism which stressed freedom above everything, Belinski suddenly discovered Hegel. Under the shock of the revelation he burst into tears. This took place at midnight in his room where, like Pascal, he experienced conversion and rebirth. But in his attempt to consider the whole real world with all its injustice and pain part of the absolute spirit's intrinsically necessary process of self-revelation and hence to justify it, Belinski veered round to protest and revolt against Hegel and against all the injustice and suffering which he saw as the perennial burden of the people. Suddenly he understood: not the absolute of reason was what his soul demanded, but fullness of being for every single individual, a fullness which

embraced immortality. Thus as he says himself, negation became
his god and the destroyers of the old his heroes: Luther, Voltaire,
the Encyclopedists, the terrorists of the French Revolution, and
Byron with his *Cain*.

BELINSKI

All the themes of the metaphysical revolution reappear in Belinski.
In a letter from the year 1841 he writes: " A wild, insane, fanatical
love of freedom and personal independence has been growing in
me. . . .Now I understand the French Revolution; I also understand
Marat's bloody love of freedom, his bloody hatred of all that cuts
itself off from the brotherhood of man. A new extreme grips me:
love of socialism which has become for me the idea of ideas, the
being of all being, the question of questions, the understanding's
alpha and omega. Everything from, for, and toward socialism!
More and more I become a citizen of the world. . .the human
personality. . .this is the point on which I fear to lose my mind.
I have begun to love mankind as Marat did; in order to make even
its smallest part happy I could, I believe, destroy all the rest by
fire and sword. "

Unable to clarify his own attitude toward the problem of God and
reach an independent decision in the matter, Belinski was completely
shattered by Marx's thesis that for Germany the criticism of religion
was essentially completed and that it was the premise of all other
criticism. For long years the problem of the existence of a personal
God continued to burn in Belinski's soul. " We have not yet
answered the question of a personal God, " he once reproached
a friend, " and you want to go to table! " A few years before
his death he wrote in a letter, " What is man without God?. . .
a cold corpse. " Without ever professing outright atheism, Belinski
gradually succumbed to the influence of Bakunin's demon of
blasphemy and to his own rancor against God and the world.
Since youth the theodicy problem had been the crux of Belinski's

religious difficulty: How is a good and holy God to be reconciled with the evil in the world?   In a youthful attempt to dramatize his own revolt Belinski wrote a play entitled *Dmitri Kalinin* in which after prolonged indecision the hero rejects all trust in Providence and blasphemes God as a tyrant who delights in the screams of his victims and intoxicates himself on their tears.   It is Belinski's arguments which a few decades later Dostoevski puts in the mouth of his " atheist, " Ivan Karamazov.   Ivan too does not begin by denying the existence of God but rather by rejecting the world as a work of God.   No ultimate universal harmony can ever justify the tears of a single pain-racked child.   Hence Ivan feels obliged to return his admission ticket to the world, for a world founded on innocent suffering should never have been created.   Such bitter rejection of God's world leads logically to the denial of God himself, although Belinski personally never seems to have taken this ultimate step.

As the theologian Sergius Bulgakov points out, the soul of the Russian intellectual, the pillar of revolutionary thought, is the same maze of contradictions that is to be found everywhere in Russian life.   On the suffering face of Russia next to blackest shadows, indeed next traits of backwardness and outright barbarity there are traits of great spiritual beauty which make that face like " a rare and precious flower blooming amidst our gruesome history, the ' red flower ' of tears and blood that one of Russia's most worthy sons, the noble Garschin, beheld in a symbolic vision. " Yet in spite of the intelligentsia's basically religious attitude, Dostoevski's comparison of the intellectual with someone possessed by demons was drawn from experience.   " The comparison, " says Bulgakov " still holds.   A legion of demons has taken possession of the enormous body of Russia, which as a result writhes in convulsions and is tortured and lamed.   Intellectual Russia has rejected Christ, but she is unable to restore her balance.   Even after repudiating Christ she remains marked by him.   Russia's spiritual anxiety is what makes her excesses so vacillating and so strange.

During the course of the 19th century the activists among the intellectuals gradually assumed command over the mere enthusiasts. As Berdyaev once remarked, the intelligentsia was willing to accept any system as long as it sanctioned their ideal.   Thus the

Marxist doctrine of revolution based on Hegelian dialectics was bound to impress them as *the* great ideological remedy they were seeking. Here at last was the theory of absolute revolution, revolution for its own sake. Any possible improvement through reforms was rejected on principle and the proletarian revolution proclaimed as the final dialectical about-face, after which the road would lead straight to paradise. Hence compromises, realistic reforms, and the removal of current abuses one by one would only postpone the ultimate apocalyptical triumph. For the sake of this magnificent end, all the inhumane means employed by the revolution must be affirmed.

BAKUNIN

Through passionately affirmed revolution Mikhail Bakunin, "the apostle of universal destruction," arrived at atheism. Bakunin's earliest childhood memories were of indignation at brutality and revolt against injustice, for like many others, the Bakunin family had suffered heavily from the consequences of the Decembrist Uprising, which was quelled by blood.

There are similarities between Bakunin and Nietzsche. Like Nietzsche, Bakunin in his youth was sincerely religious. In fact, the early religious statements of both are marked by a certain touching exaggeration. Both Nietzsche's and Bakunin's early styles were considered pontifical; both lacked the training and self-discipline for any enduring faith. Unstable, erratic and disorderly, the young officer Bakunin was notorious for his lack of discipline. He was incapable of concentrated, steady, or strenuous work.

First Bakunin studied Kant; next he became a Fichte enthusiast; soon he was worshipping Hegel, the idol of idealistic philosophy; finally he succumbed to the influence of the Hegelian Left, to Feuerbach, Strauss, and Marx. (Bakunin saw a lot of Marx but the two quarelled incessantly.) Bakunin was full of unbalanced contradictions, full of the devil as he called it. This imbalance coupled with fomenting passions made him a drastic disturber of the family peace, for again like Nietzsche, Bakunin never matured enough to establish a family of his own. He remained bound to the family into which he was born, but the bond was one of hate. He nursed a deep resentment against his father. The son never really transcended the narrow bounds of a family member in revolt to develop his own personality. In the egocentricity of puberty he remained basically disinterested in the world except as a useful stage for his personal revolt, which he projected on a universal scale.

Bakunin was beset by a wild impatience to revolutionize the world from within by a single titanic effort of the will. Behind the torrent of pseudophilosophy was nothing but self-centered coldness. Basically Bakunin remained a Russian landowner totally indifferent to the lot of his serfs.

Fichte's pathos of the liberation of the ego goaded this " unruliest of his readers, " who broadened the Fichtean concept immeasurably. Bakunin's God was depersonalized to an empty idea that could be filled at will as " the meaning of life, the object of love, and so forth. " No longer was God someone whom man can approach only by humbling himself; no longer someone who judges from a stand beyond the world. God now dwells within mankind, " exalting himself in the exalted human being. " In " the new boundless religion " God is equated with the perfect man. " The religious substance which Fichte had so to speak dissolved now crystallized anew in a boundless self-confidence that was particularly attractive to its followers because its apparently monistic features relieved its disciples of the burden of any personal existence of their own. " During the period in which he came closest to Fichte's views Bakunin equated himself with the coming God-man who as the ultimate goal of human evolution would serve as the new Messiah. Thus religious hopes for the beyond were completely secularized. Scheibert speaks of Bakunin's " almost insane self-confidence " in spite of his depressions, a self-confidence that was to maintain itself in the ambiguity of its lack of reference to place and condition. After freeing itself from all given conditions with the help of idealistic philosophy, this overwrought, totally abstract self-confidence could be filled at will with its own *nomos*. The Russian intellectual's consciousness of mission " culminated in the figure of Bakunin, a thoroughly un-humanistic figure who, when it became clear that philosophemes failed to change the world from one day to the next, had no solution to offer but destruction. " [7]

Now in Berlin, now in Paris, Bakunin worked at his radically revolutionary ideas. He demanded the complete annihilation of the prevailing social and political order. In 1851 he wrote his " confession " to Czar Nicholas I. " A new world has revealed itself to me, a world into which I have plunged with the avidness of one dying of thirst. It seemed as though I heard a new promise, the revelation of a new religion of sublimity and dignity, of universal happiness and liberation. " According to Bakunin the new order could come into being only through the destruction of the old. Only after all positive religions had been wiped out could the one saving church of liberated mankind come into being. In sharp contrast to the old Christian world stood modern philosophy's principle of the autonomy of the spirit as proclaimed by Kant, Fichte, Schelling, and Hegel. This is the spirit that is called to revolutionize the poorest stratum of society. " Let us place our trust in that eternal spirit, " Bakunin continues, " which destroys only because it is the unfathomable, eternally creative wellspring of all existence. The lust for destruction is a creative lust. Enough of theory! Plunge into the world of action, of real life! " [8]

During his long years of imprisonment Bakunin had but one fear, that his indignation and rebellion might weaken. Escaped from the yoke of subjugation he surrendered himself completely to the frenzied intoxication of freedom, which led him to a radical fanatical atheism. Either God exists and man is a slave, his freedom having been appropriated by God, or God does not exist and man is free. For the sake of the Revolution man wills and must have freedom, hence God dare not exist. The argument is a classical example of " postulatory atheism " in which God is not allowed to exist because if he did, man could not be free. According to Bakunin, then, God is an idea (in the Feuerbachian sense) which men have invented for their own selfish interests. Only the abdication of God can guarantee human freedom. In a paper entitled *God in the State*,

---

[7] E. Briem and Schultze, *Kommunismus u. Sozialismus in der Sowjetunion.*
[8] P. Scheibert, *Von Bakunin zu Lenin. Geschichte der russichen revolutionaeren Ideologien 1840-1895*, I. Bd. (1956), p. 77.

Bakunin celebrates the Biblical Satan as the first revolutionary, who is to be thanked for his attempts to liberate man from the slavery intended for him by the Creator. Yet for all Bakunin's cynical mockery of faith in God, one last typical remnant of his Russian religiousness remains; the thought of Christ calms the storm of revolt within him.

In all the so-called proofs that Bakunin arrays against God there is a flagrant lack of moderation, clear indication that they spring from rebellion and that the " objective reasons " he advances are only a camouflage. His fanatical hate pushed him to the point of rejecting any form of government at all, even a transitional form to the proclaimed stateless society. Bakunin's thought is still very much alive in current Russian atheism; to this day his notions, pseudoproofs of the nonexistence of God, and travesties of religion have remained the heavy artillery of aggressive atheism.

NECHAEV AND DOSTOEVSKI

Caught between the popular expectation of *pravda* and the impact of Western ideas that were flooding the country, destroying the religious foundations of Russian revolutionary hopes and efforts, Dostoevski wrestled with the problem of whether or not a man can live a meaningful life without God. Therein lies the enormous significance of Dostoevski's own life: that with his novels he succeeded in plumbing the psychological depths of the atheism of his day, weighing its consequences for mankind and exposing the absurdity to which they logically lead.

The Possessed is more than a novel. It was written under the powerful impact of the sensational trial of the revolutionary Nechaev, who after the publication of the secret archive following the Bolshevist Revolution in 1917 was celebrated as a top-ranking revolutionary figure. The detailed testimony on the revolutionary ideas and plans brought to light by the trial enabled Dostoevski not only to recreate faithfully the ideological world of the accused, but to test its vital worth. From the first fruits of this revolutionary ideology a man of Dostoevski's psychological depth was well able to prophesy the future of the coming communism. Moreover, Dostoevski was acquainted with the ideas of radical Western thinkers, with Max Stirner's *The Individual and his Property* (1845), for instance, which was widely read in Russia and whole sentences of which Kirilov quotes practically verbatim in *The Possessed*. For years Dostoevski struggled for clarity in his own darkness, which he describes in a letter to a friend soon after his release from prison in March 1854. " I...am a child of this age, a child of unbelief and doubt, and probably—indeed I am certain of this—I shall remain so to the end of my days.... How agonizingly the longing for faith tormented and still torments me, a longing that only grows stronger the more negative evidence I have. " [9]

Nechaev was probably the most fantastic figure among the Russian revolutionaries, a man who as a master of the revolutionary phrase knew how to befuddle and fascinate men in order to terrorize them. He kept his shallow elaborate " secrecy " transparent enough to reveal himself as the head of a band of conspirators and dramatically warned everyone that the revolution was on the march, and one must decide *now* whether one would march with the people or against them. He demanded absolute obedience of all who joined his organization and—as his trial revealed—did not hesitate to murder anyone who failed to carry out his orders with the proper obsequiousness.

Nechaev was really not a Marxist, but he attempted to gain control of the Marxist organization for his own purposes. It is largely due to his *Catechism of a Revolutionary* (often erroneously attributed to Bakunin) that he came to be considered the Father of the Revolution. A copy in code of this catechism, which was probably written in 1869, fell into the hands of the secret police, who published it. It is a unique document of sadistic rage, of destructiveness unrelieved by a single constructive idea.

Quoted from the *Catechism:* " 1. The revolutionary is marked by Fate. He knows no personal interests, concerns, feelings, ties; he possesses no property, indeed not even a name. Everything in

[9] Dostojewskij, *Briefe*, hg. v. A. Eliasberg (1914), pp. 61 f.

him is dominated by one all-exclusive interest, one single thought, one passion—revolution. 2. From the depths of his being not only by words but also by deeds he has severed all ties to the bourgeois order and to the whole world of culture with its laws, customs, and manners. He is the relentless enemy of that world, and if he continues to live in it he does so only to destroy it the more surely. 3. The revolutionary. . .knows but one science, the science of destruction. . .his only goal is the swiftest possible destruction of this evil order. 4. He despises public opinion, despises and hates the present public morality in all its forms. For him what is moral is that which furthers the triumph of the revolution; immoral and criminal everything that hinders it. " [10] The remaining 18 paragraphs are nothing but enlargements of the same anarchistic fanaticism. One dictum says blatantly: " Plundering is one of the most honorable forms of Russian national life. The brigand is a revolutionary minus the rhetoric, he is the merciless, tireless, untameable revolutionary of the deed. " [11]

The Nechaev trial exposed a spirit of cold cynicism aimed solely at destruction and subjugation. It was a terrible blow to the idealism of the remaining intelligentsia. Nechaev's was a program for the annihilation of everything these young people held sacred. Here all sentiments of sympathy and love are abolished as detrimental to revolution. Man is to become a flawless robot in the hands of the revolutionary leader. The impression which the trial left on Nechaev's contemporaries was so shattering that for a while revolutionary activist youth almost ceased to exist.

Nechaev's defense, which collected all possible excuses as grounds for clemency, pleaded Russia's cultural impoverishment as the cause of such radicalism. It presented an excellent picture of Russian student life with its social instability and the lack of a stabilizing cultural tradition. Even a Pole, declared the defense, can look back on a rich past which contains much to make his heart beat higher. " The Russian's past is destitute, and his present is as dry, poor, and naked as the endless steppes bare of all permanent landmarks. Radicalism, the most prominent trait of youth today, comes from

[10] M. Prawdin, *Netschajew — von Moskau verschwiegen* (1961), pp. 73 f.
[11] *Ibid.*, p. 79.

the lack of anything solid which might give that youth a hold; radicalism may be explained by the lack of a traditional culture. " [12]

Nechaev received a relatively mild sentence, but his own behavior repelled all his former followers.   He was accused of leading them into destruction and then unconscionably abandoning them while he saved himself by fleeing abroad.   For decades the term " Nechaevism " was used as a household word for slyness, political swindle, and the hoodwinking of comrades reduced to slaves.   Later revolutionaries protested against any connection with Nechaev.   All this makes it understandable why the name of Nechaev was long tabu.   After 1917 he was briefly eulogized then again suppressed. At some point between the eulogy and the suppression certain Bolshevistic historians established the thesis that Nechaev should be designated the Father of Bolshevism, and that Bolshevism was in reality more a fresh wave of Nechaevism than authentic Marxism. In his book on Nechaev Prawdin presents proof that this notion is to be found even in Lenin, and that the question of whether the Bolshevistic system owes more to Nechaev or to Marx is justifiable.

At any rate it was under the impact of the Nechaev affair that Dostoevski, inspired by the reports released at the trial, wrote his novel, *The Possessed,* a devastating portrayal of Russian society in all its shallowness, hypocritical sentimentality, and confused cynicism.   The romantic enthusiasts and phrasemongers who hold forth on the happiness of the people and pretend to speak in their name haven't the faintest notion about the peoples' true condition.

Apparently much in Dostoevski's merciless description of the consequences of the czarist system applies also to the Soviet system, which for a long time suppressed the novel.   Nechaev's *Catechism* certainly inspired Shigalov's " system of how to run the world " in *The Possessed.*   He says, " I've entangled myself in my own arguments, and my conclusion stands in diametric opposition to the idea from which I started.   After taking uncurbed freedom as my point of departure, I arrived at uncurbed despotism.   However I must add that any solution to the problem of a social system other than mine cannot exist at all. "   Finally as the ultimate solution Shigalov proposes " the division of mankind into two

[12] *Ibid.,* p. 81.

uneven categories. One-tenth will be granted individual freedom and full rights over the remaining nine-tenths, who will lose their individuality and become something like a herd of cattle. Gradually, through unlimited obedience and a series of mutations, they will attain a state of primeval innocence, something akin to the original paradise on earth, although, of course, they'll have to work. The procedure Mr. Shigalov suggests, which would deprive nine-tenths of mankind of their free will and transform them into a herd through re-education of entire generations, is very interesting; it is based on data gathered from the natural sciences and is very logical. " [13] What is herewith proposed is not baseness but paradise, an earthly paradise, and no other is possible at all.

To what extent this fantastic suggestion dictated actual revolutionary measures we see from the fact that at the height of his power Lenin actually tried to find some method of organized re-education with which to overcome the inertia of the human material with which he had to work and which he considered the greatest hindrance to the realization of the socialist state. The physiologist Pavlov impressed Lenin deeply with his mechanistic explanation of the life of the soul in terms of direction through nervous reflexes. Lenin considered such direction the most appropriate means of implementing his policy of re-education. Like all dictators he was totally lacking in respect for human freedom. The freedom of the personal ego was to retire behind the collective soul. The ego was Enemy Number One of the Soviet system; it was *sin*. Hence the personal ego with its intimate life of the soul must be rooted out in order to make room for a collective state conscience and a collective state doctrine the slightest criticism of which was strictly forbidden. " In this way millions of people were depersonalized, rendered hysterical, neurotic, and infantile. In brief, it was truly a painstakingly wrought strategy which was planned in advance for whole decades at a time and in which nothing was left to chance. Every reaction of the people was to be the exactly calculated reaction to a complex of environmental stimulants assembled in the social laboratory and applied by the proper authority. " [14] It is obvious

---

[13] F. Dostoevski, *The Possessed* (New York: The New American Library of World Literature, Inc., 1962), p. 385.
[14] L. M. Heitfeld, *Gehirnwaesche* (1963), p. 10.

that a logical line of reasoning stretches from Nechaev through Shigalov, Pavlov, and Lenin to the professional brainwashers of the Red Chinese.

For Dostoevski atheism is no mere doctrinaire thesis for intellectual discussion. Profound psychologist that he is, he gazes into the depths of men's souls and knows that their intellectual arguments and counterarguments play only a minor role. The problem of belief and unbelief is primarily one of a decision of the heart. Dostoevski regards the rebellious aggressiveness of the humiliated as one of the chief motives for decisions against God. He knows also atheists for whom forgetfulness of God has become a permanent attitude; for these the problem of God has been settled. Dostoevski is acquainted too with the noisy atheism of the man of the herd, who simply trots along with the others, incapable of making a decision of his own. But it is not among any of these that the problem of the true psychical origin of atheism is to be studied, but among those others who have taken the problem of God with terrible earnestness and who try to live the consequences of their denial. Dostoevski is aware that most forms of atheism spring from a vengeful heart and consist in the refusal to accept the world as it is. This type of atheist does not deny God from the start, rather he insists that a God of absolute goodness as the First Cause of this world is inconsistent with the actual suffering in the world; hence he abrogates the existence of God. Ivan Karamazov, for example, does not actually deny God; he refuses to accept God's world because in his supposed creation nothing of the divine love and justice preached by Christianity is evident. For him no theological promise of ultimate justice in another world counts; he sees only the fact of the present, the undeserved suffering of innocents.

Atheism from the motive: God *or* freedom! is to be found in Kirilov, another character in *The Possessed*. "If God exists, then the whole will is his and I can do nothing. If he doesn't exist, then all will is mine and I must exercise my own will, my free will. . . . So I'll kill myself to begin with. . . . To recognize that there's no God without recognizing at the same time that you yourself have become God makes no sense. . . . I'm unhappy because I must prove my free will. . . . I'm terribly unhappy because I'm terribly afraid. Fear is the curse of man. But I shall establish my free will. It is my duty to make myself believe that I do not believe in God. I'll be the first and last, and that will open the door. And I'll save them. This alone can save people, and the next generation will be transformed...For three years I've searched for the attribute of my divinity and I've found it—my free will! ... This is all I have at my disposal to show my independence and the terrifying new freedom...." [15]

Kirilov is a man who takes his atheism extremely seriously; he is fully aware of the far-reaching consequences of his undertaking. Once man succeeds in demanding absolute autocracy from God and appropriating it, a new day will dawn in the history of mankind. The revolt of the engineer Kirilov does not stop at the political level but reaches down into the religious foundations of existence. Political revolution is no more than a brief prelude to the one essential revolution: the repudiation of God. Kirilov believes that he has been called to take this decisive step. He considers himself a Messianic atheist, the apostle of the new man. He fails to see the absurdity of his act. The only way he can express his autonomous will is to destroy a life which he has not given himself and which with his limitations as creature he can never make so completely his own that his autonomous ego can become the source of that life. Actually, as the final pages of *The Possessed* reveal, the end of the attempted revolt against God and usurpation of his divinity by a man possessed of demons is the terrible destruction of that man.

After Dostoevski's *The Possessed*, " this unique and impassioned pamphlet against the revolutionaries, there could be no further doubt: religion was *the* opposing principle, and it was by a man's attitude toward the problems of religion that he was labeled friend or foe. "

For decades the intelligentsia was the standard-bearer of an atheistic counterfaith with which the simple people would have nothing to do. Eckardt gives a brilliant description of the intelligentsia's assiduous wooing of the infinitely complex and contra-

[15] F. Dostoevski, *The Possessed* (New York: The New American Library of World Literature, Inc., 1962), pp. 637-638.

dictory Russian people. "Evil and piety; violence and childlike faith; humaneness, vengefulness, and greed; love of earth, of the plough's furrows; prudent thrift and the lapidary pronouncements of the Sermon on the Mount; rustic fraternity and long stifled yearning for freedom; self-indulgence and poverty, the crude, indestructible, eternal poverty of the poorest *muzhik*—this life on the edge of death with its birchbark bread and the hunger-bloated bellies of children, this bare existence in tumbledown huts of rotting straw—all this flares up. The longing of these dazed, long-abused souls suddenly manifests itself as outcry, as the torch-flung impatience of frenzied masses who have had enough of death on the battlefields of the Russo-Japanese and First World Wars. One hope, only one, land! At last to own land! To make an end of the old for the sake of a fresh start!" [16]

And yet, characteristically, "the only popular movement which Narodnitshtsvo, a leading revolutionary of the 1870's, succeeded in mustering obeyed in the name of the Czar! Among the simple people the idea of the kingdom of justice on earth (vanished until Christ's return at the end of time, when a kind of Heavenly Jerusalem would become an empirical reality) was still very much alive. "As late as the middle of the last century it was not uncommon for whole villages and even larger areas to behave as if in the grip of a whirlwind. The peasants would load their possessions into their carts and depart in tight columns for an unknown Utopia. They battled the military units that blocked their way and returned to their homes only under the threat of armed force, manfully bearing all their trials and holding fast to their conviction that the forbidden land did exist, where a wonderful life awaited them....This dreamland retained its power up to the eve of the Revolution, continually luring new citizens...to Kitez, the city of the faithful beyond the reach of the ruling *non-pravda*, and to their death." [17]

---

[16] H. V. Eckardt, *Russisches Kommunismus* (1947), pp. 197 f.
[17] *Ibid.*

THE DAWN OF CRITICISM

It is well known that the 19th century and the beginning of the 20th in Russia brought a renewal of religious thought and with it a dynamic conception of the world. Since the early 19th century the awakening of a Russian national consciousness had been accompanied by the growth of a movement that was both patriotic and religious. The so-called Slavophiles were convinced that Russia's mission in the world could be only of a Christian nature. For them the Russian people were plainly *the* Christian people and the cornerstone for the kingdom of God on earth. But this many-branched movement of Christian philosophers of religion came too late to be effective against the steadily growing weight of atheistic intellectuals, who hardly could be blamed for not having sufficient judgment to recognize the dominant materialism of the West for what it was, the result of ideological decline. For them materialism was not merely the latest concern but an ultimate truth worthy of complete veneration. Accordingly, religion was the main prejudice to be overcome if salvation through revolution was to become a reality.

However, by the end of the century Western criticism of materialism had also reached Russia, causing a serious crisis in Marxism. Re-enforced by Western criticism and by positivism, a strong, almost religious reaction against massive materialism and exaggerated faith in science set in. The Soviet term for former Marxists who felt the challenge of religion was "God-seekers." To these belonged Berdyaev, Bulgakov and Merezhkovsky. Other Marxists rejected the shallow dogmatism of Engels' natural philosophy and returned to Hegel. Thus a considerable Hegelian renaissance took place in Russia. Above all after the unsuccessful revolution in 1905, there was a new tendency to question revolution as a panacea and to tackle moral problems anew in an effort to find new approaches to socialism. The half philosophical, half literary clique to which Gorky and Lunacharsky belonged attempted to construct a religion without God. Nonetheless its members were called "the God-makers." The new interest in philosophy penetrated even the Bolshevist faction of Russian social democracy. Moreover, religion began to interest certain revolutionaries not only in the form presented by the official church, but also in the religion of Tolstoy, who regarded personal ethics as the starting point of a universal renewal and who had the courage to lead the way by his own exemplary life.

LENIN'S PROGRAM OF ATHEISM

On the one hand Lenin had strong roots in the Russian revolutionary tradition; on the other, he differed from all other revolutionaries in that he succeeded in imposing his law on the Russian Revolution by the force of his relentless will to power. In spite of many rejections and personal defeats, by sheer, unlimited, unwavering energy, Lenin made himself so completely lord of Bolshevik Russia that even after his death his law remained unchallenged, except for a brief interval by Stalinism, after which Leninism was again ceremoniously elevated to the official norm. Possibly the new dynamic element in Lenin which exalted him above his surroundings and ultimately led to his success was a special inheritance from his forebears. His mother was a Volga German, and the family life of both parents supposedly was quite different from that to be found in the usual Russian home.

Lenin recognized in the budding criticism of cut-and-dried materialism and in the intellectual refinement of the criticism of Russian society a dangerous softening of the revolutionary's conceptual machinery. In his determination to place himself in command of all revolutionary action, Lenin rejected renewed discussion of principles as a threat to the uniformity of classical party doctrine, hence his book *Materialism and Empiro-criticism* (1909) which Scheibert calls "sheer denunciation." In it Lenin ignores the essential, the empirio-criticism of Mach, insisting that the new philosophy of immanence was nothing but a new defense of God. Marx brands everything that suggests the slightest criticism of the old crude materialism as "religion." Thus he remarks of the

American physicist Carus, who expressly declared himself to be a monist but who refused to join the chorus of those who denounce all religion as superstition: " It is quite evident that we have here a leader of a gang of American literary swindlers who are doping the people with religious opium.   Obviously Mach and Kleinpeter have joined this gang as the result of a little ' misunderstanding. ' " [18] Polemics of this kind betray a total lack of will to objective discussion.

Lenin succeeded in establishing mid-19th-century materialism, which with its categorical rejection of all faith in God and all religion, became the principal doctrine.   In contrast to the earlier intelligentsia, Lenin's new generation was one for whom faith and religion had never been serious problems.   For young Lenin the break with the faith of his fathers did not involve any kind of crisis.   One day the youth simply tore off the medal of a saint that hung round his neck, spat on it, and threw it away.   With this the burden of religion was discarded once and for all.

Ever since his studies at the *Gymnasium* Lenin had been consumed by the will to follow in the footsteps of his elder brother, who had been executed for involvement in an attempted assassination of the Czar.   Lenin was an atheist and revolutionary long before he even heard the names of Marx and Engels.   From these Lenin merely acquired the new, ultimate formulas which he welcomed as ready-made instruments for action and as the justification of his own revolutionary impulses.

It was clear to Lenin from the start that the desired revolution would turn on a struggle for power that would be fought with political weapons.   Never to lose sight of this goal, never to allow himself to be sidetracked—this remained the law of his life.   He knew that discussion of ideological principles would only weaken the impulse to revolution, hence his unprecedented sharpness whenever he mentioned religion.   His dictatorial censorship cut short any possibility of objective examination of basic ideological questions.   With the appearance of Lenin's book, philosophical discussion between Russian Marxists was essentially over.

[18] V. I. Lenin, *Materialism and Empiro-Criticism* (New York: International Publishers Co., Inc., 1927), pp. 229 f.

As the " engineer " of the new " human factory " Lenin represents the programmatic new antifaith. Even Marx was convinced that the intellectual and spiritual battle against belief was over; that faith in God was obsolete. Although in his younger years Marx had been such a passionate enemy of Christianity that his fanaticism cost him the loss of all objective criteria, in later life he practiced a certain reserve in matters of faith. Hermann Duncker, a Communist authority on religion, points out that only in private and in his correspondence did Marx specifically demand battle against religion. Occasionally he gave orders to harry the priests in Catholic sections of the country. Both Marx and Lenin, says Duncker, dismissed religion from their lives so early and so completely " that the fundamentally atheistic nature of their mature world view was self-understood and seemed to require no particular emphasis or explanation. The same was true of Lenin. Hence it is natural that the great leaders of Marxism did not leave behind any systematic statement of their atheism, which was so axiomatic to their whole thinking that a detailed presentation of atheistic doctrine seemed superfluous. Engels considers atheism " self-understood " for the workers' unions of 1874, just as Lenin in 1909 speaks of " class-conscious Social Democrats, who are of course atheists. "

Whereas the original program of German Social Democracy, the Eisenach Program of 1869, demanded " separation of church and state as well as separation of school and church, " the Gotha Program of the Socialist Worker's Party of 1875 declared religion to be " a private matter, " a formula which later sparked a passionate struggle. In a note scribbled on the margin of this program Marx demanded that men's conscience " be freed from the bugbear of religion, " though he prudently took care not to push this idea beyond the limits of " bourgeois " tolerance. Engels' program had demanded the strict abolition of religion, but as this was not accepted, the compromise formula, " religion is a private matter " (1901) had to be substituted. This formula was so ambiguous that the German Social Democratic Party's compromising attitude was branded by more consistent Communists like Hermann Duncker as a " terrible reaction " and " backsliding into the crudest Christian ideology. "

Nowhere in Lenin's remarks do we find a trace of real interest in the possibility of truth in religion's claims. For him " religion " is merely a term used in the polemics of class warfare. He also shares the revolutionary's view of the origin of religion and the demand that religion be combatted. " Religion is one of the forms of spiritual oppression which everywhere weighs down heavily upon the masses of the people, overburdened by their perpetual work for others, by want and isolation. Impotence of the exploited classes in their struggle against the exploiters just as inevitably gives rise to the belief in a better life after death as impotence of the savage in his battle with nature gives rise to belief in gods, devils, miracles, and the like. Those who toil and live in want all their lives are taught by religion to be submissive and patient while here on earth, and to take comfort in the hope of a heavenly reward. But those who live by the labour of others are taught by religion to practice charity while on earth, thus offering them a very cheap way of justifying their entire existence as exploiters and selling them at a moderate price ticket to well-being in heaven. " [19]

Lenin takes up Marx's old refrain, " Religion is opium for the people, " and coarsens it by adding that it is the spiritual bathtub-gin in which the slaves of capitalism drown their human dignity and the claim to an existence halfway worthy of man.

For Lenin religion is opium because it preaches patience and prevents the worker from participating in a slaves' uprising. " But a slave who has become conscious of his slavery and has risen to struggle for his emancipation has already half ceased to be a slave. The modern class-conscious worker, reared by large-scale industry and enlightened by urban life, contemptuously casts aside religious prejudices, leaves heaven to the priests and bourgeois bigots, and tries to win a better life for himself here on earth. The proletariat of today takes the side of socialism, which enlists science in the battle against the fog of religion, and frees the workers from their belief in life after death by welding them together to fight in the present for a better life on earth. " [20]

To prevent " misunderstandings " Lenin unequivocally interprets

[19] V. I. Lenin, *Collected Works* (New York: International Publishers Co., Inc., 1927), vol. X, p. 83.
[20] *Ibid.*, p. 84.

the controversial declaration of religion as "a private affair."
Actually, his interpretation is a reinterpretation which sharpens
the concept considerably as an offensive weapon. According to
Lenin, as far as the state is concerned religion may be regarded as
a private matter, but by no means is it to be considered a private
matter by the party. "Religion must be of no concern to the state,
and religious societies must have no connection with governmental
authority. Everyone must be absolutely free to profess any religion
he pleases, or no religion whatever, i.e., to be an atheist, which
every socialist is, as a rule. Discrimination among citizens on
account of their religious convictions is wholly intolerable. Even
the bare mention of a citizen's religion in official documents should
unquestionably be eliminated. No subsidies should be granted to
the established church or state allowances made to ecclesiastical
and religious societies. These should become absolutely free associations of like-minded citizens, associations independent of the state.
Only the complete fulfilment of these demands can put an end to the
shameful and accursed past when the church lived in feudal
dependence on the state, and Russian citizens lived in feudal
dependence on the established church, when medieval, inquisitorial
laws (to this day remaining in our criminal codes and on our
statute-books) were in existence and were applied, persecuting men
for their belief or disbelief, violating men's consciences, and linking
cosy government jobs and government-derived incomes with the
dispensation of this or that dope by the established church. Complete separation of church and state is what the socialist proletariat
demands of the modern state and the modern church." [21]

It is important to remember that Lenin made this demand in
1905 when the Orthodox Church was still the privileged established
church. His demand for "absolutely free associations" can by no
means be interpreted positively as a protection of the full religious
freedom which every man is to enjoy, but merely as the Church's
complete severance from the guardianship of the Russian state.
If this formulation is later repeatedly misinterpreted to mean freedom
of religion in the Soviet Union this is due to ignorance or neglect
of Lenin's historically conditioned and unmistakable meaning. The

[21] *Ibid.*, pp. 84 f.

Communists' demand for religious freedom is solely the demand for freedom from religious interference as the prerequisite to full political freedom.

Adroitly Lenin uses the ferment within the lower clergy of the Orthodox Church for his own purposes. "However abject, however ignorant Russian Orthodox clergymen may have been, even they have now been awakened by the thunder of the downfall of the old, medieval order in Russia. Even they are joining in the demand for freedom, are protesting against bureaucratic practices and officialism, against the spying for the police imposed on the ' servants of God. ' " [22]

Lenin warmly welcomed revolutionary assistance from the lower clergy and demanded full freedom of religion for them; however, he never dreamed of allowing the battle against religion to die down. " So far as the party of the socialist proletariat is concerned, religion is not a private affair. Our Party is an association of class-conscious, advanced fighters for the emancipation of the working class. Such an association cannot and must not be indifferent to lack of class-consciousness, ignorance or obscurantism in the shape of religious beliefs. We demand complete disestablishment of the Church so as to be able to combat the religious fog with purely ideological and solely ideological weapons, by means of our press and by word of mouth. But we founded our association, the Russian Social-Democratic Labour Party, precisely for such a struggle against every religious bamboozling of the workers. And to us the ideological struggle is not a private affair, but the affair of the whole Party, of the whole proletariat. " [23]

Next Lenin introduces the question to which he will return time after time. " If that is so, why do we not declare in our program that we are atheists? " Why are Christians and other believers not allowed to join the Party? The answer is briefly: for tactical reasons. From the start the need for a struggle against the roots of " religious obscurantism " is made abundantly clear. " Our program is based entirely on the scientific, and moreover the materialist, world-outlook. An explanation of our program, therefore, necessarily includes the propaganda of atheism; the publication

[22] *Ibid.*, p. 85.
[23] *Ibid.*, pp. 85 f.

of the appropriate scientific literature, which the autocratic feudal government has hitherto strictly forbidden and persecuted, must now form one of the fields of our Party work. We shall now probably have to follow the advice Engels once gave to the German Socialists: to translate and widely disseminate the literature of the 18th-century French Enlighteners and atheists. " [24]

But essential as the combatting of religion is for Lenin, under no circumstances, he warns, should one attempt to solve the problem by itself as the radical bourgeois democracies often do. The struggle against religion is to be carried out only within the framework of the universal class struggle. " It would be stupid to think that, in a society based on the endless oppression and coarsening of the worker masses, religious prejudices could be dispelled by purely propaganda methods. It would be bourgeois narrow-mindedness to forget that the yoke of religion that weighs upon mankind is merely a product and reflection of the economic yoke within society. No number of pamphlets and no amount of preaching can enlighten the proletariat, if it is not enlightened by its own struggle against the dark forces of capitalism. Unity in this really revolutionary struggle of the oppressed class for the creation of a paradise on earth is more important to us than unity of proletarian opinion on paradise in heaven.

" That is the reason why we do not and should not set forth our atheism in our program; that is why we do not and should not prohibit proletarians who still retain vestiges of their old prejudices from associating themselves with our Party. " [25]

Lenin belabors the point that to give priority to the religious issue would only cripple the revolutionary striking-power of the class struggle, for which reason one must exercise, temporarily, a certain patience with those ideologically immature proletarians who are still " Christians. "

In 1909 Lenin expresses himself on the subject in more detail. First he explicitly stresses the fact that dialectical materialism is the philosophical foundation of Marxism, which has completely adopted the historical tradition of French 18th-century materialism

[24] *Ibid.*, p. 86.
[25] *Ibid.*, pp. 86 f.

as well as the German materialism of Feuerbach—a materialism that is unconditionally atheistic and the decided enemy of every religion. Religion is opium for the people; this verdict of Marx is the pillar of Marxism's world-outlook on the religious question. Invariably Marx considers all contemporary religions and churches, all religious organizations and offshoots of religious organizations as the organs of bourgeois reaction which serve to exploit and befog the working class.

In spite of Marxism's unshakable goal, the complete destruction of religion, Lenin warns against the stupidity of openly declaring war on religion, which would only be a repetition of the stupidity of Bismarck's anticlerical struggle. Bismarck's *Kulturkampf* " only *stimulated* the militant clericalism of the Catholics, and only injured the work of real culture. . .and diverted the attention of some sections of the working class and of the other democratic elements away from the urgent tasks of the class and revolutionary struggle to the most superficial and false bourgeois anticlericalism ". [26] Lenin is convinced that through the organization and enlightenment of the proletariat, religion will die a natural death. He defends himself against accusations of unprincipled wavering and a cowardly desire to " play up to " religious workers for fear of frightening them away.

In the years following 1919 public debate between Party representatives and priests was allowed. Peter Scheibert points out that the open war of the Militant Atheists' movement in all its brutality was launched after 1921, when as the result of a stroke Lenin was forced to leave the political field to others.

In Lenin's view although religion was to be persecuted cautiously, it was nonetheless absolutely necessary that it be persecuted: " Marxism is materialism. As such, it is as relentlessly hostile to religion as was the materialism of the 18th-century Encyclopedists or the materialism of Feuerbach. This is beyond doubt. But the dialectical materialism of Marx and Engels goes further than the Encyclopedists and Feuerbach, for its applies materialist philosophy to the domain of history, to the domain of the social sciences. We must combat religion—that is the ABC of *all* materialism, and

[26] V. I. Lenin, *Collected Works*, vol. XV, p. 403.

consequently of Marxism. But Marxism is not a materialism which has stopped at the ABC. Marxism goes further. It says: We must *know how* to combat religion, and in order to do so we must explain the source of faith and religion among the masses *in a materialist* way. The combatting of religion cannot be confined to abstract ideological preaching, and it must not be reduced to such preaching. It must be linked up with the concrete practice of the class movement, which aims at eliminating the social roots of religion. Why does religion retain its hold on the backward sections of the town proletariat, on broad sections of the semi-proletariat, and on the mass of the peasantry? Because of the ignorance of the people, replies the bourgeois progressive, the radical or the bourgeois materialist. And so: 'Down with religion and long live atheism; the dissemination of atheist views is our chief task!' The Marxist says that this is not true, that it is a superficial view, the view of narrow bourgeois uplifters. It does not explain the roots of religion profoundly enough; it explains them, not in a materialist but in an idealist way. In modern capitalist countries these roots are mainly *social*. The deepest root of religion today is the socially downtrodden condition of the working masses and their apparently complete helplessness in the face of the blind forces of capitalism, which every day and every hour inflicts upon ordinary working people the most horrible suffering and the most savage torment, a thousand times more severe than those inflicted by extraordinary events, such as wars, earthquakes, etc. 'Fear made the gods.' Fear of the blind force of capital—blind because it cannot be foreseen by the masses of the people—a force which at every step in the life of the proletarian and small proprietor threatens to inflict, and does inflict 'sudden,' 'unexpected,' 'accidental' ruin, destruction, pauperism, prostitution, death from starvation—such is *the root* of modern religion which the materialist must bear in mind first and foremost, if he does not want to remain an infant-school materialist. No educational book can eradicate religion from the minds of masses who are crushed by capitalist hard labour, and who are at the mercy of the blind destructive forces of capitalism, until those masses themselves learn to fight this *root* of religion, fight *the rule of capital* in all its forms, in a united, organized, planned and conscious way.

" Does this mean that educational books against religion are harmful or unnecessary? No, nothing of the kind. It means that Social-Democracy's atheist propaganda must be *subordinated* to its basic task—the development of the class struggle of the exploited *masses* against the exploiters. " [27]

The dialectical progress of the social revolution demands a certain elasticity, accommodation to the yet " backward workers who are still connected with the countryside and with the peasantry, and who believe in God, go to church, or are even under the direct influence of the local priest. " Such elasticity forbids over-hasty atheistic propaganda not for the sake of compromise, but in order to allow moribund religion to die a natural death. Hence Lenin orders a study of what he calls " the concrete situation, " but he warns against falling into the abstract, declamatory, empty revolution of the anarchist. All the individual religious problems which affect the relation of social democracy to religion are to be approached from his, Lenin's, clearly outlined standpoint. Repeatedly he insists that to take the concrete situation into account is anything but cowardly opportunism.

Lenin explains that although German social democracy was forced to take a stand against Bismarck's anticlericalism and renounce vociferous opposition to religion, in Russia conditions are quite different. The proletariat is the leader of our civil democratic revolution. The Party of the Proletariat must take the ideological lead in the struggle against everything medieval, including the old established religion, and against all attempts to revive or re-establish it in another form. Although Engels had only gently reprimanded the German social democrats for their opportunism when after the State's declaration of religion as a private matter they interpreted this to mean that religion was a private matter even for social democrats and for the Social Democratic Party, he would have castigated the following of this German example by Russian opportunists a hundred times more sharply.

[27] *Ibid.*, p. 405.

LENIN'S JUDGMENT OF TOLSTOY AND GORKY

For Russian intellectuals Count Leo Tolstoy was the personification of piety, and Tolstoyism a powerful means of reforming social conditions. The judgment Lenin passed on Tolstoy in 1908 on the occasion of his eightieth birthday is highly revealing. " The contradictions in Tolstoy's works, views, doctrines, in his school, are indeed glaring. On the one hand, we have the great artist, the genius who has not only drawn incomparable pictures of Russian life but has made first-class contributions to world literature. On the other hand we have the landlord obsessed with Christ. On the one hand, the remarkably powerful, forthright and sincere protest against social falsehood and hypocrisy; on the other, the " Tolstoyan, " i.e., the jaded, hysterical sniveler called the Russian intellectual. . .on the one hand, the most sober realism, the tearing away of all and sundry masks; on the other, the preaching of one of the most odious things on earth, namely, religion: the striving to replace officially appointed priests by priests who will serve from moral conviction, i.e., to cultivate the most refined and, therefore, particularly disgusting clericalism. " [28]

For Lenin, Tolstoy's ideas reflect all the limitations and weaknesses of the Peasant Revolt, which had slightly relieved pressures grown intolerable but lacked the courage for genuine revolution. " On the one hand, centuries of feudal oppression and decades of accelerated post-Reform pauperization piled up mountains of hate, resentment, and desperate determination. The striving to completely sweep away the official church, the landlords and the landlord government, to destroy all the old forms and ways of landownership, to clear the land, to replace the police-class state by a community of free and equal small peasants—this striving is the keynote of every historical step the peasantry has taken in our revolution. . . . On the other hand the peasantry, striving toward new ways of life, had a very crude, patriarchal, semireligious idea of what kind of life this should be. . . .Most of the peasantry wept and prayed,

[28] *Ibid.*, p. 205.

moralized and dreamed, wrote petitions and sent 'pleaders'... begged, haggled, reconciled and promised to reconcile—until they were kicked out with a military jackboot. " [29] For Lenin, Tolstoy's passive resistance illustrated perfectly how the opium of religion paralyzes revolutionary action.

In 1918 Maxim Gorky, a contemporary of Lenin who shared his views, wrote a newspaper article in which he said: "This 'search for God' business must be forbidden for a time—it is a perfectly useless occupation. Where nothing has been placed, there is nothing to seek. He who does not sow will also not reap. You have no God because you *still* have not managed to create him. Gods are not sought—*they are made*: life is not invented but begotten. "

But even this allusion to the possibility of a search for God enraged Lenin, who replied in two letters to Gorky in which the remarks about faith in God are of a crudity seldom surpassed. On November 14, 1913, he writes: "This search for God humbug is as different from image-making or god-making or god-creating or what have you, as a yellow devil is from a blue devil. Even to mention a search for God instead of fighting against all devils and gods, against every kind of spiritual body snatching (every god is a body snatcher, even the purest, the most ideally fashioned or created godling—it's all the same); to speak out only to state one's preference for a blue devil rather than a yellow one, that is a hundred times worse than not to speak at all....Precisely because every religious idea, every idea about any god whatsoever, even the slightest flirtation with God is an unmentionable abomination tolerated (indeed often encouraged) by the *democratic* bourgeoisie, it is the most dangerous abomination, the most loathesome ' plague. ' Because more easily recognized by the masses, millions of crimes, villainies, atrocities, and physical plagues are far less dangerous than the sly spiritualized notion of a dear God tricked out in splendid ' ideological ' raiment. " [30]

"God-making, " says Lenin, " is the worst way of spitting in one's own face.... Religion teaches a person inclined to 'piety'

[29] *Ibid.*, pp. 206 f.
[30] V. I. Lenin, *Ueber die Religion*, Aus Artikeln und Briefen, (Berlin: Dietz Verlag, 1956), p. 44.

to ' meditate ' on the stupidest, filthiest, most servile aspects of his own ' ego ', supposedly deified by this idolatrous humbug. " Again —a month later—Lenin writes Gorky " . . .*every* defense of the idea of God, even the most refined, well-meaning defense or justification, is a justification of reaction. " [31]

DEMANDS FOR THE SEIZURE OF POWER

Lenin's attitude toward religion, says Duncker, is apparent from the wording of the program of the Russian Communist Party (March, 1919). Among the demands " in the domain of religious relations " we read: " With regard to religion, the Communist Party does not satisfy itself with the already-decreed separation of Church from State and of the School from the Church, i.e., with measures which bourgeois democracy proclaims in its programs but which were carried out nowhere in the world, thanks to the many actual links existing between capitalism and religious propaganda. . . .

" The Party works for the actual liberation of the toiling masses from religious prejudices and organizes the widest scientific-instructive antireligious propaganda. However, it is necessary to carefully avoid every kind of insult against the sentiments of worshippers because this would lead only to an intensification of religious fanaticism. " [32]

After the Communist seizure of power Lenin contributed an article entitled " The Importance of Militant Materialism " to the 1922 issue of the journal *Under the Banner of Marxism*. In it he declared that any journal that wishes to be an organ of militant materialism must devote a great deal of space to atheistic propaganda, thereby " complementing, correcting, and stimulating the work of the appropriate government organ. The masses must be provided with every imaginable kind of atheistic propaganda. To this end one should not hesitate to ally oneself with bourgeois

[31] *Ibid.*, p. 50.
[32] L. Brown, A. A., *Religion in Russia* (Paterson, N. J.: St. Anthony Guild Press, 1959), pp. 78 f.

atheists, even with those who have not quite weaned themselves from a religious ersatz. Lenin stresses the fact that the battle cannot be fought without " solid philosophical foundations. " First of all the editors of the journal are expected to organize a systematic study of Hegelian dialectics from the point of view of materialism, the dialectics which, according to Lenin, awakened hundreds of millions of people all over the world from their slumbers. Lenin is well aware of the extraordinary difficulties of Hegelian dialectics, still they must be developed in all directions and translated into the language of materialism.

Lenin's view of religion became the official doctrine of Russian Bolshevism and has since undergone countless changes at the hands of Russian theorists. Foremost among these was Bucharin, who worked with Lenin after 1912 and who was " liquidated " by Stalin in 1938. In his writings Bucharin developed a program for world revolution which included a detailed plan for the campaign against religion. " One must combat religion not with force but with conviction. The Church must be separated from the State. This means that although priests may exist, let those who desire their poison support them. There is a poison called opium. Those who smoke it dream fantastic dreams; they simply lie there as though in paradise. But the effects are soon evident in damaged health; gradually the opium smoker becomes a silent idiot. It is exactly the same with religion. There are people who want to smoke opium, but it would be absurd for the state at its own cost, that is, at the cost of the entire nation, to support meeting places for opium smokers and people to wait on them. Therefore the Church must be treated as follows: the State should deprive priests, bishops, metropolitans, patriarchs, abbots, and the rest of the lot of all support. Let the believers if they wish at their own expense feed the holy fathers with salmon and sturgeon and other favorite delicacies. At the same time everyone must be guaranteed freedom of worship. The rule is: religion is a private matter, but this does not mean that we should not fight for our antireligious convictions. It means that the State should not support any Church organization. " [33]

[33] E. Briem, *Kommunismus u. Sozialismus in der Sowjetunion* (c. J., etwa 1948), p. 84.

It is common knowledge that in Bolshevist Russia Lenin's atheistic program has been not only thoroughly implemented, but often outdone, as the many thousands—experts say millons—of victims attest.

SOVIET RUSSIA'S
STRUGGLE AGAINST RELIGION

The combatting of religion which had been programmed for decades, says Schapiro, was an essential of Leninist policy.   Hence it is possible to correctly relate the many seemingly contradictory measures of the religious struggle as well as of church policy simply by taking Lenin's program as the point of departure.   In such a complex development, above all in a matter so deeply felt and so passionately contested, it is easy to overemphasize one aspect and distort the entire picture.   Western visitors to the Soviet Union, among them prominent church leaders, have allowed themselves to be so impressed by government policy towards the churches as to deny energetically the existence of the religious persecution which others equally loudly lament.

In order to make a fair judgment on this point it is necessary to examine closely what Roman Roessler calls the " tactical double track system " outlined from the start in Lenin's program.   Despite many political and ideological changes during the half century since the Bolsheviks came to power, basically the policy of war to the death against " religious superstition " has remained unchanged. By contrast, Soviet policy toward the churches has gone through many phases, sometimes giving the impression that actual government policy repudiates its fundamental antireligious tendency.

Lenin's plan for the period following the victory of the revolution never envisioned a frontal attack against all religion that would deprive the people of their spiritual " opium " or " vodka " by force. Rather social conditions were to be so improved that people would no longer need such drugs.   In reality, however, militant dialectical materialism soon far exceeded the programmed goal, and today it is extremely difficult to judge to what extent the Draconic measures taken against believers were personally approved by Lenin. This much is certain, that originally fear of alienating many yet undecided potential Party members motivated a tactical caution.

Moreover, in the beginning the civil war slowed things down, and few attacks against religion were launched. Even after the Party was firmly entrenched its leaders, aware that religion was anchored deep in the Russian people, left the war against religion to the Cheka and ostensibly to the private initiative of zealous Communists.

Theoretically religion was expected to vanish as a perfectly natural result of a long process of social reform; however, Communist leaders were by no means so convinced of the necessity of this development as to be inclined to allow the so-called law of religious disintegration to solve the problem. " Communism will always consider all existing religions, churches, and varieties of religious organizations as organs of bourgeois reaction which only serve to exploit and stultify the working class. " The support which religion enjoys in the capitalistic countries of the West and the influence of " the lackeys of cult " in their own country—these, it is hammered in unceasingly—must be broken, for it is the aim of these lackeys to keep religious sentiment alive among the members of Soviet society. Consequently the party dare not sit back and wait for the natural decline of religion but must actively spur the process by pulling the foundations of religion out from under it.

The Orthodox Church took advantage of the collapse of czarism to provide itself with a spiritual sovereign such as it had had in the days before Peter the Great. In 1917 a hastily summoned church synod elected Metropolitan Tikhon Patriarch. Under his direction the Church adopted a belligerent stand against the atheistic attitude of Bolshevism. There was real heroism in the Church's curt rejection of the new rulers, which hardly prevented the Bolsheviks from pursuing their established course. This sharply counterrevolutionary attitude of the Orthodox Church was understandable; formerly she had been too closely allied with the political power of czarism. But the fact that the new regime turned with particular vehemence on the Catholic Church in Russia, which could not be accused of sympathy with the vanished czarist regime, indicates that the measures taken by the Bolsheviks were not aimed solely "against reactionary and antirevolutionary elements" in the churches, but against religion as such. The inhuman oppression not only of the "Orthodox lackeys of cult" and of Orthodox believers, but of the clergy and faithful of all churches and religious congregations cannot be excused as reaction to political attitudes.

At first there were spontaneous mass demonstrations all over Russia, even in Moscow's Red Square, protesting Bolshevist measures against religion; however, the demonstrations never developed into revolt, as the Orthodox leaders had hoped. Instead the people took the relentless antichurch measures of the State more or less in silence.

After the total separation of church and state in Russia, further measures were planned to cut the churches of from all participation in public life and to isolate them completely. The civil rights of "the lackeys of cult" were revoked. Religious instruction of the young was forbidden under threat of penal servitude. Church property was confiscated, rights of citizenship were denied to priests, all religious literature was forbidden, church schools and monasteries were closed. Naturally it was not easy to enforce all these laws, but their mere existence provided an excuse for the bloodiest persecution.

The Communist Program of 1919 (Article 13) informs its members that the guideline of the Party is its conviction that only the complete systematization and conscious direction of the entire economic and social life of the masses will lead to the disappearance of religious prejudice. There follows an ambiguous description of the Communist goal: The laboring masses are to be assisted in their struggle for true emancipation from religious prejudice by a propaganda based on the broadest possible scientific and antireligious instruction, which must guard against offending the feelings of believers and thereby strengthen religious fanaticism.

Although the Constitution of 1918 had promised every citizen freedom of religious as well as of antireligious expression, the right of the Cheka to decide what was valid "religious expression" and what was "counterrevolutionary propaganda" made it easy to stifle religion from the start. The occasional suggestions of moderation from official quarters were completely ignored. Above all, in the early years of the war on religion the Communists employed extreme violence against "the lackeys of cult." Priests were arrested, sentenced, deported, and frequently tortured to death.

To understand how far actual religious persecution departed from the official program one must read the testimony of at least one reliable eye-witness. The Russian Orthodox bishop, Paul Meletiev, was originally a monk at the famous Cloister Soloviecki, where in 1908 he was consecrated deacon and in 1910 priest. After World War I he managed to escape from prison in Siberia to Germany and to make a report whose simplicity speaks for itself. " On February 20, 1922, I was arrested as a counterrevolutionary and sent under heavy guard to the Cheka prison in Archangel. I wish to make an objective report of what I heard and witnessed there.

" The Chekists beat the prisoners with steel rods and horsewhips; they threw them from the bridges into the water. In winter they poured water over these unfortunates until they were frozen to pillars of ice. I have seen priests crucified in the prison courtyards. During interrogations prisoners had to submit to all sorts of afflictions: to beatings with billy-clubs and bunches of keys, to hunger and thirst, electric chair, thumb-screw, and gas chamber. The torturing of officers was especially hideous; their wives and daughters were raped and maltreated before their eyes. There is no atrocity that was not practiced in the Cheka prisons. Only the devil can be so inventive of every kind of torture and abuse.

" The Chekists took particular delight in offending the religious sentiments of their prisoners. They commanded them to deny God and to speak blasphemously of him, of Christ, of the Mother of God, and of the saints. Icons were nailed to the seats of the prison stools. To sit at all one had to sit on these sacred pictures. Because believers considered this a desecration and refused to sit, they had to stand in their cells for days, sometimes even for months until they finally collapsed.

" The following account of a fellow prisoner is a typical example of the satanic cunning used to dishonor the cross. The man told me that he operated a machine the lowest lever of which was a pedal. He had seen the guards fasten a cross to this so that in order to operate the machine he would be forced to tread on the cross. When he refused he was beaten so savagely with a ringful of keys that he died that same day. (He passed away in my cell minutes after confiding to me the reason for his martyrdom.) It dawned on me later that the poor man had been brought to my cell as a warning to me. . . .

"At the very beginning of the interrogation I was beaten until I bled. Blows and curses accompanied this 'interrogation.' I was accused of deeds which I never committed and which I truthfully denied. Next they demanded a confession that in the past I had deceived people by preaching God and Christ to them. If I was now ready to deny Christ and to make a public denial in church on the following Sunday I would be released. They demanded that I defame God. When I energetically refused to do so they threw me into a bunker full of hungry rats. This was a special bunker reserved for particularly loyal Christians, priests, intellectuals, and officers. As a rule the starving animals flung themselves upon the poor victim and bit him to death. Many of the condemned could not bear even the sight of the creatures and went mad. I was forced to remain several days and nights in that bunker. Upon entering I crossed myself like one going to his death. But God wanted me to survive that martyrdom unscathed. When the Chekists saw that I did not die in the bunker they flung me into an ice-cell, where I had to withstand the terrible cold for five days and nights without bread or water. Since I did not die there either one of the soldiers beat me so hard on the head that I collapsed. I lay on the floor of the cell in my blood; they poured water on me to revive me, then the mishandling continued. Finally I was led before a revolutionary tribunal where I was questioned by ignorant, hate-filled judges. The sentence was five years of confinement in a dungeon for counterrevolution." [34]

This report throws light on several facts that are worth noting. First, here is a clear case of religious persecution; there is absolutely no question of criminal offense. The obvious aim of the persecution was to force the tortured victims to apostasy. In order to attain this goal the religious sentiments of the faithful are certainly not "scrupulously spared"; they are cunningly or brutally attacked. Outlawed and defenseless persons are exposed to the hate, fury,

[34] *Sie hoerten seine Stimme.* Zeugnisse von Gottsuchern unserer Zeit. Gesammelt und herausgegeben von Bruno Schafer. Band I (1955), pp. 14 ff.

and bestiality of their persecutors for no reason other than that they are Christians. Yet the charges are never laid to their religious attitude. Invariably the victims are accused of and sentenced for "counterrevolutionary action." It is evident from other instances in this same report that in later persecutions the methods employed were essentially the same. "By 1938 only ten or twelve of Moscow's 1,600 churches were still open. All others were razed, destroyed, plundered, or converted into warehouses, depots, cinemas, or theaters. Stalin allowed a few churches to remain open for political reasons. Above all, he wanted foreigners to get the impression that he countenanced churches. But the remaining Muscovite churches are really only advertisements for naive visitors. There is no freedom of religion in Russia." [35]

The same eye-witness complains that in Europe and the rest of the world little is known about these atrocities. "Forces were at work to cover up these crimes, or where this was no longer possible, to bagatellize them. Otherwise how can one explain the strict silence of the famous League for the Protection of Human Rights headed at that time by Victor Basch? One so often hears protests against Spain, Italy, Poland, or Argentina. The world press was beside itself when two Italian terrorists in the United States, Sacco and Vanzetti, were sentenced to the electric chair. But when millions of believers were murdered in Russia and Mexico the world press along with the League for Human Rights remained silent." [36]

In the encyclical on atheistic Communism, *Divini Redemptoris*, Pope Pius XI castigated the silence of the world press on the religious persecution in Soviet Russia. In reply, a religious who had lived for years in Moscow wrote: "It is indeed a conspiracy. How else can anyone explain the fact that news agencies professionally eager to publish daily human-interest stories from all corners of the globe remain silent about the accumulated horrors of Communism's battle against God?" [37]

In the early years of the Soviet regime the success of the religious persecution lagged far behind Party expectations. In 1923 the

[35] *Ibid.*, p. 20.
[36] *Ibid.*, p. 21.
[37] L. Brown, A. A., *Religion in Russia* (Paterson, N. J.: St. Anthony Guild Press, 1959), p. 74.

Central Committee of the United Worker's Union, and soon after, the Twelfth Congress of the Communist Party of Russia were forced to admit that countless workers still believed in God, and that religion simply could not be suppressed by government measures. Two further attempts to break the backbone of the churches proved unsuccessful: a mock trial which ended with the sentencing of 54 Orthodox and Roman Catholic dignitaries (1922) and simultaneously the establishment of a State or " Living Church " which was to entice members away from the Orthodox Church.

About that time too antireligious propaganda began to grow louder. With the aid of pamphlets, newspapers, antireligious seminars (68 of them in the year 1927) and antireligious universities (44 in 1930), the new attitude of Communism toward religion was explained to the people. Lecturers assured them that Communism neither supported any religion nor suppressed freedom of conscience, that with the help of science, it was merely trying to liberate mankind. But after so many years of persecution with their drastic examples of " freedom of conscience, " the Russian people knew how to evaluate such claims.

The tenacity with which the people upheld their faith plus the fact that the patriarchs finally capitulated to Soviet pressure led to the double tactic of a long-range policy against orthodox religion in general, and a short-range policy of seeking an acceptable *modus vivendi* with the Church hierarchy. Whenever the prelates proved their willingness to abandon their hostility, government officials demonstrated their willingness to reinstate certain Church rights; at any rate, great pains were taken to win over the priests to an attitude of loyalty toward the Soviet regime. On the other hand the regime complained when as a result of such efforts Communists grew lax in their antireligious struggle. Such complaints were voiced again and again in the leading newspapers, at Party congresses, and at the special congresses for atheistic propaganda. Thus " the securing of a better legal status by no means ended the tribulations of the Church. " [38]

To a delegation of American workers Stalin frankly declared that " the party cannot be neutral toward the reactionary clergy

[38] J. S. Curtiss, *The Russian Church and the Soviet State, 1917-1950* (Boston: Little, Brown & Company, 1953), p. 195.

who poison the minds of the toiling masses....The unfortunate thing is that it has not been completely liquidated. " [39] Hence the goal of antireligious propaganda, Stalin continued, was to complete the liquidation of the reactionary clergy.

One indefatigable propagandist of militant atheism to appear on the scene was Emelian Yaroslavsky. On the great religious festivals such as Christmas and Easter the militant atheists organized masquerades and carnival parades. Costumed as bishops, priests, monks, and nuns, and bearing icons, they marched noisily through the streets, hooting wild songs, dancing, guzzling vodka, and mockingly incensing the onlookers. In 1925 Yaroslavsky founded the League of Militant Godless, of which he became president. The purpose of the League was to combat actively, systematically, and consistently all aspects and forms of religion as barriers to social development and cultural revolution. Yaroslavsky himself published several atheistic newspapers and journals, one of them *Besboshnik (The Godless One)*. In 1932 and 1933 his collected writings appeared in five volumes under the title *Against Religion and Church*. At first the crude blasphemy of the Militant Godless revolted the people more than it persuaded them. Yaroslavsky then attempted to raise the intellectual level of the struggle.

In order to break the peasants' resistance to forced collectivization the antireligious movement instigated " resolutions " demanding the closing of the churches. A large number of country churches became the victims of this campaign. The zeal of the faithful appeared to flag. There were complaints that only old people could be seen in the churches that did remain open. Meanwhile there were other developments, and the League suspended its activities. In 1943, after 20 years of service to his cause, Yaroslavsky mysteriously disappeared.

In the Thirties Party policy toward the Church and religion fluctuated between direct attacks and indirect persecution, as in the country. Where the closing of churches was related to collectivization, armed clashes between the peasantry and the regime frequently arose. " The lack of success of this campaign, which took the form of the compulsory closing of churches and which led to frequent

[39] W. Kolarz, *Religion in the Soviet Union* (New York: St. Martins Press, 1961 and Macmillan Company of Toronto, Canada), p. 12.

armed clashes with the peasants, was virtually admitted by the Central Committee in a decree of March 14, 1930. As usual, those who had merely carried out the orders of the Party leaders were blamed for practices which ' bear no relationship to the policy of our party '—the closing of churches ' without the consent of the overwhelming majority of the villagers, ' and mockery of religious beliefs. " [40]

The abrogation of Sunday could not be enforced for long; nor could the taboos on the sale of " articles of cult "—Christmas trees for example—permanently stifle religious customs. The moment the pressure was removed they spontaneously revived.

Nonetheless further legal measures against religion followed. The article of the Constitution guaranteeing the freedom of public religious practice as well as of antireligious expression was amended to allow in future only antireligious expression, only the right to the free practice of religion was still permitted. A few years later the 1936 Constitution of the USSR again changed the formula, substituting the word " cult " for " practice, " obviously in order to further narrow the religious activity of believers. Continual antireligious instruction geared to the age of the pupils was introduced into Soviet schools.

The vicennial celebration of the Revolution was intended to bring the proclamation of the complete triumph of atheism. Kremlin leaders were convinced that the time had come to give religion its *coup de grâce*. Holy Russia was breathing her last. So sure did they feel about this that it was decided to officially ask the entire populace if they still believed in God. A national census was elaborately planned with questionnaires carrying 14 items. The ninth question was: Are you or are you not a believer? This was a direct question on the subject of religion and as such abrogated the still valid decree of 1918 on the separation of church and state, which forbade any questioning about religion.

" After months and months of preparation, public lectures, newspaper articles in *Pravda* and *Izvestia,* radio announcements and other methods of mass communication, they launched a veritable army of trained personnel in a house-to-house canvass of the whole

---

[40] L. Brown, A. A., *Religion in the Soviet Union* (Paterson, N. J.: St. Anthony Guild Press, 1959), pp. 37-38.

nation. . . .When the returns were tabulated in the capital, particularly on the ninth question as to who did or did not believe in God, bewilderment soon gave way to consternation. From an absolutely incontrovertible source the author learned that seventy per cent of the population dared to put themselves down on the census-blanks as believers. It is also known from the same source that vast numbers refused to answer that question for fear or reprisals. In many instances citizens betrayed their intimidation. It is therefore quite safe to say without fear of exaggeration that the startling figure of seventy per cent, actually computed by the Central Bureau of Statistics, does not give a complete picture of the total number of Russians who believe in God. " [41]

The League of Militant Godless wrapped itself in silence. In his day Yaroslavsky had admitted that two thirds of the villagers and one third of the urban population were to be considered believers. " According to reliable evidence about fifty million Soviet citizens proclaimed themselves ' believers. ' This caused such embarrassment to the authorities that they scrapped the census returns and arrested the census officials. In the subsequent censuses of 1939 and 1959 all reference to religion was omitted. " [42]

With the German attack on the USSR in 1941 the situation rapidly changed. The Orthodox Church supported resistance to the invaders by appeals and collections. Metropolitan Sergius greeted Stalin as the nation's " divinely appointed leader " who would lead Russia to victory. As a reward for servility antireligious propaganda was stopped, antireligious museums were closed, and the Church was allowed a certain freedom of movement. In 1943 Stalin and Molotov received the three Metropolitans, Sergius, Alexis, and Nikolay, and permitted the calling of a Church Council *(Sobor)* at which Metropolitan Sergius was elected patriarch. After a ten-year interdiction the newspaper of the Muscovite patriarchate was again permitted to appear. Seminaries for priests were reopened. The government lavished decorations on priests who had leaped to the defense of the nation during the War. As de Vries expresses it in his book on religion in Russia, improved relations between church and state " were bought at the price of weighty ideological

[41] W. Kolarz, *op. cit.*, p. 12.

concessions. " Thus the Orthodox newspaper was not adverse to lauding Communism as the true realization of *pravda*. Understandably, many believers began to consider the priests of the official Church agents of the secret police and to despise them.

Further evidence of the servility of the Orthodox Church to the Soviet was to be seen in the foreign travels of princes of the Church who allowed themselves to be misused for the purpose of winning back " apostasizing " foreign churches to the patriarchate of Moscow and thus strengthening Soviet influence over the rest of the world from a new angle. The voyages of the Russian hierarchy were directed and controlled by political escorts.

After the War the antireligious propaganda suspended during the conflict was renewed. Worried officials noted that religion began to exert a new attraction on youth. What was to be done? When in July 1947 the All-Union Society for the Propagation of Political and Scientific Knowledge was founded many people regarded it as a resurrection of the League of Militant Godless which had been dissolved at the beginning of the War.

Out of the concern of Communist leaders over the tenacity of religion came ever new efforts to intensify antireligious propaganda. Thus in 1957, 350 experts on atheistic propaganda from all parts of the Soviet Union were invited to a congress in Moscow. All twenty lectures, since published in book form, reflect the anxiety caused by the continued life of faith among the people. Owing to the lack of official statistics, Gubanov, the first speaker, was able to deny that the number of faithful had increased, but he was forced to admit that individual congregations and religious groups had succeeded in attracting new members. Equally disturbing were reports that not only were the religious die-hards among the people holding their own, but that even among members of the Communist Party there were dire fluctuations in the loyalty to atheism. Many members listened for a time to the atheists but then returned to the Church, in fact became strictly religious. To these must be added a still larger group within Soviet society. The Communist Party of the Soviet Union may not agree on the number of religiously affiliated people in Russia today, but on one thing everybody agrees: that the role of religion in the life of the Russian people is by no means played out.

For all Khrushchev's policy of coexistence between Church and State there was little real change in the established goal in regard to religion. Khrushchev's speech on the party program at the meeting of the Twenty-Second Soviet made this very clear. He declared: " Communist education presupposes the emancipation of the consciousness from those religious prejudices and superstitions which still hinder certain Soviet members from employing their full creative powers. What is needed is a clear, orderly system of scientific atheistic education which embraces all strata of society and all racial groups, and which checks the spread of religious views, particularly among children and growing youth. " [42]

In the new party program of 1961 the need to combat " superstition " and " religious prejudice " is expressly mentioned as a major point of Bolshevist education. Here again it is stated that the Party considers the struggle against signs of bourgeois ideology, against remnants of bourgeois mentality, against superstition and prejudice elemental to Communistic education....The Party uses ideological influences as a means of educating people in the spirit of a scientific-materialistic world view and of overcoming religious prejudice, but it does not tolerate injury to the feelings of believers. It is necessary to implement a systematic and broadly based program of scientific-atheistic propaganda.

Current Soviet rulers still dream of stamping out all religion in Russia within the next decades. Although theoretically this is to be a purely ideological victory, in order to make any progress at all it has been necessary to revert to the harsh persecutions of the early years of Bolshevik rule. Again churches and seminaries have been closed. In 1962 the monks of the famous Cloister of the Assumption in Pochaev sent a desperate appeal for help to Khrushchev, Kennedy, and the World Council of Churches. Before World War I this great cloister, founded on the steppes of Volhynia in the 13th century by refugees fleeing the Tartars, counted over a thousand monks. In 1962 (the Revolution had already taken its toll) fresh persecutions reduced the remaining 140 monks to 36. The appeal read: " We live in a land of freedom guaranteed by the Constitution and by the regulations of the Central Committee of

[42] *Pravda* (Moskan) vom 18-X-1961, p. 11.

the Communist Party; but only on paper! We suffer all possible suppressions, insults, disturbances, ridicule, threats; we have no legal protection whatsoever; anyone can do with us what he wills. Our protests never reach the government—is there any place at all where we can register complaints? The officials, the public offices, the godless have reverted to reactionary methods of combatting believers—with a club. They destroy our spiritual culture, wreck and blaspheme our churches and holy places. The laws on freedom of belief which Lenin laid down for the believers of the Orthodox Church are being trampled on, misinterpreted, mocked, and abused. " [43]

During the first decades of the Bolshevist regime a worried world listened intently for the bits of news which managed to escape through the cracks of the locked laboratory in which the godless Soviet man was being produced. To what extent was the human substance succumbing to this violent process of re-education? Today we know that religion did not yield. "Throughout the history of the Soviet Union religion has remained the most visible ideological alternative to Communism. " Says Walter Kolarz, "It has remained the only opponent of Communism able to preserve at least some of its institutional forms. " [44] Unbelievers admit this, however grudgingly. In Russia as in other industrial countries a process of cold secularization, a turning away—particularly of the workers—from their inherited religion is quite evident, but this should not be considered a victory of the campaign to destroy religion. It is impossible to give exact figures, but for millions of Russians today religious faith is very much alive. The Communists' failure to root out religion is due to the ineffectiveness of antireligious propaganda and to Communism's inability to provide men through the collective with new spiritual foundations and create a new morality and culture strong enough to overcome that by which men have hitherto lived.

Communist technology (which frequently refers to itself as culture) has repeatedly emphasized the symbol of Prometheus. In 1956 a "Soviet publishing house issued Aeschylus' *Prometheus Bound*

---

[43] *Kommunismus ohne Zukunft* Das neue Parteiprogramm der KPdSU herausgegeben und erlaeutert von Guenther Wagenlehner (1962), p. 230.

[44] Digest des Ostens. 6 vg. 1963, 3, p. 81.

in a mass edition of 150,000 copies, not because of its literary value, but because it was considered useful from an antireligious propaganda point of view. The preface drew attention to the attraction which Prometheus, ' the noble fighter against the gods, ' held for Karl Marx and other ' progressive thinkers. ' " [45] In this age of forced technicalization Prometheus, who through technological aid gave sorely plagued man the means to help himself, should be revived. Technical inventions and new machines long since standard equipment in Western countries were the great hope of the Bolshevist administration. These machines were expected to overwhelm the poor *muzhik* as " miracles of atheism. " The antireligious propagandists were confident that the mere appearance of tractors would have a magical effect on the peasants. Characteristically one of the brochures of the first Five-Year Plan offered its readers " the choice " between prayers and tractors, and a poster plastered over enormous areas of Russia crassly depicted the alleged conflict between tractor and cross. But the results were hardly those anticipated. Enthusiastic peasants welcomed the newly arrived tractors by affixing crosses to them, and priests directed services of praise and thanksgiving to God.

Another Promethean project referred to as the " assault on heaven " was to prove equally disappointing. This slogan was revived by Communists when Russian aeronautics began the conquest of space. The sputniks were supposed to have brought back " proof " that there was no God in heaven. Never had true faith in the Heavenly Father been so naively, crudely, anthropomorphically tied to a sensible image. Before the propagandists had finished making the most of " the conquest of the stratosphere " they were silenced by a tragedy. Upon attaining an elevation of over twelve miles, the three-manned spaceship USSR crashed. The faithful could hardly be expected to regard this event as a triumph of the godless Prometheus.

The effectiveness of using the sputnik as an argument against God may be gauged from the fact that because of the frequently exposed exaggerations of Soviet propaganda many Russians refused to believe that the sputniks existed at all. Kolarz concludes that

[45] W. Kolarz, *op. cit.*, p. 1.

the fourth of October, 1957, the day on which the first sputnik
was launched, may have been a turning point for many people in
the world, but it was not a turning point in the struggle between
Soviet Communism and religion. It is important to understand
this because it makes a lie of the constantly renewed claim that
modern atheism may be traced to the change in the world view
brought about by science, a view which supposedly precludes any
place for God.

Neither the Russian *muzhik* nor the early Christian entertained
any such naive conception of the "heavenly Father." Educated
or not, the real believer is perfectly aware that all images—sensible
or insensible—are merely lame expressions of the inexpressible
and inconceivable. All authentic knowledge of God, though the
individual believer may be hard put to formulate it, is an intellectual
passing beyond the world of time and space to that world's all-
transcending Maker.

THE RELIGIOUS STRUGGLE IN RED CHINA

For years the nations of the free world were led to believe in the
existence of a uniform block of Communistically controlled countries
all of which were exponents—practically indistinguishable from one
another—of Marxist faith. Now that this semblance of unity no
longer prevails, the important differences have the limelight. As
far as religion is concerned, it has long been clear that the difference
between Soviet Russia and Red China is largely one of degree.
Determined to follow the example of Soviet Russia in the antireligious struggle, the Chinese attempted to achieve the same end
more quickly through more drastic measures. They were convinced
that by a hectic "leap forward" it would be possible not only to
catch up with Russia, but to surpass her.

On the religious front Red China's overzealousness seemed to
bring swifter success than Russia was ever able to attain. Although
the Soviets never lost sight of their goal of the complete annihilation

of religion in Russia, a continual change of tactics proved necessary. The admissions of failure to achieve that goal which are wrung from the responsible bureaus invariably place the blame on those in charge of atheistic propaganda: the agents of " scientific enlightenment " have just not shown the necessary zeal. Thus the well-known Italian journalist Virgilio Lilli could conclude an article on the difference between Soviet Russia and Red China with the remark that whereas in the Communist countries of Europe the Communist storm " has ripped the leaves from the tree of Christianity but left its roots unharmed [in Red China] wherever Christian culture did manage to take root it has been torn up by the storm-winds of materialism, nationalism, and racism. "

Certainly in China the application of Marxist ideology by force was facilitated by conditions quite different from those in Russia. The Chinese people never had any religious awakening which resulted in a morality comparable to that developed by Christianity in Russia over a period of more than a thousand years. Chinese ethics were never re-enforced by the individual's awareness of being face to face with an absolute, personal God; of absolute answerableness to one's own conscience. In all the millennia of China's history no such confrontation ever became an integral part of Chinese culture. As a result the fundamental attitude of the individual Chinese is quite different from that of the Russian. As Klaus Mehnert points out, the Chinese is much more closely related to his surroundings than the Russian is; indeed than any Westerner can imagine. The Chinese has not developed a sense of personality which, independent of the evaluation of others, makes him conscious of his own worth and answerable for his thoughts and deeds to God alone. The intellectual system which for the Chinese coordinates his acts and values is always geared to his surroundings; his worth is always measured by the evaluation of others, hence the importance of having and saving " face. " Because the Chinese knows no absolute vis-à-vis, because no omniscient Face confronts him, he has no individual conscience. Hence what he fears most is not guilt or the blameworthiness of wrongdoing that would disgrace him in his own and in God's eyes, but rather the shame of the decreased worth in men's eyes which exposure of his wrongdoing would bring.

Mehnert even goes so far as to contrast what he calls shame-cultures with the guilt-cultures that have developed in Christian countries. Compared with the peoples of the Communist-dominated countries of Europe with their essentially Christian " guilt-cultures, " which give them a highly personal power of resistance to totalitarian pressure, the Chinese usually lack the inner strength to resist because the shame-culture teaches conformity and weakens the will and the readiness to resist. Whereas in Russia Christian dualism created a spiritual dynamic that was bound to express itself in resistance to attacks on religion, the absence of such dualism in China put the religious struggle there on an entirely different basis.

The failure to develop spiritual immunity to atheism is traceable to a peculiarity of millennia-old Chinese culture. Although originally the concept of a supreme god (Shang-ti) existed also in China, it gradually faded to the anonymous, impersonal power known as Tao. The once personal transcendent godhead was reduced to the immanent, world-determining principles such as the masculine and feminine principles underlying all nature. Typical Chinese philosophy became more a pragmatic linking of facts than the intellectual penetration of facts in the Greek or Western sense, which attempts to discover their essence. This is the only kind of thought that leads to the transcendent, to a surpassing of the world in the direction of its divine Establisher. Confucius emphatically rejected his disciples' questions about the ground of existence, exhorting them to content themselves with that which reveals itself in man. Confucius does often mention heaven (Tien), but he leaves the concept so vague that the god of heaven as originally conceived is lost in an impersonal cosmic power. Agnosticism in China did not proceed to the express denial of God and gods as it did in the West; rather with typically pragmatic caution it was inclined to accept an indeterminable number of gods. The safe, down-to-earth behave-as-if tactic generally adopted resulted in an abundance of magical practices.

On the whole it is true that the Chinese transferred ultimate spiritual authority from the gods to the ancestors, to whom man's appeals were to be directed. By consciously linking himself to the long chain of his ancestors the Chinese finds an ersatz for gods now reduced to mere formulas. In any case, the gods never meant much to the Chinese intellectual, in whom it was difficult for an existential sense of religion to develop.

The passionate quest for God, the struggle for answers to the fundamental problems of deliverance and harm, good and evil, redemption and holiness, problems that in Russia were never allowed to rest, these problems hardly existed in China. " The powerful polarization existing between God and the world is to the Christian a positive experience, and from the Volga to the Atlantic it has been *the* subject not only of religious history but of all intellectual history as well. In China, however, there has been scarcely a trace of it since Confucius. " [46]

What the first European in China, Marco Polo, observed was an attitude seemingly oblivious to religion in the true sense. Clearly religion had never been a dominant force in China. One must agree with Mehnert that whereas rationalism and enlightenment came relatively late to Europe, in the Orient they were so victorious in the first millennium B.C. that ever since the educated Chinese has had very little sense of revealed religion. When the cultivated Chinese speaks of gods he does so in a vague metaphorical way that makes the actual existence of such beings questionable. For him as for the product of Western enlightenment and idealism the essential content of faith has been reduced to a mere metaphorical schema. In much the same way, the Chinese speaks of heaven, the absolute, natural law, and the principle of order, or *Tao*, which embraces also human existence. For him immortality is not the deathlessness of his personal spirit, but merely a figurative kind of continuity in his children, grandchildren, and great-grandchildren. Completely alien to the Chinese's whole way of thinking is the religious concept of sin, which is in essence the disobedience of responsible man, a disobedience for which he must answer personally to a personal God.

China's thousands-of-years-old intellectual attitude almost predestines her to a collective pattern of existence. Virgilio Lilli begins his first-hand report on China with the significant observation that for the Westerner in Communist China there are times when the

[46] K. Mehnert, *Peking and Moscow* (New York: G. P. Putnam & Sons, 1963), p. 39.

Chinese resembles an animal more than a man, so completely has
he been " conditioned. " Unfamiliar as he is with the richness of
a personal existence, the Chinese allows himself to be pressed into
a pattern amazingly like that of the anthill. No one seems to
possess his own unique, irreplaceable personality and in so doing
to enjoy what Goethe calls supreme happiness.

That the Communist Revolution could bring about such a radical
break with the past is understandable only in view of the fact that
for many Chinese, religion and the temple had already become
" completely alien, even uncanny phenomena. " These belong to a
past which, though actually only a decade or so away, seems to lie
thousands of years back. As a result the Westerner is much more
inclined to be attracted to a temple than is the native. Possibly
Red China is the first country in the world in which one can truly
speak of God as " the unknown. "

For a long time venerable China presented the simultaneously
grand and pathetic spectacle of noble ruin. Old age encroached upon
her gigantic land and people, on what Lilli calls her " millennia-old
fields, millennia-old peasants, millennia-old gods and godlessness...
her millennia-old wisdom thoroughly decrepit yet incredibly rich in
superstition as in poetry, in vitality as in disease, in kindliness as
in violence, in destitution as in wealth. "

After Confucianism, Buddhism and Taoism played a certain role
in the spiritual life of China without ever being actually founded
there by a specific religious founder. Chinese history as a whole
is unique in its lack of religious awakeners and reformers. Wing-tsit
Chan says: " Not only were these three systems not founded by
new leaders, but there have been comparatively few religious
leaders in Chinese history. Not a single member throughout Confucianism's long history of 2,500 years may be labelled a religious
leader. There were great priests in both Buddhism and Taoism,
to be sure, but most of them existed before the 12th century, and
since that time there have been fewer and fewer prominant religionists. In recent Chinese history one cannot find a Ramakrishna or
even a Kagawa. Today, aside from a few outstanding Buddhist
abbots, one cannot think of a prominant religious teacher, preacher,
theologian or prophet, whether Confucian, Taoist, Islamic, or

Christian. When Ch'en Tu-hsiu said that China is not a land of great religious leaders, he was stating a concrete historical fact. It is amazing how few religious leaders China has produced, especially compared to her great number of eminent philosophers, poets, painters, statesmen....If the life of Chinese religion had depended on a few leaders, it would have died out long ago. " [47]

In the main, the Chinese masses never knew a religious awakening, that stirring of the spirit which, once it occurs, can never be expunged. Once converted, a man can never again return to his earlier indifference. Should he fall away from his religious faith he necessarily becomes a fanatic who must yell down the voices within him.

To speak of Confucianism, Buddhism, and Taoism as the three religions of the Chinese masses is misleading; all three are really agnostic systems in which God's place has been left open. The member of any of these " religions " does not select any one particular god to the exclusion of the others, which he would then consider idols. Buddhist monks do not hesitate, says Chan, to venerate also non-Buddhist gods. Most of the many millions of Chinese " do not follow three separate, parallel, and conflicting religions at the same time, but a syncretic religion embracing the ancient cult as its basis and Buddhist and Taoist elements as secondary features. Even when they visit a strictly Buddhist or Taoist temple, they do so not as Buddhists or Taoists but as followers of the religion of the masses. " [48]

The religious activity of the masses was directed at winning the favor of all kinds of powers. Buddhists, Taoists, and other religionists venerated thousands of idols and natural objects and brought offerings, above all to those deities whom they expected to lend them power and to grant their desires. The enlightened venerated only " heaven, " their ancestors, and occasionally also Confucius, Buddha, and Lao Tzu, but they did not venerate spirits. The ignorant believed in 33 Buddhist heavens, 81 Taoistic heavens, and 18 Buddhist hells. Although the masses believed in astrology,

[47] W. Chan, *Religious Trends in Modern China* (New York: Columbia University Press, 1953), p. 138.

[48] *Ibid.*, p. 141.

geomancy or "diagrams of omen," ghosts, the interpretation of dreams, medical formulas, magic, and the symbolic sounds of birds and animals, the enlightened rejected such " beliefs. "

The simple folk visited temples and shrines of all kinds; the educated avoided these, with the exception of the Temple of Heaven, the Temple of Confucius, and the halls of their ancestors. Magic was despised by the educated, but the masses were convinced of its efficacy and used it to protect themselves against evil spirits or to make these more propitious to them. The weird potpourri of superstitions was so distasteful to the educated that, as Wing-tsit Chan reports, "Not a single book on Chinese folk religion has been published in the last five decades, " nor has statistical material on China ever bothered to include the question of religious affiliation.

This lack of interest, often even disdain, for popular religion on the part of the educated naturally led to its decline. Thousands of images have been smashed. Priests, monks, and nuns have been driven out of temples. Temples have been used for nonreligious or antireligious purposes or have been confiscated or destroyed. The City God, guardian of urban life, has vanished from many cities, and no new city has a place for him. The God of Grain, the chief deity of a rural community, no longer reigns majestically. Instead his arena is used in secular or unholy ways. Few new villages honor him with an altar. This was the situation even before the Communist revolution. According to one report, in a group of 175 temples, fifty-eight per cent were being utilized for nonreligious purposes.

In pre-Communist China there were three-and-a-half million Christians, percentage-wise an almost imperceptible minority. Whereas in Europe Christianity quickly became an integral part of Western culture, in China Christianity was generally considered an exotic import. It is difficult to judge the fairness of current criticism of the missionaries' methods, which are presently being denounced for failing to take into account the unique characteristics of the Chinese people. Today all foreign missionaries have been deported, Chinese who still believe are harshly persecuted, and the churches are deprived of all support. The Catholic church-buildings that still stand are mere facades behind which Christianity is being pulled down. To what extent an invisible Church continues to live in the hearts of those who remain loyal will not be evident until after the storm has spent itself.

Before 1949 the Western visitor to China could not escape the impression of a gigantic cemetery in which very few values remained vital. What China still offered was the fading sunset glow of a culture so ancient and so devitalized as to be as good as dead. Communist China has cut away layer after layer of history. As a consequence of this drastic operation the China of Mao Tse-tung is a child that looks firmly to the future, avid to build a new life. Communism's initial rigorous surgery dispensed with no less than China's whole highly developed social order based on the family, including much of her rich tradition, culture, literature, philosophy, mythology, arts, and ethical values. This was done in order to create an entirely new man, the product of a radical re-education that penetrates to the profoundest, most hidden mystery of the individual.

To this end the Communistic leadership of China employs methods quite different from those used so far in Soviet Russia. The Bolsheviks " liquidated " entire classes. The aristocracy, the middle class, and hordes of Kulacs were wiped out, yet the goal, which was " to sterilize the country against religion " was never completely realized. In the beginning of the Chinese Revolution the old orders and institutions were usually permitted (outwardly) to remain. The idea was to hollow them out completely without damaging the shell. Radical re-education was to destroy all memories of the past and to mold people into impersonal units of the collective. The greatest barrier to this re-education of men into draft animals is religion. Confronted by the divine Thou, man discovers his own inalienable personality. Virgilio Lilli notes that this is why man's relation to God is vociferously branded " the greatest of all prejudices, the worst superstition, the most dire waste of energy. "

It is understandable that during the early period when the anti-religious pressure was still slight, some bishops and priests were convinced that by making certain concessions they could save the Church in China. Meanwhile they have had the bitter experience of finding themselves in the grip of an ideological re-education that threatens them with the complete loss of the substance of belief.

Yet the night is not without stars. A temporary slackening of the totalitarian reins in the conviction that a certain amount of criticism could be risked, indeed should be promoted, revealed that the people's resistance has by no means ended. Many of those who now bend supple as young bamboo under the storm will one day find the courage to be themselves. Perhaps under the pressure of Communism, the will of the individual Chinese to discover his own personality and seek and find durable foundations for it will at last be strengthened. From such a beginning the Chinese could come to a new and authentic encounter with God.

12. *Crisis*

THE SITUATION IN THE
RELIGIOUS CONFLICT TODAY

We have just reviewed some of the major engagements, especially those in the West, in the conflict between belief and unbelief. If we accept Goethe's word that that conflict is the true and ultimate theme of history we begin to realize that the phase in which we now find ourselves is particularly dramatic and harsh. The whole world feels itself threatened by an atheistic system whose unwavering goal for half a century has been and remains world revolution.

Although Communist leaders claim absolute faith in the advent of universal Communism, they do not dream of leaving that advent to its own irresistible power, but on the contrary consider themselves bound to assist its ultimate victory by arduous personal effort. Douglas Hyde, onetime Communist leader in England, replied to the question, " Can Communism be overcome? " roughly as follows: Communists know that a titanic struggle is taking place, a struggle that embraces all mankind, all countries, and every human being. What is at stake is no less than the hearts and souls of men. The *Daily Worker*, the party newspaper in England, has frequently alluded to Communism as a faith for moderns. Communists are not embarrassed by this definition; on the contrary, they purposely appeal to the religious instinct in man, to his deep longing for a religion. I know from my own experience that the majority of Communists in the free world know exactly where Communism is heading and how it intends to get there. They are convinced that they will live to celebrate the universal victory of Communism. For them victory is inevitable if they work hard enough for it and seize every opportunity that presents itself.

In the free world there is no consolidated defense against Communism's militant aggressiveness. In keeping with the spirit of the age religious problems are considered a matter of individual conscience with which the state has no right to interfere, or at best only indirectly. Already in antiquity, this favorite theme of liberals was categorically denied by Plato, for whom religion was by no means a private matter which the state concerned with the general welfare should ignore. On the contrary, like most men of his day Plato was convinced that religion is the necessary spiritual basis for sound and flourishing communal life in the *polis,* and that the weakening of religion inevitably leads to the flagrant corruption of the community. For this reason Plato demanded the protection of religion by law. Even Nietzsche was aware of the fact that faith in God is the intellectual and spiritual foundation of Western culture and that with the collapse of religion also Western culture must fall. Meanwhile the liberal standpoint on this matter has thoroughly established itself in public opinion.

According to that standpoint religion is so exclusively a private matter that any official manifestation of even the most general belief in the Deity should be illegal; the only action which the state may take in this regard is to prevent frivolous attacks on the religious sentiments of those who still believe. The result is that only a few isolated individuals are aware of the significance of the spiritual struggle that is taking place around them, certainly the majority stand aside uncomprehending.

Another important fact belongs here, namely, that the Western world under fire from militant atheism is not only generally lacking in the will to resist, but also is, itself, the intellectual hotbed of modern atheism, although the tired skepticism of the West does not draw the same conclusions that are drawn by the aggressive, revolutionary East.

The forms of atheism in East and West appear to be so different that one wonders if they could possibly be part of the same phenomenon. In fact certain manifestations of atheism in East and West differ to such an extent that we are moved to ask: Can we really speak at all of atheism as " a " power or of " the " forces of atheism? Doesn't its confusing diversity easily lead to over-simplification and the danger of interpreting the atheism of today in terms of values of yesterday, so that we fail to come to grips with the actual enemy? And most important of all, are the concepts " atheism " and " godlessness " identical?

The concept " godlessness " seems to be burdened by the ancient definition clearly and sharply expressed in the Psalms: " The fool says in his heart, ' There is no God. ' " The godless fool of the Psalms is not really claiming that there is no God. What he does is ignore God and withhold traditional reverence.

As we have seen, also the so-called atheism of antiquity was more a matter of frivolous contempt for the official cult of Greece than of actual denial of the existence of gods. Socrates and Plato, who rebuked the unbelief of their day with objective arguments for the existence of the gods as well as with appeals to the individual conscience, were suspected by the undiscriminating masses of being themselves " *atheoi,* " much as Xenophanes had been accused of atheism earlier, and Aristotle and Athenagoras were to be accused later. Even Christians, the martyr Polycarp for one, had the same accusation flung at them. Today we frequently hear the question: Is it justifiable to apply the historically burdened and ambivalent concept of atheism in one unalterable sense to all the variants of modern atheism, irrespective of their widely differing fundamental attitudes? Are there not attitudes toward the problem of God that are basically the opposite of utilitarian frivolity and moral destructiveness, attitudes that spring from the desire to create the prerequisite for a new morality and the construction of a new social order? Isn't the " postulatory atheism " of a Nicholas Hartmann for example the opposite of what the usual concept atheism stands for, since the last thing Hartmann desires is to encourage libertinism? On the contrary, he is attempting to safe-guard the possibility of establishing what he considers a truly human morality.

Postulatory atheism moves on the same level as the old atheism inasmuch as it too is not primarily concerned with the existence or nonexistence of God. Had the question of God's existence been put to Hartmann point-blank he probably would have backed out of it by way of atnosticism. Like other types of atheism, the postulatory atheism of Nicholas Hartmann too sets out from an a priori standpoint to exclude God "postulatorily," although his point of departure and that of most other atheistic postulates lie poles apart.

From a comparison between the atheism of an educated modern natural scientist with the militant atheism of the Bolshevist Godless Movement, we see how erroneous it is to equate all forms of atheism. On principle the first is as tolerant as the second is intolerant. Can we be sure that in the case of the scientist it is really a question of true atheism? Might it not be rather a matter of superannuated church restrictions which because they are outgrown result in a temporary estrangement that will right itself with further intellectual development on both sides? This is probably what Teilhard de Chardin meant with his answer to the question circulated by *La Vie Intellectuelle* on the reasons for current unbelief. "The world," he says, is on the way to becoming converted to a natural religion of the cosmos which should not cut it off from the God of the Gospels. Herein lies the world's 'unbelief.' Let us convert this conversion on a higher level by demonstrating with every act of our lives our conviction that Christ alone *in quo omnia constant* is capable of animating and guiding a new understanding of the universe. It may be that out of an extension of today's unbelief tomorrow's faith will grow."

How far apart the so-called atheism of Nietzsche with its tidings of "the death of God" is from Marx's militant atheism! Isn't Nietzsche's real intention to open people's eyes to the fact that for generations men have been "murdering" God without admitting it? Isn't his deepest desire to be the prophet of the darkness and chaos into which atheistic nihilism must plunge the world? Doesn't his desperate will to superhumanity spring from the hopeless effort to resist the threatened extinction of humanity?

Marxist atheism is quite another matter. It considers traditional faith an obstacle to the new faith in the autonomous power of man and his new social order, an obstacle that must be stubbornly combatted and destroyed. Communistic faith inflames its faithful with the fanatically impatient will to force a world revolution, so that on stripped and levelled ground the new social order that leads to the Communist paradise may be built. Compared with the Marxist's faith in progress, which is unshaken by doubt or by nihilistic discouragement, Nietzsche's profound pessimism really seems to deserve his own adjective, " decadent. "

Even within Russia today there are several distinct types of atheism. However, two forms of unbelief especially need to be distinguished. If Russian atheism has made progress in recent decades this is certainly not due to irreligious and antireligious education or to Bolshevist terror. What has taken place in Russia is a process analogous to that which followed the industrial revolution in other countries: the secularization of the proletarian worker suddenly uprooted not only from the land but also from his culture, including his religious culture, to find himself totally unprepared in the throes of urban life. The modern worker was stripped of his old cultural pattern and given no recognizable new cultural pattern to replace it. Exhausted by hard work (or as in the case of the leaders of industry absorbed by the fascination of ever new technological goals) the strength and will to the religious decisions of Christian life grew lax even without any denial of God. In the process of industrialization this cold secularization would have taken place in Russia's large towns and cities also under a democratic regime, as it has in the urban centers of the West. That Marxism ideologically influences this process in both East and West cannot be denied. Thus it is very likely that the outwardly different forms of atheism stem from the same root.

The complexities of atheism become still more apparent when we consider that side by side with the negative concept of denial of God there exists a knowledge that really includes the idea of God. Herein Schopenhauer agrees with the authentic religious believer; for both, the notion of an *impersonal* God is self-contradictory. For the same reason pantheism remains unacceptable as a truly religious attitude. Pantheism, says Schopenhauer, was invented by philosophers for the sole purpose of decently ridding themselves of God. That is why Schopenhauer calls Spinoza, along with Kant and other philosophers, an atheist. It is well known how frequently toward the end of the 18th century judgment swung round in favor of Spinoza. To Jacobi's remark to Goethe referring to Spinoza as an atheist Goethe replies that on the contrary, Spinoza is " *theissimus et christianissimus.* " In the periods of neo-Classicism and the Romantic Movement Spinoza is promoted to a " Father of the Church, " and Herder, Goethe, Novalis, Friedrich Schlegel, and Schelling all venerated him as " St. Spinoza. "

But for real light on the essence of atheism it is not enough merely to sort out and label its various forms. What must be clarified is the difference between original and derivative forms of atheism. For example many forms of atheism which do not include a definite and total unbelief are perhaps no more than misunderstandings or protests against inadequate forms of faith and should be recognized as such.

When we examine original forms of atheism, especially when we analyze the reasons for the unbelief of their various founders as we have attempted to do here, we realize that the word " atheism " is a great deal more than a nominalistic term that covers utterly different types of unbelief. In the last analysis all forms of atheism are based on something they all have in common, on one element which, admittedly, reveals itself in many different ways. In all our investigations we found one invariant.

The questions posed at the beginning of our discussion took as their starting point the unmistakable cue which modern atheism itself offers: the word " event. " Modern atheists consider atheism an event, the necessary outcome of a process of maturization whose completion is only a matter of time. Universal atheism will be a milestone in human progress that is biologically determined by evolutionary as well as intellectual and historical development. Ernst Juenger describes atheism as an " event of high order " comparable to the breaking out of an electromagnetic field. His conception of atheism leaves no room for the question of guilt. For Heidegger the nihilism proclaimed by Nietzsche is the " fate " of present day man, which he must shoulder resolutely. The question is left open as to whether or not the night of nihilism will be followed by a new morning of faith and holiness as rediscovered by poets.

Meanwhile, for all his proclaimed faith in the irresistible advent of the new paradisiacal reign, the atheistic Communist does not dream of renouncing his own active contribution to the establishment of that reign. On the contrary, he considers the advent of the kingdom without God dependent on his untiring efforts. As Douglas Hyde testifies, the Communist regards history as a titanic struggle into which every country and every person is drawn. With this statement alone he makes a lie of his own words and actually supports the opposite view, which holds belief and unbelief to be neither a matter of fate nor of degree of cultural evolution, but rather a matter of man's personal responsibility. The truth is that every man must take a stand for or against God: he can deny or ignore his divine vis-à-vis, or he can enter into dialogue with him. Particularly in the realm of faith the individual is called to make a truly personal decision. This is the last level on which man should lightly surrender himself to an anonymous power, whether it exists in the name of Evolution, Historical Fate, or any other. He who willingly and without careful consideration simply surrenders to this or that historical current risks mistaking a passing fad for an inescapable fate. Such a man easily becomes guilty. If the history of mankind is basically the intellectual and spiritual struggle between two mutually exclusive opposites, for the individual, critical examination and responsible choice are essential duties.

As we have demonstrated, atheism is by no means the stamp of our age alone, nor is it the only dominating force. Nietzsche intended his philosophy of nihilism to be an appeal for decision and action—in favor of atheism. For him too all obstacles to its establishment were to be trampled down. Similarly the Communistic atheist's " faith " is obligated to personal effort and contribution toward the great goal of world revolution.

Although both belief and unbelief may be considered matters of a man's individual and personal decision, this does not imply that the history of mankind or of a particular culture is simply the sum total of a series of isolated acts of decision by individuals who, for all their proximity to one another, do not affect one another's decisions, as Kierkegaard seems to claim. The decisions of individuals do mutually affect one another. Every individual finds himself in the currents of superindividual movements which certainly do influence, though they do not force, his decisions. It is up to the individual personally to weigh the values involved and responsibly affirm or reject them. Even the failure to make a decision is basically a decision, as is the decision to drift with the strongest current although it would be possible to hold out against it. Frequently in history the seemingly hopeless resistance of the one against the collective force of the many has met with astonishing success.

Whenever the spiritual struggle of an age demands that a man line up with one front or the other, it is absolutely necessary to have a clear understanding of the *essence* of each side, regardless of the compromises or entanglements which belief or unbelief when translated into the actual life of that man may entail. Behind all the various forms into which current atheism seems to be disintegrating one must discover the invariable that is common to all.

Unquestionably all atheism has such an underlying motive. First emerging in antiquity, it clarified its terms in the literature of the modern age, gradually becoming the root of philosophical world views as well as of political programs. It has been a powerful stimulus to the eschatological expectations of youth, and once fixed, its mythical image became the stirring symbol of generation after generation of young people. Goethe classically formulated this attitude (which he resisted and ultimately rejected) in his poem *Prometheus*. To the end of his life, as Goethe himself admits, the Promethean attitude remained a fixed idea for him, as it did for all those of his day whose influence was on the side of atheism. It was over Prometheus that men's spirits parted company. Either men became the slaves of the Promethean idea, which they made the basis of all further philosophy, or they turned away from it and attempted to find some compromise with the old belief in God, as was the case with most of the German idealists. It was precisely this recoiling from the consequences of the destruction of religion (originally the goal of the idealists) along with the attempt to leave the problem of Christian faith in suspension by reinterpreting it in the equivocal sense of Hegel which made German idealism so hazy that it was interpreted contradictorily time and again. Meanwhile Lenin is not far wrong with his claim that dialectical materialism is the true heir of German idealism. As Martin Buber remarks of the perfecter of idealism, Hegel's revolutionary suspension of religion really has " denuded it of reality for the era now closing. "

By dismantling the whole structure of enlightened thought Hegel created that monumental system of idealism which in our own age has engendered two intellectual offspring, existentialism and dialectical materialism. On examination these prove to be far more intimately related than they seem at first glance.

The concept " nature " dominated the thought of the Enlightenment. Nature was something posited, unalterable and unambiguous, an easily recognized norm from which one could draw all other conclusions. Because the bow was overspanned and too much was expected from the concept of nature, a crisis resulted which found its logical termination in Hegel, who substituted " freedom " in place of " nature " as the basic concept of his system. Moreover, Hegel demanded freedom as an absolute concept, thereby abrogating the opposing concept of nature, which restricts freedom and limits it to its place in the larger order of nature.

The rival heirs of Hegelian philosophy, existentialism, and dialectical materialism are intoxicated by the power of creative self-realization. Both underestimate given reality with its resultant norms of being and action as voiced by conscience and enlightened by objective norms. Both forbid the question of the origin of existence, striking it from the structure of human existence and making being in the state of becoming solely dependent on the creative will. Whereas earlier world views in the search for the ground of being took *theoria,* the objective contemplation of the given, as their point of departure, the fundamental approach of modern thought is the other way round: it is the action of man rather than of God that is considered creative, either intellectual action such as thought, which creates an intellectual world, or practical action, which creates a material civilization. In this view the reality that precedes human acts, in other words nature, is considered no more than man's self-alienation, which may be corrected by absolute self-confidence and self-creation. To this day " Prometheus " remains the principle of modern atheism. In the introductory contribution to the official educational journal of East Germany, *Cosmos, Earth, Man,* a professor of chemistry, Robert Havemann, " establishes " atheism with a long quotation from Goethe's *Prometheus.* According to Havemann, now that the socio-economic revolution has been completed, it is high time that the last God of monotheism be dethroned.

In the key speech of an academic celebration at Jena's Friedrich Schiller University in 1957 (where 116 years earlier Karl Marx

submitted his *Dissertation* with its apotheosis of Prometheus), it
was declared that the great Socialistic October Revolution of 1917
was Promethean man's cue to shake off forever the chains with
which the powers of the Unspirit bound him. The October Revolution struck the hour of liberation for the Promethean spirit of man.
In its control of the historical process, the Revolution represented
the greatest triumph of scientific thought yet known. For the first
time in history social development was directed by a group of
determined men voluntarily united unto death, men whose political
action was guided solely by the criteria of science. The Soviets
have incorporated the mythical Prometheus into their ideology
because he goes well with the basic Marxist ideas, which stress the
supreme goal of revolutionary self-confidence attainable only after
complete liberation from " religious superstition. "

It is noteworthy that neither the chemist who undertook to
establish atheism on " purely scientific " arguments nor the academic
speaker at the Jena celebration offered a single result of scientific
research in the field of natural science to prove his argument against
the existence of God. The abrogation of the Deity is demanded
simply as an act of revolt that is part of the revolutionary re-forming
of society. Supposedly it is self-understood that the notion of God
belongs to the ideology of a form of society that is now extinct.
Such arguments reveal the affective foundation of the Communists'
rejection of God.

The taproot of all forms of modern atheism is the will to autonomy.
Because absolute self-assertion and self-creation conflict with a God
whose superabundance includes all freedom, thereby seemingly
abrogating all human freedom, God must go. *Modern atheism is
the dethronement of God for the sake of the freedom of man.*
It is revolt. The antithesis of the divine Positor of reality with
his given order, which every conscience is capable at least of
glimpsing, is the will to self-glorification and autonomy, which turn
in resentment and violent protest against the personal God as a
tyrant and enemy of man. A strained and lopsided theological-
philosophical concept of the divine makes the Creator appear to
threaten and consume creaturely reality with its independence and
relative freedom, to cripple men's efforts to shape their own lives,
and to cloud the pure intoxication of human achievements with

the stain of the forbidden. Man's reason as the ultimate norm of judgment, his conception of values according to which all values are to be weighed—this is the attitude in which history as the work of God is summoned before the tribunal of mankind and condemned as immoral. The will to replace the old deformed world by a new, rational one of man's own planning becomes the leitmotif of modern action. Only on ground from which also God has been cleared away can a brave new world be constructed.

Thus Bolshevism interprets the greatest and most radical experiment ever undertaken in the history of the world: the attempt to substitute the norms deeply embedded in human nature as well as the conscience which those norms form and inform by a master plan of the new supreme tribunal which is presided over by Science. There can be no doubt that the tremendous energy lavished on this experiment springs from a will to faith which, no longer finding a satisfying cause to champion in crumbling Christian faith, abandons it and seeks an ersatz elsewhere. The fanatical, unconditional will behind atheism indicates that its source lies in the religious depths of human nature. On the other hand, one must beware of over-simplifying and of viewing this substitute for religion as something due solely to error.

The hallmark of atheism today stands out most clearly when we compare current atheism with pre-Christian paganism. The first time the Apostle Paul walked through the streets of Athens, the intellectual and spiritual capital of ancient paganism, he was so impressed by the signs of religious longing and intuition which he saw everywhere in the altars and monuments of the city that he took that longing as his cue, and spontaneously interpreted it to his listeners as the deep yearning which he had come to satisfy with the Gospel's joyful revelation of the One whom the Greek spirit had so long and assiduously sought. To be sure, Paul met with resistance. Only a few were open enough to accept his message. Unquestionably in the piety of antiquity there existed a lively expectation that the Deity would one day reveal himself. As Sigrid Undset wisely remarks in one of her essays on Christianity and Germanic culture, classical paganism was a love song to a yet hidden God, whereas neopaganism is a declaration of war against a God who has revealed himself. Were St. Paul to stroll through

Bolshevist Moscow, metropolis of the new paganism, looking for signs of religious faith on the cold bare blocks of modern buildings, he would find few. What he would find would be churches transformed into stores, cinemas, and clubs, and until a short time ago, prominently displayed in huge letters, the credo of the new paganism: Religion is the opium of the people. If he dared to stop on one of Moscow's huge squares and speak to the passers-by of the God who had graciously revealed himself to men, he would meet only astonished questioning glances. Hardly anyone would find the courage even to listen. And were the Apostle to the Gentiles eventually to turn to one of the remaining representatives of the official church for help, he would very likely be reported to the State " security agents, " who would silence him altogether.

In the denigration of religion as " spiritual gin " and " opium " there is a positive value which we should try to see. Narcotics are used by dreamers who lack both the courage to a clear consciousness of self and reality and the responsibility and mettle to mold their own lives. Both believer and nonbeliever should beware of what Baudelaire calls the " artful paradises " which constantly dissolve into nothingness. However, behind the defamation of religion as opium lurks the determined will to unqualified autocracy. According to Hegel the history of mankind is the record of man's spiritual ascent up ever widening steps of self-liberation from inner and outer chains until, in a supreme act of self-comprehension, the human spirit will one day achieve absolute self-possession.

Marx remains true to Hegel in this fundamental view, which he shares with Hegel, though he relativizes Hegel's final step by breaking through the web of idealistic theory to demand one further step in the liberation of humanity: the working man's autonomous shaping of his own life.

" PHILOSOPHY OF SELF-CONSCIOUSNESS "

The term " dialectical materialism, " which the Marxist-Leninist world view applies to itself, suggests a particular conception of matter, which authentic materialism considers the fundamental principle and essence of being. The philosophical world view presented by Karl Marx is not primarily materialistic. Rather he aims at a philosophy of the human consciousness which on the first page of his first publication he exalts to the "supreme deity" beside which no other may exist. From Marx's Promethean point of view, the criticism of religion was finished long ago. Religion is no longer a theme that can claim to be of topical interest; its problems have little bearing on Marxian thought. Marx simply discards religion as something of no more interest than an outgrown shoe.

In order to stress the superiority of his *Weltanschauung* over old-fashioned faith, Marx loftily refers to it as a science. Proudly man has scaled the heights of modern science, leaving far beneath him the mists and bogs of a dream landscape.

For the modern atheist the awakened consciousness is as far superior to religion as modern science is to magic. By the 19th century many people were convinced that the great achievement of the 18th century had been its completion of the criticism of religion; obviously, then, in the 20th century religion could hardly be a theme still worthy of objective consideration.

However, for all the atheists' claims to a scientific rejection of God, their standpoint is not based on scientific, that is to say, positive, objective evidence. The foundations of atheism are not intellectual but emotional, not arguments but rather the suppression of arguments; atheism rests on an affective *Frageverbot* or tabu on all discussion of God as the ultimate ground of being. The arguments against the existence of God which the modern atheist does present are not his own but go back to Kant and to the French materialism of the 18th century, at which time, supposedly, the criticism of religion found ultimate, classical expression. Meanwhile it has become increasingly evident that to invoke Kant's authority against the existence of God is as fateful an error as it is widespread. For Kant's criticism was directed at the rationalists' overemphasis of human knowledge, not at belief in the existence of God, which he was attempting to establish on new foundations. Whether or not Kant achieved that lofty goal is another matter.

As for French materialism's rejection of faith in God and religion, it too is rooted not in objective, scientific argument, but in profound resentment against abuses within the Church. Irritation and resentment, not critical analysis, were the beginning of that metaphysical revolution which instinctively identified itself with the mythical figure of Prometheus. Although that revolution takes different forms in the East and in the West, on both sides the ground from which it springs is the same.

Sympathy with the needs of primitive man dreaming in his cave had moved the Titan Prometheus to help man by bringing him the blessings of civilization, giving him the courage to seek self-possession, autonomous power, and lordship over the earth. It was the resistance of things to man's attempts to bend them to his purposes which at last awakened man, the dreamer adrift on the stream of sensual impressions. Not until he had defied the resistance of matter was he able to enjoy the experience of being and possessing himself.

Every experience of power is accompanied by a strangely intoxicating longing for higher power, from which in turn springs what Nietzsche calls the will to power. The touchiness of the ambitious Titan inclines him to interpret the resistance of matter to his efforts as the envy and ill will of the gods, even of heaven's highest. Moreover his intellectual awakening has made him conscious of rights that are inalienably his, and he is quick to rebel at the least real or imagined threat to them. As Lassalle points out, the spirit is a born rebel.

Prometheus' revolt began with his forgetting himself so far as to quarrel with Zeus. The suspicion that the wielder of supreme power might not be, as it behooved him to be, simultaneously absolutely just and absolutely holy grew constantly stronger. Obviously Zeus was withholding certain good things from men; might this not be for selfish reasons? Naturally enough such suspicions led to a certain tension. At the slightest irritation Prometheus vented his growing rebelliousness in wild accusations.

After long nursing similar suspicions the resurrected Prometheus of modernity brought action against the Christian God, charging him with injustice and despotism. The trial of God that began in the Enlightenment lasted for centuries; he was found guilty and sentenced to banishment.

The least suspicion of divine injustice robs God of his central, most essential attribute, his holiness. During the trial God was treated as a mere principle of absolute justice in order that "the case against God" might proceed in his name. Modern man holds moral law to be the direct road to the world of the spirit; for him it is to moral law that all spiritual beings, God included, must bow. Once God has been deposed in the name of this absolute principle, the question of his existence loses its weight. Agnosticism is a bridge not only to forgetfulness of, but ultimately to the denial of God. For a while his shade lives on in the so-called "principle of absolute justice."

The genesis of atheism is usually ignored or suppressed. This is understandable, for the provable fact that atheism grew out of an emotional protest in which objective arguments played only a secondary role hardly substantiates modern atheism's claim to be a child of science. Consciously or unconsciously objective argument on the subject of God is avoided in order to circumvent an embarrassing truth. One clutches gratefully at Theodore Vischer's dictum, "Morality is always self-understood," as a kind of figleaf with which to cover one's nakedness. Under the spell of that dictum the science of belief has hitherto found it tactless to trace the true, psychological roots of unbelief; instead it persisted in considering unbelief an error in reasoning to be combatted by apologetics and above all by "proofs" of God's existence. Today amazed theologians are beginning to realize that nobody is really interested in such proofs.

Besides the reluctance to expose the true root of unbelief there is another mistake common among believers regarding unbelievers. One is inclined to explain unbelief as the result of frivolously discarded moral restraints, in other words, the readiness to equate unbelief with libertinism. It cannot be denied that such an equation is valid for many circles in which faith in God has cooled to the point where religion is considered no more than a irritating checkrein which is best discarded. But this attitude is typical only of the lukewarm and indifferent who lack the strength for resistance and the will to personal decision. In every age such people make up the willing herd that succumbs so easily to tyranny.

But side by side with this type of unbelief is another which is the opposite of moral torpor or libertinism. It is the result of a willful interpretation of morality which makes it a man's *duty* to reject faith in God. This logical development of the Promethean attitude has been expertly analyzed by Max Scheler who says, " In this form of ' posited atheism ' the negation of God is certainly not felt to be a release from responsibility or a lessening of man's independence and freedom but precisely the greatest imaginable increase of responsibility and sovereignty. " [1] This is quite a different view of the opponents of Christianity from that usually held by Christian thinkers. Here is true atheism, unbelief in which faith is neither lost in the jungle of other interests nor starved for lack of sustenance but dutifully and emphatically rejected.

To sum up, modern atheism is not a conclusion reached by objective reasoning, nor is it the result of an examination of reality which includes new aspects or probes deeper than earlier examinations and thereby discovers either some new truth or some error in the old reasoning. Atheism is to be sought not in the reason but in the will. Atheism springs from the revolt of the man who has written personal freedom large on his banner. Like Prometheus modern man desires to shake off the burden of God " and the dream of service to God " to awaken to conscious possession of himself. He refuses to obey anyone or bend a knee to anyone, including God, because he insists on being his own lord and lawgiver.

REVOLUTIONARY IDEOLOGY

In antiquity there were of course uprisings of enslaved and subjugated individuals or groups who rebelled and attempted to throw off the yoke of servitude by force, but revolutions in the true sense are a typically modern phenomenon. Incomparably more far-reaching than any mere revolt, a revolution is an attempt to bring

[1] M. Scheler, *Philosophische Weltanschauung* (Dalp-Taschenbuecher, 1954), p. 85.

about a carefully programmed new social order based on an ideology.

Our age has been aptly called the age of ideologies, and the great revolutions belong to it: the American, the French, the German, and the Russian. Ideology and revolution go together. Whereas all earlier philosophies were aware that the will to knowledge could lead at best only to a fragment of truth, rationalistic philosophy knows no such modesty. It believes in reason as in a god. Not satisfied with fragmentary knowledge, it designs what it considers a closed system of truth which is on principle all-inclusive and in which all the problems of existence are totally resolved.

Convinced that it possesses the fountainhead of universal knowledge, " the philosophical age " is inclined to ignore the evidence of empirical truth. It does not hesitate to construct out of insights and definitions of its own what it considers to be the system of systems, a rational world order. Thus the makers of ideologies, often the most influential philosophers of their day, feel that they possess the ultimate in valid knowledge of the right order of the state and of society, and that the rational rearrangement of the age in which they live insures a radical improvement in the human condition. They are convinced that unplanned existence, which has grown naturally from invisible historical roots, is dis-ordered and an inherently unjust existence. Therefore it is doomed. By definition the ideologist is the builder of a better world carefully planned according to abstract principles. When this ideal world of his fails to tally with reality, the fault lies not in the theory but in the reality, which must be abolished. Thus to present an ideology to the world is simultaneously a challenge to men to realize it. The broader, more radical and grandiose an ideological theory of existence is, the more chance it has not only of inspiring enthusiasm but also of gaining fanatical support. The fanaticism of its apostles clouds everything but the one idea; mankind's veritable panacea alone is spotlighted. Since fanaticism dictates even the framing of ideologies, it is only natural that in their implementation no contradiction may be countenanced.

Aside from the great ideologies, which have gained widespread influence, there are a number of smaller ones, programs for world betterment which also trace all evils to a single root and conduct crusades against the chosen offender with equal zeal, whether this obstacle to earthly paradise be alcohol, interest rates, monarchy, private property, or meat-eating. Inchoate at the bottom of every ideology lies an almost religious idealism.

Like all fanatics, ideologists turn a deaf ear to the realism of the prudent, disregarding on principle all warnings that man, being what he is, cannot redeem himself. Fanatics are recognizable by their rejection of existing possibilities. The ideologist refuses to act on the basis of partial but real knowledge or to undertake gradual, realistic improvements. He insists on a sweeping solution to all the problems of mankind. Almost invariably his motto is " Everything or nothing! " As a result, ideologies tend to become utopian. Abstract principles override concrete reality, and men are taught to sacrifice actual, individual, fellow men for the sake of a phantom Mankind.

At the same time the arrogance of the new ideological constructs only serves to augment already existing evils. In the long run those, who like Prometheus attempt to defy the gods and seize by cunning what these do not freely give, must fail. The chorus of the daughters of Oceanus warns Aeschylus' Prometheus, " The will of man shall never break the harmony of God. " Because the divine order of existence is the essential order it can be rejected or rebelled against; it cannot be replaced. He who attempts to create a new order of existence only destroys.

Prometheus' fate makes this abundantly clear. " This I have learned beholding your destruction. " [2] Rebellion against God ends with the rebel's own destruction.

Since universal values are primal, created, God-given, man's task can only be to preserve those values, and whenever they fall into disorder to correct the resultant wrongs. Every attempt to recreate actuality according to invented or contrived principles ignores not only the nature of things but the essence of the universal law and order to which they belong.

The great European revolutions aimed at deposing not only the human opponents of revolution but essentially also the Creator, for the will to world betterment springs from the conviction that

[2] Aeschylus, *Prometheus Bound*. Translated by Philip Vellacott (Penguin Classics, 1961), p. 36.

man can do better than his Maker, who must be abolished so that man may redeem himself. Pascual Jordan remarks in his book, *The Revolt that Failed,* " The spectacle of the foundering of mankind's universal uprising against God is *the* shattering yet reassuring experience of recent years. " [3]

POSTULATORY ATHEISM TODAY

Dietrich Kerler and Nicholas Hartmann are unmistakable champions of postulated atheism. Both take as their starting point " the funda-mental facts of the moral life, " above all, " the fact that the purely and absolutely moral person knows no value of an intellectual or nonintellectual nature comparable to the value represented by a man selflessly performing the duties of his state. " [4] According to this philosophy, since moral man is affirmed as the highest possible value, that which is part of moral action, man's autonomous creation of moral values, must be affirmed along with that value. " In its urge to create, morality wills that its morality be its own supremely personal act. The idea that morality might be in any way indebted to powers outside itself, whether divine or anonymous, is intolerable to it. " [5] It considers the submission to divine powers taught by humility as " a denial of man's personal creativity " and therefore rejects it as immoral. In sovereign, conscious self-affirmation, man, who considers himself the absolute master of his works, presses his own seal upon them. A sense of moral freedom and autonomy is considered inseparable from the truly moral attitude.

The notion that in his autonomous realization of moral values man himself is " an infinite value not to be outshone by earthly or heavenly splendor, not even by the glory of the Godhead, "

---

[3] P. Jordan, *Der gescheiterte Aufstand* 2 Aufl. (1957), p. 156.

[4] D. H. Kerler, *Max Scheler und die impersonalistische Lebensanschauung* (1917), p. 5.

[5] *Ibid.*, p. 24.

springs from an attitude that diametrically opposes the authentic religious attitude. What is claimed here is the notion of a mutual cancellation, an " irreconcilable conflict " between the religious life and moral autonomy.

Only the subject actually experiencing values himself can evaluate, hence " it is *we* who prescribe the ideal laws to reality, indeed, even to God. . . . We are the begetters, in some instances the affirmers of the demands of the ideal and in this capacity, naturally *only* in this, we are the mightiest and most sublime beings in the entire cosmos. " [6]   Even if God were the inventor or begetter of the ideal, once it came into existence, he would be its " servant. "   Then, subordinating himself to the ideal, God would have surrendered his sovereignty to it.   " The glorious freedom of the moral man reveals itself in his intellectual-psychical unrestraint when confronted by the transcendent. " [7]

Similarly the postulatory atheism of Nicholas Hartmann is based on man's moral freedom.   For if the world were really created according to a divine plan, everything in it would be so perfectly arranged that there would be no room for human freedom.   Man as a moral being, as *person*, would be destroyed.   With this the problem of the existence of God as the ground of the universe becomes inconsequential.   Regardless of man's knowledge or lack of knowledge on the subject of God's existence, God *ought not to exist*.   Man must be entirely free to fulfill his existence by himself on his own responsibility.

When Hartmann discusses the need to reject God, the usually sober, objective thinker gives way to an emotionalism that completely warps his judgment.   Fearful of heteronomy, the total destruction of man as a moral being, Hartmann refuses to consider the objective question of God's existence.   In what Bela von Brandenstein calls Hartmann's " harsh male pride " he rejects the possibility of a relative, creaturely freedom for man.   Whenever Hartmann mentions God the high calibre of his philosophy suffers; his whole presentation sinks to the level of uncritical popular philosophy with its *argumenta ad hominem*.   Von Brandenstein seems to hit the mark when he diagnoses Hartmann's emotional

---

[6] *Ibid.*, p. 26.
[7] *Ibid.*, p. 37.

attitude toward the question of God as the result of an "unhealed trauma." Like Nietzsche, what Hartmann rejects is the Reformers' freedom. One must agree with Brandenstein that "Nietzsche's influence on this peculiar conception of heroism, which is entirely in keeping with Hartmann's own nature, certainly makes itself felt."[8]

If the problem of God in the philosophy of Karl Jaspers often seems tragically fragmented and insoluble, one substantial reason for this is that Jaspers' thought is burdened by the principle of the false infinitude of the Faustian urge. According to this view too the *Weltanschauungen* dominated by the notion of an all-decreeing God, sprang from man's inability to bear his own chaotic infinitude. This is Jaspers' understanding of the world views of Plato, Aristotle, Aquinas, and Descartes. According to Jaspers it is man's reason which produces such philosophical "boxes." Compared with other psychic powers reason is superficial. Like Lessing, Jaspers recoils from the discovery of ultimate truth because he senses that it might limit to the finite man's infinite, roving search. The norm by which Jaspers judges everything, including faith in God, is man's absolute will to his own existence. Hence man cannot, dare not commune with God because this would stifle his human freedom.

The Protestant theologian Ricoeur, a friend of Jaspers, rightly defines his philosophy as " an incipient atheism which springs from a vacillating compromise between Kierkegaard and Nietzsche." Jaspers rejects Christianity as an absolute religion primarily in order to assert the complete freedom of human existence. No absolute religion can exist, he says, because God cannot express himself absolutely in time and space. Divine self-revelation, for example in the form of an incarnation, would abrogate God's transcendence and destroy man's freedom. For this reason the doctrine of the Godman is a contradiction and an impossibility. Ricoeur remarks that his repeated reminders to Jaspers of the importance of moderation in such arguments have been unavailing. In spite of all the philosopher's assurances to the contrary, here obviously " *hybris,* or *la vanité philosophique* was somehow being resurrected." For not only theological sin exists, but also philo-

---

[8] B. Von Brandenstein, *Teleologisches Denken.* Betrachtungen zu dem gleichnamigen Buche Nicolai Hartmanns (1960), p. 104.

sophical sin, and the philosophy of existentialism is not immune. According to Ricoeur, " its sin consists in its preoccupation with the self; man is completely encircled by the self...Existentialism makes as proud a claim for its origin as the *cogito* of Cartesian philosophy or ' the spirit ' of Hegelian. " [9]

The principle from which Jaspers' thought takes its point of departure and by which it evaluates all things is the personal freedom of man. This leads to a crippling of faith in God, but it does not lead to a denial of him. Because for Karl Jaspers man's freedom must be unconditionally preserved, God is not permitted to lay aside his transcendency and enter into history.

AGAINST THE STREAM: KIERKEGAARD

The Danish philosopher of religion, Sören Kierkegaard, is an outstanding example of man's freedom of decision and ability to fight clear of the intellectual mainstream of his day, even though initially he had been drawn into it. Kierkegaard came to grips with Hegel and managed to free himself from Hegel's influence. Kierkegaard's own decision fell in the opposite direction. He recognized in Hegel's philosophy of the spirit a threat to the fundamental substance of man's being with all its burden and bliss.

Man is spirit. This is the starting point for Kierkegaard, much as it is for Hegel. But Kierkegaard goes on to ask: What is spirit? Spirit, he replies, is self-being *Selbst-Sein)*. It is having a relationship with the self. In other words, it is the possession of an intellectual self, for also the animal possesses a self, albeit only a sensual self incapable of entering into a relationship with itself. The uniqueness of the human self consists in its ability to turn back upon, enter into a relation with itself. When a man achieves intellectual self-consciousness he discovers that this includes the knowledge that he does not possess this self-being of himself, rather

[9] P. Ricoeur, in: Karl Jaspers, Hg. v. P. A. Schilpp (1957), p. 633.

that his self has been posited by another. For a being that relates itself to itself " must either have posited itself or have been posited by another. " The human self is a derived, posited relation. " By relating itself to its own self and by willing to be itself the self is grounded transparently in the Power which posited it. " [10]

Man cannot even *will* to receive his being unconditionally from himself. Every forced attempt to do so is against human nature and must therefore lead to despair. All attempts to overcome despair by one self only lead to deeper despair, for the dis-relation of despair exists not only within a man but is also in his dis-relation to that " third term " by whom a man in his relation to himself knows himself to have been posited. Hence he can overcome despair only by affirming his own self *as it is* and by clearly positing that self " in the Power which posited it. " As Kierkegaard insists, this is the formula for belief, recognition that the self is posited by another. It is " the expression for the total dependence of the relation (the self namely), the expression for the fact that the self cannot of itself attain and remain in equilibrium and rest by itself, but only by relating itself to that Power which constituted the whole relation. " [11]

Hegel's philosophy is the psychologically impossible attempt to force the self to the level of a system of absolute thought, thereby freeing the self from the actual concrete situation of human existence. It is the usurpation of an eternity—to be sure, of a false eternity, as of a poor infinitude—by which man deludes himself into believing that he possesses absolute knowledge and is therefore beyond the need of a decision.

With this man believes, as the young Hegel clearly states, that he can claim the predicate of holiness for himself and completely ignore the possibility of " sin. " However a man is never pure ego, his personal *cogito* can never wing its way to the absolute *cogito*; always and forever it remains after-thought, re-flection, a later retracing of the fore-thought which determined existence and hence necessarily preceded human thought. Moreover, man's thought is always a medium of his existence, which is always open

[10] S. Kierkegaard, *The Sickness Unto Death*. Translated by Walter Lowrie (Princeton, N. J.: Princeton University Press, 1948), p. 19.
[11] *Ibid.*, p. 18.

to the possibility of blameworthy failure to be what it was meant
to be. This is "sin," and the ability to sin is part of human
existence; even the attempt to escape this situation by means of
an absolute intellectual system which leaves no place for sins is
itself sin, says Kierkegaard in *Philosophical Fragments*.

Nothing is more natural to the man awakened to intellectual
self-consciousness than to desire to know the ground of his own
being. Contemplation of one's being leads simultaneously to the
realization that that being does not exist on its own, is not absolute;
hence an absolute is indicated. For peculiar to being is what
Fuerstenberg calls its "addiction to the absolute"; existential
autonomy *(Seinsautonomie)* is not possible for contingent being.
In the last analysis no form of atheism is simply one of several
possible opinions about the world, an opinion that needs only to
be objectively verified or refuted. Atheism necessarily ends in
contradictions, as is already indicated by Hegel's suspension of the
law of contradiction. Ultimate antinomies seem to split the ground
of being. Perverse deification of human thought, of "the whole
man," or of the world necessarily results in the dialectical about-
face to nihilism, meaninglessness, and declarations of the world's
absurdity.

There is an inner self-contradiction in atheism that for the time
being is camouflaged by simply denying the legitimacy of the
questions about being as a whole or about the subject that formulates
those questions. All atheism is threatened from within. To the
degree that atheism seriously attempts to understand itself it must
necessarily destroy itself.

The denial of God causes man to misconstrue his own essence,
resulting in an attitude of self-contradiction for which man has
only himself to thank. Elimar von Fuerstenberg's book, *The Self-
contradiction of Philosophical Atheism*, is a study of precisely this
phenomenon. He concludes: "A philosophy that must contradict
itself in order to trace being back to nothingness is basically a
futile philosophy which can only rivet man to despair." [12]

---

[12] E. von Fuerstenberg, *Der Selbstwiderspruch des philosophischen Atheismus*
(1960), p. 8.

CAMUS AND "INHERITED" ATHEISM

The question so natural to man concerning God as the absolute ground of being leads through doubt to an objective insight that when scientifically formulated according to the facts of the world and of man amounts to what is called a proof of the existence of God. However, such proving has long since fallen into disrepute, and not only the proofs that were rationally misunderstood, but even the existential demonstrations of the absolute through insights into being itself.

When two years before his death Hegel began his famous lectures on the proofs of the existence of God he found that he had to defend his undertaking against the so-called cultural prejudices of his day. He was forced to admit, " Such proofs are so little esteemed that they are seldom known, and then merely as historical phenomena. It is possible to meet even theologians who for all their eagerness to prove religious truths with scientific arguments, are totally unfamiliar with these proofs. " Since Hegel's day the prejudices against them have become even more tangible. The tabu on theological questions, on which Hegel's own philosophy originally stood, proved an amazingly resistant and effective historical force that has held generation after generation under strict censure. Here, says Fuerstenberg, is a sorry example of succumbing to a tabu which is itself dogmatic, unskeptical, and unscientific.

The servile obedience of whole generations of philosophers to this ban on theological discussion led to the spiritual crippling of many intellectuals, who were neither willing nor able to restate the timeless question of man's origin and honestly struggle to answer it. The result was the appearance of what may be called " inherited " forms of atheism. Camus is one of the so-called heirs we shall examine.

The French existentialist Albert Camus no longer poses the ultimate questions at all. He simply starts from the premise that there is no meaning to existence, a premise he has decided upon not because of any philosophical insight, but because of what he calls the sense of the absurd so widespread in our age. When

questions about the last things are no longer posed, the old answers
have a hollow ring. The whole problem is dismissed from the start
as absurd. Quite arbitrarily the absurd is selected as the point of
departure and is on principle not to be questioned. Thus a wall
is erected which no one dares pull down. For Camus the absurd
is the fruit of a philosophical notion of his day which he simply
accepts. If Camus insists on taking absurdity as his starting point,
says Blanchet, it is because he is an atheist " by birth " and " from
a sense of solidarity. "

For Camus filial piety toward his mother was an inner obligation.
This simple, uneducated washerwoman, who battled her way through
life by sheer drudgery, becoming deaf, ill, and dull from exhaustion,
had renounced religion as a dispensible luxury, preferring to stand
up to the obvious absurdity of existence without pious " claptrap. "
For this woman only two things mattered: life, which is worth
mastering without why's and wherefore's, and after it death.
Unremitting suffering had ground her last remnant of faith and
hope to dust. She had become a nameless cipher in the legions
of the toiling masses.

Camus identified himself with the masses because of his mother
and felt obliged likewise to strip himself of all " illusions " concerning this world and the next. " The working masses, worn out
with suffering and death, are masses without God. Our place is
henceforth at their side, far from teachers, old or new. " [13] To the
old " teachers " belong the Evangelists with their religion of salvation in the beyond; to the new, the Marxist materialists with their
religion of salvation here on earth. Also this decision comes under
the heading of revolt. He who condemns himself to live like the
poor and humiliated, who cannot live as he does, condemns himself
to live without God. On this point Camus explicitly identifies
himself with Dostoevski's rebel, Dmitri Karamazov. He writes:
" The movement of pure rebellion is climaxed in the shattering cry
of Karamazov, ' If all cannot be saved, what's the good of saving
one! ' " With this the inner dichotomy is certainly made permanent,
for Camus knows that nostalgia for union, the longing for the
absolute, is the driving force in the drama of human existence.

[13] A. Camus, *The Rebel*, An Essay on Man in Revolt (New York: Alfred
Knopf), p. 303.

When birth and solidarity " oblige " even an intellectual like Camus to remain true to atheism, it is no wonder that among " the toiling masses " unwillingness to pose the old questions led to the nihilism so often depicted in current literature.

Even before Nietzsche nihilism had been an important and threatening phenomenon, but by the turn of the century, due largely to his influence, it became the leading ideology of the day. The first generation considered nihilism merely an intellectual plaything. They were attracted by its dangerous destructiveness but never seriously expected its realization. But the first enthusiastic generation was followed by a second, whose mood after the First World War's " hailstorm of steel " veered round to a radical cynicism for which all ringing words were nothing but lures to catch the unwary. This sapping of values did not succeed in stamping out the masses' will to faith immediately. Thus it was necessary for so-called leaders to abuse that will by cynically distorting the sacred works of the past in order to quicken the struggle for a new " great religion. " The sterility of the new religion was soon evident in its obvious inability to accomplish anything constructive on the strength of its own autonomous will because its motivating force was not creative love but destructive hate. Plumbless hatred is in itself evidence of a wallowing despair at the inability to abolish the once established laws of nature in order to set up a counternature of its own.

Already in Nietzsche we find traces of this undercurrent of hate, which is the mark of nihilism. Impelled by something within him, Nietzsche never tires of hurling his venom against Christianity as well as against all the devious paths to hidden underworlds and false deities that he runs across. He intoxicates himself on the wails of indignation at his tearing down what others hold true and sacred. In this respect Hitler was Nietzsche's disciple; he actually " made hate the center of his school of destruction, " as Hermann Rauschning points out in his book on nihilism. Here is a case, Rauschning aptly remarks, of something neither accidental nor merely personal, of an elemental quality of nihilism that becomes evident wherever nihilism is implemented or spread. If for all his conquest of the physical world, for all his science and technology, man has fallen into a phase of destructiveness and self-destruction that surpasses anything in the history of human violence, the reason lies in his will to destroy and in an autonomous urge to extinction. Although this perverse will has like a shadow always accompanied man's will to create, in the present age it has grown independent and arbitrary.

Characteristic of our day is not envy or hate, which have always been important elements of social existence, but the joy of hating, hate as a creative power and unifying element. The sworn members of the Nazi Party composed a tight community of hate. Hate takes the place of love. It creates an illusory new world. It is hate that spurs the revolutionary, not love of greater justice. Certain forms of socialism, says Rauschning, live more from hatred of the middle class than from the fire of an ideal.

The true creativity that belongs to man as creature is always limited to re-creating and creatively developing what already exists. The notion of man creating out of nothing like God remains a phantom as foolish as it is impossible. Accordingly the first step for the truly creative man is love of his given material, which he must affirm before he can sense its possibilities. This is especially true of the potentialities within man; before these can begin to be realized there must be that loving submersion in the self and in others which is the prerequisite of understanding. The arbitrary, self-glorifying person who insists on doing everything on his own is incapable of such love. For him reality is nothing but that which resists his will or is a means to his ends. He refuses to respect the views of anyone else. The will to autonomous " reform " knows no reverence for an existence that is in itself vital, valid, and worthy of respect, an existence that may not be arbitrarily tampered with, least of all when what is in question is the personal, absolute worth of every human being. Only nihilism in its abject cynicism is capable of attempting such a thing as the annihilation of an entire race.

ABSOLUTE FREEDOM
OR ABSOLUTE SLAVERY?

God is renounced in the name of man. Absolute, divine freedom appears to threaten human freedom, so God must go. However, by the law of its own inner inconsistency, the proclamation of man's absolute freedom leads to the exact opposite: to his absolute enslavement. Not even Prometheus could make charges against God without appealing to the principle of an absolute justice which, innocent of the slightest despotic arbitrariness, is the only ground for a case at all. For it is the absoluteness of moral values whose unquestionable validity remains untouched by the currents of change that are the prerequisite of man's claims to human dignity. Only when rights exist which are rooted in eternity and which will remain valid for all eternity regardless of the shifting circumstances of time and place, is there a refuge to which man can fly when his human rights are threatened.

Naturally, once man's lust for absolute freedom is unleashed, he is no longer capable of respecting any rights, not even those eternal rights which protect his own human rights. Wantonly the freedom hero longs to make himself his own lord, his own lawgiver. He dreams of establishing new universal laws in the sovereignty and perfection of his own personal power. He considers the absolute validity of the concepts of good and evil no more than the prejudice of the weak and cowardly who, fearful of putting their hand to strong things, hide behind the skirts of such concepts. The moment the unquestionable authority of eternal values is supplanted by the so-called legislative authority of a human leader, human freedom ceases to exist. What was once the unquestionableness of the divine now in the form of arbitrary and total power is conceded to a single person, into whose hands everyone is delivered. The anarchy to which revolution leads cries out for a leader to force upon the amorphous masses a new, artificial order based upon the absolute authority of the so-called "leader, *Fuehrer, duce, caudillo.*"

Dostoevski, who thought the ideas of Nechaev's notorious

Catechism for Revolution through to the end, clearly saw what its consequences would be, as the much quoted sentence that he puts into Schigalev's mouth proves: " After starting out from unlimited freedom I arrive at unlimited despotism. " Since Dostoevski's day the accuracy of this insight has been proved by the tragic fates of millions of human beings.

Lenin conceived the plan of a total re-education of men that was to be so radical as to annihilate the existing ego with its private arbitrariness. He saw in Pavlov's reflexology, with its teaching that the life of the soul is no more than the play of nerves controlled by reflexes, the perfect ideological means to such re-education. Once new reflexes more suitable to a unified system have been thus produced, the world will have " the new man " who will have no more in common with the old than his outer shell.

Red China adopted this plan from Soviet Russia and by employing the most stringent methods of brainwashing initially had some success in her efforts to produce unthinking robots who merely react to the slogans ground out to them with the persistence of a gramophone record. Yet to judge from the fragments of news from China which reach the free world today, the success is limited. After years of the most vigorous efforts, the whole process of re-education is being questioned and courageously rejected as inhuman. Naturally many bow before the gale of Communism, but they do so with the intention of righting themselves and standing erect again once the storm has passed.

THE EXPERIMENT THAT FAILED

The experiment described in the foregoing chapter may already be regarded as a failure. Much as the natural scientists questioned nature in methodical experiments and by applying the answers paved the way for modern technological living, today experts should objectively evaluate the results of *the* massive experiment of our age, atheism. By theoretically substituting the laws of a completely autonomous human reason man attempted to regulate human life anew. Hence now it is our right and duty to examine the results of this experiment and to interpret its message in order to pave the way for the decisions of our own day.

Live dangerously! This is the underlying motto of Nietzsche's whole philosophy. His own unbelief is also an experiment in the possibility of living without God. Because from his early (what he calls his experimental) years to the formulation of his doctrine of the eternal recurrence of the same, Nietzsche insisted on the experimental nature of his philosophy and evaluated every other philosopher by his ability to apply his doctrine to his own life, Nietzsche invites us to measure his stature as a philosopher by the norm of its existential validity. In view of Nietzsche's conviction that he was destined to offer himself up in Dionysian self-sacrifice in order to prove his philosophy, we are bound to accept the results of that experiment as valid. In an agony of suffering Nietzsche learned that man is not permitted to shift the limits of his given existence, that to attempt absolute autonomy splits man in two. Such tragic dichotomy leads to the exact opposite of autonomy, to enslavement by inexorable fate. Not by a hair's breadth can the slave of fate alter the fixed, never-ending cycles of fate's course.

THE DIALECTICAL LAW OF HISTORY

Under the immediate impact of the terrors of the French Revolution Alexis de Tocqueville undertook to trace the historical laws at work in it. In his analysis of the inner workings of revolution, he points out the historical validity of the law of reversal from absolute freedom to absolute tyranny. The democratic revolution, says de Tocqueville, starts with the demands for freedom and justice and, at least in the beginning, with the naive conviction that both are equally realizable. However, the stark contrast between the humaneness of the theories and the savagery of what actually occurred during the Revolution must open the eyes of all who *want* to see to the fact that behind the lofty demands lurk passions of very doubtful origin. One result of universal equality is that the individual loses himself in the anonymity of the mass. He is filled with pride and self-confidence, and his new independence gives him a heady sense of freedom. But it is precisely this intoxicating freedom without responsibility of the anonymous masses which invariably leads to anarchy and from there to slavery. For once the strong generation that brought about the revolution has spent itself, some strong individual will appear in the midst of the ensuing chaos and use it as an excuse to exercise his own boundless will to power.

Thus for de Tocqueville the historical dynamic which worked itself out in the French Revolution provides a textbook example for a general law of historical dialectic. He saw in the development that took place between July 14, 1789 and the Caesarism of Napoleon I the steps of a historical process, which he knew would repeat itself in regular cycles with increasing harshness. An egalitarian people knowing only the termitelike happiness of fearful and industrious animals practically demands the dictatorship of an absolute leader.

Despite the strenuous efforts made in the post-revolutionary period to revive and develop the lost causes of the first great Revolution and to attack the whole problem more radically in order to force a complete change, the result was always the same: always the exact opposite of what was intended. The intoxicating triad, Freedom-Equality-Fraternity, which began with the dream of a virtuous empire under the sovereignty of Reason, advanced, step by step to its despotic end, the rule of blood and the rolling heads of all who failed to comply with Reason's master-plan.

In the last analysis it was Hegel's extreme individualism with its passionate concern for the freedom of the individual which established the historical reign of absolute reason in which the individual no longer counts. The translation of Hegel's intellectual revolution into a workers' revolution annihilated anew the individual, for whom nothing remained but to dutifully sacrifice himself to the collective.

Current despots mock at the " sentimentality " of the individual's demands for fundamental human rights. What Schopenhauer called " the rascally individual" *(das lumpige Individuum)* has only one right and one duty: to sacrifice himself for the collective system, even if in the process his human features are crushed beyond recognition by the boot-heel of the collective.

Marxian socialism, which abolished the vertically structured transcendence of absolute principles, has reduced man to a radically historical being and abrogated the eternal fundamental human rights and freedoms. Meanwhile, man has had to experience the bitterness of what it means to be thrust into such a world, to live under a system that suspects an enemy in everyone who thinks for himself. Even the neutral person is considered inimical, a cancerous growth that must be removed. What is valid today may be treason tomorrow. One is expected to approve whatever measures are currently affirmed, whatever is currently expedient, indeed whatever is being currently tested; applause is expected even *before* it has proved itself.

Because absolute historicity has no criterion for tomorrow's dogma, everyone lives in constant fear of being too late with his approval of the next change. For the subject who withholds blind faith in the system regardless of the changes it undergoes commits the unpardonable sin of " resisting historical progress "; he is a heretic and must be destroyed. Neither neutrality nor lip-service suffices. Faith must be lived, translated into action, served. Happiness from any other quarter is suspect; it is potential guilt which the least slip transforms into actual guilt.

Every revolution that made " the will of the people " sovereign began by seeking that will among the masses. Failing to convert the masses to its beliefs, it soon turned its attention to the organization or " party. " The will of the people was henceforth entrusted first to a group, finally to a single leader. Thus all revolutions— except the American— have ended by strengthening the central power. If that power does not consider itself obligated to any transcendent or superhistorical values, if it regards itself as a purely historical power that owes its unique privileges to success and to that alone, everyone is forced to remain on the alert for the changes in ideology which the dictator in his new-found infallibility determines and orders implemented. To be sure, his absolute infallibility lasts only as long as he manages to keep all real power in his hands. Hence revolution runs its course by stifling every fresh revolt before it can lift its head. Even the most servile are suspected of sympathizing or of at one time having sympathized with the latest attempt at revolt. Consequently, as Camus points out in *The Rebel*, in the world of the pure historical process as realized by revolution " a race of culprits will endlessly shuffle toward an impossible innocence under the grim regard of the Grand Inquisitors. " In the 20th century, he concludes, " power wears the mask of tragedy. "

THE END OF PROMETHEUS

With the demasking of absolute power " Prometheus' " swift advance begins to congeal in failure. He had started out with love of oppressed man, for whose sake he appeared before the assembled gods to call Zeus to task in the name of " the principle of justice. " Shocked by the heartlessness of the heavenly tyrant, Prometheus had turned away from Zeus and attempted to create a better world on his own. But the Titan soon learned that men are too shortsighted to recognize their own happiness when they see it and too cowardly to take risks. Hence they must be organized, they must be pushed toward the happiness that beckons them from afar. For the sake of future generations tremendous efforts and sacrifices must be demanded of the living, in order that their descendants may one day know happiness. However, the longer the revolutionary struggle lasts and the harsher the servitude it demands, the more remote and unreal the sun-bright City of tomorrow appears. Hence first of all men must be saved from their own faintheartedness.

Camus' hero reassures the people that he, and he alone, knows the City in the sun. Those who doubt him are driven off into the desert or riveted to the rocks to become the meat of ferocious birds. The others now continue their march through the dark behind the lonely leader, who walks wrapped in thought. Prometheus has become God and rules alone over the loneliness of men. However, all he has taken over from Zeus is his remoteness and his cruelty. Prometheus is no longer Prometheus, he is Caesar. The real, eternal Prometheus now resembles one of his victims. Out of the depths man's cries still resound.

The metaphysical revolution began with doubt in the holiness of God. Men wrangled with God in the name of justice, revolted against his Delegate, and killed him. Once started along the road of revolt, there was no stopping until what remained of God in the form of absolute principles had also been destroyed. The metaphysical revolt ended with the glorification of the will to power, a will which no longer recognizes any permanent values and which, as the nihilism of all values, accepts whatever is momentarily strongest as its lord. In this system which, once launched, must continue its work of destruction with terrifying consistency, there are only two possibilities of change. Either those deprived of their rights rise up in fresh revolt and demand the restoration of their natural rights, in other words, begin the tragedy of revolution all over again, or with the passing of the despot, despotism is succeeded by a return to the state founded on law. Then by invoking " the shadow of God " in eternal principles, the way to the absolute, holy God himself is opened. But because the choice between the two possibilities lies within the sphere of man's authentic freedom of decision, it is impossible to predict (as a natural process may be predicted) what the next chapter in man's history will be. Decision is " irrational " because it is determined by man, who is free.

Authentic freedom of choice saddles man with the responsibility of serious reflection on the essence and value of the Promethean attitude, for the only way out of this devil's circle is through a change of heart. Our gravest danger lies in a false sense of superiority which causes us to lose sight of the moral ground on which decisions must stand. We must be receptive to the lesson of history which in an hour of perception even many unbelievers have acknowledged, and we must think it through to the end.

Belated recognition of the message of history has come from unexpected quarters. Heinrich Heine confessed that man in his demand for divine rights succumbs " to the temptation of the

serpent, " namely, the desire to be like God. For Heine the serpent
is "the first *Privatdozent*" of German idealism, Hegel, whereas
for Bakunin, the theoretician of revolutionary thought, the serpent
is the revolutionary.   Bakunin goes so far as to celebrate the
Biblical Satan in an essay entitled *God and the State*. Here Satan
appears as the archrevolutionary, to whom we are deeply indebted
for attempting to liberate us from the slavery intended for us by
God. Nietzsche, "the bold hunter of God," was forced to admit
that he had caught himself in his own net. He experienced the
deadly venom of the serpent in his own bloodstream. Too late
he realized that he had succumbed to its song: You will become
like God!

Modern man's own unbelief, his suspicious attitude toward God,
which provides him with an excuse for defiance and revolt, his
haughty determination to create an autonomous counterworld of his
own—all these have led to his fall. Today, caught between the
horns of tragic recent experience and the threat of the decades
ahead, man is growing increasingly ill at ease. In the best minds
everywhere attitudes are forming which gradually converge on a
new common awareness of human limitations.

THE MEANING OF OUR AGE

The 1931 issue of the oldest German philosophical journal, *The
Philosophical Yearbook,* contains a cue to the meaning of our age.
In it are to be found side by side two scholarly analyses of modern
philosophy which so complement each other that they suggest
diggings at the two ends of a tunnel. Although the workmen start
from opposite sides of the mountain, they meet in the middle.

The first paper, by Theodor Steinbuechel, was written to com-
memorate the hundredth anniversary of Hegel's death. It is a
compendium of the essence, values, and limitations of German
idealism, which despite its many historical forms is based on a
single essential will. Idealism is more than a mere philosophy;
it is an intellectual movement, a formative power which affected

an entire age, drawing even poets under its spell. Coming from the ranks of originally Christian theologians, the idealistic philosophers made titanic efforts to found all being anew in an autonomous intellectual creation whose universal system embraced the whole of reality.

One consequence of the Enlightenment's establishment of human reason as an absolute was Kant's elevation of the spontaneity and autonomy of reason to an absolute principle, which his successors developed to its ultimate logical end. Whereas all earlier philosophies from the Greeks on had attempted to understand all being by tracing it back to its ontological root, idealism tried to trace being to the creative principle of subjectivity. Kant was still convinced that for us the unknowable, divine *intellectus archetypus* is essentially different from the human *intellectus ectypus*. It was Kant's successors who made the two one and who defined it as absolute thought, the ground of all being.

In Hegel's philosophy of the intellect, the apogee of idealism, this all-supporting, all-creating, all-embracing ground is sought in the creative spontaneity of thought as the positor of reality, indeed as supra-individual, absolute spirit. This fundamental view is not a conclusion but an " elemental primary assumption *(Urvoraussagung)* and prior decision " for a particular conception of being in which all alleged being is dissolved in a process of intellectual creativity. Ignoring the dialectical contradiction, or rather elevating it to the principle of thought and of the world, Hegel's idealism transfers the infinite to the finite, the unconditional to the conditional, the universal to the particular, the rational to the phenomenal with its transitoriness.

If we concede that the prior decision for the idealistic principle does not rest on objective, judicious reasons, speculation that limits itself to the objective must stop right here. However, since its influence is so great that modern atheism is traceable to it, we are obliged to continue by examining also its nonrational, affective grounds. It can be demonstrated of both Hegel's and Fichte's idealism that they are founded on a characteristic prior decision which prefers to be anchored in the absolute freedom of man rather than in the overpowering, absolute personality of God. As Nietzsche frankly admits, this is *hybris*.

ARROGANCE
THE TRUE ADVERSARY OF FAITH

Careful to avoid undue condemnation, we must try to grasp the importance and meaning of *hybris,* or arrogance. Like Stein-buechel's paper on idealism, Aurel Kolnai's analysis of arrogance in the same volume of the *Philosophical Yearbook* can be of great help.

The best way to get to the essence of arrogance is clearly to separate it from the phenomenon of pride with which it is often confused. Justifiable pride is happy recognition of one's own proficiency when measured against a social or other kind of standard. Such pride is perfectly capable of being paired with humility, the awareness of one's creaturely limitations. Arrogance is not simply an extension of pride. It is something qualitatively new. Pride and arrogance enjoy a certain proximity, but pride invariably relates itself to values—real or imagined—in the self.

To the extent that the self is stressed for its own sake, pride approaches arrogance. Essentially arrogance is a peculiar kind of absolutizing of the self, which is thus elevated to a dispenser of values. Pride tends to overestimate the self, but arrogance is not merely exaggerated self-esteem. Arrogance begins, so to speak, further along, at the point where overestimation of the self annihilates estimation of and comparison with others; in other words, relation to any system of values is rejected in favor of the absolute esteem in which the self alone is held.

The proud man may exaggerate his relative position and importance in the world, but the arrogant man considers the world important only in relation to himself. Whereas the proud man desires to secure what he considers to be an existence worthy of him, for the arrogant man no existence other than his own really *exists.* The proud man believes he knows what he owes himself; the arrogant man feels that he owes no one anything. The proud man assumes too high a place in the order of things; the arrogant man inwardly rejects any place in any order. In arrogance, then,

Kolnai concludes, the sense of personal worth celebrates a peculiar apriority.

It would be a mistake to consider arrogance as a purely ethical phenomenon without metaphysical significance. In reality arrogance is grounded in a characteristic absolutizing of the self along with the corresponding relativization of everything and everybody else.

In the area of world views arrogance leads to a kind of pantheism which Kolnai calls a compromise between solipsism and an acceptance of reality. Here lies one of the possible intermediary levels of intention on which arrogance allows the non-ego validity. Pantheism (particularly Stoic or Spinozan pantheism and possibly to a lesser degree also that of Plotinus and Bruno) starts out by depriving individual things, persons, and matters of their ultimate, decisive significance, thus sparing the subject the need for any personal surrender to them. In the profoundest and most intimate sense, abrogation of the personal Godhead disposes of the bond, obligation, and purpose of the God-man relationship. In the pantheistic interpretation of the world the subject himself can be "God," since in reality everything is "God," and I am part of everything. Furthermore, since I am in all things I am really none of them. Substantial oneness with the universe provides the most suitable background against which my ego stands out in splendid solitude, for secretly it declines to lose itself in the universal substance. It is easier for me to isolate myself when everything other than myself is one than it would be if degrees of proximity existed, especially proximity to a separate Creator and Ruler of the cosmos who demands responsibility of me. How favorable strict pantheism is to the mood of arrogance may be seen by comparing this mood with that to be found in the occasional pantheistically overflowing love in certain Christian mystics, St. Francis for one, with his hymns to his "brothers" and "sisters" sun, water, and fire. It is not love but icy rejection to say to the things of the world: No matter what you are, do, or suffer, you are and remain one: God.

The suggested apriority of the ego's own worth, and glittering behind it contempt of all non-ego...are sure "signs of arrogant intent. For arrogance the real object of rejection is God; hence it is necessary to warn against arrogance because although initially it may be directed at some mere object, it easily shifts its direction to God. . . . " [14]

Hegel firmly rejected the label of pantheism for his system, and Hegelian pantheism is certainly not on the same level as that of the Stoa, of Spinoza, Plotinus, or Giordano Bruno. Whereas all other forms of pantheism are compromises with reality, which is understood as the " one and all, " characteristically Hegel's outstrips this type of pantheism by no longer recognizing any self-existent reality whatsoever and by taking the idealistic concept of the reality-engendering power of the thinking ego with entirely logical seriousness.

The consciously willed a priori decision which opts for the absolute ego regardless of what changes in world view this may entail is a desertion of given reality and of its ground of being in God. Arrogance is the original sin of which the Biblical Lucifer was guilty and into which he attempts to entice men.

ST. AUGUSTINE ON UNBELIEF

St. Augustine has left us an interesting analysis of the Biblical notion of unbelief. In Genesis the account of man's fall from faith begins with the wrong kind of striving for likeness to God. " For the true honor of man is the image and likeness of God, which is not preserved except it be in relation to him by whom it is impressed. The less therefore that one loves what is one's own, the more one cleaves to God. But through the desire of making trial of his own power, man by his own bidding falls. . .to a sort of intermediate grade. And so, while he wishes to be as God is, that is, under no one, he is thrust on, even from his own middle grade, by way of punishment, to that which is lowest, that is, to those things in which beasts delight: and thus, while his honor is the likeness of God, but his dishonor is the likeness of the beast,

[14] A. Kolnai, siehe *Philosophisches Jahrbuch* (1931), Bd. 44, p. 317.

' Man being in honor abideth not: he is compared to the beasts that are foolish, and is made like to them. ' By what path, then, could he pass so great a distance from the highest to the lowest, except through his own intermediate grade? For when he neglects the love of wisdom, which remains always after the same fashion, and lusts after knowledge by experiment upon things temporal and mutable, that knowledge puffeth up, it does not edify: so the mind is overweighted and thrust out, as it were, by its own weight from blessedness; and learns by its own punishment, through that trial of its own intermediateness, what the difference is between the good it has abandoned and the bad to which it has committed itself; and having thrown away and destroyed its strength, it cannot return, unless by the grace of its Maker calling it to repentence, and forgiving its sins. " [15]

Walther Rehm makes this passage from Augustine the starting point of his analysis of the spiritual content of modern literature. He then proceeds to demonstrate that Augustine's interpretation of unbelief is valid also for the modern form of unbelief or doubt. " Augustine, still under the influence of antiquity, which made man the center and measure of all things, describes man as the creature on his eternal journey between heaven and hell. Like Lucifer man in his creaturely arbitrariness lusts to make his ego the heart of the world. Here Augustine suggests Lucifer, the fallen, hence eternally falling, plunging angel, as a symbol of man's immanently dangerous and perennial longing to turn from God and return to the finite-human.

" Such estrangement from the divine must be pictured against the background of Augustine's world, in which the battle against the yet powerful Greco-pagan philosophy of life continued to rage, and the classical counterpart to the Christian Lucifer type, Prometheus, was still in command. Under such circumstances man's self-alienation from God is judged all the more sharply. It is overweening, culpable desertion, the rebelliousness and revolt of the creature against the Creator; it is ' *superbia and conversio ad se ipsum.* ' " Although Lucifer is justly called the Biblical Pro-

---

[15] A. Augustinus, " On the Holy Trinity " in *The Nicene and Post-Nicene Fathers* (Grand Rapids, Mich.; W. B, Eerdmans Publishing Company, 1956), Vol. III, p. 161.

metheus, the archangel's renunciation of the absolute, personal God of the universe was far more radical than was the Titan's, hence its irrevocability.

The tendency to unbelief is also given striking expression in modern art. The will to arbitrary self-creation has destroyed the image of man in its original meaningfulness, and all attempts to substitute a new image have failed. *The Lost Center,* subtitle of Hans Sedlmayer's critique of the pictorial and plastic arts of the 19th and 20th centuries, is significant. Symptom and symbol of the times, this art is the visible sign of man's loss of his true center, which according to Pascal means not only man's loss of God, but simultaneously his desertion of his own humanity.

After brief intoxication, the will to arbitrary new creation leads to disappointment and the bitter absurdity of a life emptied of meaning. The disappointed one faces the profoundest question of all: to be or not to be. The meaninglessness of life is the true " sickness unto death. " Its sophisticated motif is capable of temporarily diverting man's natural will to live but incapable of turning the terrible emptiness that results back toward life. Analyses of the problem of suicide have shown that to deprive the human spirit of its absolute goal in God is to deprive it of the only atmosphere in which it can breathe.

THE NEW FALL

The eternal possibilities of revolt in man, whose creaturely nature remains the same throughout the ages and who is therefore everlastingly threatened by temptations that remain basically the same— this is the gist of the Promethean myth, as it is of the Biblical account of the fall. Personal experience as well as the unbelief portrayed in literature help us to understand something of the meaning behind the old mythically garbed figures.

Genesis states that the Tempter approaches man with cunning, first arousing his suspicion that God has withheld certain good things from him out of a selfish lust for power and that he has hoodwinked man with lies. This charge infringes upon the absolute holiness of God, casts doubts upon his love, and establishes a principle of absolute justice and absolute love in whose name man can call God to account. Next the Tempter assures man that his eyes will be opened, and like God, he will know good and evil.

The Book of Job is the story of the same temptation to revolt, for to insist on one's own innocence while remonstrating with God is to summon God before the tribunal of an absolute justice. Such harping on "rights" bears the germ of creaturely revolt against the Creator, whose holiness necessarily includes absolute (although in the creature's vision not always self-evident) justice. What began with the first pair of human beings continues throughout the spiritual history of mankind until finally it reaches the point where it claims to be able to define the absolute meaning and demonstrate the absolute logic of human history. In the process mere factuality is stamped absolute justice, and world history is inevitably declared to be world judgment. The result is that man's despair is eternalized and every possible escape from it permanently blocked. Hegel's philosophy of the spirit *(Geistphilosophie)*, which Herzen called "the algebra of revolution," was at first ecstatically welcomed by Bakunin but later repudiated by him because Hegel pins himself down to the dialectics of justice-injustice.

Notwithstanding the various shapes and shades of modern world views, practically all have one fundamental point in common: they agree on the absolute, autonomous will of self-glorifying man, who for the sake of his humanity can suffer no God. This is true also of existentialism. Heidegger's philosophy strikes the objective viewer as a completely secularized theology, a theology in which the question of God has become so uninteresting that it is simply dropped.

In a series of lectures which he held during the Third Reich Heidegger attempted to reinterpret Nietzsche's "God is dead!" Nietzsche's proclamation, said Heidegger, was still an "anti-proclamation" hence still attached to what it opposed. Nietzsche's movement against God should be continued in such a manner that the Rejected does not leave a trail of emotions behind him, but quietly, unobtrusively sinks into oblivion. In other words the vanished

authority of God is to be replaced by the authority of man with
his reason and conscience. Creativity, formerly the property of
the Biblical God, now becomes the hallmark of human action.
Heidegger still considers Nietzsche's atheism to be a step in the
direction of self-consciousness, in which the essence of modern man
is to be found. The final step is taken by the man who is determined
to be the executor of the absolute will to power. However, it is
precisely this attempt on the part of man to be himself in the
absolute sense, to draw strictly upon himself for himself, that leads
him into an inner ontological contradiction and despair. Persistent dissatisfaction with this state makes man press for a solution
that will ease the tension.

Perfect nihilism is consummated suicide, regardless of the means
of self-destruction employed. Also the convulsive efforts of the
leader of the Third Reich, begun in the cramp of nihilistic despair,
went the way of collective self-destruction, a fact which certain
cynical remarks of the *Fuehrer* prove beyond the possibility of
doubt.

Nietzsche's tidings of the death of God are soberly accepted as
a fact by Jean-Paul Sartre, the prophet of an existentialism that is
frankly atheistic. Man no longer needs God because man selects
and realizes his own essence in absolute sovereignty. In one of
his essays Sartre lauds Descartes for having completely understood
that the concept of freedom necessarily embraces absolute autonomy
and that the free act is an absolutely new creation whose seed could
not have existed in a pre-worldly state. Freedom and creativity
are one and the same. Also the good and the true are grounded in
man's free act. According to Sartre, it is of no importance that
Descartes reveals precisely this original and constituting freedom
to be in God, whose infinite existence he perceives in his *cogito*.
"The fact remains that a mighty power of affirmation both of the
human and of the divine permeates and sustains Descartes' world.
Two centuries of crises—religious as well as scientific—had to pass
before man could win back that creative freedom which Descartes
attributed to God, before at last truth, the essential foundation of
humanism, understood: man is the being whose appearance causes
the world to exist. But we must not blame Descartes for giving to
God what belongs to man. Rather let us admire him for insisting

on the demands of the idea of autonomy and for understanding long before Heidegger...that the only foundation of being is freedom. " [16]

THE TASK FOR TODAY

The preceding analysis forces us to reject Heidegger's fatalistic thesis according to which current nihilism, whether in the form of declared philosophical knowledge or in that of mute gloom, is an inevitable fate that must be resolutely shouldered without asking whether after the long trek through the dark we may expect the dawn of a new faith. Who has the right to decide whether or not " existence " as such a dawn is in store for us? Who *is* existence anyhow, that it has the power to allot us this or that? Moreover, who is called to be the interpreter of its mysterious voice? Or should we suppress such questions? Who dares to demand of us that we simply drift along with the " current of history "? Haven't the great men and women of history always stood *contra torrentem?* Doesn't surrender to the drift of history require the sacrifice of personal choice and compliance with the impersonal uniformity of the masses? *This* would be a true loss of self, what Heidegger calls degeneration into an attitude of cowardly make-believe. Because the absolute freedom we demanded has proven illusory we need not, dare not renounce the relative freedom that we as humans do possess.

Although today " one " does not discuss God in public, although for average, run-of-the-mass-mill people, to whom unfortunately also many intellectuals belong, God is dead and the problem of God is unmentionable, this can be no norm for people with genuine self-confidence and a sense of personal responsibility. For often enough it is the duty of the individual to pit his conscience against the spirit—or unspirit—of the age.

[16] J. P. Sartre, *René Descartes, Discours de la Méthode* (1948), pp. 203 f.

Certainly "Fate," which did not bring on this night of atheism, will not reverse it to a morning bright with new gods of its own. Such expectations ignore the prior decision behind atheism as naively as do those miscalculations which expect the unbelief of today automatically to become the belief of tomorrow. The only way out is through the pain of disillusionment, the shock of awakening from a nightmare, and the consequent need to seek and find new bearings, this time in reality. Thus through the chorus of disillusioned voices the quick of hearing have caught the message that it is man's sovereignty, the god of modern humanism, that is dead—that never in reality existed save as a fabrication.

Intolerable as was even the report of the bestiality that annihilated millions, such staggering suffering seems to have been necessary to shock man back to awareness of the nullity of human existence and the impotence of all man's strength and power. Today those who learned the terrible lesson taught by mass agony realize the dangers inherent in enthusiastic "Greek" faith in an autonomous, man-made realm of beauty and reason. The blinded must undergo the shattering experience of the void and withstand the terrors of extreme isolation before their eyes see again and they are able to recognize the basic facts of human existence.

Today, although the yoke of slavery which those in communist countries are forced to bear is heavy, there too only suffering can open men's eyes to the errors of the ideology which the revolutionary self-consciousness has exalted to a supreme godhead. That this ideology consistently implemented necessarily leads to the abrogation and destruction of the free personality is a truth which must be experienced through suffering. One must taste the fruit to be able to evaluate the tree that bears it.

FEAR OF THE LORD,
THE BEGINNING OF WISDOM

The religious proto-experience of every age is the experience that despite his great power, man is a nonentity. The toying with an ideological nihilism seems to be an extreme form of myopia which prevents man from gauging the earnestness of that experience. But for the person who uses his " eyes " and " ears " the harshness of fate may prove to be grace, as in the case of Job, for all his—a mere creature's—presumptuous arguing with God.

Divine ordinances are always incomprehensible to man. All attempts to read meaning into fragments of life or history from the narrow viewpoint of some absolute—absolute reason for instance— proved to be *hybris* and presumption curable only by the drastic grace of being battered into recognition of one's limitations and of the given measure of things. Purged by grief, Job knows at last: Fear of God, *that* is wisdom.

Similarly over a century ago Kierkegaard discovered that he who has learned proper fear has achieved supreme wisdom. An enlightened 18th century tried to talk the masses out of the elemental religious experience of creaturely fear, which it " demasked " as an invention of sly priests. Later that experience was branded the narcotic of the masses. Yet fear of God remains the prerequisite of man's humanization without which he soon reverts to a beast. Prophetically Leibniz warned: When men cease to fear God all the passions will be unleashed, and the prevailing attitude will cause the earth to be engulfed in a new flood—this time of blood.

Because all warnings died away unheard, the heavy stick of history had to be used on men's backs to teach them over again what already the Greek tragedians knew, that fear of the gods is the beginning of wisdom. One cannot but agree with Heinrich Weinstock's biting remark that the Westerner, above all the German, who *still* refuses to demask autonomous and arbitrary freedom for what it is, a frightful illusion, is beyond help.

The comforting fact about our age is that not only many " yet-Christians " have managed to survive, but also that the number of completely new encounters with God is steadily growing. To be sure, believers in the true sense of the word are still a small minority, but was judgment in matters of truth and justice ever on the side of the great majority? Goethe's word about the epochs of faith being the only fruitful epochs still holds. Only belief, which through participation in the truth constantly preserves and strengthens the will to life, remains vital, certainly not negativistic unbelief, which barely manages to stave off the consequences of its mood of decline and *Untergang*. Nihilism, fascinated as it is by the phenomenon of death and petrified by confrontation with the void, is a philosophy of senility and decrepitude. No age intent on true progress can afford such a world view for long; whether they are aware of it or not, the nihilists are already moribund.

The authentic will to faith is not destroyed in the forge of suffering but purified. Suffering strengthens man's God-given faith in the meaningfulness of life and of history even when the fragments which lie within our ken must, *qua* fragments, remain mysteries. The will to understand the primal meaning of existence directs man's gaze to a vis-à-vis whose features under earnest scrutiny gradually become clear and personal. At last the answer to the riddle of life's meaning comes through in the joyful recognition that it is not to " the " truth or " the " good, but to his goodness and vital being that we are committed. Awakened by private grief to the wisdom of *homo sapiens*, the man who knows also the co-suffering or *Mit-leid* of sympathy discovers the image of God in the face of his brother and thus himself becomes true *homo humanus*. No longer does his gaze pass by his brother unseeing and empty; now it feeds on the reflection of the divine before it and is reminded by it of the Original, the common Father.

PROMETHEUS—MARY

Everyone who recognizes in the spirit of " Prometheus " bent upon complete, worldwide revolution the real cause of the tremendous tensions in present-day humanity recognizes also the need for a counter-image to help us out of the cul-de-sac in which we find ourselves. We need not impose on the spirit of the age a symbol that is inimical to it when we have at hand that which inspired Johann Gottlieb Fichte, the father of idealism. For later in life even he recognized in man's freely willed " revolt against the warnings of the divine ordinances " and " the resistance of our will

to the divine will" what he calls "the supreme immorality."
Unequivocally the mature Fichte declares, "self-will, which seeks
self-glorifying wisdom, is the disturbing element which quarrels
with love and blocks its way, the only way there is, to the blessed
life." [17]

As long as a man insists on being something for himself unrelated
to the high vocation he was given, this false self-love will hinder
the development of the essential life and personality within him
and block his way to blessedness. For all egocentric being, says
Fichte, "is only nonbeing and the curtailing of true being." Not
one of the objects which man's sensually aroused greed clutches
to can satisfy him for long. "On the other hand, to the extent
that in a supreme act of freedom a man voluntarily relinquishes
his own being with its freedom and independence, he preserves
and participates in divine being and in all the bliss which it
entails." [18] In other words, not until a man destroys himself
before God does he find fulfillment of that self and, with it, access
to divine being.

There is no avoiding the first step to higher morality, which is
relinquishing of one's will to autonomy. A man must "seize
his vocation and desire to be absolutely nothing but what he, and
only he, can be; what he alone in keeping with his higher nature,
that is to say, with the divine in him, ought to be." [19]

To illustrate this fundamental idea, Fichte introduces beauty,
which in this world he knows exists only as the reflection of the
beauty that is God, the source and origin of all beauty. In the
world of men only the perfect light of the divine idea, unclouded
by human self-will, is perfectly beautiful.

Fichte finds such beauty realized in the image of the "holy
Woman who, uplifted above the clouds, is surrounded by heavenly
hosts. Enraptured, these fall down before her who is robed in all
the radiance of heaven, whose supreme joy and glory she is. She
alone, completely absorbed and lost in the one overpowering
experience: I am the handmaid of the Lord, be it forever done to

---

[17] J. G. Fichte, *Die Anweisung zum seligen Leben*, ed. Medicus, Bd. V,
p. 245.
[18] *Ibid.*, p. 236.
[19] *Ibid.*, p. 239.

me according to His will, is totally unaware of all that is taking place around her. When this one experience with all that it entails is embodied in a human figure, the result is Beauty in a definite form. What is it that makes this form beautiful, its members or proportions? Isn't it rather that experience, and that alone, poured out in all these members? " [20]

Mary's conscious " *Fiat!* "—pure affirmation directed unwaveringly to God, never by a single glance of self-complacency to fall from its pure heights, makes perfect transmission of light possible. Hans Urs von Balthasar says in his book, *Prometheus,* even one full glance at the ignoble in its unspirituality mars. One such glance was enough to plunge Schiller's St. Joan from the heights. Through this supreme attitude runs a strict sense of duty and a chastity at once inexorable and sweet.

It is from this perspective that Mary confronts the mythical Prometheus. Prometheus is the symbol of the man who achieves full self-consciousness and the virility of action through arbitrary revolt against God. Mary's is an attitude of childlike humility which nonetheless through conscious, unfaltering affirmation of the divine will transcends the level of naive childlikeness and attains the fullness of beauty, the radiant maturity of the Woman lifted up above the clouds. Thus Mary becomes the prototype of the Christian, image of the perfect Christian attitude as opposed to the Promethean attitude of clear rejection of God. Transcending the limitations of sentiment and sentimentality, the Church celebrates Mary as the power that crushes the head of the serpent under her heel and triumphs over the errors which in the course of history have conflicted with Christian truth. It is to Mary that the Church applies the words from the Canticle of Canticles: " You are as beautiful as Thersa, my beloved, as lovely as Jerusalem, as awe-inspiring as bannered troops " (6,4).

In Fichte himself the battle between " Prometheus " and " Mary " raged for years. Finally the intoxication of pride in his philosophy was overthrown by the realization that he who confronted him, Johann Gottlieb Fichte, was none other than the truly transcendent One whom man by his own strength can never reach. The only

[20] *Ibid.*

attitude befitting the totally other One, the "Father of spirits,"
is the attitude of the child. " I hide my face before thee, and lay
my hand upon my mouth. How thou art, and seemest to thine
own being, I can never know, any more than I can assume thy
nature. After thousands upon thousands of spirit-lives, I shall
comprehend thee as little as I do now in this earthly house. That
which I conceive becomes finite through my very conception of it;
and this can never, even by endless exaltation, rise into the Infinite.
Thou art different from men, not in degree but in nature. In every
stage of their advancement they think of thee as a greater *man,*
and still a greater; but never as God—the Infinite whom no
measure can mete. I have only this discursive, progressive thought,
and I can conceive of no other. " [21]

With this Fichte recognizes the qualitative difference between
God and creature, the absolute otherness of divine being and
knowing, the unknowability of the divine essence, and the impene-
trability of divine decrees. Even the underlying pattern of our
own lives is visible only to One, to " the Father of spirits. "

Into the place of the self-glorifying consciousness and the virile
intellectual deed which severs all outer bonds steps the child's
attitude, aware of its own finiteness and of being face to face
with One who is infinitely, utterly different, with One by whom it
knows itself called and to whom it feels itself duty-bound. In a
free act of the will the believer submits himself not only to the
seemingly crushing majesty of a superexistence, but also to the
power of a personal God round whom in loving surrender one's
own finite existence turns. Thus the rebelliousness of autonomy
is replaced by the will to desire to be no more than the handmaid
of the Lord. " Prometheus " and " Mary " symbolize two radically
different attitudes. Until now the spirit of the age has marched
under the banner of Prometheus, but today the question arises:
To what extent does recognition of the failure of the Promethean
spirit lead to the counterspirit under the banner of Mary?

The Christian of today knows that Mary is not merely an
idea or a myth; she is not simply an image or symbol. Mary is
a highly personal reality. She does not stand by idly, a spectator

[21] J. G. Fichte, *The Vocation of Man* (New York: The Liberal Arts Press,
1956), p. 140.

of history, but turns to us, the makers of history, and demands the change of attitude necessary to avert the further catastrophies which threaten us and the species. Because of the radicalness of current unbelief, a radicalness based on a prior decision, the only possibility of a change lies in a complete reconsideration of that prior decision. Now that the popes of our own century have pointed again and again to Mary as *the* " sign on the heavens of our age " (Pius XII), now that they have backed her maternal warnings and beseechings with the full weight of papal authority, the alerted Christian can no longer stand aside and allow things to drift the way they ar, drifting and will continue to drift if he does nothing to alter their course. If penance and a change of heart are the order of the day, that order is directed to every one of us.

Heidegger says that once we have endured " the lean years, " we may expect the " poet, " who never lost touch with the vanished gods, to come and unbar the gate to the empire of the saints. But must we really wait for the poet? Already, for all who seek it, that gate stands ajar, pushed open by the saints themselves. Why should we wait for another " coming " of the Lord when new forms of belief in the living, personal God already flower among us?

Certainly the prerequisite to a full understanding of this fact is that revaluation which St. Paul calls wisdom. The Christian news of salvation is not dependent on the wisdom of philosophers, which readily stiffens with pride and becomes folly in the sight of God. " For it is written, ' I will destroy the wisdom of the wise, and the prudence of the prudent I will reject. ' Where is the ' wise man? ' Where is the scribe? Where is the disputant of this world? Has not God turned to foolishness the ' wisdom ' of this world? For since, in God's wisdom, the world did not come to know God by ' wisdom, ' it pleased God, by the foolishness of our preaching, to save those who believe " (1 Cor. 1,19).

EPILOGUE

In closing let us turn once more to what Goethe considered the leitmotif of history, the struggle between belief and unbelief which we have attempted to trace on various levels much as one tries to track a surveyor's boundary-line through the underbrush and trees. Mankind dreams perennially of an autonomous evolution of human nature and of great creative deeds of the human spirit which in a purely immanent world process will overcome evil, the shadow of the world, and lead to the victory of goodness and light. This dream has proved a fateful illusion. Its dangers are the greater because they are so well camouflaged. Indeed the whole war over God remains largely an undeclared war that is explained away as part of a perfectly natural development of the human spirit. This permits men to consider themselves excused from the obligations of personal decision and personal service and thus strengthens the forces of unbelief. For in the course of history not a single victory for goodness was won simply by passively allowing things to develop or unfold in a natural process. Victory must be hard-wrung from powers inimical to the divine, often in heroic struggle against seemingly impossible odds.

What we have surveyed here has been only part—albeit a fundamental part—of the struggle for God. Significantly Bruno Bauer's *Trumpet* against Hegel attacks him not only as " the atheist Hegel, " but also as " Hegel the antichrist, " just as Nietzsche declared himself not merely an atheist but antichrist as well. The rebellion of unbelief is aimed not only at the Lord God but also at his Envoy. " The kings of the earth rise up, and the princes conspire together against the Lord and against his anointed: ' Let us break their fetters and cast their bonds from us '! " (Ps 2,2).

Christ and his followers obviously knew that Christianity's way through the centuries would be anything but a triumphal march. Rather, the joyful tidings of the all-powerful and gracious Father would be suppressed, Christians would be persecuted, and even within Christendom itself would come the falling away of many whose faith would grow cold.

A new and important task for each of us is to try to understand the history of the world not only as the struggle between faith in God and rejection of God, but as a series of outright attacks on his anointed. Vladimir Soloviev, the Russian poet-philosopher, attempted such an interpretation in his symbolical history of the triple fall of Christendom. [1] According to Soloviev, the Western Church succumbed to the three temptations which Christ himself, as reported by the Evangelists, triumphantly resisted.

The first fall of the Western Church (to the temptation to seize earthly power) was followed by the fall of the protesting segment of Western Christianity, which in turn succumbed to the temptation of intellectual pride. Human reason usurped the place of revealed truth, ultimately taking it upon itself to trace the entire substance not only of knowledge but of faith to the creative activity of reason. What the Enlightenment began in a superficial manner German idealism completed with a thoroughness that reached its apogee in Hegel. The panlogism of Hegel attempted to transform reality into the dialectical movement of concepts.

The intellectual arrogance to which Western Christianity yielded in the second temptation has been exposed many times and from various quarters. In the first place pure reason proved helpless against the onslaught of the passions, which became decisive historical forces. Even on its own level of abstract thought, pure reason in its pride came to grief. After exalting panlogistic speculation to dramatic heights, abstract reason collapsed under the pressure of objective truth as it gradually emerged from scientific research.

From the ruins of the mammoth temple to autocratic Reason the Western spirit departed on its last and worst deviation, which may be called the arrogance of the flesh. This is the West's temptation to turn stones into bread with which to still all hunger, spiritual as well as physical. Thus historical materialism, which on principle recognizes none but man's earthly needs, takes over the last lap of the long odyssey of the Western spirit.

[1] V. Soloviev, *War, Progress and the End of History*. Translated by A. Baksky (London: University of London Press, Hodder and Stoughton Limited).

Soloviev's interpretation may at times suffer from a certain over-schematization of historical events (in reality all three temptations involve the whole man, body and spirit); nonetheless to the extent that in every age one characteristic temptation predominates, Soloviev's interpretation is valid.

Time and again thinkers and writers have attempted to extend the interpretation of history into the realm of prophecy, basing their arguments on Scriptural passages on the antichrist. Soloviev's contribution to this effort is his legend of the antichrist. [2]

However, such attempts at prophecy can never be more than arrows in the dark, for the essentially irrational factor in human freedom does not encourage authentic prophecy.

Under the circumstances, then, it is important to direct our curiosity, which readily loses itself in conjectures on the future, away from futile speculations and toward the serious and sacred tasks that await us. This active approach to the problem of the the future was Christ's approach, as it was that of his disciples and early followers everywhere.

The first step is to reflect for ourselves on the connections we have tried to trace in these pages. In a movement diametrically opposed to that of apostasy with its noise and crowds, change of heart always begins in the quiet privacy of contemplation. Only when great individuals have accomplished such conversion in exemplary fashion will others who may lack the strength and leisure for sustained intellectual effort be able to follow.

---

[2] A. Maceina, *Der Inquisitor od. Das Geheimnis der Bosheit Deutung der Erzaehlung vom Antichrist Solojews* (1955).

Supplementary reading list

Altzier, Thomas, *The Gospel of Christian Atheism* (Phila.: Westminster Press, 1966).

Augustine, Saint, *On the Two Cities,* ed. by F. W. Strothmann (New York: Frederick Unger Publishing Co., Inc.).

Baldwin, Marshall Whithed, *The Medieval Church:* the division of Western civilization, essays in the history of our Tradition from ancient Greeks and Hebrews to the present (Ithaca: Cornell University Press, 1964).

Barth, Karl, *The Word of God and the Word of Man* (New York: Harper & Row, 1957).

—, *The Terrible Crystal*, Studies in Kierkegaard and Modern Christianity, tr. by Channing Pierce (New York: Oxford University Press, 19±1).

Bentley, Eric Russell, *The Cult of the Superman* with an appreciation by C. S. Lewis. (London: Richard Hale, 1947).

—, *A Century of Hero-Worship;* on Carlyle and Nietzsche, with notes on Spengler, Stephen George, D. H. Lawrence (Boston: Beacon Press, 1957).

Bonhoeffer, Dietrich, *No Rusty Swords;* letters, lectures and notes from the collected works of Bonhoeffer (New York: Harper & Row, 1965).

Brennecke, Fritz, *The Nazi Primer;* official handbook for schooling of Hitler youth (New York: Harper & Bros., 1938).

Bretall, Robert, *A Kierkegaard Anthology*, edited by Bretall (Princeton, N. J.: Princeton University Press, 1947).

Brinton, Crane, *The Shaping of Modern Thought* (Englewood Cliffs, N. J.: Prentice-Hall, Inc., 1963).

—, *Ideas and Men:* the story of Western Thought (Englewood Cliffs, N. J.: Prentice-Hall, Inc., 1950).

—, *The Jacobins* (New York: The Macmillan Company, 1930).

—, *Nietzsche* (Cambridge: Cambridge University Press, 1941).

—, *The Anatomy of Revolution* (New York: Vintage Books, 1952).

Buber, Martin, *Eclipse of God;* studies in the relation of religion and philosophy (New York: Harper & Row, 1952).

—, *Paths in Utopia* (New York: The Macmillan Company, 1949).

—, *I and Thou* (New York: Charles Scribner's Sons, 1958).

Bultmann, Rudolph and Jaspers, Karl, *Myth and Christianity;* an inquiry into the possibility of religion without myth (New York: Noonday Press, 1958).

Burnham, James, *Suicide of the West* (New York: John Day Company, Inc., 1964).

Butterfield, Herbert, *Christianity and History* (New York: Charles Scribner's Sons, 1950).

Byrn-Jones, David, *The Dilemma of the Idealist* (New York: Macmillan, 1950).

Camus, Albert, *The Myth of Sisyphus*, and other essays, tr. by Justin O'Brien (New York: Alfred A. Knopf, 1955).

—, *The Plague*, tr. by Stuart Gilbert (New York: Alfred A. Knopf, 1948).

Casserley, Julian, *The Bent World* (New York: Oxford University Press, 1955).

Chapman, John William, *Rousseau — Totalitarian or Liberal?* (New York: Columbia University Press, 1956).

Chesterton, G. K., *The Everlasting Man* (New York: George H. Doran Co., 1921).

Cox, Harvey, *The Secular City* (New York: The Macmillan Company, 1965).

Danielou, Jean, *Holy Pagans of the Old Testament*, tr. by Felix Faber (London: Longmans Green & Co., 1957).

—, *Lord of History*, tr. by Nigel Abercrombie (Chicago: Henry Regnery Co., 1958).

Daniel-Rops, Henry, *Bernard of Clairvaux*, with a foreword by Thomas Merton, tr. by Elizabeth Abbott (New York: Hawthorn Books, 1964).

—, *The Heroes of God*, tr. by Lawrence Blockman (New York: Hawthorn Books, 1959).

D'Arcy, Martin, *Communism and Christianity* (New York: Penguin Books, 1956).

—, *Mirage and Truth*, the theistic and Christian ideal in competition with those that have taken its place (London: The Contemporary Press, 1935).

—, *The Meaning and Matter of History:* a Christian view (New York: Farrar, Straus, and Cudahy, 1959).

Dawson, Christopher, *The Tyrannies of World History* (New York: Sheed & Ward, 1962).

—, *Religion and the History of Western Culture* (New York: Doubleday, 1958).

—, *Progress and Religion* (New York: Doubleday, 1960).

Desan, Wilfrid, *The Tragic Finale;* an essay on the philosophy of Jean-Paul Sartre (Cambridge: Harvard University Press, 1954).

Dietrich, Otto, *Hitler*, tr. by Richard and Clara Winston (Chicago: Henry Regnery Co., 1965).

Dostoevski, Fedor Mikhailovich, *The Grand Inquisitor*, tr. by S. S. Koteliensky, introduction by D. H. Lawrence (London: E. Mathews & Marrot, 1930).

—, *The Brothers Karamazov*, tr. by Constance Garnett (New York, Modern Library, 1950),

Eastman, Max, *Marxism; Is it a Science?* (New York: W. W. Norton & Co., 1940).

Ebenstein, William, *Today's Isms: Communism, fascism, capitalism, socialism* (Englewood Cliffs, N. J.: Prentice-Hall, Inc., 1954).

Eliade, Mircea, *Mephistopheles and the Androgyne:* studies in religious myth and symbol (New York: Sheed & Ward., 1966).

Eliot, T. S., *The Idea of a Christian Society* (New York: Harcourt, Brace, 1940).

Ewing, Alfred Cyril, *Idealism;* a critical survey (New York: Humanities Press, 1933).

Flores, Angel, *The Kafka Problem* (New York: New Directions, 1946).

Francœur, Robert, *The World of Teilhard* (Baltimore: Helicon Press, 1961).

Gilson, Etienne, *Christianity and Philosophy* (New York: Sheed and Ward, 1939).

Gollancz, Victor, *Our Treatened Values* (London: V. Gollancz, Ltd., 1946).

—, *In Darkest Germany,* introduction by Robert Hutchins (Hinsdale, Ill.: Henry Regnery, Inc., 1947).

Gollwitzer, Helmut, *Dying We Live;* records of the Resistance, tr. by Reinhard Kuhn (New York: Pantheon Books, 1956).

Guardini, Romano, *The End of the Modern World,* tr. by Joseph Themen and Herbert Zurke (New York: Sheed & Ward, 1956).

—, *Power and Responsibility,* tr. by Elinor C. Briefs (Chicago: Henry Regnery, Inc., 1961).

—, *Faith and the Modern Man,* tr. by Charlotte Forsyth (New York: Pantheon Books. 1952).

—, *The World and the Person,* tr. by Stella Lange (Chicago: Henry Regnery, Inc., 1965).

—, *The Conversion of Augustine,* tr. by Elinor C. Briefs (Westminster, Md.: The Newman Press, 1960).

Halévy, Elie, *The Era of Tyrannies,* tr. by R. K. Webb (Garden City, N. Y.: Anchor Books, 1965).

—, *The Growth of Philosophical Radicalism,* tr. by Mary Morris (Boston: Beacon Press, 1955).

Hazard, Paul, *The European Mind,* tr. by Lewis May from *La crise de la conscience européenne* (London: Hollis and Carter, 1953).

Heimann, Eduard, *Freedom and Order,* Lessons from the War (New York: Charles Scribner's Sons, 1947).

Herberg, Will, *Four Existentialist Theologians;* a reader from works of Jacques Maritain, Nicolas Berdyaev, Martin Buber, and Paul Tillich (Garden City: Doubleday, 1958).

Hildebrand, Dietrich von, *Graven Images,* Substitutes for True Morality (New York: David McKay Co., Inc., 1957).

Hitler, Adolf, *Mein Kampf,* complete and unabridged, fully annotated, ed. by John Chamberlain, Sidney Fay and others (New York: Reynal and Hitchcock, 1940).

Hook, Sidney, *The Hero in History* (New York: The John Day Co., 1943).

—, *John Dewey, Philosopher of Science and Freedom* (New York: Dial Press, 1950).

Hsiao, Yu, *Mao Tse-tung and I Were Beggars,* with a foreword by Lin Yutang (Syracuse, N. Y.: Syracuse University Press, 1959).

Hsueh, Kuang-ch'ien, *Decision for China: Communism or Christianity,* tr. by Paul Sih (Chicago: Henry Regnery, Inc., 1959).

Hubben, William, *Four Poets of Our Destiny:* Kierkegaard, Dostoevsky, Nietzsche, Kafka (New York: The Macmillan Company, 1952).

Hunter, Edward, *Brain-washing in Red China;* the calculated destruction of men's minds (New York: Vanguard Press, 1951).

Jackson, Barbara (Ward), *The West at Bay* (New York: W. W. Norton, 1948).

—, *Faith and Freedom* (New York: W. W. Norton, 1954).

—. *Five Ideas that Change the World* (New York: W. W. Norton, 1955).

Jackson, Holbrook, *Dreamers of Dreams:* Carlyle, Ruskin, William Morris, Emerson, Thoreau, Whitman (New York: Farrar, Straus, 1949).

Jaeger, Werner, *Humanism and Theology* (Milwaukee: Marquette University Press, 1948).

—, *Early Christianity and Greek Paideia* (Cambridge, Mass.: Harvard University Press, 1961).

—,   *The Theology of the Early Greek Philosophers*, tr. from German
    by Edward Robinson (Oxford: Clarendon Press, 1947).
James, William, *The Will to Believe* and other essays (New York, London:
    Longmans Green & Company, 1927, reprint).
Kafka, Franz, *The Trial*, tr. by Willa and Edwin Muir (London: Secker &
    Warburg, 1947).
—,   *The Castle*, tr. from German by Willa and Edwin Muir with
    an homage by Thos. Mann (New York: Alfred A. Knopf, 1954).
Kaufmann, Walter, *Religion from Tolstoy to Camus* (New York: Harper &
    Row, 1964).
—,   *The Owl and the Nightingale;* from Shakespeare to Existentialism
    (London: Faber and Faber, 1960).
Kierkegaard, Soren, *The Concept of Dread*, tr. by Walter Lowrie (Princeton,
    N. J.: Princeton University Press, 1944).
—,   *Fear and Trembling and The Sickness Unto Death*, tr. by
    Walter Lowrie (New York: Doubleday, 1954).
—,   *Either/Or*, Vol, 1 tr. by David and Lillian Swenson, Vol. II by
    Walter Lowrie (New York: Anchor Books, 1959).
King, Rachel Hadley, *The Omission of the Holy Spirit from Reinhold
    Niebuhr's Theology* (New York: Philosophical Library, 1964).
Knox, Ronald, *Enthusiasm*, a chapter in the history of religion (Oxford:
    Clarendon Press, 1950).
Koestler, Arthur (and others) Silone, Gide, S. Spender, *The God That Failed*,
    introduction by Richard Crossman (New York: Harper & Bros., 1950).
—,   *Darkness at Noon*, tr. by Daphne Hardy (New York: Modern
    Library).
—,   *The Age of Longing* (New York: The Macmillan Company,
    1961).
—,   The *Sleepwalkers*, introduction by Herbert Butterfield (London:
    Hutchinson, 1959).
—,   *The Yogi and the Commissar*, and other essays (New York:
    The Macmillan Company, 1945).
Kuhn, Helmut, *Freedom Forgotten and Remembered* (Chapel Hill: University
    of North Carolina Press, 1943).
Labin, Suzanne, *The Anthill.* The human condition in Communist China,
    tr. from the French by Edward Fitzgerald (New York: Frederick
    A. Praeger, 1961).
Leff, Gordon *The Tyranny of Concepts:* a critique of Marxism (London:
    Merlin Press, 1961).
Levenson, Joseph, *Confucian China and its Modern Fate* (Berkeley: University
    of California Press).
Lewis, C. S., *The World's Last Night*, and other essays (New York: Harcourt
    Brace, 1960).
Lin, Yutang, *The Flight of the Innocents* (New York: G. P. Putnam's Sons,
    1964).
Lubac, Henri de, *The Drama of Atheist Humanism*, tr. by Edith Riley
    (New York: Sheed & Ward, 1950).
Lynch, William F., *Christ and Apollo*, dimensions of the literary imagination
    (New York: Sheed & Ward, 1960).
Malraux, André, *The Metamorphosis of the Gods*, tr. by Stuart Gilbert
    (New York: Doubleday, 1960).
Marcel, Gabriel, *Men Against Humanity*, tr. by G. S. Fraser (London: The
    Harbill Press, Ltd., 1952).
Maritain, Jacques, *The Dream of Descartes*, tr. by Mabelle Andison (New
    York: Philosophical Library, 1944).
—,   *Three Reformers: Luther, Descartes, Rousseau* (New York:
    Charles Scribner's Sons, 1936).

—, *True Humanism* (New York: Charles Scribner's Sons, 1938).

—, *Existence and the Existent*, tr. by L. Galantiere and G. Phelan (New York: Doubleday, 1957).

Mauriac, André, Ducattillon, Pere, Marc, Alexandre and others, *Communism and Christians* (Westminster, Md.: The Newman Press).

Mehmert, Klaus, *Soviet Man and His World* (Eng. ed., The Anatomy of Soviet Man) (New York: Frederick A. Praeger, 1962).

Mercier, Louis, *The Challenge of Humanism* (New York: Oxford University Press, 1933).

Milosz, Czeslaw, *The Captive Mind*, tr. from the Polish by Jane Zielonko (New York: Vintage Books, 1955).

Moeller, Charles, *Satan*, a joint translation from the French (New York: Sheed and Ward, 1952).

Mu, Fu-sheng, *The Wilting of the Hundred Flowers* (London: W. Heinemann, Ltd., 1962).

Mumford, Lewis, *The Story of Utopias*. Introduction by Hendrik van Loon (New York: P. Smith., 1941).

—, *The Transformations of Man* (New York: Harper & Company, 1956).

—, *The Condition of Man* (New York: Harcourt, Brace & Co., 1944).

—, *The Human Prospect* (Boston: Beacon Press, 1955).

Murray, John Courtney, *The Problem of God* (New Haven and London: Yale University Press, 1964).

Niebuhr, Reinhold, *Faith and History*, a comparison of Christian and Modern Views of History (New York: Charles Scribner's Sons, 1949).

—, *Pious and Secular America* (Eng. ed. *The Godly and the Ungodly*) (London and New York: Charles Scribner's Sons, 1959).

Nolte, Ernst, *Three Faces of Fascism*; Action Française, Italian Fascism, National Socialism, tr. by Leila Vennewitz (New York: Holt, Rinehart & Winston., 1965).

Nouy, Lecomte du, *Human Destiny* (New York: The New American Library, 1956).

Otto, Rudolph, *The Idea of the Holy*; an inquiry into the non-rational factor in the idea of the divine and its relation to the rational. Tr. by John Harvey (London and New York: Oxford University Press, 1950, 9th ed.).

Paléologue, Georges Maurice, *An Ambassador's Memoirs* (St. Petersburg, July 1914 to May 1917), 3 vols. Tr. by F. A. Holt (New York: George H. Doran Co., 1924-1925).

Pálóczi, Horváth, *Mao Tse-tung, Emperor of the Blue Ants* (New York: Doubleday & Company, Inc., 1963).

Parkes, Henry, *Marxism; an Autopsy* (Boston: Houghton Mifflin Co., 1939).

Pascal, Blaise, *Pensées*. Tr. with an introduction by Martin Turnell (New York: Harper & Row, 1962).

Pelikan, Jaroslaw, *Obedient Rebels*. Catholic Substance and Protestant Principle in Luther's Reform (New York: Harper & Row, 1964).

—, *The Christian Intellectual* (New York: Harper & Row, 1966).

Picard, Max, *Hitler in Ourselves*. Tr. from the German by Heinrich Hauser (Hinsdale, Ill.: Henry Regnery, Inc., 1947).

Pieper, Joseph, *The End of Time*. Tr. by Michael Bullock (London: Faber and Faber, 1954).

—, *Enthusiasm and Divine Madness*; on the Platonic dialogue of Phaedrus. Tr. by Richard and Clara Winston (New York: Harcourt, Brace & World, 1964).

Pope Pius XI, Encyclical of His Holiness, *On Atheistic Communism (Divine Redemptoris)* (New York: The America Press, 1937).

Quasten, Johannes, *Patrology*, Vol. III, The Golden Age of Greek Patristic Literature (Westminster, Md.: The Newman Press, 1950).

Robinson, John A., *Honest to God* (Philadelphia: Westminster Press, 1963).

Rousseau, Jean-Jacques and Others, *Famous Utopias*, the complete text of Rousseau's *Social Contract*, More's *Utopia*, Bacon's *New Atlantis*, Campanella's *City of the Sun*, with introduction by Charles Andrews (New York: Tudor Publishing Co., 1937).

Santayana, George, *Egotism in German Philosophy* (London: J. M. Dent & Sons, Ltd., 1940).

Sartre, Jean-Paul, *The Transcendence of the Ego*. Tr. and with an introduction by Forrest Williams and Robert Kilpatrick (New York: Noonday Press. 1957).

—, *No Exit*, a play in 3 acts (New York: Alfred A. Knopf, 1947).

—, *Nausea*. Tr. by Lloyd Alexander (New York: New Directions, 1949).

Sheed, Frank, *Man the Forgotten* (rep. ed. for USO) (New York: Sheed & Ward, 1942).

—, *Society and Sanity* (New York: Sheed & Ward, 1953).

—, *Communism and Man* (New York: Sheed & Ward, 1938).

Sheen, Fulton J., *Communism and the Conscience of the West*, (New York: Garden City Books, 1948).

Sheldon. Wilmon, *America's Progressive Philosophy* (New Haven: Yale University Press, 1942).

Shirer, William, *The Rise and Fall of the Third Reich* (New York: Simon & Schuster, 1960).

Sorokim, Pitirim, *Modern Historical and Social Philosophies*. Danilevsky, Splengler, Toynbee, Schubart. Berdyaev, Northrop, Kroeler, Schweitzer (New York: Dover Publications, Inc., 1963).

Spengler, Oswald, *The Decline of the West*, auth. tr. with notes by Charles Francis Atkinson (New York: Alfred A. Knopf, 1939).

Stravou, Constantine, *Witman and Nietzsche* (Chapel Hill: University of North Carolina Press, 1964).

Stoddard, Theodore Lothrop, *The Menace of the Underman* (New York: Charles Scribner's Sons, 1922).

Streller, Justus, *Jean-Paul Sartre: To Freedom Condemned*. Tr. from the German and with an Introduction by Wade Baskin (New York: Philosophical Library, 1960).

Teilhard de Chardin, Pierre, *The Divine Milieu* (New York: Harper & Row Torchbooks. 1965).

—, *The Phenomenon of Man*. Tr. by Bernard Wall, introduction by Julian Huxley (New York: Harper & Row, 1959).

—, *The Future of Man*. Tr. by Norman Denny (New York: Harper & Row, 1964).

Tillich, Paul, *The Courage to Be* (New Haven: Yale University Press).

—, *Ultimate Concern*; Tillich in dialogue, ed. by D. Mackenzie Brown (New York: Harper & Row, 1965).

Ussher, Arland, *Journey Through Dread*, a study of Kierkegaard, Heidegger, and Sartre (New York: Devin-Adair Co., 1955).

Walsh, Chad. *From Utopia to Nightmare* (New York: Harper & Row, 1964).

—, *C. S. Lewis, Apostle to the Skeptics* (New York: The Macmillan Company, 1949).

Warner, Denis, *Hurricane from China* (New York: The Macmillan Company, 1961).

Weil, Simone, *The Need for Roots*, with Preface by T. S. Eliot (London: Routledge and K. Paul and Boston: Beacon Press, 1952).

Wolfe, Bertram, *Three Who Made a Revolution* (New York: Dial Press, 1964).

NAME INDEX

Printed in Belgium by Desclée & Cie, Éditeurs, S. A., Tournai 10.921
D 1968 - 0002 - 31